A History of English

Blackwell Textbooks in Linguistics

1	Liliane Haegeman	*Introduction to Government and Binding Theory* (Second Edition)
2	Andrew Spencer	*Morphological Theory*
3	Helen Goodluck	*Language Acquisition*
4	Ronald Wardhaugh	*Introduction to Sociolinguistics* (Third Edition)
5	Martin Atkinson	*Children's Syntax*
6	Diane Blakemore	*Understanding Utterances*
7	Michael Kenstowicz	*Phonology in Generative Grammar*
8	Deborah Schiffrin	*Approaches to Discourse*
9	John Clark and Colin Yallop	*An Introduction to Phonetics and Phonology* (Second Edition)
10	Natsuko Tsujimura	*An Introduction to Japanese Linguistics*
11	Robert D. Borsley	*Modern Phrase Structure Grammar*
12	Nigel Fabb	*Linguistics and Literature*
13	Irene Heim and Angelika Kratzer	*Semantics in Generative Grammar*
14	Liliane Haegeman and Jacqueline Guéron	*English Grammar: A Generative Perspective*
15	Stephen Crain and Diane Lillo-Martin	*An Introduction to Linguistic Theory and Language Acquisition*
16	Joan Bresnan	*Lexical-Functional Syntax*
17	Barbara A. Fennell	*A History of English: A Sociolinguistic Approach*

A History of English

A Sociolinguistic Approach

Barbara A. Fennell

University of Aberdeen

Blackwell
Publishing

350 Main Street, Malden, MA 02148-5020, USA
108 Cowley Road, Oxford OX4 1JF, UK
550 Swanston Street, Carlton, Victoria 3053, Australia

First published 2001 by Blackwell Publishing Ltd
Reprinted 2001, 2002, 2003

Library of Congress Cataloging-in-Publication Data

Fennell, Barbara A.
    A history of English : a sociolinguistic approach / Barbara A. Fennell.
        p.   cm. — (Blackwell textbooks in linguistics ; 17)
    Includes bibliographical references and index.
    ISBN 0–631–20072–X (hardback : alk. paper)— ISBN 0–631–20073–8 (pb : alk.paper)
    1. English language–History.   2. English language–Social aspects.   3. Language and culture–English-speaking countries.   I. Title. II. Series.
PE1075 .F39 2001
420'.9—dc21   00–057918

A catalogue record for this title is available from the British Library.

Set in 10 on 13 pt Sabon
by Graphicraft Ltd, Hong Kong
Printed and bound in the United Kingdom
by TJ International Ltd, Padstow, Cornwall

For further information on
Blackwell Publishing, visit our website:
http://www.blackwellpublishing.com

Contents

List of Maps and Figures   xii
Acknowledgements   xiii

1 Introduction   1
  1.1 The Time Periods of English   1
  1.2 Language Change   3
  1.3 Sources of Information on Language Change   7
  1.4 Linguistic Preliminaries   9
  1.5 The Sounds of English, and Symbols Used to Describe Them   11
    1.5.1 Consonants   11
    1.5.2 Vowels   12
      1.5.2.1 Monophthongs   12
      1.5.2.2 Diphthongs   12
  1.6 Structure of the Book   13

2 The Pre-history of English   15
  Timeline: The Indo-European Period   15
  2.1 The Indo-European Languages and Linguistic Relatedness   17
    2.1.1 The Beginnings   17
    2.1.2 The Development of Historical Linguistics   18
    2.1.3 Genetic Relatedness   19
  2.2 Linguistic Developments: The Indo-European Language Family   23
    2.2.1 Family-Tree Relationships   23
    2.2.2 The Indo-European Family   23
      2.2.2.1 Indo-Iranian   25
      2.2.2.2 Armenian   26
      2.2.2.3 Albanian   26
      2.2.2.4 Balto-Slavonic   26
      2.2.2.5 Hellenic   28
      2.2.2.6 Italic   28
      2.2.2.7 Celtic   29
      2.2.2.8 Germanic   31

2.3   From Indo-European to Germanic   34
      2.3.1   Prosody   35
      2.3.2   The Consonant System: Sound Shifts   35
              2.3.2.1   Grimm's Law   36
              2.3.2.2   Verner's Law   37
              2.3.2.3   The Second Consonant Shift   38
      2.3.3   The Vowel System   40
      2.3.4   Morphology   40
      2.3.5   Syntax   41
      2.3.6   Lexicon   41
      2.3.7   Semantics   42
      2.3.8   Indo-European/Germanic Texts   42
      2.3.9   Neogrammarians, Structuralists and Contemporary
              Linguistic Models   43
2.4   Typological Classification   44
      2.4.1   Universals   45
              2.4.1.1   Syntactic Universals   45
      2.4.2   Morphological Typology   46
2.5   Sociolinguistic Focus. The Indo-European Tribes and the Spread
      of Language. Language Contact and Language Change.
      Archaeological Linguistics   49
      2.5.1   Language Contact   50
      2.5.2   Archaeological Linguistics   51
2.6   Conclusion   53

3 **Old English**   55
   Timeline: The Old English Period   55
   3.1   Social and Political History   55
         3.1.1   Britain before the English   55
         3.1.2   The Anglo-Saxon Invasions   56
         3.1.3   Anglo-Saxon Influence   56
         3.1.4   Scandinavian Influence   57
   3.2   Linguistic Developments: The Sounds, Structure and
         Typology of Old English   59
         3.2.1   The Structure of Old English   59
                 3.2.1.1   OE Consonants   60
                 3.2.1.2   Vowels: from Germanic to Old English 62
                 3.2.1.3   Old English Gender   64
                 3.2.1.4   Inflection in Old English   64
                 3.2.1.5   Old English Syntax   72
                 3.2.1.6   Old English Vocabulary   77

3.3   Linguistic and Literary Achievements   79
    3.3.1   Texts   79
        3.3.1.1   Prose   80
        3.3.1.2   Poetry   82
3.4   The Dialects of Old English   85
3.5   Sociolinguistic Focus   86
    3.5.1   Language Contact   86
        3.5.1.1   Latin and Celtic   88
        3.5.1.2   The Scandinavians   90

4   **Middle English**   94
Timeline: The Middle English Period   94
4.1   Social and Political History   94
    4.1.1   Political History: The Norman Conquest to Edward I   94
    4.1.2   Social History   96
        4.1.2.1   The Establishment of Towns and Burghs
                  and the Beginnings of Social Stratification   96
4.2   Linguistic Developments: Middle English Sounds and
      Structure, with Particular Emphasis on the Breakdown of the
      Inflectional System and its Linguistic Typological Implications   97
    4.2.1   Major Changes in the Sound System   97
        4.2.1.1   The Consonants   97
        4.2.1.2   Consonant Changes from Old to
                  Middle English   98
        4.2.1.3   Vowels in Stressed Syllables   98
        4.2.1.4   Vowels in Unstressed Syllables   99
        4.2.1.5   Lengthening and Shortening   99
        4.2.1.6   Summary Table of Vowel Changes from Old
                  to Middle English   100
        4.2.1.7   The Formation of Middle English
                  Diphthongs   100
    4.2.2   Major Morphological Changes from Old to Middle
        English   101
        4.2.2.1   Loss of Inflections   101
        4.2.2.2   Other Changes in the Morphological System   102
        4.2.2.3   Verbs   103
    4.2.3   Middle English Syntax   104
        4.2.3.1   Word Order   106
    4.2.4   The Lexicon: Loan Words from French   106
        4.2.4.1   Numbers and Parts of the Body   107
        4.2.4.2   Two French Sources   108

4.3	Middle English Dialects	108
	4.3.1 Linguistic and Literary Achievements	114
	4.3.1.1 Middle English Literature	114
	4.3.2 Language	114
	4.3.3 Genre	115
4.4	Sociolinguistic Focus: Social Stratification, Multilingualism and Dialect Variation. Language Contact: The Myth of Middle English Creolization	116
	4.4.1 English Re-established	116
	4.4.1.1 Language and the Rise of the Middle Class	120
	4.4.2 The Development of Standard English	122
	4.4.2.1 The Evolution of ME 'Standard' English	123
	4.4.3 Middle English Creolization: Myth?	125
	4.4.3.1 Definitions	126
	4.4.3.2 Pidgins and Creoles in England?	128
4.5	Conclusion	133
5	**Early Modern English**	135
	Timeline: The Early Modern English Period	135
5.1	Social and Political History	136
	5.1.1 Historical and Political Background	136
	5.1.1.1 Internal Instability and Colonial Expansion	137
5.2	Linguistic Developments: The Variable Character of Early Modern English	138
	5.2.1 Phonology	138
	5.2.1.1 Consonants	139
	5.2.1.2 Vowels	140
	5.2.1.3 The Great Vowel Shift	141
	5.2.2 Morphology	141
	5.2.2.1 Nouns	141
	5.2.2.2 Pronouns	142
	5.2.2.3 Adjectives and Adverbs	142
	5.2.2.4 Verbs	143
	5.2.2.5 The Spread of Northern Forms	143
	5.2.3 Syntax	144
	5.2.3.1 Periphrastic *do*	144
	5.2.3.2 Progressive Verb Forms	145
	5.2.3.3 Passives	145
	5.2.4 Sample Text	146
	5.2.5 Vocabulary	147
	5.2.6 The Anxious State of English: The Search for Authority	147

		5.2.6.1	Dictionaries and the Question of Linguistic Authority: Swift's and Johnson's View of Language	149
5.3	Linguistic and Literary Achievement			152
5.4	Sociolinguistic Focus			154
	5.4.1	Variation in Early Modern English		154
	5.4.2	Standardization		156
		5.4.2.1	The Printing Press	156
		5.4.2.2	The Renaissance and the Protestant Reformation	156
		5.4.2.3	English Established	157
	5.4.3	The Great Vowel Shift		158
		5.4.3.1	Phonological Change	158
	5.4.4	Case Study: Power and Solidarity Relations in Early Modern English		162
5.5	Conclusion			166

6	**Present-Day English**			167
	Timeline: Present-Day English			167
	Introduction			168
6.1	Social and Political History			169
	6.1.1	The Age of Revolutions, Wars and Imperialism		169
	6.1.2	Urbanization, Industrialization and Social Stratification		170
6.2	Linguistic Developments			172
	6.2.1	Morphology and Syntax		172
		6.2.1.1	Morphology	172
		6.2.1.2	Syntax	173
	6.2.2	The Lexicon		175
		6.2.2.1	Colonialism, Contact and Borrowings	175
		6.2.2.2	Neologisms	176
		6.2.2.3	Illustrative Texts	178
6.3	Modern English Dialects			179
	6.3.1	Traditional Dialects		180
	6.3.2	Modern Dialects		182
	6.3.3	Received Pronunciation (RP): The Social Background		185
		6.3.3.1	Characteristics of RP	187
	6.3.4	RP, Estuary English and 'the Queen's English'		188
6.4	Sociolinguistic Focus: English in Scotland, Ireland and Wales – Multilingualism in Britain			191
	6.4.1	English in the British Isles		191
		6.4.1.1	English in Scotland	191

6.4.1.2   English in Wales   195
6.4.1.3   English in Ireland   198
6.4.2   Immigrant Varieties of English in Britain   200
6.4.2.1   Immigration to Britain in the PDE Period   200
6.4.2.2   Colonial Immigration and Language   202

7   English in the United States   208
Timeline: America in the Modern Period   208
7.1   Social and Political History   209
7.1.1   Settlement and Language   209
7.1.2   Settlement by Region   210
7.1.2.1   The Original Thirteen Colonies   210
7.1.2.2   The Middle West   213
7.1.2.3   The South and West   214
7.2   The Development of American English   216
7.2.1   The Strength and Maintenance of Dialect Boundaries   216
7.2.2   How, Why and When American English Began to
Diverge from British English   217
7.2.2.1   Physical Separation   217
7.2.2.2   The Different Physical Conditions Encountered
by the Settlers   218
7.2.2.3   Contact with Immigrant Non-Native Speakers
of English   219
7.2.2.4   Developing Political Differences and the
Growing American Sense of National Identity   219
7.3   Language Variation in the United States   222
7.3.1   Uniformity and Diversity in Early American English   222
7.3.2   Regional Dialect Divisions in American English   223
7.3.2.1   The Lexicon   223
7.3.2.2   Phonology: Consonants   226
7.3.2.3   Phonology: Vowels   227
7.3.3   Social and Ethnic Dialects   229
7.3.3.1   Social Class and Language Change   231
7.3.3.2   Ethnicity   231
7.3.3.3   African-American Vernacular English   232
7.3.3.4   Traditional Dialects and the Resistance to
Change   237

8   World-Wide English   241
Timeline: World-Wide English   241
8.1   Social and Political History: The Spread of English across
the Globe   243

8.1.1   British Colonialism   244
    8.1.1.1   Canada   244
    8.1.1.2   The Caribbean   245
    8.1.1.3   Australia   246
    8.1.1.4   New Zealand   247
    8.1.1.5   South Africa   247
    8.1.1.6   South Asia   248
    8.1.1.7   Former Colonial Africa: West Africa   250
    8.1.1.8   East Africa   252
    8.1.1.9   South-East Asia and South Pacific   253
8.1.2   An Overview of the Use of English throughout the
    World   255
8.2   English as a Global Language   256
8.2.1   The Industrial Revolution   256
8.2.2   American Economic Superiority and Political
    Leadership   257
8.2.3   American Technological Domination   257
8.2.4   The Boom in English Language Teaching   258
8.2.5   The Need for a Global Language   259
8.2.6   Structural Considerations   260
8.2.7   Global and at the Same Time Local   261
8.3   English as a Killer Language   264
8.3.1   Language Death   265
8.3.2   Language and Communication Technology   266
8.4   The Future of English   267

Bibliography   270
Index   280

Maps and Figures

Maps

3.1	The Anglo-Saxon kingdoms	57
6.1	Traditional dialect areas	181
6.2	Modern dialect divisions	184
7.1	Sketch map of direction of settlement of America	216
7.2	Eastern dialect areas of the United States	224
7.3	An example of dialect layering in Western United States	225
7.4	Carver's major dialect regions	230

Figures

1.1	Typical developments of creoles	5
2.1	The Indo-European language family	22
7.1	An example of dialect layering in the West, hierarchically represented	226
7.2	Northern Cities Vowel Shift	227
7.3	Southern Vowel Shift	228

Acknowledgements

I should like to thank Beth Remmes of Blackwell Publishers and Valery Rose, my copy editor, for their invaluable help and support in what has been a trying year. I should like especially to thank my husband Stefan, who did not die after all, but survived and helped me through to the end of this project.

I should like also to acknowledge the following for permission to reproduce copyright material:

Blackwell Publishers, for maps 6.1 and 6.2 and table 6.1, all of which first appeared in Peter Trudgill, *The Dialects of England* (1990);

Craig Carver, for maps 7.3 and 7.4 and figure 7.1, which first appeared in Craig Carver, *American Regional Dialects: A Word Geography* (1987);

The Hindustan Times Online, for the extract from Subhash Goyal, 'A River Most Foul' (1998);

The Times of India, for the extract from Aditya Kant, 'White-Collar Crime: Cops See Red', © Bennett, Coleman and Co. Ltd.;

University of Michigan Press, for map 7.2, which first appeared in Hans Kurath, *A World Geography of the Eastern United States* (1949).

Dedicated to the memory of Michael S. Reynolds

1 Introduction

1.1 The Time Periods of English

There are a number of ways to tackle a linguistic history of this sort. One would be to trace changes in the language level by level, that is, by looking at all the phonological changes first, then all the morphological, all the lexical, all the syntactic changes, and so on. There are some books that proceed this way. Another way might be to proceed topic by topic: the spread of Indo-European, the Great Vowel Shift, the change from a type A language to a type B language, and so on. There are also texts that proceed in this way. Yet another approach might be to choose authors who typify a particular period, such as Chaucer, Shakespeare, Donne or Milton, and base any description on their work. Alternatively, one might wish to trace the history of the English language in accordance with a particular theoretical or methodological approach, for example a structuralist account or a language variation account. Needless to say, such books also exist.

The present book, however, attempts to provide a taste of a variety of ways in which the development of the English language can be approached. For this reason, each chapter contains sociohistorical and cultural background, a descriptive account of major structural characteristics from stage to stage and a particular topical focus. As a consequence of this approach, it seems most reasonable to split up the book into discrete historical periods.

Typically, studies of the development of English taking this wider approach divide the language into four stages: Old English, Middle English, Early Modern English and Modern or Present Day English. However, this is also not a straightforward task, as there are no hard and fast rules about when one period of English ends and another begins. What one has to do is decide upon a set of criteria for dating each period in a particular way. The dates for the periods of English I have chosen in this book are as follows:

Old English	CE 500–1100
Middle English	1100–1500
Early Modern English	1500–1800
Modern English	1800–present

Each of these dates actually marks a historical event (rounded to the nearest century or half-century), rather than a linguistic development. The Old English period begins about fifty years after the invasion of Britain by the Germanic tribes at the behest of the Celtic king Vortigern in CE 449. This is the time when the Germanic dialects were first brought to Britain, providing the raw material for the development of English. We round up to CE 500 here with good reason, as it probably took several generations of settlement before any distinctively Anglo-Saxon variety of Germanic established itself. The Old English period ends with the second major invasion of Britain (the third, actually, if we include the invasion by the Romans before the Germanic language came to Britain; see chapters 2 and 3). This was the conquest of Britain by William, Duke of Normandy, in 1066, which marks a watershed in the linguistic history of Britain, as it heralds almost four hundred years of intimate contact with French, the period that we call Middle English. The Early Modern period begins in 1500 and ends in 1800. The date 1500 roughly marks the beginning of the Renaissance and the introduction of the printing press, both of which had profound consequences for the development of the English language. The Early Modern English period ends with the independence of the American colonies. This event marks the end of the British monopoly on the English language and the beginning of the Modern English period, in which several national varieties of English developed, changing the profile of English for ever.

There are some important linguistic characteristics that overlap with these historical periods, of course. The year CE 500 marks the branching off of English from the other Germanic dialects. The year 1100 marks the period in which English lost the vast majority of its inflections, signalling the change from a language that relied upon morphological marking of grammatical roles to one that relied on word order to maintain basic grammatical relations; 1500 marks the end of major French influence on the language and the time when the use of English was established in all communicative contexts. From 1500 to 1800 and later, the English language absorbed a huge number of words from Latin and Greek as a result of the revival of classical learning. Towards the end of this period, and picking up momentum from 1800 on, the lexicon of English is enriched by two significant historical processes. The first is colonialism (which actually begins at the beginning of the Early Modern English period), during which process English both spread throughout the world and absorbed many hundreds of words from a rich array of the world's languages with which it came into various forms of contact. And from the end of the eighteenth century the Industrial Revolution and, eventually, the emergence of the United States as a world power, coupled with the development of technology (particularly electronic and computer technology), also had a profound influence on the vocabulary of English.

1.2 Language Change

Why do languages change? This entire book is about language change, and it illustrates the fact that languages change for a wide variety of reasons. Firstly, languages have an internal structure, which is itself dynamic, and may change for internal reasons. Secondly, languages might also change because people do not learn them perfectly: as people come into contact with others, they might learn the contact language imperfectly, which could ultimately cause the language to change, perhaps causing a 'substratum' effect on the language, that is, an underlying effect from language A on the structure of language B. It is underlying by virtue of the fact that A is usually a language that existed but is no longer spoken in the territory of B.

And a second question we might ask here is, why don't people always speak the same way all of the time? Linguists believe that all children who are born without special needs are linguistically equal: that is, they are all born with the potential to learn any language. Thus, a child of British parents who is born in Japan is just as able to learn Japanese as a first language as any Japanese child born in Japan to Japanese parents. Moreover, all normally developed human beings are born with the same articulatory apparatus, which is why we are all potentially able to make the same range of sounds (indeed, it used to be believed that at the 'babbling' stage, babies went through the entire range of possible human language sounds). However, there is always the potential for slight variation in the production of sounds: some people produce 'sh' sounds that are closer to 'th' than others, while some people pronounce 'r' sounds that are closer to 'w' or 'l' than others. Or, if we look at the vocabulary choice of individuals, we know that sometimes we consciously or subconsciously take a liking to a particular word and use it with particular frequency and in a specific way. (For example, in Britain in late 1999 and early 2000, teenagers and young adults used the word *pants* to mean *bad*, as in *I don't like this dinner – it's really pants!*) This individual variation provides the potential for change. It might be that the way a particular individual pronounces or uses a word becomes a marker of prestige, in which case other members of his or her cohort will, possibly subconsciously, begin to change their speech in the direction of the prestige pronunciation, in order to express their solidarity and identify with that person. We are all aware of the fact that we often shift our speech according to the person we are talking to: if we want to express solidarity with that person, we shift towards his or her speech, while we shift away from it if we want to keep our distance. In social psychology, this quite natural process is called 'linguistic accommodation'. When this occurs on a one-to-one basis and is a temporary phenomenon, no language change ensues from it. But when such accommodation spreads from individual to individual and happens repeatedly over time, it can lead to language change.

Another reason why language changes is that speakers of a language come into contact with speakers of another language or languages. This can be because of migration, perhaps because they move to more fertile lands, or because they are displaced on account of war or poverty or disease. It can also be because they are invaded, as in the case of the earlier periods of English, when first the Germanic tribes, then, later, the Vikings and, later still, the Normans invaded Britain. Depending on the circumstances, the home language may succumb completely to the language of the invaders, in which case we talk about **replacement**. Alternatively, the home language might persist side-by-side with the language of the invaders, and, depending on political circumstances, it might become the dominant or the dominated language. If there is close contact between the invaders and the invaded, it is possible for there to be significant influence from one language on the other. Cultural and physical separation, on the other hand, could lead to the persistence of both languages in their separate domains with very little influence of one on the other (for example, in the case of Welsh and English throughout the Tudor period; see chapter 5).

If the contact is between a dominant language and more than one other language, and the speakers of these languages have no language in common, then an interim contact language might develop. This language would have a reduced linguistic system in the first instance; it would be subject to variation and would not be equal to all the communicative tasks that a native speaker is likely to need to perform (from, say, ordering goods to saying prayers to composing songs or poems). In this case, we would call the variety a pidgin. The pidgin might persist over time and stabilize in terms of its forms and functions. If it is passed on to subsequent generations, which need to use it as their main or only language, it will expand to fulfil those linguistic functions it was not equal to in its earlier form. In this case, we would speak of a creole developing. More often than not, such languages end up shifting in the direction of the dominant language as social conditions improve and access to power and the mainstream society increases. It is usually the case that a society in which a creole develops displays a continuum of language varieties, which we refer to as a post-creole continuum. The varieties that coexist in such circumstances range from a still relatively reduced 'basilectal' variety, through a range of more standard-like 'mesolectal' varieties to 'acrolectal' varieties, which are very close to the dominant (lexifier) language, but which retain features of grammar, lexicon and pronunciation that still mark them off from the national (often European) standard variety. I illustrated this process in Fennell (1997: 82) (see figure 1.1).

But language contact is not always a necessary or sufficient condition for language change: its opposite, separation, also very often leads to language change. When the English language was taken to America in the seventeenth century, for

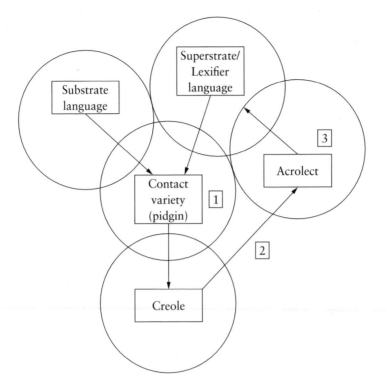

Figure 1.1 Typical developments of creoles

example, it began to diverge from British English for a number of reasons. Firstly, it developed from not one (standard) dialect of English, but from a number of regional varieties that were all brought to America by different waves of settlement. Once in America, English changed in response to the new conditions that the settlers encountered, from physical geography to forms of government, and as a result of contact with many other indigenous and immigrant languages. Furthermore, and this was particularly the case after political separation from Britain, American English diverged from British English in the absence of, or indeed in reaction to, an acknowledged British model. And since there was no one particular American state or city to which all Americans looked as their linguistic model, a large number of regional focal centres developed, each acquiring its own regional prestige.

We must bear in mind, however, that a discussion of language change such as this necessarily simplifies matters. Most languages change across time for a variety of reasons. For example, American English also diverged from British English because of contact with other languages, and in African-American Vernacular English (AAVE) this divergence is considerable. In the standard language, however, the influence from other languages is comparatively minimal, and confined for the most part to lexical elements (though some of the differences, such as pronouncing 'r'-sounds that occur after a vowel, have become emblematic of the differences between the national varieties; see chapter 7 on American English).

The factors involved in language change that we have discussed so far depend on language-external conditions. But there also appear to be language-internal reasons why languages change. A prime example of this is the change in system in English from a synthetic or inflectional language, which relies on morphological endings to mark grammatical function, to an analytic one, which relies on word order to convey grammatical relations. From a structural point of view this is the most significant change that has occurred in the history of English. As we shall see in greater detail in chapters 2–6, the reason why English developed in this way is also internal. The major stress on a word, which in Indo-European could originally fall on any syllable in the word (though not haphazardly, but according to rule), eventually fixed on the word-initial or nuclear syllable. This meant that attention was drawn away from the end of the word, ultimately leading to the obscuring, and eventual loss, of inflectional endings. This in turn caused English to become heavily reliant on word order to signal the basic grammatical role of a noun phrase (as subject, direct object, indirect object, etc.), resulting in a major typological change. Ultimately we do not know what caused the stress to fix on the nuclear syllable, and it may indeed have been on account of some extralinguistic factor such as those we have discussed above, but we have no way of knowing this. Once the stress became fixed, however, it triggered this succession of internal changes.

Another example of system-internal change is the phenomenon known as front mutation or i-umlaut, which occurred between Germanic and Old English (and occurred in all West and North Germanic languages). If an unstressed syllable in Germanic containing [i] or [j] followed a stressed syllable, the vowel of the stressed syllable was fronted or raised in anticipation of it (that is, it partially assimilated to the following vowel). Thus *beran* 'to bear' produces *bireþ* 'bears' (3rd person singular) *mūs* ('mouse') becomes *mys* ('mice') because of the form from which they derived in earlier Germanic (see chapter 3). Again, this change cannot be attributed to anything other than system-internal factors that have to do with the articulation of sounds within the English system.

The development of the verb *do* in English from a full verb with its own lexical content to a support or auxiliary verb after about CE 1500 is another example of system internal change. In this instance the original meaning was bleached out of the full verb *do*, and it became a lexically empty grammatical function word, used for example in yes–no questions (*Do you know the way home?*) and to support the negative particle *not* (*I don't smoke*). (See chapter 5 on Early Modern English.) We refer to this kind of system-internal change as *grammaticalization*.

This last example could also be termed a form of *reanalysis*, that is, where a word that historically has been associated with one particular structure becomes associated with another. There are lots of morphological examples in English of a sub-type of reanalysis, namely *metanalysis*, where morpheme boundaries come to be reinterpreted or reanalysed. Thus, English *naddre*, *napron* and *noumpere* have become *adder*, *apron* and *umpire* by reanalysis of the morpheme boundaries in combinations such as *a naddre*. The converse has also happened; for example, the morpheme boundaries in the phrase *an ewt* have been reanalysed to produce *a newt* (cf. Trask, 1996: 103). This is another type of internal source of language change.

To summarize the causes of language change, then, we can say that languages change because of:

- geography (separation of one language or variety from another; alternatively closeness – language contact);
- contact with new vs. old phenomena (the need to adapt to new, different, or changing aspects of society);
- imperfect learning;
- a substratum effect;
- social prestige factors (the attempt on the part of speakers to imitate or acquire linguistic features that are considered 'better' than their own).

Where internal factors are concerned, we can cite as motivation such reasons as:

- ease of articulation (is X easier to say/pronounce than Y?);
- analogy (the application of one phenomenon to others by association);
- reanalysis;
- randomness (see Crystal, 1987: 333, and Trask, 1996, for good discussion of the cause and types of language change).

We will have cause throughout the chapters that follow to look at numerous examples of external and internal linguistic change.

1.3 Sources of Information on Language Change

Thomas Alva Edison did not invent the phonograph until 1877, and David Hughes invented the microphone the following year. The first crude magnetic sound recordings became a possibility in 1899, though it was not until 1942 that magnetic recording tape was invented. In this age of DVDs, CDs, VCRs and videophones, it is perhaps difficult for us to imagine a time when it was not possible to record what people say. I remember once in North Carolina several years ago a mature student in one of my seminars told a first-year student that she 'sounded like a broken record'. The younger student looked blank and asked, quite genuinely, 'What does a broken record sound like?' This incident brought home to me the fact that in the 'postmodern', or to use a term coined recently by Eric Idle, the 'post*modem*' era, young students take for granted the ability to record and retrieve written and spoken information by depressing a key on a keyboard or operating a remote-control device.

When we attempt to investigate the history of any language, however, we have no such aids in our investigations. Indeed, we start not merely in pre-technological but even in pre-literate times, and evidence from archaeology and theoretical reconstruction is all we have to go on in the earliest stages. To assist us in our analysis of Old English we are fortunate to have written texts in English from the seventh century CE onward; many languages of Europe had no written records until several hundred (in some cases more than five hundred) years later (see chapter 2).

However, we have relatively few texts from that time, as we shall discuss in the chapter dealing with Old English, and the texts we do have do not cover all types of language. For example, we do not have many examples of everyday speech, domestic language or the dialects of particular areas. This means that whatever generalizations we do make about Old English, we always have to bear in mind the gaps in our data, and the fact that we are *interpreting* the past, not objectively describing it.

Another limitation of using written texts is that they often conform to a written standard of speech, so that spellings do not necessarily reflect the pronunciation of the writer. The fact is that the orthography of standard English conceals a variety of pronunciations, and that since it is not a phonetic system, linguists have difficulty guessing how a word is 'really' pronounced by a particular speaker at a particular time. To take a modern example, a research student of mine doing fieldwork on Scots in the North-East of Scotland had great difficulty eliciting pronunciations of the word *good* in North-East dialects from a dialect word list. At first she tried using a quasi-phonetic spelling <gwid> in the list to prompt the informants in the pilot study, but they explained that the spelling 'put them off', because they don't say [gwid]. Once she replaced the spelling with standard <good>, however, and simply asked the informants to say the word as they would in their own dialect, they responded much more readily, and provided a variety of different local pronunciations.

However, all is not lost when it comes to investigating pronunciation in older periods of English. Luckily, there are also written texts from people who are only semi-literate, and their spelling is a clue to their pronunciation: <sarvent> for *servant*, for example. Poetry is also often useful, as rhyming words give us a further indication of how they were pronounced.

Far from always being helped by the existence of written documents, however, we are also often misled by written texts in the earlier periods of English because they were frequently translated from other languages, particularly Latin and French, and contained interference from the source language, thus giving us a false impression of idiomatic English of the period. This seems to have been particularly the case with vocabulary (for example, using borrowed words that resembled the source word very closely, where a word from the native word stock was more usual) and with syntax (slavishly following the word order of Latin instead of using English word order, for example). Even morphology was sometimes influenced by the source language in translations.

1.4 Linguistic Preliminaries

In attempting to look at the structure of any language linguists customarily divide the language into different levels.

Phonetics is the science of the production or articulation and reception of human speech sounds, and can be studied without looking at the sound system of any one particular language, while **phonology** is the study of sounds as they operate in the system of a language. Thus we talk about the **phonetics** of human speech sounds, but the **phonology** of English or Swedish or Swahili. **Phone** is the term for any individual sound, while a **phoneme** is any meaningfully distinctive sound in a language. Thus while the difference between the articulation of /p/ in [pʰɪn] and [pɪn] is audible in English (there is a little breath after the first /p/ which is not heard after the second), it does not make a distinction in meaning. On the other hand, the difference in pronunciation between /p/ and /b/ in *pin* and *bin* [pɪn] and [bɪn], while still relatively slight (the only difference between the two sounds is whether the vocal folds are vibrating in their production), does make a significant contrast (that is, in meaning); therefore these two sounds are **phonemes**, while [p] and [pʰ] are not, but rather variants or **allophones** of the phoneme /p/.

Morphology is concerned with the arrangements of and the relationships amongst **morphemes**, which we classify as the smallest meaningful units in a language. Thus, *cat* is a morpheme, since it represents a unit of meaning, but so also is *-s*, which has the meaning of 'plural', that is, 'more than one'. On its own *cat* is also said to be a **lexeme**, a member of a language's **lexicon** (popularly referred to as 'vocabulary'), or set of 'words' (see below). *Cats* is therefore made up of two morphemes, the difference between them being that *cat* can stand on its own (*I've just bought a cat*), while *-s* cannot (**I've just bought a -s. Two *-s are better than one*). (Note that in this chapter an asterisk before an example denotes that it is not grammatical.) Morphemes that can stand alone are called **root** or **free** morphemes, while those that cannot are called **bound** morphemes. It is important to note that a morpheme is not equivalent to a syllable: *banana* consists of three syllables in English, but it constitutes only one morpheme (it cannot be broken down into smaller units of meaning). **Affixes** (that is, prefixes and suffixes) are bound morphemes. For example, *-er, -or* as in *eater, sailor* are affixes which allow us to derive an agentive noun from another root (e.g., the verb *sail*); consequently, affixes like these are known as **derivational** affixes. Other affixes, however, have a grammatical rather than a lexical function, so that, for example, the suffix *-ed* is used to change certain verbs into past tense verbs: *jump > jumped*; *cross > crossed*. This latter type of affix is called an **inflectional** affix, of which Old English had many more than any subsequent period of English, as we shall see in the coming chapters.

In **syntax** we study the way in which words are ordered into larger elements, namely phrases, clauses and sentences. The two sentences *The dog bit the man* and *The man bit the dog* contrast in meaning in English, not merely on account of any particular property of the phrase *the man* or *the dog*, but because of their order in relation to the verb (the subject of the sentence occurs before the inflected verb here; the direct object appears directly after it). Another important contrast in meaning occurs between the sentences *It is raining today* and *Is it raining today?*, where the order of the elements subject and verb (together with the intonation of the sentence) signals whether the sentence is a statement or a question.

All the words and morphemes of a given language in one exhaustive list would constitute the **lexicon** of that language. The lexica of languages are notoriously unpredictable and idiosyncratic, and not so subject to rule and regularity as are the phonology, morphology and syntax. The lexicon of a language is subject to continual and often rapid change, and vocabulary is the one part of our language that we continue to learn for much of our lives, while the basic grammatical rules of our language are learned by and large by the time we reach puberty.

Semantics is the study of the meanings of individual morphemes, words, sentences and whole texts or utterances. When we relate our knowledge of utterance formation to the real world, that is, when we bring in notions of appropriateness and context, we are operating on the level of **pragmatics**. For example, it would be inappropriate to greet a grieving widow at a funeral with 'Long time no see!', even though in terms of its form it is beyond reproach. This level of language is very difficult for us to examine in older forms of English, since we are unable to observe face-to-face contact and other contextual constraints on linguistic behaviour of the time, though we can venture some analyses of the way utterances function in social context (see chapter 5 on address forms in Early Modern English).

1.5 The Sounds of English, and Symbols Used to Describe Them

The phonemic inventory of English is provided below. Note that it is the *sounds* that are the key, not the spelling (a given sound can be represented by more than one written symbol in our alphabet); to represent the basic sounds of the language we use the IPA – the International Phonetic Alphabet – which differs from our own orthography wherever the latter is unable to reflect the reality of the sounds of a given word.

1.5.1 Consonants

Stops: the flow of air is interrupted during the articulation of the sound:

p	b	t	d	k	g
(*pearl*;	*bird*;	*tongue*;	*different*;	*king, curl*;	*gambol*)

Fricatives or spirants: the flow of air is not interrupted during articulation, but is continuous:

f	v	s	z	θ	ð
(*five*;	*very*;	*strong*;	*zebra*;	*thing*;	*this*;

ʃ	ʒ	h
shirt;	*pleasure*;	*heart*)

Affricates: complex sounds made up of a stop element + fricative simultaneously articulated:

ʧ ʤ (*child*; *jungle*)

Nasals: the flow of air passes through the nasal, not the oral, cavity:

m n ŋ   (*my*; *needle, knee*; *sing*)

Liquids: vowel-like, with uninterrupted flow of air:

r l   (*ring, wrist*; *lung*)

Semivowels or **glides**: consonants articulated in the same position as the corresponding vowels [u], [i], but involving constriction of the lips [w], and tongue against the palate [j]:

w   j   (*w*aist; *y*oung)

1.5.2 Vowels

1.5.2.1 Monophthongs

Symbol	*as in*
i	s**ea**t, f**ee**l, rec**ei**ve
ɪ	h**i**t, **i**llness
e	r**ai**n, fr**ei**ght, gr**ea**t (NB: this sound can be realized as monophthongal or diphthongal, depending on the variant/dialect). In general, however, the sound does not appear in its 'pure' form in Modern English. It might be useful to compare these words with French *thé*, German *Tee* (tea).
ɛ	s**e**t, **e**lephant
æ	f**a**t, tr**a**p
u	tr**ue**, bl**ue**, m**oo**t
ʊ	l**oo**k, w**ou**ld
ʌ	st**u**ff, ab**o**ve, en**ou**gh, fl**oo**d
o	sp**o**ke, r**oa**d, harm**o**nious
ɔ	**aw**e, fl**aw**, br**oa**d, t**a**ll, d**o**g, fr**o**g (in British English)
a	f**a**ther, l**ah**-dee-dah
ə	p**ie**ces, p**e**ruse, sof**a** (though some speakers of British English use ɪ in words such as *pieces* [pisɪz]).

Note: Throughout the book a colon will appear, where appropriate, to mark a long vowel, e.g. [iː], [eː].

1.5.2.2 Diphthongs

aj (also **aɪ**)	f**igh**t, b**i**nary, l**ie**
aʊ (also **æʊ**)	pl**ough**, ab**ou**t, H**ow**ard
ɔj (also **ɔɪ**)	pl**oy**, r**oy**al

1.6   Structure of the Book

In accordance with what we said above about our approach to the development
of English and the dating of the periods of English, most chapters of this book
are written in chronological order. Chapter 2 provides us with a discussion of the
pre-history of English, concentrating on where English came from and how it got
to Britain in the first place. A particular focus of this chapter is the question of
how and why the ancestors of the English-speakers, the Indo-Europeans, spread
the language group out from the original homeland. Chapter 3, 'Old English',
discusses the development of English from its arrival in Britain until the Norman
invasion in 1066. It describes the structure of Old English, the nature of Old
English vocabulary, and the various influences upon its character. In this chapter
we look particularly at the effects of contact with other languages on the English
language. The Middle English chapter, chapter 4, traces the development of
English from the time of the Norman invasion up to the Renaissance. We see that
this is a particularly important time for the structure of the English language,
since it is the period in which English loses its inflectional character and begins to
look more like the English we use today. The vocabulary of English in this period
is, as always, an important aspect of its development, since it shifts away from
being Germanic in character on account of the long and intimate contact with
French. Since the changes in the Middle English period are so striking, we discuss
the question of whether English became a creole at this time, reflecting the influence of Scandinavian and French. Chapter 5 focuses on Early Modern English,
which is a very long period, scanning as it does three hundred years and a
number of important sociohistorical and cultural events. Since during this period
the Great Vowel Shift occurs and British class-based society develops, we investigate whether there is any connection between the two events. As we said above,
the Modern English period, the subject of chapter 6, is the era of two significant
developments that changed the world, making international travel and international communication and therefore contact with diverse languages and cultures
commonplace. Consequently this chapter explores the effects of colonial expansion and the development of technology on the English language. From 1800 on
we can say that British and American English are the two major varieties of the
language, and that other national varieties also develop. For this reason, we concentrate at the end of chapter 6 on modern British dialects. Chapter 7 is devoted
entirely to a discussion of the development of American English, beginning with
the first settlement in Jamestown, Virginia, in 1607 and ending with a discussion
of the relationship of modern American dialects to the original patterns of settlement on the one hand, and to British English on the other. Chapter 8, 'World-
Wide English', examines the expansion of English throughout the world and the

development of its role as a global language. In this chapter we look at the changing role of English in the former colonies and the varieties of English that have developed in these contexts. We ask how it is that English has become a global language in the past half-century, and why there is so great a demand for English language teaching. We end chapter 8, and with it the book, by looking to the future and speculating about the role of English as a world language in the new millennium.

Suggested Readings

Crystal, David (1987) *The Cambridge Encyclopedia of Language*, 1st edn. Cambridge: Cambridge University Press.

Finegan, Edward (1999) *Language: Its Structure and Use*. London: Routledge.

Trudgill, Peter (1986) *Dialects in Contact*. New York: Basil Blackwell.

2   The Pre-history of English

Timeline: The Indo-European Period[1]

8000 BCE	Hunter groups move into Lapland
7000 BCE	Wheat, barley and pulses cultivated from Anatolia to Pakistan; goats and pigs domesticated
	Farming developed on Indian subcontinent; barley main crop
6500 BCE	Adoption of farming in Balkan region; beginning of the European Neolithic spread of domestic animals, probably from Anatolia
6200 BCE	Farming villages established in the west and central Mediterranean
5200 BCE	First farmers of central Europe spread northwest as far as the Netherlands
4500 BCE	Cattle used as plough animals in lower Danube region
	First megalithic tombs built in western Europe
4400 BCE	Domestication of horse on Eurasian Steppes
4200 BCE	Earliest copper mines in eastern Europe
	Agriculture begins south of the Ganges
3800 BCE	Ditched enclosures around settlements in western Europe, forming defended villages
3500 BCE	New farming practices: animals increasingly used for traction, wool and milk. Simple plough (ard) now used in northern and western Europe
3250 BCE	Earliest writing from western Mesopotamia: pictographic clay used for commercial accounts
3200 BCE	First wheeled vehicles in Europe (found in Hungary)
3100 BCE	Cuneiform script developed in Mesopotamia
3000 BCE	Construction of walled citadels in Mediterranean Europe and development of successful metal industry
2900 BCE	Appearance of Corded Ware pottery in northern Europe
2500 BCE	Bell beakers found in western Europe, often associated with individual burials

	Development of urban civilization in the Indian Plain
	Earliest syllabic script used in Sumerian literature
2300 BCE	Beginning of full European Bronze Age
2000 BCE	Fortified settlements in east and central Europe point to increasing social and economic pressures
1900 BCE	Cretan hieroglyphic writing
1850 BCE	Horses used for the first time to pull light carts in the western Steppes
1650 BCE	Linear A script (Crete and the Cyclades)
	City-states of central Anatolia unified to form the Hittite kingdom with a strongly fortified capital at Boğazköy
1400 BCE	Linear B script (mainland and islands of Greece)
	Development of pastoral nomadism on the Steppes: cattle herded from horseback
1300 BCE	Westward spread of urnfield cemeteries
1200 BCE	Collapse of Hittite empire
1000 BCE	Hillforts in western Europe
	Full nomadic economy on the Steppes based on rearing horses, cattle and sheep
850 BCE	First settlement at Rome; cluster of huts on Palatine Hill
800 BCE	Establishment of culture north and east of Alps – first stage of Celtic Iron Age (Hallstatt)
	Rise of Etruscan city-states in central Italy
	Rise of cities and states in Ganges Valley supported by rice farming
750 BCE	First Greek alphabetic inscription
	Ironworking spreads to Britain
	Earliest Greek colonies set up from western Mediterranean to the eastern shores of the Black Sea
690 BCE	Etruscan script developed from Greek
600 BCE	Trade between Celts north-west of Alps and Greek colonies of the west Mediterranean. Rich wagon burials attest to wealth and power of Celtic elite
	Latin script
	Central lowlands of northern Europe first settled
	First Greek coins
480 BCE	2nd stage of European Bronze Age (La Tène).
	Emergence of classical period of Greek arts and architecture
	City-states reach height of importance
460 BCE	Parchment replaces clay tablets for Aramaic administrative documents

450 BCE	Athens, the greatest Greek city-state, reaches the peak of its power
400 BCE	Carthage dominates the west Mediterranean
390 BCE	Celts sack Rome
334–329 BCE	Alexander the Great invades Asia Minor, conquers Egypt and Persia and reaches India. Hellenism established in Asia
331 BCE	Alexandria founded
250 BCE	Brahmin alphabetic script in India All of peninsular Italy controlled by Rome
206 BCE	Rome gains control of Spain
146 BCE	Romans destroy the Greek states but Greek culture still important and Greek artists brought to Rome Roman destruction of Carthage
27 BCE	Augustus sole ruler of Roman empire
CE 50	Rome largest city in the world – population 1 million
CE 117	Roman empire reaches its greatest extent
CE 125	Hadrian's Wall built
CE 285	Administrative separation of eastern and western halves of Roman empire
CE 313	Edict of Milan: toleration of Christianity in Roman empire
CE 330	Constantine founds Constantinople as new eastern capital of the Roman empire
CE 410	Sack of Rome by Visigoths leading to collapse of western Roman empire
CE 429	German (Vandal) kingdom in north Africa
CE 449	Angles, Saxons and Jutes invade Britain

2.1 The Indo-European Languages and Linguistic Relatedness

2.1.1 The Beginnings

As we will discuss further later in this chapter, the pre-history of English is linked with the pre-history of a society that eventually spread to an area as far east as India and Persia (modern-day Iran) and as far west as Ireland and perhaps beyond. We know relatively little about the pre-history of what came to be called the Indo-European language group, to which English belongs, largely because there are no written records to go on. However, we are not completely without ideas about how the Indo-European language developed and spread across such a wide geographical area, thanks to the archaeological record, a process which we call linguistic reconstruction, to be discussed later in the chapter, insights from modern dialectology, and otherwise educated speculation in areas such as anthropology and agriculture.

The timeline of history above illustrates some of the cataclysmic sociohistorical and technological developments that took place within an 8500-year span, from the first indications of nomadic tribes in Lapland to the settlement of Britain by the Angles, Saxons and Jutes in CE 449. While we are all aware of the importance of events such as the rise and fall of the Greek and Roman empires, we must also recognize the extreme significance of peaceable developments in agriculture and transport, such as the development of arable farming and the domestication of animals, and the use of the plough to help in sowing crops. Linguistically, what is most important is the spread of spoken varieties of Indo-European, probably along with the development of agricultural practices and the societal organizations that accompanied it, and the later development of writing. We will discuss the link that has been posited between the spread of language and the spread of agricultural practice at the end of this chapter.

We must also realize, however, that the study of language history itself is a relatively recent phenomenon, and that this fact, too, has consequences for the types of tale we can tell in a chapter of this kind.

2.1.2   *The Development of Historical Linguistics*

Historical or diachronic linguistics is evolutionary in nature. In the nineteenth century Darwin's theory of evolution had a profound influence on all areas of science, including linguistics, though it has also been shown (Sampson, 1980) that the influence flowed in the opposite direction as well. It is therefore not surprising that in the last century mainstream linguistic work was historical and comparative, while theories of language development were analogous to biological theories. For example, it was maintained that languages have a life-cycle and develop according to evolutionary laws. Furthermore, linguists used biological metaphors, suggesting that language, like *Homo sapiens*, has a genealogical or family tree, or, in other words, that every language can be traced back to a common ancestor. This theory of language, developed by the German linguist August Schleicher, is referred to by the German term *Stammbaumtheorie*: 'family tree theory'. According to this theory there are genetic relationships amongst languages and the similarities and differences amongst them, if they are related, are regular and systematic, that is, reducible to rule. The push to recognize systematicity is very important to linguistic history, since it helped lift linguistics out of the realm of philosophical speculation and into the arena of scientific (empirical) observation.

2.1.3 Genetic Relatedness

On the whole, all languages of the world are considered by most linguists to be (at least potentially) 'equal'. By this they mean that no one language is more or less complete than any other, and that all languages have an equal capacity or potential to develop the expressive functions needed by their speakers. However, in terms of form, there are natural indications that some languages seem closer to one another than others. For example, German speakers can usually learn Swedish far more readily than they can learn Russian, though this would not necessarily be the case for Bulgarians, and even less likely for Malaysians or Inuits. This is because German and Swedish are closely related languages – they are both members of the **Germanic sub-family** and have many linguistic features in common – whereas Russian and Bulgarian are members of a different sub-family, Slavonic. Just as members of one nuclear animal or human family resemble each other more than they resemble their cousins or members of other species, so languages within the same language subgroup resemble each other more than they resemble languages descending from other branches of the family tree, or completely unrelated families. Borrowing the biological metaphor, then, we might indeed say that the various languages of the world belong to different families and bear offspring. These similarities and differences amongst them support the theory that there is a 'genetic' relatedness amongst languages. For example, if we count to ten in German, English and Swedish, we observe similarities amongst these languages that are not shared when we count from one to ten in, say, Finnish, a language that, despite its geographical proximity, is from a different family altogether, Finno-Ugric:

English	German	Swedish	Finnish
one	eins	en	yksi
two	zwei	två	kaksi
three	drei	tre	kolme
four	vier	fyra	neljä
five	fünf	fem	viisi
six	sechs	sex	kuusi
seven	sieben	sju	seitsemän
eight	acht	åtta	kahdeksan
nine	neun	nio	yhdeksän
ten	zehn	tio	kymmenen

Because German, English and Swedish are all **human languages** we expect to
find some similarities amongst them, of course, but in this case there are more
similarities than chance would dictate. Their similarity stems from the fact that
they are related, that is to say that at one point in history they must have been (at
least dialects of) the same language – the language spoken by the Germanic
tribes. The sub-family Germanic is related to other sub-families in the major
language family, Indo-European. The similarity amongst the Germanic languages
is pervasive. With some words it is extremely obvious: German *Mann*, Swedish
man, English *man*; German *Hand*, Swedish *hand*, English *hand*. Sometimes the
similarity is less transparent: German *Tier*, Swedish *djur*, English *deer*. The individual differences depend on the history of each language after it has split off
from the larger group and developed independently for a number of centuries.

If we look at the following word lists from three Germanic languages and three
representatives of the Romance subgroup, we observe that the similarities within
the subgroups are greater, but there is an undeniable overall similarity amongst
all the members of both groups.

English	German	Swedish	French	Italian	Spanish
winter	Winter	vinter	hiver	inverno	invierno
foot	Fuß	fot	pied	piede	pie
two	zwei	två	deux	due	dos
me	mich	mig	moi	me	me

This is because Germanic and Romance languages are all members of the parent
group Indo-European. Though similarity in the actual shape or form of the words
forms the basis of such comparison, closer scrutiny reveals that the similarity is
in fact based on systematic and **regular sound correspondences** between component segments in semantically related words, which we refer to as **cognates**. For
example, where English and Swedish have initial [t], German has the affricate [ts]
and the Romance languages French, Italian and Spanish have [d]. Similarly, where
all the Germanic languages have [f], the Romance languages have [p]. The similarities are too numerous and fundamental to be coincidences or the result of
borrowing through contact with speakers of other languages. The only plausible
explanation is that the different word forms developed over varying intervals of
time as a result of the gradual divergence of the languages involved from an
earlier linguistic phase in which their predecessors constituted something like a
single language (itself of course an abstract entity composed of different dialects).
This is what is meant when we say that historically a language derives from
another language, and that particular words derive from earlier words.

Although it would appear that some sort of relationship amongst the languages of Europe had already been posited by Marcus Boxhorn (1612–53), and

that William Wooton had related Icelandic, the Romance languages and Greek in 1713 (Blench, 1997: 5), it was the work of Sir William Jones, a British scholar living in India, that fired the imagination of European historical linguists. In 1786 he delivered a paper in which he observed that there was amongst Sanskrit, Greek and Latin 'a stronger affinity . . . than could possibly have been produced by accident'. He suggested that these languages had 'sprung from a common source', and that Celtic and even Germanic might possibly belong to this group.

Sir William Jones
Third Anniversary Discourse, 1786
The Sanskrit language, whatever be its antiquity, is of a wonderful structure; more perfect than the Greek, more copious than the Latin, and more exquisitely refined than either, yet bearing to both of them a stronger affinity, both in the roots of verbs and in the forms of grammar, than could possibly have been produced by accident; so strong indeed, that no philologer could examine them all three, without believing them to have sprung from some common source, which, perhaps, no longer exists: there is a similar reason, though not quite so forcible, for supposing that both the Celtic, though blended with a very different idiom, had the same origin with the Sanskrit; and the Old Persian might be added to the same family.

(We note that Jones certainly does not share the view of modern-day linguists that all languages of the world are equally 'good' and that none is qualitatively superior to any other. But we need to disregard this old-fashioned attitude here and concentrate on the main observation, which is the relatedness amongst the languages.) Contemporary classical philologists hoped and tried to disprove Jones's theory, since it went against the religious and conventional wisdom of the day. (Many believed, for example, that Hebrew, the language of the Old Testament, was the original 'God-given' language.) The story is often told of a Scottish philosopher named Dugald Stewart, who suggested that Sanskrit and its literature were inventions of the Brahman priests, who had used Latin and Greek as a base to deceive Europeans. As one might imagine, Stewart was not a scholar of Sanskrit.

In 1816 the German linguist Franz Bopp confirmed the relationship amongst Sanskrit, Latin, Greek, Persian and Germanic. Rasmus Rask, a Danish scholar, corroborated this finding and produced evidence that Armenian and Lithuanian were also related. Rask was the first linguist to describe formally the regularity of certain phonological differences amongst related languages; that is, he was the first to attach formal significance to the notion of sound change. Jakob Grimm (the ethnographer of fairy-tales) followed up Rask's phonological investigation with a four-volume treatise expressing the regular sound correspondences amongst Latin, Greek, Sanskrit and the Germanic languages. We will discuss his ideas in detail, after we explore the Indo-European family tree in section 2.2 below.

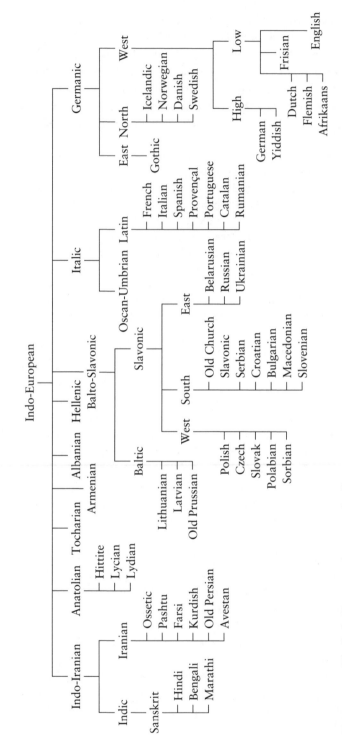

Figure 2.1 The Indo-European language family

2.2 Linguistic Developments: The Indo-European Language Family

2.2.1 Family-Tree Relationships

As a result of the research of Jones, Bopp, Rask, Grimm, Schleicher and others we now speak of the **Indo-European family** of languages from which we derive English, German, French, Greek, Latin etc. (see figure 2.1). **Linguistic reconstruction**, that is, educated guesses or calculations about earlier unattested or unrecorded forms of language, based on observed sound correspondences, enabled linguists to posit the **proto-language**, *Indo-European, as the original or **unitary language** for a group of languages that now range geographically from India and Iran in the East to Britain and North America in the West. (Note that in this chapter an asterisk before the name of a language is used to denote the fact that the language is reconstructed and unattested.) Such a unitary language, the common source of all the languages in a particular family, is termed the **Ursprache**, a fictitious, **reconstructed** entity, the **parent** language of the whole group. A common language from which some of the languages of a group sprang is called a **Grundsprache** (basic language). Thus, as we can see in figure 2.1, Latin is the Grundsprache for French, Italian, Spanish, Portuguese and Rumanian. Latin and Greek are termed **sister** languages and French is called a **daughter** language of Latin, according to the matrilineal terminology of genealogical linguistic theory.

We will now take a necessarily brief look at this family tree, pointing out major sources of information about a number of the languages and the relationship of the branches to contemporary vernacular languages.

2.2.2 The Indo-European Family

Not all linguists agree on the exact relationship amongst the branches – or nodes – of the I-E language family. Some relationships amongst individual branches can be quite complex and difficult to recognize, while others are more obvious. If we now broaden our observation of the words for 'one' to 'ten' to encompass other sub-groups of Indo-European and compare these again with Finnish we can exemplify more closely the way in which sound correspondences were detected.

English	Gothic	Latin	Greek	Sanskrit	Finnish
one	ains	unus	heis	ekas	yksi
two	twai	duo	duo	dva	kaksi
three	threis	tres	treis	trayas	kolme

four	fidwor	quattuor	tettares	catvaras	neljä
five	fimf	quinque	pente	panca	viisi
six	saihs	sex	heks	sat	kuusi
seven	sibun	septem	hepta	sapta	seitsemän
eight	ahtau	octo	okto	asta	kahdeksan
nine	niun	novem	ennea	nava	yhdeksän
ten	taihun	decem	deka	dasa	kymmenen

We see here from the basic quality of the sounds in the same positions within these cognate words (dental vs. nasal, for example) that English and Gothic appear particularly closely related to each other, as do Greek and Latin, while all of these first five languages together exhibit a basic relatedness which is not shared by Finnish. The exact relationship between English and Gothic and between Greek and Latin and Sanskrit demands much painstaking analysis of the correspondences between individual sounds assessed in terms of the history of each language. The following lists of cognates for *sun* and *moon* in selected Indo-European languages further illustrate how obvious some of the correspondences are, especially for the word *sun*, while others remain more obscure. Note particularly the sharp division of I-E languages into two groups for *moon*: those with /ln/ combinations, and those with /mn/:

Sun

Classical Greek	helios	Middle English	sonne
New Greek	ilios	New English	sun
Latin	sōl	Dutch	zon
Italian	sole	Old High German	sunna
French	soleil	Middle High German	sunne
Spanish	sol	New High German	sonne
Rumanian	soare	Lithuanian	saulé
Old and Middle Irish	grīan	Lettic	saule
New Irish	grian	Church Slavic	slŭnĭce
Welsh	haul	Serbo-Croatian	sunce
Breton	heol	Czech	slunce
Gothic	sauil, sunnō	Polish	słońce
Old Norse	sōl, sunna	Russian	solnce
Danish	sol	Sanskrit	suar (Vedic)
Swedish	sol	Avestan	hvarə
Old English	sunne, sunna		

Moon

Greek	selēnē	French	lune
New Greek	selini	Spanish	luna
Latin	lūna	Rumanian	luna
Italian	luna	Old and Middle Irish	ēsce (luan)

New Irish	gealach, rē	Middle High German	māne
Welsh	lleuad, lloer	New High German	mond
Breton	loar	Lithuanian	ménuo,
Gothic	mēna		ménulis
Old Norse	māni	Lettic	mēnesis
Danish	maane	Church Slavic	luna, mesęc
Swedish	måne	Serbo-Croatian	mjesic
Old English	mona	Czech	mesic
Middle English	mone	Polish	księżyc
New English	moon	Russian	luna
Dutch	maan	Sanskrit	candra-
Old High German	māno	Avestan	māh-

Source: Buck, 1988

We now turn to a brief overview of the distribution of the Indo-European languages around the world, before we concentrate more specifically on characteristics of the Germanic subgroup.

2.2.2.1 *Indo-Iranian*

This group comprises two large subgroups, known as Indic or Indo-Aryan and Iranian.

Indic

Over 500 Indo-Aryan languages exist, spoken by about 500 million people in Northern and Central India. The earliest Indic text is the Rigveda, dating back to before 1000 BCE, and passed on as a sacred text by word of mouth. Vedas are hymns, and as they became gradually more obsolete and difficult to interpret, owing to linguistic change, the Brahman priests wrote what later proved to be invaluable grammatical commentaries, and even pronunciation guides, on them. This resulted in a standardization of the language – in Indic, *samskrta*, from which we derive the name of the language **Sanskrit**, which dates from well before 400 BCE, the time of Pānini, its greatest grammarian. Sanskrit is still used by a small number of Brahmans today and is comparable to other religious languages such as Latin, Church Slavonic and Classical Arabic. Some time before 1000 CE (the Middle Indic period), some of the languages branched off, ultimately leading to the development of the modern vernacular languages spoken today by over 700 million people – **Hindi** (India), **Urdu** (Pakistan), **Bengali** (Bangladesh) and others (e.g. **Marathi, Gujerati, Punjabi, Singhalese**). **Romani**, the language of the Romanies or 'gypsies' is also an Indic language. A number of Indic languages have also been spoken in the twentieth century in immigration countries such as Great Britain and, more recently, the United States of America. We will discuss the language situation in South Asia in chapter 8.

Iranian

There are sacred texts dating from the sixth century from both Old Persian and Avestan, the language of the Zoroastrians (to which the Three Wise Men are said to have belonged). At present the Iranian languages still in use include **Balochi** (western Pakistan), **Pashtu** or **Afghan** (Afghanistan), **Farsi** or **Persian** (Iran), **Kurdish** (western Iran, Iraq, Turkey, USA and Canada). There are many others, however, and there are a total of about 60 million speakers in this subgroup. Much of this group was displaced by the Turkic languages and for this reason it has significantly fewer speakers than the Indic dialects.

2.2.2.2 Armenian

This is an isolate language of the Southern Caucasus with about five million speakers. Little is known of its early history, though we know of the existence of the Armenians from inscriptions dating back to the sixth century BCE. The first record we have of written Armenian is a translation of the Bible which dates from the fifth century CE. There are currently branches of Armenian speakers in Iran, as there were formerly in Turkey, now the Lebanon, as well as in other parts of Europe and the United States. There is a gypsy dialect of Armenian that contains virtually no native vocabulary, while it retains native phonological and syntactic structures.

2.2.2.3 Albanian

Albanian is another isolate language with about six million speakers, 4.5 million of whom live in Albania and 1.5 million in Kosovo. Once again, very little is known about the early history of Albanian, as its written records are the most recent of all the sub-families, dating only from the fifteenth century CE. Currently, there are two main dialects of Albanian, the northern dialect, Gheg, and the southern dialect, Tosk, though there are, of course, other varieties within these two major divisions. The recent war in Kosovo brought with it the displacement of a large number of Albanian speakers, and linguists will be monitoring the spread of Albanian to other countries of the world as a result.

2.2.2.4 Balto-Slavonic

This subgroup has only been attested for the last 1000 years, yet the languages in it retain relatively archaic features, such as a comparatively large number of case forms (I-E had eight: nominative, vocative, accusative, genitive, dative, ablative, locative, instrumental) of which Lithuanian and some of the Slavonic languages retain seven and others six, while still others (Bulgarian and Macedonian) have essentially lost the distinction of case in the noun and adjective. The oldest extant Slavonic texts date from the ninth century CE, making it difficult to determine the exact interrelationships within the group, so that linguists dispute, for example, whether the subgroup is Balto-Slavonic, or whether Latvian and Lithuanian constitute a completely separate subgroup. The former is still the position preferred by many linguists, as the structures and lexica of the Baltic and Slavonic languages are too close to one another to assume a completely separate dialectal base within I-E. At the very least, these two groups must have been together for a considerable length of time, either from I-E times or at some time following their development as separate groups of dialects.

Slavonic

Slavonic speakers were located in western Russia and south-east Poland already during Roman times. Their earliest known writings were translations of the Bible, composed specifically for the introduction of Christianity in the West Slavonic lands (Moravia, shortly after CE 860) by Saints Cyril and Methodius and their followers. The earliest translations were in a south Slavonic dialect based on Old Bulgaro-Macedonian, although extant texts date – at the earliest – from the tenth century. The language of these texts is now referred to as 'Old Church Slavonic'. There is great uniformity amongst the Slavonic dialects, much more than amongst the Germanic languages, for instance. It may therefore be assumed that there has been no long period of separation, and this assumption is confirmed by the reconstruction of Proto-Slavonic, since it closely resembles Old Church Slavonic.

The modern Slavonic languages are subdivided into three groups, traditionally consisting of:

South Slavonic	**Bulgarian** (Bulgaria), **Serbo-Croatian, Slovenian, Macedonian** (former Yugoslavia)
West Slavonic	**Czech** (Czech Republic), **Slovak** (Slovakia), **Polish** (Poland), **Upper** and **Lower Sorbian** (eastern Germany)
East Slavonic	**Russian** (Russia), **Ukrainian** (Ukraine), **Belarusian** (Belarus)

Through political expansion, Russian spread throughout the whole area formerly known as the Eastern Bloc, into East Germany and other satellite countries. However, the recent break-up of the Soviet alliance means that the situation is changing rapidly, and it would appear that Russian is retracting in the face of the advance of English, at least as a second language (see chapter 8). There are currently perhaps 300 million speakers of Slavonic languages.

Baltic

This subgroup now consists of **Latvian** (in Latvia) and **Lithuanian** (in Lithuania), with about two and three million speakers, respectively. **Old Prussian**, a Baltic language once spoken in what is present-day eastern Poland, has been extinct since the eighteenth century.

2.2.2.5 Hellenic

The Hellenic subgroup has currently relatively few speakers, but it is historically a very important group. **Modern Greek** (Greece) has about 11.5 million speakers.

It is assumed that present-day Greece was inhabited by I-E speakers before 2000 BCE. Place names like **Corinth** with typically Greek nasal **n** plus **dental** (*-nth*) are also found in Asia Minor. The Doric migrations into Greece took place between 2000 and 1200 BCE. In the nineteenth century early Greek texts were discovered in Crete and on the Greek mainland. The writing systems employed here are known as Linear A and Linear B. Though there was already a significant number of dialects in earlier times, the most important of these was the Athenian, or **Attic**, dialect. Intellectual domination in later centuries caused this dialect to spread throughout Greek-speaking areas and become the common medium of communication, the **Koine** or **Hellenistic Greek**. Alexander the Great and others spread this language far beyond the Hellenic peninsula: this is the Greek of the New Testament. However, the decline of Greek power eventually brought with it a reduction of the area in which Greek is spoken, illustrating the changing fates of linguae Franche that we allude to in the final chapter of this book. Modern Greek is classified into two variants: 'demotic Greek', which is based on the vernacular, the language of the people, and 'pure' Greek, which is based on the classical koine and contains classical features. The latter variety is used for more formal communication. At present it is largely confined to Greece, Cyprus and Turkey, though emigration has led to there being a considerable number of speakers in the United States.

2.2.2.6 Italic

Indo-European was brought in successive waves to the Italic Peninsula in the second millennium BCE. Comparatively little is known about the language situation in Italy before 600 BCE, and we can only speak about it with relative certainty from 250 BCE. Early Italic is divided into two groups: Oscan-Umbrian and Latin-Faliscan. Expansion of the Roman Empire tended to hinder the spread of earlier dialects, focusing attention on Latinate Rome.

Classical Latin was therefore long maintained as the written language of the Roman Empire, and subsequently as the international lingua franca of the learned.

Vulgar Latin was the dialect spoken during the decline of Classical Latin, and from it descend the **Romance languages,** though these are attested only long after the collapse of the Roman Empire. Since the Renaissance, the dialect of Florence, **Florentine Italian,** has been the basis for **Standard Italian. Italian** (Italy, with approximately 58 million speakers) is attested from the tenth century; **Provençal** (southern France, with an estimated ten million speakers) from the eleventh century; **French** (France, Canada, with about 70 million first-language speakers and 150 million second-language speakers world-wide); **Portuguese** (Portugal, Brazil, Angola, Mozambique, Guinea Bissau, etc., with 150 million speakers, 130 million in Brazil) from the eleventh century; and, finally, **Rumanian** (Rumania, with about 23 million speakers) is attested only from the sixteenth century.

Through colonial expansion into South and Central America, **Spanish** has become one of the most widely spoken languages in the world. It is the first language of approximately 280 million people and is also spoken by bilingual speakers of Spanish, Catalan and Amerindian languages. The Brazilians alone speak Portuguese rather than Spanish, which replaced many of the indigenous languages of South America.

2.2.2.7 Celtic

Celtic has many characteristics in common with Italic, but the exact relationship between these two groups is uncertain and therefore they are classified as separate subgroups. From place names such as **Bohemia** (< *Boii,* the name of a Celtic tribe), we assume that the Celts inhabited central Europe at an early date. We know they expanded greatly in the second millennium BCE and established themselves in Spain and northern Italy and later almost conquered Rome. They penetrated into Asia Minor as far as modern-day Ankara, Turkey, and were clearly distinct from other groups at the time of St Paul's missionary journeys, as his Epistle to the Galatians attests. St Jerome reported that they had maintained their Celtic speech until his day, the fourth century CE. During their expansion they figured greatly in Gaul, Britain and Ireland. Since the beginning of the modern era, however, the Celtic languages have been in decline. We will have more to say about the Celts when we discuss the languages of Britain before the English settlement.

The Celtic languages are traditionally classified as two subgroups: P-Celtic or **Brythonic,** and Q-Celtic or **Goidelic.** This classification is based on a significant difference in the development of sounds in the two branches. In Proto-Indo-European there is thought to have been a consonant that may have been pronounced as a velar stop with rounded lips [k^w], rather like the <qu> in English *question.* According to Price (1984: 16), in languages where this sound occurs it frequently changes to a /p/ because, instead of the air being stopped at the velum, it is stopped at the lips (thus, Latin *equus* is equivalent to Greek *hippos* 'horse'). In Brythonic Celtic (i.e., Welsh, Cornish and Breton) [k^w] developed into /p/.

However, in Goidelic or Gaelic (Irish, Scottish Gaelic and Manx) the [kʷ] was retained for a while (and written as <q>, though it was later simplified to /k/ and written as <c>).

Irish (Goidelic) Welsh (Brythonic)

Q-Celtic	P-Celtic	
cé	pwy	*who*
ceathair	pedwar	*four*
ceann	pen	*head*
ċoire	pair	*cauldron*
cruth	pryd	*appearance*

(adapted from Price, 1984: 17)

Brythonic

Gaulish was a continental Brythonic dialect, and is no longer spoken. The remaining Brythonic dialects, **Welsh** (Wales), **Cornish** (Cornwall) and **Breton** (northern France), are continuations of the dialects spoken in Britain before the Roman invasion. The earliest manuscript materials are **glosses** from *c*.800 CE of Welsh and Breton. There is a wealth of Welsh literary material from the twelfth century. Like the other Celtic languages, the Brythonic Celtic group has largely given way to English in Britain and French in France (see chapter 6 for a discussion of English in Scotland, Wales and Ireland). If we take Welsh as an illustration here, while the census of 1891 listed 494,000 Welsh monoglot speakers (which constituted one-third of the population at the time), by 1901 no more than 15 per cent of the population were monoglot Welsh speakers. By 1911 the proportion had dropped to 9 per cent and by 1921 it was 6 per cent; in 1931 there were only 4 per cent monoglot Welsh speakers (Lockwood, 1975: 37). By 1961 there were only 26,000 monoglot Welsh speakers in all and we can assume that in the year 2001 there may well be none at all. Modern Welsh has 500,000 speakers in total, and Breton fewer than 500,000, while Cornish reportedly became extinct in 1777, when Dolly Pentreath, the last recorded speaker, died. While there are still a handful of people who profess to know Cornish, they can be considered in no way either fluent or native speakers of the language, which is, speaking realistically, extinct.

Goidelic

Two languages have been attested in this subgroup: **Irish** (Erse or **Irish Gaelic**) and **Manx**. The last Manx speaker, Ned Mandrell, died in 1974 (Edwards, 1985: 65). While Brythonic Celtic had been spoken in the Lowlands and along the eastern coast of Scotland – Lockwood (1975: 18) refers to this as 'Pictish Celtic' – Irish Gaelic was taken to Scotland from the middle of the fifth century, starting with Argyll in the West, and the language there is referred to as **Scots Gaelic**.

In Ireland several dialects developed, some of which have been completely supplanted by English. With the establishment of Eire, the Irish Republic, one of these dialects, **Munster**, was proposed as the national language, but political and economic circumstances and the prestige of English have thwarted the attempt to revive Irish as a viable international language.

The future of this branch of Celtic is therefore also severely threatened. Irish has 30,000 first-language speakers, though fewer than about 5,000 were registered as monolingual in Irish even in 1981; many more (up to a million) have learned some Irish as a second language in school, though with radically varying levels of proficiency. Although at the end of the nineteenth century there were a quarter of a million Scots Gaelic speakers, it is now still spoken in the Highlands and the Western Isles by fewer than 80,000 first-language speakers.

We will discuss the linguistic situation in Wales, Ireland and Scotland in greater detail in chapter 6.

2.2.2.8 *Germanic*

Much of the displacement of the Celtic languages was brought about by the Germanic peoples, who migrated for over 1000 years and penetrated westward to Iceland, Greenland and America, eastward to former Baltic and Slavonic territory, and south-west as far as Africa. From the sixteenth century on, Germanic speakers, particularly the English, embarked on programmes of colonial expansion and were subject to other migrations, which carried them westward to North America and southward to South Africa, India, Australasia and other, lesser, landmasses.

Classical writers such as Caesar (*c.*50 BCE) and Tacitus (*c.*CE 98) give us our first recorded mentions of the Germanic peoples. The Romans seem to have confused Germans with Celts, and it is speculated that the ethnonym *German* itself may in fact have been taken from the name of a small Celtic tribe.

Apart from Germanic place names, personal names and a few relics of older forms in Finnish, we have no data on Germanic until the fourth century CE. For this reason the early history of Germanic is largely based on **reconstruction**. *****Proto-Germanic** is the unattested, hypothetical Grundsprache of English, German, Yiddish, Dutch, Afrikaans, Flemish and the Scandinavian languages. The numbers of speakers of the various Germanic languages are approximately as follows:

English	350 million as first language; over 400 million as second language
German	100 million
Dutch	14 million
Swedish	8.3 million (including Swedish-speaking Finland)
Danish	5 million

Flemish	5 million
Norwegian	4.3 million
Yiddish	200,000 as first language; two million as second language
Icelandic	250,000

The Germanic languages are thought to have been relatively unified until the beginning of Christianity, displaying only minor dialect differences, and they were undoubtedly mutually intelligible. Separation eventually led to the development of what are generally regarded as three subgroups: **East**, **West** and **North Germanic**.

East Germanic

The most important East Germanic dialect was **Gothic**, though there were others (Burgundian, Gepidic, Rugian, Vandalic, etc.). Our information about Gothic comes from Ulfilas's fourth-century translation of the Bible, which exists only in large fragments. The Goths expanded into present-day France, Italy and Spain, where the language eventually succumbed to the Romance languages by about the ninth century, with isolated groups in southern Russia. However, Busbecq, a Flemish ambassador of Charles V, observed Crimean Gothic still being spoken in Turkey as late as the sixteenth century and recorded some of the words he encountered. No modern Germanic languages descend from Gothic, although at one time it was believed they all did. Moreover, there are no Gothic loan-words in the other Germanic languages.

North Germanic

Swedish, Danish, Gutnish, Norwegian, Faroese and **Icelandic** are the Scandinavian languages. Our earliest information on these languages comes from **runic inscriptions** from the third to the eighth centuries CE (though there are runic inscriptions from early varieties of Frankish, Frisian, English and other central German tribes, and there are other runic inscriptions dating back to the second century CE). The northern runic inscriptions are relatively uniform in character, since they represent the conservative language of ceremony and the Nordic priesthood. The common Scandinavian language is known as **Old Norse** and lasts until the thirteenth century. From about the eleventh century onwards, dialectal difference becomes considerable and from this time on two groups are differentiated:

| **East Norse** | Swedish, Danish, Gutnish |
| **West Norse** | Norwegian, Faroese, Icelandic |

Although the Scandinavian languages are politically separate, they have continued to influence each other and are today still mutually intelligible to a large extent (except for Icelandic, which preserved more archaic features than the other languages as a result of geographic separation). Because of a long-standing close political relationship, Danish and Norwegian are closest, so much so that it is occasionally difficult to tell which is which when they are in written form. While Icelandic has only a small number of speakers, approximately 250,000, it is nevertheless an important member of the subgroup, partly because of its conservative grammar and particularly because of its extensive and excellent literary tradition.

West Germanic

West Germanic is especially important to us as the group to which English belongs. It is also subdivided into two groups, **High Germanic** and **Low Germanic**, on the basis of the operation of the **Second** or **High German Consonant Shift**, which we discuss in detail below.

Low Germanic

Old Saxon is the essential constituent of Modern Low German, while Old Low Franconian (with Frisian and Saxon) is the basis of Modern **Dutch** in the Netherlands, **Flemish** in Belgium and **Afrikaans** in South Africa. **Frisian**, a coastal German dialect, had close commercial links with English until the eighteenth century, and was sometimes, though rather controversially, posited as part of a separate **Anglo-Frisian** subgroup. In the modern period, however, it has come under the influence of High German and has diverged considerably from English.

High Germanic

This subgroup comprises several dialects (Middle, Rhenish and East Franconian, Bavarian, Allemannic, Swabian) and is attested from the eighth century onwards. The **Second** or **High German Consonant Shift** (see section 2.3 below) split up the Germanic area into two distinct dialect regions. German dialects had existed before this change, but it was this second sound shift that broke the unity of the Germanic languages, and a clear division was made between those dialects which underwent the shift and those which remained unaffected by it. The dialects which were receptive to the change are called **High German dialects**, and those that were not are called **Low German dialects**. These terms derive from their geographical reference to the highlands and lowlands of Germany, and do not in historical linguistics have the connotations of 'prestige dialect' vs. 'non-prestige dialect' that they do in common German parlance today.

The major dividing line separating High German from Low German as a whole is the **Benrath Line**, named after a town on the river Rhine. Starting on the French border just south of Limburg the line runs first northwards and then east through Germany to Poland, crossing towns such as Düsseldorf, Kassel and Fürstenburg/Oder. It also goes through Magdeburg, but this is an exception, since it is the only one of these cities which is Low German.

It is largely because of the retention of the West Germanic consonant system (sixth–eighth centuries) that the sound system of Low German preserves its similarity to English, while the Modern German literary language, based on High German dialects, displays quite striking differences. We will look at these changes in detail below. Germany did not unify politically as a country until 1871 (and has subsequently separated and reunified), and hence there is no long-established geographical centre for Standard German, as there is for, say, Standard French or, indeed, English. Instead, Standard German pronunciation is based on stage pronunciation, *Bühnenaussprache*. Modern German-speaking countries each provide their own competing models of German on both the national and local levels. German is the official language of Austria and Liechtenstein, and one of the official languages of Switzerland, and while all of these varieties are mutually comprehensible in their more standardized forms, there are notable individual differences at all levels of formality.

Yiddish

Yiddish is a Germanic language that developed out of High German and was strongly influenced by Aramaic and Hebrew. It exhibits strong lexical influence from the surrounding languages with which it came into contact (e.g., Slavonic in the eastern European variant). When the Jews were emancipated in the late eighteenth century, Western Yiddish declined, disappearing altogether in Germany itself, and the Yiddish that is spoken today is that of the East, exhibiting strong Slavonic influence. In 1939 there were approximately 12 million speakers of Yiddish, two-thirds of whom were in eastern Europe. During World War II the number of Yiddish speakers was tragically decimated, and partly because of the Germanic provenance of Yiddish, (modern) Hebrew was chosen to become the official language of the new state of Israel. Yiddish subsequently declined even further, so that more pessimistic linguists are predicting its demise (see chart on pp. 31–2 for number of speakers). There are, however, still groups of Yiddish speakers throughout the United States, particularly concentrated in the largest cities, such as New York; literature is still being produced in the language, and there are a number (albeit dwindling) of speakers who speak Yiddish fluently and natively.

2.3 From Indo-European to Germanic

At this point an important question interposes itself in our description: how did the Germanic languages develop from Indo-European? At the end of the chapter we will discuss the socio-economic and demographic circumstances that may have caused the Indo-European peoples and their languages to migrate and split off from one another. In the following section we address the question from a structural point of view, and discuss a number of important differences between Germanic and Indo-European, which contribute to the uniquely Germanic character shared by English and the other Germanic languages in the subgroup.

2.3.1 Prosody

Firstly, where Indo-European had a free pitch accent, which basically meant that the accent, based on pitch, could be found on any syllable of a word, Germanic developed a strong fixed stress accent, based on loudness. Thus, primary stress was fixed on the root or nuclear syllable, with weak stress falling on the syllables that followed, and a second-level stress fell on the second element of compound words and a number of prefixes. German *Urlaub* ('leave, holiday') shows initial stress, while *erlauben* ('allow, permit') shows the later nuclear stress. This shift proves to be extremely important to the whole system of what was to become English: when the primary stress settled on the initial syllable in Germanic, it directed focus away from the ending of words, eventually causing the weakening and loss of morphological endings in English and a concomitant reliance on word order to signal grammatical relations. In other words, this shift of stress is believed to be the underlying cause of the major change in English from a synthetic to an analytic language, one with less morphology, relying on word order for the marking of syntactic relationships. We shall have more to say about morphological and syntactic typology in this chapter, and the breakdown of the case system and the development of English word-order patterns will be a major theme of the chapters that follow.

2.3.2 The Consonant System: Sound Shifts

On the basis of observations made by Rasmus Rask in 1818, Jakob Grimm codified the correspondences between certain consonants in the Germanic languages and those in Sanskrit, Latin and Greek, in 1822.

Following the Stammbaumtheorie of the genealogical classification of languages, the Germanic languages diverged from the other Indo-European languages as a result of the operation of the First Germanic Sound (or 'Consonant') Shift, which is said to have begun perhaps as far back as the first millennium BCE. It is not known what exactly caused this shift, which is described below, but it must have occurred after the segregation of the Germanic tribes from neighbouring tribes and the parent language. As we have already intimated, certain Germanic borrowings into Finnish, a phonologically very conservative language, do not display these changes and must therefore be the result of contact between the languages before the shift occurred. It has been assumed that the shift was still in progress as late as the fifth century CE, and linguists have speculated that the change occurred because of contact with non-Germanic-speaking peoples, as a result either of the migration of the Germanic tribes, or of infiltration by foreign tribes into established Germanic territory. This assumption will be discussed further below. Whatever its cause, the Germanic consonant shift is the most striking difference between the Germanic group and the other Indo-European languages.

Let us now look in detail at the major sound changes that separate Germanic from its sister families in I-E.

2.3.2.1 Grimm's Law

Indo-European Consonant Phonemes: The Stops

Stops	Labial	Dental	Velar	Labio-velar	Palatal
[−voice]	p	t	k	kw	k′
[+voice]	b	d	g	gw	g′
[+voice, +aspiration]	b^h	d^h	g^h	ghw	g′h

Some scholars dispute the existence of a palatal series of velars, but there is enough evidence from a number of languages to warrant their inclusion; for example, *k′ and *g′ yielded Slavonic [s] and [z], respectively, whereas plain *k and *g remained unchanged. We can describe the changes that took place from I-E to Germanic in general as a function of manner of articulation; there was no limitation on the changes based on place of articulation, as the consonants involved clearly show (labials, dentals, and velars). The first two changes were the merger of palatal and labial velars with plain velars, which can be seen as the loss of palatality and labiality as distinctive features. In the development of the Germanic system, each set of stops lost one constituent element: aspirated stops lost aspiration, voiced stops lost voice, and voiceless stops lost the only feature left – the stop quality itself. These changes then yielded the following simplified system, in which only the phones [f], [θ], [h] are actually new:

Germanic Consonant Phonemes from the Indo-European Stops

f	þ [θ]	h
p	t	k
b	d	g

We can summarize the changes that resulted in the Germanic system quite simply as follows:

voiceless stops	>	voiceless fricatives
voiced stops	>	voiceless stops
voiced aspirated stops	>	voiced stops

Thus we have for example Latin *pes* corresponding to German *Fuß* (foot); Latin *ager* and German *Acker* (cultivated field); German *Gast* (guest) corresponding to Latin *hostis* (which in turn resulted from a voiced aspirate [gʰ] changing to the pharyngeal in Latin).

These changes were originally described by Jakob Grimm (expanding on Rasmus Rask's findings) and came to be known collectively as **Grimm's Law**. (This law has been challenged in more recent years – see summary in Collinge, 1985 – but this need not concern us here.) The law summarized above did not work without exception, however, and in true neogrammarian style, an explanation for the exceptions was sought. The exceptions were first noted to be dependent upon the **phonetic environment** in which a sound occurred. For example, no shift occurred after another voiceless stop or after *s*, so that OE *eaht* 'eighty' and *spit* 'spit' do not feature a changed consonant, but rather retain the original I-E **t** and **p**.

2.3.2.2 Verner's Law

In 1875 Karl Verner (and others) explained other exceptions to Grimm's Law. While in Latin *centum* and English *hundred* the correspondence between initial [k] and [h] was according to the rule, the correspondence between medial [t] and [d] was not, since Grimm's Law predicted that the latter should have been [ð], not [d]. Verner showed that two environmental features were crucial: the new sound correspondences were in force when (1) the stress was not on the vowel immediately preceding, and (2) the sound in question was bounded by elements that had the feature [+voice] (either vowels or voiced consonants). When either of these two factors was in evidence, voiceless spirants became voiced in Germanic; thus, in West Germanic the þ (which itself developed < *t according to Grimm's Law) became a d in the word *hundred*. Compare also I-E *patér* 'father' and Latin *pater*, but OE *fæder*, with [d] not [ð].

This explanation also helped to account for the forms of the preterite in many strong verbs. We refer to this process, which is evident in verbs of four different verbal classes, as **grammatical change**; it can justifiably also be termed **morphophonological** or **morphonological change**, with reference to the intersection of phonological change and the morphological role of the elements in question. The infinitive, preterite singular and present tense of such verbs have a root-final consonant that differs from the root-final consonant of the preterite plural and the past participle. For example, the OE preterite singular of *cweðan* (to say) is *cwæð*, but the plural is *we cweden*. In the latter, the accent was originally on the ending, as it was also in the past participle *cweden*, which also has <d>, and the consonant is surrounded by vocalic elements. Far from listing exceptional forms, then, Verner's Law maintained the crucial neogrammarian tenet that sound change is regular, which is what Grimm's Law itself had attempted to show. Grimm's and Verner's Laws together are referred to as the **First Germanic Consonant Shift**.

Thus, I-E [p], [t], [k] > [f], [θ], [x] (Grimm's Law) or [b], [d], [g] (Verner's Law) depending on the position of the stress accent in the I-E etymon concerned. The picture is further complicated in the development of OE, as Germanic [f], [θ], [x] could be voiced > [v], [ð], [g] or [x], with the voicing of the voiceless spirant [s] > [z]. In OE the voiced consonants [ð], [g], [z] then underwent a secondary development to [d], [g], [r] – hence the opposition of *wearð* 'became' and *word-en* 'become' (p.p.), *freas* (froze) and *fror-en* (frozen), etc. The preterite plural and the past participle go back to ancient I-E forms bearing the stress accent in post-consonantal position; in other words, they again depended on inherited stress patterns. Modern English *was* and *were* preserve the [s]–[r] contrast within one and the same paradigm.

2.3.2.3 *The Second Consonant Shift*

In all of the above discussion, the changes are then essentially bound to the core I-E voiceless stop sounds /p/, /t/, /k/. They did not change in the same way in the Germanic languages as a whole, however: this voiceless sequence remained in Low German/English but was liable to change in High German. Compare the following examples, which illustrate the next stage – the Second Consonant Shift – affecting Modern High German but not English (though note that for k- > kx the change only appears in some dialects of High German, exemplified here by Swiss German).

(1)   **p-, t-, k- > OHG pf, ts, k(x)**

Eng.	Ger.	Eng.	Ger.
pipe	Pfeife	shape	schöpfen
tongue	Zunge	sit	sitzen
cow	Kuh	wake	wecken
	(**Swiss** German Kxu)		(**Swiss** German wekxen)

(2)   **-p-, -t-, -k- > -f(f)-, -s(s)-, -x-**

Eng.	Ger.	Eng.	Ger.
hope	hoffen	up	auf

water	Wasser	it	es
cake	Kuchen	book	Buch
	(**Swiss** Kxukxen)		

According to the neogrammarian principles of sound change we expect to find that all the late Proto-Germanic -*k*-, -*k* sounds have changed to [x] over the whole High German territory because sounds in the same environment were expected to change consistently and without exception. However, although the isoglosses for *ich* and *machen* are virtually identical from the eastern extent of German speech to the Rhine area, at that point they separate, and this is not predicted by the principles of sound change. The isogloss for *machen* crosses the Rhine near Benrath, somewhat south of Ürdingen, the point at which that for *ich* crosses the river. These two isoglosses are called the Benrath and Ürdingen lines, and their divergence near the Rhine, along with other isoglosses that flare out at this point, have led to the label the 'Rhenish Fan'. The Benrath line corresponds to the extent of Cologne's influence from the fourteenth to the sixteenth century. Similarly, there is an area where *dat*, *wat*, *allet* are found on the Mosel and in Franconia, that is, where *t* did not change to *s*.

One can account for these different isoglosses by assuming that a sound change [*k*] > [*x*] had taken place in southern German and that its effects were gradually extended northward, leaving some pockets as relic areas (though alternative theories about the actual direction of change have been posited). The extent of spread of innovation in any word is determined by the cultural prestige of the speakers who use it, and ultimately, this change became emblematic of a prestige form of German.

Possible explanations for the High German (Second) Sound Shift

While no one can be exactly sure of the cause of the High German Sound Shift, it has been suggested that the fixing of word stress on the first syllable affected the pronunciation of all other sounds. The ethnological theory states that the inhabitants of the Main, Rhine and Danube areas were originally Celtic and retained the native articulation of the vanquished tribes when attempting to speak the language of the conquerors. If this were true, we would be dealing here with a possible example of substratum influence; unfortunately, there is no way of verifying this hypothesis.

Another cause that has been suggested is that similar phonetic changes may happen spontaneously in different languages and at different times. In this regard it is fascinating to note that when Armenian branched off from Indo-European it underwent a similar series of consonant changes to those characteristic of Germanic. Ironically though, it has also been suggested that Armenian might have been one group with which the Germanic tribes came into contact, causing the consonant shift through substral influence. In other words, there is no reason to assume any link between what happened in Armenian and what happened in

Germanic. In the absence of evidence (linguistic, archaeological, or other), there is no way to answer the question about the cause of the High German Sound Shift. The best we can do seems to be to find universal laws according to which the sound systems of all the world's languages are prone to change.

2.3.3 *The Vowel System*

The vowel system of Indo-European also changed in Germanic, though the changes were not so far-reaching and were usually in the direction of simplification. The I-E vowel system has been depicted as consisting of the following:

```
  i            u
     e  ə  o
        a
```

All of these vowels – with the exception of [ə], schwa, which was only ever short – were either long or short; in addition, the system had the diphthongs [ei], [ai], [oi], [eu], [au], [ou]: that is, mid and low vowels + front or back glide.

I-E *[a] became Germanic [o], so that there was one vowel less in Germanic. I-E *[o] and [a] also merged, reducing the number of short vowels and reducing the number of diphthongs by one. I-E *[ei] simplified to Germanic [i] so that Germanic had only three diphthongs, whereas I-E had had six.

Although the I-E vowel inventory was relatively small, its members were active in morphological processes. There was an extensive system of ablaut or apophony (vowel gradation) relationships, indicating changes in tense and number within paradigms and, occasionally, parts of speech. Modern English has lost this as a productive morphological process, but retains relics of this system: hence, *sing* becomes *sang* and *sung* in past tense and past participle respectively (see chapter 3).

2.3.4 *Morphology*

I-E had three numbers (singular, plural and dual) and three genders (masculine, feminine and neuter), and all of these were preserved in Germanic, though the dual person soon died out in OE.

Case morphology was also simplified. Whereas I-E had eight cases, Germanic ablative, locative and dative merged in the dative case, leaving only six cases. This in turn triggered the development of the system of prepositions, as the meaning relations conveyed by the lost cases had to be expressed in some other manner, and this marks another step on the eventual road of the development of English into an analytic, as opposed to a synthetic, language.

I-E had only one set of adjective endings, but Germanic developed a second: the so-called strong and weak (-*n*) consonantal declension: thus in OE we have the weak form *se goda man* (the good man) after a determiner, as well as the (older) strong form *god man* ((a) good man) with no preceding determiner. This will be discussed further in chapter 3.

In I-E the verb marked person, number, aspect, voice and mood. Aspect included present, imperfect, perfect, aorist (a momentary action in the past), pluperfect and future. In the course of its evolution the focus of the verb conjugations in Germanic from aspect to tense and time relations was simplified to two time categories (present and preterite).

I-E had three voices, active, passive and middle (or reflexive). Germanic lost the inflections for the last two and developed phrasal alternatives (cf. Modern English *The books are being read*). Germanic had five moods: indicative, subjunctive, optative (expressing wishes/probability), imperative and injunctive (expressing unreality).

I-E had seven major classes of verbs, distinguished by their root vowels and following consonants. Germanic retained this same basic system (indirectly) and added a new category of verbs, the dental (-t-) past tense or dental preterite verbs. Thus German *machen* (make, do) infin., *machte* (ma**de**, did); Swedish *göra* (make, do), *gjorde* (made, did) (see chapters 3 and 4).

2.3.5 Syntax

As we note in the texts later in this chapter, the syntax of Germanic was a great deal more flexible than that of present-day English, because basic grammatical relations (subject, direct object, indirect object, etc.) could be expressed by morphological means. This greater flexibility of word order is illustrated for example by the fact that in Ulfilas's translation of the Bible into Gothic it was possible to transfer the Greek word order fairly directly, suggesting that there was still a lot more freedom in Germanic word order than there was in later periods. However, this situation soon began to vary in the different Germanic languages. For instance, when translators rendered considerable portions of the Latin Bible into OE by about 1000 CE, they did not have the same freedom to vary word order that their predecessors had exploited, a clear reflection of the changes in the system. In the next chapter we shall look in greater detail at the developing word-order patterns in Old English.

2.3.6 Lexicon

There are enough cognates throughout the I-E tree to posit a common ancestor – for example, kinship terms *father*, *mother*, basic verbs *be*, *lie*, *eat*, terms for

natural phenomena *sun, moon*, body parts *foot, head*, numerals, and basic adjectives *long, red*, as well as cognate elements for common grammatical concepts
such as interrogative and negative forms.

Proto-Germanic retained a large number of words inherited from I-E, but at
the same time it displays many lexical innovations: *back, bless, blood, body,
bone, bride, broad, child, dear, earl, eel, game, gate, ground, oar, rat, rise, sea,
soul, theft, womb*, for example. These words were either borrowed following
contact with other, non-I-E, tribes (though, once again, we cannot know this for
sure) or generated spontaneously. New words were also derived from old ones
already present in Proto-Germanic by the process of suffixing; thus, for example,
Proto-Germanic **iskaz* (-ish) was added to other elements to create nouns and
adjectives denoting nationality.

2.3.7 Semantics

Over the history of I-E, which can be taken as a period lasting several thousands
of years, the number of semantic shifts from I-E to Germanic must have been
very significant; but since there are neither I-E texts nor Common Germanic
texts, we can only resort to comparisons of linguistic forms from such early
written languages as Latin, Greek, and Sanskrit with their Germanic cognates.
Thus, for example, Latin *vesper* 'evening', although phonologically changed, is
related to the Germanic words for *west*, e.g. Swedish *väst*, Dutch *western*; I-E
*gembh- 'bone, tooth' is realized as Germanic *comb*, both suggesting a shift from
the original form to the new function: from the sun setting in the west to the
evening, and from one 'tooth' to a collection of 'many teeth' – a comb. A similar
set of forms are the words *book, beech* (tree), the former possibly originally
related to the substance out of which a book could have been made, while the
actual words *book*, German *Buch* are related to the Gothic *boka* 'letter of the
alphabet'; in the latter instance we have the extension of the idea of 'one written
element' (i.e., a letter) to one encompassing a large written work as a whole: a
collection of letters.

2.3.8 Indo-European/Germanic Texts

There are no extant texts that can be taken to represent either Proto-Indo-
European or Proto-Germanic. Although linguists have tried to reconstruct stories in
Proto-Indo-European, these would certainly not do for linguistic research, since
they themselves are artificial creations, artefacts. Instead, therefore, linguists frequently use the earliest Latin, Greek, Hittite, and Sanskrit texts to represent I-E,
while Old English, Old Norse or Gothic texts are used to represent Germanic.

2.3.9 Neogrammarians, Structuralists and Contemporary Linguistic Models

After the initial flurry of linguistic reconstruction – and the birth of comparative linguistics – in the first half of the nineteenth century, the new linguistic science developed into one founded on empirical rigour and the search for rule-ordered observations about language. By the end of the century the neogrammarians (in German *Junggrammatiker*, a wonderful pun on 'novel' and 'young') had developed the idea that language change was regular and rule-governed, and that 'exceptions' to rules must themselves be subject to other rules that still needed to be worked out. The basic premise was a sound one, in that the reconstruction of any proto-language such as I-E had to take place within strict parameters: language X was related to language Y and Z, and Y to Z, as a function of predictable phonological and morphological change – as far as that is possible (compare the discussion of Grimm's and Verner's Laws, above). However, this basic tenet eventually proved too strong: not every exception can be explained by means of rules, as human language is neither a perfect system nor ideally symmetrical, and it is certainly not unchanging over time. (In fact, there are two maxims in linguistics that seem to completely contradict each other. One is that 'sound-laws admit of no exception', and the other that 'every word has its own history'!)

The realization of the limitations of comparative and historical linguistics, coupled with research on new non-Indo-European languages that did not fit the Latin and Greek mould on which neogrammarian models were built, heralded a new approach to language study: structuralism. Language was now studied as a structure, as a system that admitted change within it. Structuralists over the next century developed various means of linguistic analysis, from close phonetic descriptions of forms and sounds to the development of theories regarding the essential building blocks underlying these sounds. Essential sounds or phones that could change meaning from one word to the next were termed 'phonemes', essential morphs expressing discrete grammatical meaning were labelled 'morphemes', and so on (see chapter 1). The emphasis on linguistic structures allowed for greater flexibility of linguistic analysis, such that the basic elements of language X could be compared with those of language Y, without the two languages having to be related.

This is not to say that comparative-historical linguistics gave way completely to structuralism, but rather that historical linguists were able to make use of structural principles in their analyses and reconstructions. Thus, for the history of a given language such as English, it became possible to discuss any change (whether phonological or morphological) in terms of what was critical for the *system* at a given time. The Saussurean principles of **synchrony** (i.e. at one point in time) and **diachrony** (i.e. over a period of time) were not mutually exclusive, but could intersect: no longer would one be limited to atomistically describing the development of, say, one vowel, from 4000 BCE to 2000 CE; rather, one could compare the system as it was in 500 BCE with the system of 1000 CE, for example. It is true to say, however, that more emphasis was placed on synchronic than on diachronic linguistics for several decades in the twentieth century.

Later developments in linguistic enquiry, such as transformational-generative grammar, then government and binding and now minimalist theory, took the structuralist ideas further by emphasizing and trying to describe underlying processes of language in general, that is in terms of the syntactic processes involved in their generation, rather than in terms of the underlying forms themselves.

Of course, over the last century the major schools of linguistic thought have been complemented by the development of many other approaches to the study of language, such as psycholinguistics, computational linguistics and artificial intelligence. Historical linguistics has been complemented especially by sociolinguistics, which focuses on the nature of language as a social phenomenon and the correlation between social and demographic features and the use of linguistic tokens, and the way in which language functions in society. The social dimension of language is crucial to the present study of English, and is developed throughout the book.

2.4 Typological Classification

While it is usually fruitful to classify the languages of the world according to their genetic relatedness to other languages, we also benefit from analysing formal linguistic correspondences *across* language families. It stands to reason that all human languages share the common property that they are just that, naturally occurring human (as opposed to, say, artificial or machine) languages, and as such they must have certain things in common. One thing they all have in common, for example, is that they have to have at least one vowel in their sound systems. This is what we call an absolute universal. By looking at language universals and language types, we can discover the limits of what defines a human language, and we can discover the limits of variation across languages. Such work has been the focus of numerous linguists since the 1960s, in particular Joseph Greenberg and Bernard Comrie. It is important for us to look at language universals and particularly linguistic typology in the present study, since English is a language which has dramatically changed in terms of linguistic type since Old English. In order to appreciate the full significance of that change, we need to have some idea of the theory and methods behind the study of language universals and linguistic typology.

2.4.1   Universals

As broad-based definitions, we can start by saying that language universals are those properties of language that are common to all human languages, while language typology assigns languages to different types according to the formal differences amongst languages.

There are three fundamental questions that we need to ask when developing a theory of language universals:

(1)   Which properties are necessary to any human language?
(2)   Which properties are possible in a human language but not necessary?
(3)   Which properties are impossible for any human language?

When we develop typologies, we base them on some particular parameter, such as the absence or presence of nasalized vowels. A certain number of logically possible types are establizhed (e.g., in the above instance +/– nasal vowels) and each language in the sample under study is assigned to one of these types. If indicated by the sample, languages can then be cross-classified on different parameters. Sometimes, all the types that are logically possible are represented in the sample with no marked skewing, but this is not particularly interesting to language universals. However, when some of the possibilities are not represented, the typological result becomes important for the statement of language universals.

2.4.1.1   Syntactic Universals

Greenberg postulated that languages with V(erb), S(ubject), O(bject) – i.e., VSO – basic word order have prepositions. There are four logical possibilities: VSO + prepositions, VSO – prepositions, non-VSO + prepositions, non-VSO – prepositions. A large number of languages fall into the first, third and fourth categories, but none into the second. Thus, cross-classifying languages in terms of basic word order (VSO vs. non-VSO) and the presence vs. absence of prepositions led Greenberg to establish a language universal.

Greenberg also postulated that in basic word order the subject *tends* to precede the object. There are three basic clause constituents, S, V, O, which gives six logical possibilities for linear arrangement: SOV, SVO, VSO, VOS, OVS, OSV. The first three types are all consistent with the stated universal and the vast majority of the world's languages conform to these types. The fourth type has very few members, the fifth even fewer and the sixth hardly any (possibly a few Amazon Basin languages). Thus, typologizing languages in terms of six logically possible types leads us to the recognition that subjects precede objects in unmarked word order. Thus, in Modern English we see the contrast in markedness between the following two sentences:

Strawberries taste good.
S   V   O
Strawberries, I like; blackcurrants make me sick.
O   S V

While the first sentence is perfectly fine as a unit on its own, the second sentence only works if the first clause is *contrasting* with something else. In other words, the second sentence features marked word order.

Languages that are closely related can differ markedly along typological parameters. For example Hawkins (1985) illustrates the remarkable differences between German and English with reference to word order and semantic relations. To take just one example, while in German the grammatical subject of the sentence tends to be the semantic subject, in English there is not always such a direct correspondence between grammatical and semantic roles:

English: The key slowly opened the door.
German: *Der Schlüssel öffnete langsam die Tür.
              The key opened slowly the door.
              Mit dem Schlüssel öffnete man langsam die Tür.
              With the key opened (some)one slowly the door.
              (= Someone slowly opened the door with the key.)

This is yet another example of the way in which the shift from an inflectional (case-marking) to an analytic language has affected the structural make-up of English. Interestingly, while word order is more restricted, semantically there appears to be greater licence than in German, as with these 'personification-based' examples.

2.4.2 *Morphological Typology*

The major typological shift in English that we have just alluded to requires us to understand how morphological typology works. In 1818 August von Schlegel proposed a typological classification in terms of morphological structure. Morphological typology usually recognizes three canonical types of language: **isolating**, **agglutinating**, and **fusional** (occasionally also **polysynthetic** or **incorporating**).

An (ideal) isolating language has a 1:1 correspondence between words and morphemes. Vietnamese is quite close to such an ideal isolating type:

Khi to den nha ban toi, chung toi bat dau lam bai.
when I come house friend I, PL I begin do lesson PL
'when I came to my friend's house, we began to do lessons'

(Comrie, 1989: 43)

Generally in Vietnamese one word consists of one morpheme (except **bat dau**, here, which is made up of two: 'seize' plus 'head'). The term **monosyllabic language** is also used to refer to an isolating language.

In an agglutinating language words may consist of more than one morpheme, but the boundaries between them are clear-cut, and a morpheme has a reasonably invariant shape, so that identifying them in terms of their phonetic shape is also relatively straightforward.

Turkish nouns vary for number (singular/plural) and six cases (nominative, accusative, genitive, dative, locative, ablative). However, because Turkish is an agglutinating language it is always possible to segment any given noun clearly into lexical stem, number affix and case affix:

	man	
	sing.	**plur.H**
Nom	adam	adam-lar
Acc	adam-i	adam-lar-i
Gen	adam-in	adam-lar-in
Dat	adam-a	adam-lar-a
Loc	adam-da	adam-lar-da
Abl	adam-dan	adam-lar-dan

In a fusional language there is no clear-cut boundary between morphemes: the expression of different categories within a word is fused together to give a single, unsegmentable morph.

Russian distinguishes two numbers and six cases, and even fused affixes have variant shapes, because different affixes are used in different declension classes:

	table		**lime tree**	
	sing.	**plur.**	**sing.**	**plur.**
Nom	stol	stol-y	lip-a	lip-y
Acc	stol-y	stol-y	lip-u	lip-y
Gen	stol-a	stol-ov	lip-y	lip
Dat	stol-u	stol-am	lip-e	lip-am
Instrumental	stol-om	stol-ami	lip-oj	lip-ami
Prepositional	stol-e	stol-ax	lip-e	lip-ax

As we can see from the following table, the German model represents a reduced fusional system in comparison with the Russian, and much of the 'morphological weight' is borne by articles, as the following noun declensions with definite articles illustrate:

	man		**woman**	
	sing.	**plur.**	**sing.**	**plur.**
Nom	der Mann	die Männ-er	die Frau	die Frau-en
Acc	*den* Mann	die Männ-er	die Frau	die Frau-en
Gen	*des* Mann-es	*der* Männ-er	*der* Frau	*der* Frau-en
Dat	*dem* Mann	den Männ-ern	*der* Frau	*den* Frau-en

As we can see from the chart, in the case of 'man' there are only two overt case markers in each number, and where a nominal ending does not express the case, the article does; in a feminine noun like 'woman', there are no longer *any* case markers outside of the article. Of course the German system is further complicated by vocalic changes such as fronting (e.g., in *Mann–Männer*). English goes even further along the continuum from fusional to analytic, however, and represents a 'slightly fusional' system verging on the isolating. While it retains some case marking, particularly in the singular pronouns, it has lost its case system almost entirely in the noun and adjective, though it does retain possessive markers 's and s' and a plural marker in the noun.

sing.	**plur.**	**sing.**	**plur.**
son	son-s	young son	young son-s

'Inflecting' and 'flectional' are terms also encountered along with 'fusional'. These are unfortunate labels because both agglutinating and fusional languages have inflections; 'fusional' is therefore a better term.

Polysynthetic or incorporating languages constitute a fourth broad morphological type. However, while they have traditionally been lumped together, they do in fact involve different processes. Incorporation involves taking a number of lexical morphemes and constructing them into a single word, e.g. *lighthouse*. This process is extremely productive in some languages and gives rise to extremely long words which can be the equivalent of whole sentences of English:

Chukchi (a north Siberian language)

təmeyhəlevtəpəgtərkən
tə –   meyŋə – levtə – pəɣt – ərkən
1 pers.sg.subj. great   head   ache   have
'I have a big headache'

(Comrie, 1989: 45)

Polysynthetic languages also permit the combination of a large number of grammatical morphemes into a single word, often corresponding to a whole sentence of English:

Eskimo (Siberian-Yupik)

angyaghllangyugtuq
angya – ghlla – ng – yug – tuq
boat AUGMENT   ACQUIRE DESIDERATIVE 3 pers.sg.
'he wants to acquire a big boat'

(Comrie, 1989: 45)

However, in Eskimo there is only one lexical morpheme, so Eskimo is polysynthetic, not incorporating.

There is no language that represents an ideal morphological type, as it is the nature of language to change over time, and not all parts of the language system change at the same rate and at the same time. Instead, morphological typology represents a typological continuum, and we can assign each language a place along a cline from synthetic to analytic. Originally, many proponents of typological classification absurdly associated excellence as well as evolutionary standard with their classes, but this is no longer the case and all types are recognized as equally well suited to the communicative needs of their speakers.

We must also note that languages can change in their typological classification, and English is a case in point. In the following chapters we will be examining the typological development of English from a clearly inflecting, or fusional, language in its earliest manifestations in OE, to one that is now only slightly fusional, and much more analytic in type. Furthermore, we will discuss the concomitant change in syntactic type, from a Pragmatic Word Order language to a Grammatical Word Order language.

2.5   Sociolinguistic Focus. The Indo-European Tribes and the Spread of Language. Language Contact and Language Change. Archaeological Linguistics

In the introduction to this book we asked the question 'Why do languages change?' With respect to the great spread and diversity of the Indo-European languages, we must look at geography as a major factor. The movement of peoples from one habitat to another – whether as aggressors, or for reasons of safety (avoiding or escaping conflict), or in order to improve their way of life (moving to lands better suited for agriculture or pasturing) – is an especially significant factor that had far-ranging consequences for language change within the Indo-European language family.

2.5.1 *Language Contact*

The term 'language contact' can be taken to describe a number of sociolinguistic situations. In its most straightforward sense, contact between peoples who speak different languages results in contact between their languages: people must communicate, and might learn each other's tongues. More often it is the language of the culturally more advanced of the two peoples that becomes the focus for the speakers of the other language. Thus, for example, during the course of their history, the Baltic Finns borrowed substantial numbers of lexemes from the Germanic and Baltic, and at later times from the Slavonic, dialects, in order to express notions that had been absent from their own languages. Agricultural, economic, architectural and ecclesiastical lexemes are amongst those that were most frequently borrowed, and they are still part of the modern lexica of such languages as Finnish and Estonian. Change of this kind is clearly primarily lexical, but given a long enough period of contact, other changes can take place as well – most often in the realm of phonology, but at times also in the morphological and syntactic systems. Deeper change of this kind will take place only (a) after centuries of contact and (b) if the 'taker' language is not a codified literary language. Speakers of the latter will over time become bilingual, and, if use of their first language declines, they can become monolingual speakers of what was earlier their second language. The final stage is of course 'language death', and there are many examples of this phenomenon from around the world (compare, for example, Cornish and Old Prussian mentioned above). Linguistic change caused by the coming together of two peoples and their languages can be termed 'adstratum' influence, while the eventual dominance of one language over another has been described as a 'superstratum' phenomenon.

The landmass known as 'Eurasia' has been neither uninhabited nor mute for several millennia, and speakers of Indo-European dialects/languages have systematically moved into areas populated by others, usually speakers of non-Indo-European languages. If the group moving into a region (again, for whatever reason) is sufficiently superior in terms of numbers, power and culture, leading to their establishment as the dominant people, over time they can completely absorb the smaller people. In many instances, traits of the language of the latter can appear in the language of the former, a phenomenon which is referred to as 'substratum' influence. Thus, again in the Baltic realm, Slavs moving into what is now north-west Russia dominated smaller tribes of Baltic Finns, and numerous studies have been devoted to phonological and morphological features of Russian that could be attributed to such influence from Baltic Finnic.

In the course of this book frequent reference will be made to language contact, as this is critical to the development of English throughout its history.

2.5.2 *Archaeological Linguistics*

The earliest records we have of any Indo-European language date only from about 1500 BCE, which makes it impossible to talk with any degree of certainty about the earlier history of the Indo-Europeans. We know from archaeological evidence that sometime after 3000 BCE the Indo-Europeans began a series of migrations across Europe and into Africa. However, we do not know where they started from or indeed what motivated them to move in the first place.

A long-standing theory in historical linguistics has been that an original language or Ursprache developed in the early Bronze Age somewhere in what is now western Russia, north of the Black Sea. Basing their theory on archaeological finds, particularly Corded Ware burials, and using the presence of certain core words in the languages of the region in question as a second source of indirect evidence, it was suggested, first by Childe, and then in an expanded version by Marija Gimbutas, that mounted warriors from this region migrated ever farther, conquering the indigenous peoples they encountered on their way and imposing the Indo-European language on them. This eventually led to the development of the modern languages of today. Gimbutas called these migrations of the Indo-Europeans the 'Kurgan invasions' (*kurgan* is Russian for 'burial mound').

More recent research, however, calls this Kurgan theory into question. First of all, the archaeological evidence on which it rests is not convincing, as the Corded Ware burials are now considered to be local phenomena associated with emerging local aristocracies, which is hardly indicative of successive waves of mounted warriors. Secondly, the core words theory can also be disputed, since words for flora and fauna have been shown to change over time. An example we might cite is that the words *robin* and *oak*, while in common usage in the United States today, do not refer to the same species of bird or tree they refer to in British English.

Most importantly in the context of the present book, which seeks to consider sociohistorical explanations for linguistic phenomena, the question 'why' remains very firmly unanswered by the Kurgan theory. Just why would vast numbers of mounted warriors have invaded in westward sweeps as they supposedly did? Why would they subjugate the people they encountered, and why would they impose their Indo-European language on the vanquished?

The question of motivation is central in modern sociolinguistics, and is referred to as the **actuation** problem. What actually triggered the migration of the Indo-European people? It seems implausible that for centuries hordes of people would have maintained sufficient aggression to carry out the sustained invasions that Childe and Gimbutas suggested. Moreover, there surely must have been some vast increase in the population of the steppes to motivate the warriors to go out in search of new territory in this way, and there is no archaeological evidence of this.

More recent research on archaeology and language has concentrated on the cultural evidence provided by groups of artefacts and on the process of cultural change. To paraphrase Colin Renfrew (1997), on the basis of such evidence we might ask what social, economic and demographic processes might be correlated with the changes in language that must have taken place, and how might language change be reflected in the archaeological record?

While it is not without its – sometimes severe – critics, Renfrew's attempt to link historical linguistics with archaeology has led to most thought-provoking revision of the Kurgan theory. Renfrew argues that linguistic correspondences derive from a significant number of 'dispersal episodes' over the past 10,000 years. These linguistic dispersals are linked with demographic, economic, technological and social processes.

Not all language areas of the world are spread as widely and offer as comparatively little diversity as the Indo-European area. Renfrew maintains that areas like the Indo-European are the result of language dispersals, which for the most part took the form of language replacements that occurred from the Pleistocene period onward. The major reason for these dispersals, that is, what actuated them, was the need to migrate for demographic reasons, particularly for the sake of subsistence as new farming culture spread, a process Renfrew calls 'farming dispersal'. It makes intuitive sense that people would be constantly on the move in order to improve the quality of their existence: to have more land, to grow more and to eat better. Modern waves of so-called economic refugees bear witness to this sort of migration as a fact of life.

Renfrew argues that people migrated into areas that were able to sustain the herds and the crops that were supported by emerging agricultural technologies. Successful new agricultural practices and plentiful food led to an increase in the birth-rate and a decrease in the death-rate, which produced more people, and hence a demographic imperative to spread out and find more suitable land to sustain more and more lives. Thus Renfrew posits an iterative, self-perpetuating process, which could easily be sustained over thousands of years, and which could be augmented as new technologies (such as the invention of the plough) developed.

Research has shown that agricultural economies, however simple, tend to be characteristically fifty times more productive in terms of the output of food calories produced than mobile hunter–gatherer economies (Renfrew, 1997: 85). The model proposes that successful languages are transmitted along with the plants and animals from the nuclear area culture, either in a wave of advance, or when hunter–gatherers become acculturated to the nuclear group's way of life.

We might want to compare this scenario to the situation in Tudor Britain, when English-speaking trader–settlers established towns along the Welsh borders, enticing the Welsh to come into the towns to trade, but requiring them to use English in order to do so. (In fact, Welsh speakers were officially excluded from these boroughs by charter, thus further promoting the economic necessity of developing facility in English – see chapter 6.)

Renfrew's theory is powerful, as it can be applied to the dispersal of other languages, not just the Indo-European family. It is also plausible in that it can be backed up by archaeological findings that support the emergence of new farming culture, such as farming implements, crop samples and the like.

2.6 Conclusion

In this chapter we have seen that the roots of English stretch far back into pre-historic times. We are uncertain as to where exactly Indo-European began and how and when it diverged to form the subgroups that make up the Indo-European language family today. Much of the work of historical and comparative linguistics comprises informed speculation or educated guesses about the way things might have been. Occasionally new archaeological finds are made that either reinforce our theories and models, or cause us to start again. One of the most famous such cases is that of Ferdinand de Saussure's laryngeal theory from the late nineteenth century, in which he claimed that an extra set of sounds, later called laryngeals, would need to have existed in order to account for some of the changes that had taken place in the vowels of early Indo-European. Very little attention was paid to this theory until 1927 when Hittite (which had been deciphered after Saussure had formulated his theory) was found to have a symbol approximating an *h* in certain places where Saussure had proposed the presence of a laryngeal. While linguists still argue about the details of the laryngeals, it is generally agreed that this finding constitutes corroboration of the reconstructive method, suggesting that we can indeed pursue the prehistory of languages with some degree of confidence.

In the next chapter, our discussion of Old English eventually becomes less speculative, since from about the 700s we have some tangible documentation to help us through our analyses. Nevertheless, there is still considerable doubt about the *facts* of the history of Old English, which begins with an undocumented invasion and unfolds in a time when literacy was scarce and what written resources there were were open to destructive attack and the ravages of time and the elements.

Note

1 HarperCollins (1999) *Past Worlds Atlas of Archaeology*.

Suggested Readings

Blench, Roger and Matthew Spriggs (1997) Archaeology and Language I. Theoretical and Methodological Orientations. *One World Archaeology 27*. London: Routledge.

Collinge, N. E. (1985) *The Laws of Indo-European*. Amsterdam: Benjamins.

Comrie, Bernard (1989) *Language Universals and Linguistic Typology*, 2nd edition. Chicago: University of Chicago Press.

Crystal, David (1987) *The Cambridge Encyclopedia of Language*, 1st edition. Cambridge: Cambridge University Press.

Greenberg, Joseph H. (1960) A quantitative approach to the morphological typology of language. *International Journal of American Linguistics*, **26**, 178–94.

Keiller, Alan R. (ed.) (1972) *A Reader in Historical and Comparative Linguistics*. New York: Holt, Rinehart and Winston.

Lehmann, Winfred P. (1992) *Historical Linguistics: An Introduction*, 3rd edition. London and New York: Routledge.

Renfrew, Colin (1987) *Archaeology and Language*. London: Jonathan Cape.

Renfrew, Colin (1997) World Linguistic Diversity and Farming Dispersals. In: Blench, Roger and Matthew Spriggs (1997), pp. 82–90.

3   Old English

Timeline: The Old English Period

55 BCE	Julius Caesar attempts to invade Britain
43–50 CE	Emperor Claudius invades Britain
410	Romans withdraw from Britain
449	Beginning of invasions of Britain by Germanic tribes
597	St Augustine introduces Christianity to the English
787	Scandinavian invasions begin
793	Sacking of Lindisfarne
878	King Alfred defeats the Danes at Eddington
	Treaty of Wedmore
899	King Alfred dies
1016	Danish King Cnut rules England
1042	Accession of Edward the Confessor to the English throne

3.1   Social and Political History

3.1.1   Britain before the English

The lack of written records means that we know relatively little about language use in Britain before the Anglo-Saxon invasions, though the islands were clearly inhabited for thousands of years before that point. The first inhabitants we do know about are the Celts or Scots, who probably inhabited Ireland first and spread from there to the Isle of Man and Scotland, the Cymric or Brythonic Celts arriving later. Apart from them there were the Picts, who have left a number of inscriptions in the ogham alphabet from around the fourth century CE, and who probably were also eventually Gaelic speakers. This topic will be discussed further in chapter 6.

Though Julius Caesar had already attempted to invade Britain in 55 BCE, it took the troops of Emperor Claudius in 50 CE to subjugate Britain. In so doing, they supplanted the Celts, killing many and expelling many others to the farthest corners of Britain, though obviously leaving enough Celts in place to have contact with the Romans, and to regroup once the Romans left Britain altogether.

3.1.2   The Anglo-Saxon Invasions

Once the Roman Empire began to disintegrate, Roman troops were withdrawn from their British outpost and by 410 CE a power vacuum existed there. Though there had been some sporadic groups of Germanic peoples in the country for a couple of hundred years before, the invasions by the Jutes, Angles and Saxons began in 449 CE. The Jutes had been asked by Vortigern, one of the Celtic kings, to help repel the Picts and Scots who had viciously attempted to fill the power void, causing havoc amongst the Celtic tribes. The place name *England* derives from the name of one of the Germanic tribes, known by the Romans as *Angli*, and adopted as the national name about 150 years after the original invasions (*Englaland* – 'land of the Angles', with the repeated consonant – vowel sequence reduced, giving *England*).

3.1.3   Anglo-Saxon Influence

The influence of the Germanic tribes was extreme. Either the native Britons were driven into isolated and inaccessible areas of the country, or the Anglo-Saxon way of life was imposed upon the native people, as was the language.

The settlement of the Angles and Saxons was made easier by the fact that they spoke closely related Germanic dialects of the Great North German Plain, so that they could communicate with each other, and they did not look too dramatically different from the Celts, enabling them eventually to blend in with the local population. The first Germanic tribesmen to arrive, the Jutes, settled mostly in Kent, while the Saxons occupied what became Wessex and Sussex, the lands south of the River Thames. The Angles settled the huge area from north of the Thames to the Highlands of Scotland.

Eventually seven Germanic kingdoms were formed, known historically as the Anglo-Saxon Heptarchy: Mercia and Northumbria (sometimes referred to collectively as Anglia), East Anglia, Wessex, Sussex, Essex and Kent (see map 3.1). Superiority shifted from tribe to tribe in the OE period. Kent dominated early on, and in the sixth century King Ethelbert claimed sovereignty over all the kingdoms south of the Humber. In the seventh and eighth centuries Northumbria came to predominate, largely because of the influence of centres of learning at Lindisfarne, Wearmouth and Jarrow (the monastery of the Venerable Bede). The ascendancy

Map 3.1 The Anglo-Saxon kingdoms

subsequently passed to Mercia and finally to Wessex, starting with King Egbert and continuing to his grandson Alfred the Great and on to Edward the Confessor, who became *Rex Anglorum* (King of the English) in 1042.

3.1.4 Scandinavian Influence

According to the Anglo-Saxon Chronicle (see below), the Scandinavian invasions began in 787 CE; the period from the middle of the eighth century to the middle of the eleventh century is known as the Viking Age. It is clear that some sort of change occurred in Scandinavia that spurred on the Viking dispersals, but we cannot be sure whether it was famine or some other economic crisis, or a need to explore and conquer, or a combination or succession of these. There are two possible etymologies for the word *Viking*: one is that it could derive from the Old Norse word *vik*, which means 'bay', suggesting 'a man from the bays or inlets of the North Sea', while the other is that it derives from the Anglo-Frisian word *wic*, meaning settlement, so that it means, quite simply, 'settler'. These possible etymologies reinforce the ambiguity surrounding the nature of the Scandinavian invader, one suggesting the marauding seafarer, and the other the farmer who settles side by side with his Germanic kin. In the light of our discussion of the spread of Indo-European in the previous chapter, it is most likely that the Scandinavian invasions indeed developed out of a combination of aggressive spirit and economic necessity.

In any case, it is well documented that the Vikings were moved to attack all of the lands in the adjacent North Sea and Baltic areas. What began as a series of unplanned raids ended as an organized series of conquering attacks: the Swedes established a kingdom in Kievan Russia (known as Rus'), the Norwegians colonized areas of the British Isles, the Faroes and Iceland and thence pushed on to Greenland and the coast of Labrador. The Danes founded the Dukedom of Normandy and eventually conquered England.

There are three broadly definable stages of Scandinavian attacks on Britain, the **raiding** stage (from 787–850), the **settlement** stage (850–78) and the period of political **assimilation** (878–1042). During the early raids towns and coastal monasteries were plundered by small marauding bands with no centralized organization. Their main routes were from Norway to Shetland, Orkney, the Isle of Man and Ireland, and from Jutland to Friesland, the Rhine and the Channel. Lindisfarne Priory and Bede's monastery in Jarrow were amongst the targets of these early attacks. In the settlement stage, larger, more organized units raided widespread areas, settlements were established, and Ivar the Boneless and his brother Halfdan, sons of Ragnar Lothbrok, invaded East Anglia. The entire eastern part of England eventually fell to the Danes, who then set their sights on Wessex, of which Alfred had become king in 871. After seven years of resistance Alfred eventually attacked the Danish under Guthrum and defeated them completely at Eddington, causing the Danes to capitulate.

The Treaty of Wedmore, signed by Guthrum and Alfred in this same year (878), marks the culmination of the second stage in the Danish invasion. The Danes withdrew from Alfred's territory, although they did not leave England. The treaty prescribed a line, from approximately Chester to London, to the east of which the inhabitants were under Danish law. We refer to this part of the country as the Danelaw. In addition, the Danes agreed to accept Christianity, and Guthrum was baptized into the Christian church, taking Alfred as his godfather.

Though there were frequent lapses, this last development is of great significance, since it settled religious differences, the last major barrier to intermarriage, thus facilitating settlement and the ultimate fusion of the two groups.

From 900 on there was a new phase of invasion of Norwegians from the Norse kingdom in Dublin. They penetrated into the North-West, the Wirral, the Lancashire coast, Westmorland, Cumberland and as far north as the Solway Firth. Until about 990 eastern England, though still strongly Danish in blood and custom, remained under English rule; then a new and overwhelming succession of invasions began, led by Olaf Tryggvason, who later became King of Norway. At first, bribes were offered to dissuade the invaders from plundering, but their demands escalated out of control and in 1014 Æthelred the Unræd ('the ill-advised') was driven into exile, leaving the Danish King Cnut to accede to the throne. England remained under Danish rule until 1042, when the line of Alfred was restored with the unanimous election of Æthelred's son, Edward the Confessor.

3.2 Linguistic Developments: The Sounds, Structure and Typology of Old English

3.2.1 The Structure of Old English

Old English is said (technically) to begin in 449 CE with the invasion of Kent by Hengest and Horsa, although we place its start at 500 CE, since it must have taken one or two generations – at least – for it to develop its distinctive character; we do not have the first manuscript attestations of English until about 700 CE. We know that the Anglo-Saxons spoke West Germanic, a sister dialect to Old High German, Old Frisian, Old Low German, Low Saxon and Old Low Franconian.

Several very important features characterize OE:

(1) Old English was synthetic, or fusional, rather than analytic or isolating.
(2) The noun, verb, adjective, determiner and pronoun were highly inflected. Consequently, word order was not as rigid as in Present-Day English.
(3) There were weak and strong declensions of nouns and adjectives.
(4) There were also weak and strong conjugations of verbs.
(5) The vocabulary of OE was overwhelmingly Germanic in character (approximately 85 per cent of the vocabulary used in OE is no longer in use in Modern English).

(6) Word formation largely took the form of compounding, prefixing and suffixing; there was relatively little borrowing from other languages.

(7) Gender was grammatical (dependent on formal linguistic criteria), not logical or natural (contingent on sex).

3.2.1.1 OE Consonants

Old English Consonant Chart

From the following chart we see that the consonants of Old English were very similar to those of Modern English:

	Bilabial	Labio-dental	Inter-dental	Alveolar	Alveo-palatal	Velar
Voiceless stop	p			t		k
Voiced stop	b			d		g
Voiceless affricate					tʃ	
Voiced affricate					ʤ	
Fricative		f	θ	s	ʃ [ʒ]	h
Nasal	m			n		
Lateral				l		
Retroflex				r		
Semivowel	w				j	

The differences between this set of consonants and that of modern English are essentially orthographic in nature, as some graphemes can represent a variety of sounds:

(1) The consonants **w, b, d, m, l, t** and **p** were all similar to their counterparts in Modern English.

(2) OE r was not like the retroflex /r/ of British or American English, but was trilled; that is to say, it was similar to the trilled /r/ of Scots English.

(3) sc and cg were pronounced [ʃ] and [ʤ] respectively: *disc* 'dish' was pronounced [dɪʃ] and *ecg* 'edge' was pronounced [ɛʤ]. Since /sk/ becomes [ʃ] in OE, all OE words that pronounce sc as [sk] are clearly loans from Scandinavian.

(4) The fricatives f, þ, ð, and s each represented two separate sounds:

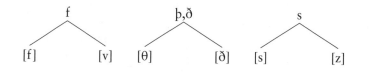

Voicing was predictable by context; that is to say whenever the sound in question was between voiced sounds it was itself voiced: *cēosan* → [ʧeːozan] 'choose'. Elsewhere it was unvoiced:

initially:	sæt	[sæt]	'sat'
finally:	hūs	[huːs]	'house'
before another			
voiceless sound:	ēast	[east]	'east'
doubled:	cyssan	[kyssan]	'to kiss'

Thus we see that there are no voiced fricative phonemes in Old English; the voiced fricatives are predictable allophones, in complementary distribution with the voiceless fricatives (that is, where the voiceless fricatives appear, they cannot, and vice versa).

(5) The sound spelled with the letter <n> was either [n] or, before [g] and [k], the velarized nasal [ŋ]: *singan* → [sɪŋɡan] 'to sing'.

(6) The sounds represented by the letter <h> were: [h] initially, including in the clusters /hl-/, /hr-/, /hw-/, [x] after back vowels, and [ç] after front vowels: *hām* > [haːm] 'home'; *leoht* > [leoxt] 'light'; *hlāf* > [hlaːf] 'loaf'; *hring* > [hrɪŋg] 'ring'; *miht* > [mɪçt] 'might, could'. In other words, OE had a velar fricative, with a possible palatal fricative allophone.

(7) The sound spelled with the letter <c> was either [k] (before a consonant or back vowel) or [ç]/[ʧ] (next to a front vowel): *cēosan* → [ʧeːozan]; *clǣne* → [klæːnə] 'clean'.

(8) Similarly, <g> was either [j] (before or between front vowels and finally after a front vowel): *gēar* → [jæːər] 'year'; or [g] before consonants, back vowels and front vowels resulting from umlaut: *gōd* → [goːd] 'good'; or [ɣ] (a voiced velar fricative) between back vowels and after /l/ or /r/: *sagu* 'saw', *fylgan* 'follow'. This voiced velar fricative coalesced with [g] by late OE or early ME.

(9) <cg> was pronounced [ʤ] in medial or final position: *brycg* 'bridge'.

(10) /ʒ/ appeared late in OE and is still rare in present-day English (beige, garage).

(11) OE had phonemically long consonants, so that *bēd* 'prayer' contrasts with *bedd* 'bed'.

(12) OE had a number of consonant clusters that are no longer in the language. As well as the /h/ clusters discussed above, there were /kn/ and /gn/, which are no longer pronounced as [kn] and [gn], but whose origin remains visible in the modern spellings *knee* and *gnaw*.

3.2.1.2 Vowels: from Germanic to Old English

There were four major changes in the vowels from Common Germanic to Old English:

Germanic		Old English
ɑ	>	æ
ɑi	>	ā
ɑu	>	ea
eu	>	ēo

Each of them is different in terms of the change in place of articulation: the first involves fronting of the original vowel, the second monophthongization, the last a lowering of the second element; the third (au > ēa) is most peculiar, as the resulting sound bears no resemblance to the original.

In addition to these changes three other types of change occurred: breaking, back mutation and front mutation.

Front mutation is the most important, and it is often referred to as **i-umlaut** or **i/j-mutation**. It is shared by all West and North Germanic languages, pre-dates written Old English and perhaps took place around the sixth century. If a stressed syllable was followed by an unstressed syllable containing [i] or [j], the vowel of the stressed syllable was fronted or raised. In other words, it partly assimilated to the following high front [i] or [j]. After the mutation occurred the [i] or [j] that originally caused mutation dropped out or changed to [e] so that it does not occur itself in the mutated words: ****bankiz** > **benc** 'bench'; **mūsiz** > **mȳs** 'mice', plural of **mūs**.

This phonological change had profound morphological consequences, producing the vowel mutation plurals, e.g. **fōt–fēt** 'feet', **bōc–bēc** 'books'. Some OE comparative and superlative adjectives also showed mutation: **strang, strengra, strengest**. There is one survival of this in the adjectives in modern English: **old, elder, eldest**, while all the others have been regularized.

Modern transitive–intransitive pairs derive from the mutation of old intransitive forms to transitives: **lie/lay, sit/set**. Second- and third-person singular indicative strong verbs mutated because an original [i] in their endings produced a different stem vowel for these persons, as in some Modern German verbs (e.g., **ich helfe, du hilfst, er hilft**: 'I help, you help, he helps'; see under Verbs, below). These verbs have all subsequently regularized in English, however.

Old English vowels

While we cannot be sure of their exact quality or quantity in Old English, we know that there were 14 full vowel sounds plus schwa and four diphthongs in Old English which we can schematically represent as in the following diagrams:

Old English monophthongs

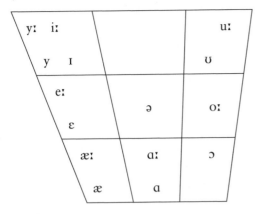

Old English diphthongs

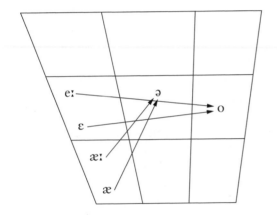

Thus we see that unlike Modern English, Old English had high front rounded vowels. The diphthongs consisted of two backing diphthongs [eo] and [ɛo] and two rising diphthongs [æːə] and [æə]. The chart below illustrates the OE vowel sounds, providing an example of the type of word in which they feature, an approximate pronunciation and a gloss for each example:

OE vowels

Spelling	Sound	OE word	Pronunciation	Meaning
a	[ɑ]	camp	[kɑmp]	battle
ā	[ɑː]	wā	[wɑː]	woe
æ	[æ]	hæft	[hæft]	captive
ǣ	[æː]	lǣst	[læːst]	last
e	[ɛ]	tellan	[tɛlɑn]	count

ē	[eː]	eðel	[eːðəl]	native lord
i	[ɪ]	hit	[hɪt]	it
ī	[iː]	īs	[iːs]	ice
o	[ɔ]	from	[frɔm]	from
ō	[oː]	hrōf	[hroːf]	roof
u	[ʊ]	hund	[hʊnd]	dog
ū	[uː]	fūl	[fuːl]	foul
y	[y]	yrre	[yrre]	anger
ȳ	[yː]	ȳstig	[yːstɪj]	stormy
ea	[æə]	heall	[hæəl]	hall
ēa	[æːə]	ēage	[æːəjə]	eye
eo	[ɛo]	seolc	[sɛolk]	silk
ēo	[eːo]	bēo	[beːo]	be

3.2.1.3 Old English Gender

Gender in OE is grammatical, not logical or natural. This means that nouns and pronouns followed different patterns of declension as a function of linguistic characteristics of the words (often inherited from I-E and not visible in OE itself). Thus *wif* 'wife' is a neuter noun and *mann* 'man' is a masculine noun, and *wifmann* 'woman' is therefore masculine also, as dictated by the second element of the compound. The switch to logical gender occurred partly because of the attrition of the system of inflections, though it actually began in the OE period and was complete by the end of Middle English. It has been suggested on the basis of recent work in corpus linguistics that feminine nouns kept their gender longer than masculine or neuter nouns, and this is perhaps the reason why in Modern English 'she' is occasionally still used to refer to inanimate nouns such as names of countries, ships and the like.

3.2.1.4 Inflection in Old English

Old English was an inflected language like Latin or, to a somewhat lesser extent, Modern German. There were generally speaking four cases in the noun systems depending on the grammatical function of the noun. The **nominative** case was used primarily for subjects, the **accusative** case for direct objects, the **genitive** case for possessives; and the **dative** case was used primarily for indirect objects, but had other functions as well. There were also rare traces of a fifth case, the **instrumental**, where in Modern English we would use a preposition such as 'with' or 'by means of' (e.g. *sweorde* 'He slew him **with a sword**'). In most instances we find that the instrumental forms have coalesced with those of the dative. This parallels the general coalescence of the dative and ablative (equivalent to the instrumental) in such languages as Classical Latin, especially in the plural noun. The Old English system retained the singular and plural numbers, but had lost the dual number (used in reference to pairs of things or persons), which was present in I-E and is retained in a few modern languages. All three original genders, i.e. masculine, feminine and neuter, were retained in Old English.

The noun

Nouns in Old English are divided into either vocalic or consonantal stems, depending on the element in which the noun-stem originally ended. There are four vocalic stems -*a*, -*o*, -*u* and -*i*, though the vowel itself was often lost in Old English, the declension being actually inherited from an earlier form of Germanic. The *i*-stems, e.g., *wine* 'friend', for the most part joined the masculine *a*-nouns and the two are therefore treated together below. The largest group of consonantal stems was marked by the presence of *n* in Indo-European; other minor groups of nouns included *r*- and *nd*- stems. Among vocalic stems, masculines consist of *a*-stems (and old *i*-stems), neuters of *a*-stems and feminines of *o*-stems, while *u*-stems were either masculine or feminine. Consonant stems could be any of the three genders.

The chart below provides a sample paradigm, in this case the masculine *a*-stem noun 'fish', showing the forms which directly underlie the regular forms of the two remaining Modern English inflections on the noun, the plural and the possessive:

Old English masculine *a*-stem noun

	Singular	Plural
Nominative	fisc	fiscas
Accusative	fisc	fiscas
Genitive	fisces	fisca/fiscana
Dative	fisce	fiscum
(Instrumental	fisce	fiscum)

The nominative/accusative plural form *fiscas* is the source of plural -*s* in Modern English, while the genitive singular -*es* form is the source of the Modern English -'*s* possessive.

Over one-third of OE nouns were masculine *a*-stems, while a quarter were feminine *o*-stems, a quarter were neuter *a*-stems and 10 per cent were masculine consonant stems. Added to this were some other, minor, declensions, such as mutated plurals (*fot, fet*), -*ru* plurals (*æg, æg[e]ru*), a number of nouns of relationship (*fæder, fæderas*), *r*-stems (mentioned above). Compare the following masculine consonantal *n*-stems *guma* 'man' and *hunta* 'hunter' to the vocalic stem above:

Old English masculine *n*-stem noun

	Singular	Plural
Nominative	guma, hunta	guman, huntan
Accusative	guman, huntan	guman, huntan
Genitive	guman, huntan	gumena, huntena
Dative	guman, huntan	gumum, huntum

It is striking that there is no longer any differentiation in the singular outside of the nominative, and, while the nominative and accusative plural are opposed to the genitive and dative plural, the nominative and accusative plural are also exactly the same as the accusative, genitive, and dative singular.

While the *u*-declension originally comprised masculines, feminines and neuters, almost all the neuters and a large number of the masculines changed declensions. The majority of the *u*-stems are still masculines, however. The chart below features one masculine (*magu* 'man') and one feminine (*duru* 'door') *u*-stem noun:

Old English masculine and feminine *u*-stem noun

	Masculine		Feminine	
Nominative	magu	maga	duru	dura
Accusative	magu	maga	duru	dura
Genitive	maga	maga	dura	dura
Dative	maga	magum	dura	durum

The following overview of the set of OE nominal endings is based on Strang (1970: 296). It illustrates clear cases of syncretism (falling together) of case endings: the masculine and neuter vocalic stem endings in the singular are identical, as are the genitive and dative plural; in fact, all dative plural forms are the same in all stem types (vocalic as well as consonantal), and the tendency is for all genitive plural forms of vocalic stems to be the same. Greater harmony is found in the consonantal stems, in which all genitive and dative singular forms are the same across all genders, while there is no longer any differentiation according to gender in the plural. (NB: elements in parentheses may or may not occur.)

	Vocalic stems				Consonantal stems		
	M	N	F	M/F	M	N	F
N	-(e)	-(e)	-(u)	-(u)	-a	-e	-e
A	-(e)	-(e)	-(e)	-(u)	-an	-e	-an
G	-(e)s	-(e)s	-e	-a	-an	-an	-an
D	-(e)	-(e)	-(e)	-a	-an	-an	-an

N/A	-as	-(u)	-a, -e	-a	-an
G	-a	-a	-(en)a	-a	-ena
D	-um	-um	-um	-um	-um

The use of the cases is described below (see p. 72).

The Adjective

The OE adjective is especially interesting for a variety of reasons. First, there are two sets of forms, termed 'strong' and 'weak': the strong endings are used when the adjective is *not* accompanied by a marker of definiteness – in this case an article or a demonstrative or possessive pronoun; the weak endings occur when the adjective is preceded by a determiner. In the previous chapter, we pointed to this second adjective declension type as being characteristic of the Germanic languages. Thus:

Gōd mann '(a) good man' vs. *Sē gōda mann* 'the good man'

Second, the cases of the adjective preserve a greater degree of formal differentiation than do the cases of the noun; this is especially true of the strong adjective, in both numbers. In addition, the adjective preserves five distinct cases (i.e., preserving a separate instrumental, something that is no longer obvious in the noun). In the weak adjective, on the other hand, and especially in the plural, syncretism is the rule. There are striking parallels if we compare the weak declension of the adjective with the consonantal declension of the noun above. The full set of adjectival forms, here with the example *gōd* 'good' is as follows:

	Strong			**Weak**		
	M	**F**	**N**	**M**	**F**	**N**
Sg						
N	gōd	gōd	gōd	gōd-a	gōd-e	gōd-e
G	gōd-es	gōd-re	gōd-es	gōd-an	gōd-an	gōd-an
D	gōd-um	gōd-re	gōd-um	gōd-an	gōd-an	gōd-an
A	gōd-ne	gōd-e	gōd	gōd-an	gōd-an	gōd-e
I	gōd-e		gōd-e			
Pl						
N	gōd-e	gōd-a	gōd	gōd-an		
G	gōd-ra	gōd-ra	gōd-ra	gōd-ena *or* gōd-ra		
D	gōd-um	gōd-um	gōd-um	gōd-um		
A	gōd-e	gōd-a	gōd	gōd-an		

Special points to notice are:

(1)   the loss of a distinction among the three genders in the nominative singular;
(2)   the realization of most forms of the weak singular adjective as *gōd-an*;
(3)   the stabilization of one form each in the genitive and dative plural for all genders; and
(4)   the complete lack of gender distinction among weak adjectives in the plural.

OE personal pronouns

Like present-day English, OE has singular and plural forms of personal pronouns. It also preserves (until early ME) the **dual** pronouns (from I-E), which are used to refer to a pair of people, e.g. a married couple. All three persons and genders are preserved in the singular. OE has also four cases in the pronouns, still distinguishing the dative and accusative forms, which fell together by Middle English, producing what is in ModE often referred to as the 'objective case'.

	Singular	**Dual**	**Plural**
First person	I	we two	we
Nominative	ic	wit	wē
Accusative	mec, mē	unc, uncit	ūsic, ūs
Genitive	mīn	uncer	ūser, ūre
Dative	mē	unc	ūs
Second person		you	
Nominative	ðū	git	gē
Accusative	ðec, ðē	inc, incit	ēowic, ēow
Genitive	ðīn	incer	ēower
Dative	ðē	inc	ēow

Third Person	**Masc**	**Neut**	**Fem**	**All genders**
		Singular		**Plural**
	he	it	she	they
Nominative	hē	hit	hēo, hīe	hēo, hīe
Accusative	hine	hit	hēo, hīe	hēo, hīe
Genitive	his	his	hire	hira, heora
Dative	him	him	hire	him, heom

The Old English verb

In the most general of terms, the verbal system as a whole was greatly simplified in comparison with the I-E system. Old English had only two simple tenses, present and past (or preterite); markers of the passive – present in I-E – were lost, and formal categories were limited to the indicative, subjunctive, and imperative.

Old English inherited a verbal system from Germanic (and ultimately from I-E) that was frequently characterized by vowel alternations within the root, known as *Ablaut*. The nature of the vowel alternations within a paradigm depended on the class of the verb, as well as on the tense and mood of a given form. The alternations themselves were not greatly changed from Germanic to OE, with the exception of regular sound changes within OE and instances of analogical level-ling. In addition to the existence of different classes of conjugation (or conjuga-tional types), the verbs are described as either 'strong' or 'weak', but the 'weak' verbs constitute the vast majority of the verbs, and the total number of 'strong' verbs was only slightly higher than 300. In essence, the weak verbs differed from the strong primarily in the shape of the preterite: the former had stable root vowels and tended to add a dental ending, sometimes consisting of an extra syllable, while the latter were characterized by Ablaut word-medially.

Strong verbs

Strong verbs are traditionally subdivided into six classes, depending on the sequences of root vowels that appear in the different tenses. While some authors include a seventh class, which consists of reduplicating verbs, these make up a relatively insignificant group, which we will ignore here. The six principal classes are commonly described as follows:

Class I

	pres. *i*	pret. sing. *a*	pl. *i*	past part. *i*
drīfan 'to drive':	drīfþ	drāf	drīfon	drīfen

Class II

	pres. *eo, u*	pret. sing. *ea*	pl. *u*	past part. *o*
cēosan 'to choose':	ciest	cēas	curon	coren

Class III (with some variation depending on the verb stem)

	pres. *i*	pret. sing. *a*	pl. *u*	past part. *u*
bindan 'to bind':	bint	band	bundon	bunden

Class IV

	pres. *e*	pret. sing. *æ*	pl. *æ*	past part. *o*
beran 'to bear':	bi(e)rþ	bær	bǣron	boren

Class V

	pres. *e*	pret. sing. *æ*	pl. *æ*	past part. *e*
cweþan 'to say':	cwiþþ	cwæþ	cwǣdon	cweden

Class VI

	pres. *a*	pret. sing. *o*	pl. *o*	past part. *a*
faran 'to go':	færþ	fōr	fōron	faren

As suggested above, different vowels could appear not just from one tense to another, but also within a given paradigm – especially in the past. The simplification of the system as a whole is mirrored in the paradigms of the indicative and subjunctive, as syncretism often took place in the set of personal endings used. This phenomenon is especially true of the forms of the subjunctive, but is seen in the plural of the indicative as well, as illustrated by the following sample verb, *drīfan* 'to drive':

	Indicative	**Subjunctive**
	Present	**Present**
	Singular	
1	drīf-e	drīf-e
2	drīf-st (-est)	drīf-e
3	drīf-ð (-eð)	drīf-e
	Plural	
1	drīf-að	drīf-en
2	drīf-að	drīf-en
3	drīf-að	drīf-en

In the present tense forms, then, syncretism has taken place in the plural of the indicative (in which one form expresses all persons), while the subjunctive distinguishes only between singular and plural. The same is true of the past tense forms, but note the root-vowel alternation in the indicative:

	Indicative	**Subjunctive**
	Past	**Past**
	Singular	
1	drāf	drīf-e
2	drif-e	drīf-e
3	drāf	drīf-e
	Plural	
1	drif-on	drīf-en
2	drif-on	drīf-en
3	drif-on	drīf-en

We note that the system is further streamlined in the following ways:

(1) the present and past forms of the subjunctive as a whole are differentiated from one another only by vowel length in the root (long: short);
(2) there is no longer any differentiation between the first and third persons singular past indicative;

(3) the second person singular past indicative is identical to the subjunctive form.

Clearly the gradual loss of distinction among a great many forms had to affect the further development of verbal paradigms; the tendency towards underdifferentiation (or, to put it another way, simplification) continued into the Middle English period. As we shall see, however, this primarily concerns the identity of specific morphological *endings*; vowel alternations within the root tended to remain, as is reflected in the system inherited by Modern English.

Weak verbs

The forms of the weak verbs depended entirely on the ending, as there were no vowel alternations (that is, no Ablaut) within the root. Many verbs could be cited as examples here, but one will suffice, *dēman* 'to judge' (NB: final *-e* is represented in some linguistic sources as *-æ*; here *-e* may be taken as a normalized variant attested during the OE period):

	Indicative	**Subjunctive**
	Present	**Present**
	Singular	
1	dēm-e	dēm-e
2	dēm-(e)st	dēm-e
3	dēm-(e)ð	dēm-e
	Plural	
1	dēm-að	dēm-en
	Past	**Past**
	Singular	
1	dēm-de	dēm-de
2	dēm-des(t)	dēm-de
3	dēm-de	dēm-de
	Plural	
	dēm-don	dēm-den

The same remarks regarding syncretism of forms made for the strong verbs apply equally to the weak.

Irregular verbs

'Irregular', or anomalous, verbs form an extremely small group in OE, namely the four verbs 'do', 'go', 'will', 'be'. The verb 'to be' can be cited here as an example, as it is especially noteworthy for having two present tense paradigms, the first of which foreshadows the Modern English verb, while the second is evident in the Modern German paradigm:

Indic. sing.			**Present**	**Past**
	1	eom	beo	wæs
	2	eart	bist	wǣre
	3	is	biþ	wæs
Indic. pl.		sind, sindon	beoþ	wǣron
Subj. sing.		sie	beo	wǣre
Subj. pl.		sien	beon	wǣren

3.2.1.5 Old English Syntax

The use of the cases

Since the case distinctions have been lost in Modern English, it is worthwhile to describe the function of the OE cases in context. The following sentences illustrate the primary grammatical functions of the case markers in Old English (note that the instrumental is left out, as it has to all intents and purposes been lost as a discrete case marker):

Nominative

Subject: **Hroðgar** maþelode.
                             Hrothgar spoke.

Subject complement: Bēowulf is **min nama**.
                             Beowulf is my name.

Vocative: **wine mīn, Bēowulf . . .**
                             Beowulf, my friend . . .

Accusative

Direct object: And him Bryttas sealdan and geafan **eardungstowe**.
                             And to them the Britons granted and gave (a) dwelling place.

Adverbial of time: Wunundon þær **ealne þone winter**.
                             They lived there all the winter.

Preposition of motion: Gewat þa ofer **wægholm**.
                             Went then over (the) sea.

Genitive

Possessive: feower hundra wintra . . . fram **ures Drightnes meniscnysse**
                             four hundred years . . . after our Lord's birth

Measure: þær wearþ Cirus ofslægen ond twa þusend **monna**
                           mid him.
                           There was Cirus slain and two thousand men with
                           him.

Object of verb of   Cynewulf benam Sigebryht **his rices**.
  depriving: *Cynewulf took from Sigebryht his kingdom.*

Dative
Most prepositions: Crīst wæs on **rode**.
                           Christ was on (the) cross.

                           eode þa to **setle**
                           went then (she) to (her) seat

                           sweord ofer **setlum**
                           sword(s) over seats/benches

                           an æfter **eallum**
                           one for (them) all

Indirect object: Se kyng þa geaf gryð **Olafe**.
                           The king then gave (a) truce to Olaf.

Object of certain verbs: Hyra feore burgon.
                           Their life (they) saved.

Manner/means: Ic him þenode deoran **sweorde**.
                           I him served (with) an excellent sword.

(**Note**: The last example is technically an old instrumental, which has by now
merged with the dative.)

Word order

As we have just seen in the morphology section, nouns in Old English were
inflected for number, case and person. Since the grammatical category was marked
by inflection, this meant that constituents of a sentence were 'moveable'; in theory
all six possible permutations of the constituents **S**(ubject), **V**(erb) and **O**(bject)
(or, better, Complement – which we label as X here) could be varied in order to
convey special emphasis within the clause. In practice, however, some word
orders were more frequent than others. The most frequently found orders were
(as, for example, in Modern German), verb-second order in main clauses (that is,
any order of subject and complement, provided that the verb was the second
constituent in the string), and verb-final order in dependent clauses.

In other words, in Old English main clauses without special emphasis, the word order was as follows:

SVO/SVX
se cyning het hie feohtan
   S   **V** **X**
the king ordered them to fight

and seo landfyrd com ufenon
        S   **V**   **X**
and the land army came from above

& þa Deniscan ahton sige
    S   **V**   **O**
and the Danes gained victory

In dependent clauses introduced by either a subordinating conjunction or a relative pronoun the verb usually appeared in clause-final position, with any auxiliary usually following the infinitive or participle thus:

þæt hie þone Godes mann abitan scolden
 S   **O**   **V**
that they the man of God devour should
'in order that they should devour the man of God'

For stylistic variation, or for the sake of emphasis, or to topicalize an element, the object or complement might be placed first in the sentence, in which case the finite verb would be in second position, followed by the subject (that is, the order would be OVS or XVS, where X stands for complement):

OVS
þa stowe habbaþ giet his ierfenuman
O   **V**   **S**
that place have still his successors
'his successors still have that place'

The object could also be found between subject and verb:

& him eac geheton þæt hiera kyning fulwihte onfon wolde
                   S   **O**   **V**
and (they) him also promised that their king baptism receive would.

Very often, especially in the chronicles and other historical-narrative documents, a main clause would be introduced by an adverbial such as *þa* 'then' or *þy ilcan geare* 'in that same year'. In such instances, the verb immediately followed the adverbial, with the subject coming immediately after that (that is, XVS order):

XVS
ða   ongan ic
X   V   S
then began I
(= *Then I began*)

þy ilcan geare gesette Ælfred cyning Lundenburg
      X   V   S
The same year besieged king Alfred London

However, other orders were possible with other introductory demonstratives and adverbs than *þa*. The following sentences are reminiscent of Modern English word order, since they begin with a demonstrative or an adverb which is followed by subject and verb (that is, XSV order):

XSV
& þy ilcan geare Tatwine was gehalgod to arcebisc
        X   S   V
and in the same year Tatwine was consecrated as archbishop

& on Pasches he weas on Northamtune
      X   S   V
and at Easter he was in Northampton

Since the auxiliary verb *do* had not developed in Old English to any significant extent, OE questions were formed with subject–verb inversion:

Hwæt segest þu, yrðling?
X   V   S
What say you, farmer?

Wære þu todæg on huntoðe?
V   S   X
Were you today (a-)hunting?

And in negative sentences the negative particle *ne* appears at the beginning of the clause and is usually followed by verb and subject:

ne geseah ic næafre þa burg
Neg V   S
not saw I ever that town

We must conclude that Old English word order was much 'freer' than it is today, in terms of the possible orders of constituents, and we must therefore ask why this should be the case, and why the word order changed.

We must recognize that the relatively free word order in Old English was inextricably bound with the fact that the morphology of Old English was richer than that of Modern English. While the system was far from perfect, it was nevertheless still the case that basic grammatical relations such as 'subject of', 'direct object of' and 'indirect object of' were often marked on the noun phrase in question. In discussing linguistic typology in chapter 2 above we had occasion to mention that in the course of its history English underwent a major change from being a synthetic to an analytic language in terms of its morphology; that is, it lost almost all of its inflections. The major reason for this has also been mentioned: sometime during the shift from Indo-European to Germanic the primary stress on a word was fixed on the initial or nuclear syllable, instead of occurring on any syllable, depending on the individual word type. This change meant that attention was drawn away from the grammatical suffixes at the ends of words, and it ultimately caused the erosion of most of these endings. This in turn caused the language to rely more heavily on word order to convey grammatical relations, and to develop prepositions to compensate for some of the grammatical information that was lost with the endings. For example, in the Modern English sentences below, we only know the subject and direct object relations because of the position of each noun phrase relative to the verb:

(a)   The girl kisses the boy.
      S   V   O
(b)   The boy kisses the girl.
      S   V   O

Since in (a) *the girl* directly precedes the verb and *the boy* is immediately after it, we know that the first noun phrase is the subject and the second is the direct object. Because the positions of the noun phrases in (b) are reversed, we know that the grammatical functions are also reversed, that is, *the boy* is the subject and *the girl* is the object. There is nothing in the actual noun phrases themselves to indicate these functions; it is simply their position *vis-à-vis* the verb that marks their function.

By contrast, in Old English, because the grammatical function is actually marked on the words themselves, they are not tied to any one position and the word order can be varied to change the emphasis in the sentence. Thompson (1978) referred to languages that rely on word order to convey grammatical relations as Grammatical Word Order (GWO) languages and those that can vary word order for the purposes of changing emphasis or topicalization as Pragmatic Word Order (PWO) languages. It is the case that this syntactic typology co-varies with morphological type, and that one usually finds more fixed word order in languages that have relatively little inflectional morphology, such as English or Chinese, and more flexible word order in those languages that have more inflectional morphology, such as Czech and Russian. As with other typologies we discussed above, there appear to be no languages that are absolute types.

3.2.1.6 Old English Vocabulary

Although we do not have vast amounts of material from Old English, we have enough poetry and prose to convince us that the lexicon of Old English was extensive. There are two major features of the OE lexicon that deserve mention. The first is the system-internal means of word formation, and the second is the extent and nature of loan words in Old English.

Word formation

As throughout the rest of its history, England in Old English times was experiencing dramatic change and the development of new concepts, products and ideas, and new words needed constantly to be added to the word-stock to reflect these developments. Moreover, since Old English poetry was alliterative, meaning that it was based on the repetition of sounds at the beginning of words, a large stock of words with different initial sounds was needed in order to keep the poetry fresh and exciting. The system of Old English provided for the coining of new words from the existing word-stock in two ways: compounding and affixing.

Compounding

Compounds were usually used to make nouns or adjectives. The final element of the compound always dictated the part of speech and the gender. In nominal compounds, either another noun, an adjective, or an adverb was attached to a noun to make a compound noun as in *lar + hus* 'school'; *dim + hus* 'prison'; *eft + cyme* 'return'. The first noun was not usually inflected, but there were exceptions, such as *dæges + eage* 'day's-eye' = 'daisy'; *Engla + land* 'Angles' land' = 'England'. Adjectival compounds could be formed by an adjective preceded by a noun, another adjective or an adverb, and participles could function as the adjectival element: *blod + read* 'blood-red'; *efen + eald* 'contemporary'; *fela + synnig* 'very guilty'; *cyn + boren* 'of royal birth'; *lind + hæbbende* 'armour-bearing'. The last of these examples is an interesting case of an adjective that can be used as a noun – an adjectival noun. There were also occasionally compound adjectives that had nouns as their second elements, e.g., *dreorig + mod* 'sad'; *brun + ecg*

'bright-edged'. The sample passage from *Beowulf* in section 3.3.1.2. below illustrates these compounds very well.

Affixing

Affixing is a term that covers prefixing and suffixing in Old English (some other
languages have infixes, which are morphemes that can be placed in the middle of
a word, but English does not, except in cursing and swearing, interestingly, as in
fan-blinking-tastic).

Suffixes in OE were usually used to transform one part of speech into another,
while prefixes were generally used to change the semantic force of a particular
word. Thus a suffix like *-dom* could create an abstract noun from another noun
or adjective: *þeow + dom* 'slavery'; *wis + dom* 'wisdom'. A suffix such as *-ig* was
used primarily to derive adjectives from nouns: *blod + ig* 'bloody'; *græd + ig*
'greedy'. The suffix *-ing* is an interesting nominal suffix, which was used to form
nouns from adjectives and other nouns. It usually had the sense of 'belonging to'
or 'coming from' and could be used as a patronymic. Thus *wic + ing* 'Viking' =
'coming from the bay' (or 'settler'); *earming* 'wretch' (*earm* 'poor'). From nouns
like *æðeling* 'nobleman' the ending *ling* was detached, becoming a suffix in its
own right, as in *deor + ling* 'darling'.

Prefixes in Old English could be bound morphemes, like *be-*, or independent
morphemes, such as *ofer* 'over'. They often had multiple functions, but did not
change parts of speech. For example, the prefix *be-, bi-* could be used to lend the
semantic dimension 'across, over' to a verb, e.g. *gan* 'to go', *began* 'to cross, walk
over'; it could also make an intransitive verb transitive: *sittan* 'to sit', *besittan* 'to
besiege'.

The perfective prefix *ge-* was most often used to form past participles: *ceosan*,
gecoren; *findan*, *gefunden*. It could also be used to change the meaning of a
word: *hatan* 'to (be) call(ed)', *gehatan* 'to promise'. As in Modern German still, it
could also be used to make a collective out of a noun, e.g. *broðor*, *gebroðor*
(brothers, brotherhood).

Baugh and Cable (1993: 53) report that English has lost 85 per cent of its
Germanic vocabulary. One of the reasons for this loss is that during and particularly after the Old English period, the language became receptive to borrowing
words to enrich its word-stock, rather than creating its own using the mechanisms described above. Saunders (1995: 102) pondered what Modern English
would look like if it had maintained the OE methods as the primary ways of
lexical enrichment, rather than borrowing words from other languages. He came
up with words such as *tug* for *train*, *flything* for *aeroplane* (cf. *Zug* and *Flugzeug*
in German, which uses this mechanism of vocabulary enrichment more than
English does). Below is a list of other suggested alternatives for words that have
been borrowed into English:

Current word	Alternative
airport	flyhaven
station	standstead
telephone	farspeak
television	farsee
pram (baby carriage)	childwain
psychology	soullore
geology	earthlore
ferrous sulphide	ironish brimstoneling

Loan words

The English lexicon has been influenced by the vocabulary of other languages since even before English itself developed. This is a natural process, since English (and, before it, the Germanic languages on the European mainland) has always been in contact with other languages and cultures, which meant it needed terms to describe new concepts and objects encountered through this contact. Borrowing words from the contact languages was one way to accomplish this. In section 3.5 below we will discuss the kinds of language contact that took place before and during the Old English period and their effects on the vocabulary of English.

3.3 Linguistic and Literary Achievements

3.3.1 *Texts*

Both poetry and prose have survived in manuscript form since Old English times, though hardly huge amounts of either. One must bear in mind that at that time literacy was a scarce facility, confined mostly to clerics. The copying of books was carried out by hand, and producing and owning any manuscript was a costly business reserved for the privileged few. Moreover, it was not self-evident that works should be written in English at all, since Latin (and, to a lesser extent, Irish Gaelic) was the language of learning. One reason why we have lost many Old English manuscripts is, of course, the ravages of time: large numbers of manuscripts must have been lost throughout history, destroyed for example by fire or flood, and at different periods, such as during the Norse invasions, especially in the early stages. Ironically, though, as Millward (1989: 115) points out, the Viking invasions originally led to the production of more manuscripts in English, because they engendered a severe decline in Latin scholarship.

3.3.1.1 *Prose*

English was the first of the European languages of the time to develop a respectable written prose tradition, partly, as we have said, because after the decline in Latin learning brought on by the Viking invasions, it became more practical for English scholars to write in English than in Latin. Much of the Old English prose that survives is translated from Latin, such as King Alfred's (own or commissioned) translations of Bede's *Ecclesiastical History of the English People* (completed around 731 CE), Pope Gregory the Great's *Cura Pastoralis* (*Pastoral Care*), Boethius' *Consolation of Philosophy*, and Orosius' history, *Historiarum Adversarum Paganos Libri vii*. Parts of the Old Testament, some of the Psalms and the Gospels were translated into Old English. Thus, most of the prose we have from this period is religious in nature. However, a few fragments of prose fiction do survive, including *Apollonius of Tyre*, *Alexander's Letter to Aristotle* and *Wonders of the East*.

The *Anglo-Saxon Chronicle* was also most likely instigated by King Alfred. It survives in seven manuscript versions and is a continuous record of annual events, starting with the first landing of Julius Caesar (55 BCE) and ending with the coronation of Henry II in 1154. But no one knows exactly when, or by whom, it was started, though the oldest chronicle, the Parker Chronicle, indicates that it may have been started in 891.

The Parker Chronicle is perhaps based on a compilation of various chronological summaries, royal genealogies, a list of the bishops of Winchester to 754, etc., originally written in Latin but no longer extant. The history of chronicles (or annalistic writing) stems from the need to draw up Easter tables to determine the day on which Easter Sunday should fall. The clerics who calculated these dates occasionally wrote about important events in the textual margins. By 930, the details recorded began to fall within living memory and they become much more detailed. The chronicle contains a number of poetic inserts, e.g. the *Battle of Brunanburh*, a poem of just over 70 lines dealing with the victory of king Æthelstan of Wessex over the Norwegian Vikings and Scots in 937. The chronicle was maintained through both the Danish invasions and the Norman Conquest. Only the Peterborough Chronicle is continued after 1079, however, perhaps as the hobby of one or two monks, and it was discontinued after 1154.

There is also a considerable body of religious prose writing from Abbot Ælfric and Bishop Wulfstan. Wulfstan was Bishop of London and Worcester, and Archbishop of York. As legal counsel to Æthelred the Unræd and subsequently to Cnut he drew up the entente between the Danes and the English.

The *Blickling Homilies* and the *Vercelli Homilies* also give us insight into religious prose of the Old English period, though they are largely anonymous.

There also survive a number of genealogies, glossaries to Latin works, laws, charters, letters, leech books and herbal catalogues, as well as Byrthferth's *Manual*, which contains information on astronomy and mathematics.

Almost all the extant Old English prose is in the West Saxon dialect, and in the modern era the Early West Saxon of Alfred has been used as the basis of a kind of standardized academic Old English, but this dialect does not appear to have functioned as a standard in the time of Old English. However, a genuine standard, based on Late West Saxon, does seem to have developed in the latter part of the tenth century. Indications of this are that there are common spellings in use by scribes from different areas, as well as a possible standard lexical stock. Below is an example of Old English prose, from the translation of *Historiarum Adversarum Paganos Libri vii*, with interlinear and following prose translations. It has been chosen partly because it is one of the more readily comprehensible texts in Old English prose, but also because it gives us some insight into the state of knowledge of the world in the so-called Dark Ages.

The voyages of Ohthere and Wulfstan

Lines 59–71 (from the Lauderdale or Tollemache or Additional MS), pp. 13ff. From Dorothy Whitelock (1984), *Sweet's Anglo-Saxon Reader in Prose and Verse*, fifteenth edn. Oxford: Oxford University Press. (My glosses.)

He sæde ðæt Norðmanna land wære swyþe lang and swyþe smæl.
He said that Northmen's land was very long and very narrow.

Eal þæt his man aþer oððe ettan oððe erian mæg, þæt lið wið
All that is one either or graze or plant may that lies with

ða sæ; and þæt is þeah on sumum stowum swyþe cludig; and
the sea; and that is however on some places very stony and

licgað wilda moras wið eastan and wið uppon emnlange þæm bynum
lie wild moors to the east and up along the cultivated

lande. On þæm morum eardiað Finnas. And þæt byne land is
land. On the moor dwell Lapps. And the cultivated land is

eastweard bradost, and symle swa norðor swa smælre.
to the east widest, and ever the further north the narrower.

Eastwerd hit mæg bion syxtig mila brad, oððe hwene bradre,
To the east it may be sixty miles wide, or even wider,

and middeweard þritig oððe bradre; and norðeweard he cwæð,
and in the middle thirty or wider; and to the north he said,

þær hit smalost wære, þæt hit mihte beon þreora mila brad
there it narrowest was, that it might be three miles wide

to þæm more; and se mor syðþan, on sumum stowum, swa brad
to the moor; and the moor then, in some places so wide

swa man mæg in twam wucum oferferan; and on sumum stowum
that one may in two weeks cross; and in some places

swa brad swa man mæg on syx dagum oferferan.
so wide that one may in six days cross.

'He said that the land of the Northmen was very long and very narrow. All the land that lies by the sea may either be grazed on or ploughed; in some places however it is very rocky; wild moors lie to the east and up along the cultivated land. Lapps (Sami) dwell on the moors. And the cultivated land is broadest to the east and grows increasingly narrow the farther north one travels. To the east it may be sixty miles wide, or even wider, and in the middle thirty miles or wider, and he said it was narrowest in the north, it might be about three miles wide in the north; and then in some places the moor is so wide that one may cross it in two weeks and in others one may cross it in six days.'

Ælfric's preface to his Latin grammar

Ic Ælfric wolde þas lytlan boc awendan to Engliscum gereorde of þam stæf-cræfte
I Ælfric wanted this little book to translate into English language of the art of letters

þe is gehaten *grammatica*, siþþan ic þa twa bec awende on hund-eahtatigum
that is called grammar, since I the two books translated into one hundred and eighty

spellum, for þæm þe stæfcræft is seo cæg þe þara boca andgiet unlycþ;
discourses, for which the grammar is the key that these books' knowledge unlocks;

and ic þohte þæt þeos boc mihte fremian geongum cildum to anginne þæs cræftes,
and I thought that this book might benefit young children to begin this craft,

oþ þæt hie to maran andgiete becumen.
until they more knowledge to acquire come.

3.3.1.2 *Poetry*

The 30,000 lines of Old English poetry that survive today come down to us from the tenth and eleventh centuries, and are for the most part contained in four manuscripts:

(1) The British Museum manuscript of *Beowulf* and *Judith* which is part of the seventeenth-century (Robert) Cotton manuscript collection, and which is referred to as MS Vitellius A 15. It also contains several prose texts.

(2) The Bodleian manuscript, called Junius XI after Franz Junius, who gave the manuscript to Oxford University in the seventeenth century. This manuscript includes *Genesis, Exodus, Daniel* and *Christ and Satan.*

(3) The Exeter Book or Codex Exoniensis at Exeter Cathedral, which contains a large collection of Anglo-Saxon poetry dating approximately from 970 to 990; there are also two later editions. The main text contains 123 pages with the originals of *Phoenix, Julian, The Wanderer, The Seafarer, Widsith, Deor, Wulf and Eadwacer, The Wife's Lament* and *The Husband's Message.* It also contains a number of maxims, *Maxims I,* and *The Cotton Gnomes (Maxims II).*

(4) The Vercelli Book, Codex Vercellis, from the cathedral library of Vercelli, Italy. This manuscript contains *The Dream of the Rood, Elene, The Fates of the Apostles,* and *Address of the Soul to the Body.* In it are also found a number of prose homilies and the *Life of St Guthlac.*

There follows a sample from *Beowulf* with an interlinear translation (my glosses) and a prose translation (Donaldson, 1966: 5). Beowulf is an epic poem written by an unknown author or authors, which comes down to us from a tenth-century manuscript. It was probably composed in the first half of the eighth century. It is a 'folk epic' of 3,182 lines which tells the story of the young warrior Beowulf and his exploits against the monster Grendel in the land of Hrothgar, king of the Danes. It is the only surviving complete secular epic poem; the subject matter is Scandinavian, and the poetry is alliterative, with stress on the first syllable. The tradition of alliterative verse in English eventually died out.

Hwæt syndon ge searohæbbendra
What are you armour-bearers

byrnum werede, þe þus brontne ceol
mail-coats wearing, who thus in your high ship

ofer lagustræte lædan cwomon,
over the sea-road sailing come,

hider ofer holmas? Hwæt, ic hwile wæs
hither over the sea? Lo, I for a while was

endesæta, ægwearde heold,
guard of the coast, sea-watch held

þe on land Dena laðra nænig
that on the land of the Danes foe none

mid scipherge sceðþan ne meahte.
with a force of ships harm might.

No her cuðlicor cuman ongunnon
No warrior more boldly came ashore

lindhæbbende, ne ge leafnesword
shield-bearers, nor you word of leave gave

guðfremmendra gearwe ne wisson,
from our men of battle, fully not knew

maga gemedu. Næfre ic maran geseah
kinsmen consent. Never I mightier saw

eorla ofer eorþan, ðonne is eower sum,
warrior on earth, than is of you one,

secg on searwum; nis þæt seldguma,
a man in battle-dress; not is that retainer

wæpnum geweorðad, næfre him his wlite leoge,
by his weapons made worthy, unless him his appearance belies,

ænlic ansyn. Nu ic eower sceal
singular form. Now I your shall

frumcyn witan, ær ge fyr heonan
lineage know, before you from here

leassceaweras on land Dena
spies on the Danes' land

furþur feran. Nu ge feorbuend,
further go. Now you far-dwellers,

mereliðende, mine gehyrað
sea-voyagers, to my listen

anfealdne geþoht: ofost is selest
simple thought: haste is needed

to gecyðanne, hwanan eowre cyme syndon.
to know, from where you come are.

(237a–57b)

What are you, bearers of armour, dressed in mail-coats, who thus have come bringing a tall ship over the sea-road, over the water to this place? Lo, for a long time I have been guard of the coast, held watch by the sea so that no foe with a force of ships of might work harm on the Danes' land: never have shield-bearers more openly undertaken to come ashore here; nor did you know for sure of a word of leave from our warriors, consent from my kinsmen. I have never seen a mightier warrior on earth than one of you, a man in battle-dress. That is no retainer made to seem good by his weapons

– unless his appearance belies him, his unequalled form. Now I must learn your lineage before you go any farther from here, spies on the Danes' land. Now you far-dwellers, sea-voyagers, hear what I think: you must straightway say where you have come from.

(My glosses; prose translation from Donaldson, 1966: 5.)

3.4 The Dialects of Old English

There were four major dialects in Anglo-Saxon England: Kentish, an offshoot of the Jutes who settled in Kent; West Saxon, spoken south of the Thames; Mercian, spoken from the Thames to the Humber (except in Wales, of course, where (Brythonic) Celtic was still spoken); and Northumbrian, spoken north of the Humber (hence the name), excluding Scotland, where, again, (Gaelic) Celtic was spoken. Since Mercian and Northumbrian share common features not found in West Saxon and Kentish, they are sometimes spoken of together under the name Anglian, because most of the Germanic tribes north of the Thames were Angles. There were definitely other dialects, but we have no written record of them. Anglian and Kentish are also only barely attested. We have much more documentary evidence of West Saxon, and scholars tend to use this dialect to represent Old English, often editing other texts to make them conform to the West Saxon norms, and adding macrons, or length signs, as a reading aid, though length was certainly not indicated on vowels in the original texts. West Saxon is used to represent Old English even though Modern Standard English is largely a descendant of the Mercian speech of the eastern section of the Midland area. This is because Winchester, the capital of Wessex for a long time from the time of King Alfred, was a centre of culture and learning, thanks to Alfred's patronage. London was already a thriving commercial city at the time, but it did not assume its central role for many years to come.

Northumbrian is represented by Caedmon's Hymn and Bede's Death Song from the eighth and ninth centuries, by glosses on the Lindisfarne Gospels, Rushworth Gospels and the Durham Ritual, all from the tenth century, and by the Leiden Riddle and the runic inscriptions on the Ruthwell Cross, the Franks Casket and elsewhere.

Mercian is attested in a large collection of charters of the Mercian kings, interlinear glosses on the Vespasian Psalter from the mid-ninth century, part of the Rushworth Gospels from the tenth century; the Corpus Glossary from the eighth–ninth century, the Leiden Glossary from the eighth century; glosses from the eighth-century Blickling Psalter and the Lorica Glosses and Prayer from the ninth century, as well as the Royal Glosses of about 1000.

The Kentish dialect is represented in the eighth century from glosses in Latin charters, while in the ninth century there is a series of charters in the dialect itself. There are four Latin charters with Kentish names. After 900 it is only attested by the Kentish Psalm, the Kentish Hymn and glosses to Proverbs.

West Saxon is poorly represented in the early period, even though it later became something of a literary standard. Early West Saxon is based on the Parker Manuscript of the Anglo-Saxon Chronicle, the two oldest manuscripts of Alfred's translation of Gregory's *Cura Pastoralis* and the Lauderdale MS of the OE translation of Orosius, all from the late ninth or early tenth century. Later West Saxon writing is represented by the works of Ælfric (*c.*1000) and by the glosses on the Junius Psalter, the Leech Book (both early tenth century), the Abingdon MSS of the Anglo-Saxon Chronicle (late tenth and eleventh centuries), the West Saxon Gospels (*c.*1000), boundaries in the charters of the West Saxon kings, and numerous royal writs.

The attested dialect differences that have come down to us from Old English were comparatively slight, and not at all as marked as modern spoken dialects (e.g. a Geordie youth vs. a West Country farmer), so that it does not hamper us to use texts from West Saxon. Occasionally, however, a distinctive Mercian or Anglian text may be compared and cited as more obviously similar to the standard modern form than West Saxon, e.g. Anglian *ald* which develops regularly into ModE *old* as opposed to West Saxon *eald*. While this early West Saxon (from as late as the ninth century) is the English of the age of Alfred, by about the late tenth and early eleventh century, the time of the writer Ælfric, an early literary standard developed, which is often called Classical Old English.

The Old English period spans just under 600 years, and changes naturally occurred in sounds, grammar and vocabulary during this time, which we can see when we compare older texts with earlier ones. We must also be aware that, in comparison with this early period, Old English changed drastically – though slowly and systematically – to become Modern English.

3.5 Sociolinguistic Focus

3.5.1 Language Contact

We mentioned briefly above in our discussion of the vocabulary of Old English that borrowing words is one way to enrich the word-stock of a language. Borrowing results from contact between people, in which new concepts and ideas are encountered for which new words have to be developed. Throughout the course of its history, English has been in contact with other languages, through either migration or invasion, colonization, or cultural or economic domination, and language contact is a major topic throughout this book.

But not all language contact is the same. Some contact situations are casual and may result in the simple borrowing of a few non-essential words from the prestige language (**prestige borrowing**). A more intense contact situation, on the other hand, might lead to large-scale borrowing of words, as well as interference from the contact language with the structure of the original language. In the most extreme cases, language contact might lead to the complete loss of language A, whose speakers shift entirely to language B. Thomason and Kaufman (1991: 74–6) devised a detailed borrowing scale, that is, a system which can help to gauge the level or degree of interference by one system in another as a result of contact.

Thomason and Kaufman's borrowing scale

(1)   Casual contact: lexical borrowing only.
Lexicon: Content words. For cultural and functional (rather than typological) reasons, non-basic vocabulary will be borrowed before basic vocabulary.

(2)   Slightly more intense contact: slight structural borrowing
Lexicon: Function words, conjunctions and various adverbial particles.

Structure: Minor phonological, syntactic and lexical semantic features. Phonological borrowing here is likely to be confined to the appearance of new phonemes with new phones, but only in loan words. Syntactic features borrowed at this stage will probably be restricted to new functions (or functional restrictions) and new orderings that cause little or no typological disruption.

(3)   More intense contact: slightly more structural borrowing.
Lexicon: Function words: adpositions (prepositions and postpositions). At this stage derivational affixes may be abstracted from borrowed words and added to native vocabulary; inflectional affixes may enter the borrowing language attached to, and will remain confined to, borrowed vocabulary items. Personal and demonstrative pronouns and low numerals, which belong to the basic vocabulary, are more likely to be borrowed at this stage than in more casual contact situations.

Structure: Slightly less minor structural features than in category (2). In phonology, borrowing will probably include the phonemicization, even in native vocabulary, of previously allophonic alternations. This is especially true of those that exploit distinctive features already present in the borrowing language, and also easily borrowed prosodic and syllable-structure features, such as stress rules and the addition of syllable-final consonants (in loan words only). In syntax, a complete change from, say, SOV to SVO syntax will not occur here, but a few aspects of such a switch may be found, as, for example, borrowed postpositions in an otherwise prepositional language (or *vice versa*).

(4) Strong cultural pressure: moderate structural borrowing.
    Structure: Major structural features that cause relatively little typological change. Phonological borrowing at this stage includes: introduction of new distinctive features in contrastive sets that are represented in native vocabulary, and perhaps loss of some contrasts; new syllable structure constraints, also in native vocabulary; and a few natural allophonic or automatic morphophonemic rules, such as palatalization of final obstruent devoicing. Fairly extensive word-order changes will occur at this stage, as will other syntactic changes that cause little categorial alteration. In morphology, borrowed inflectional affixes and categories (e.g., new cases) will be added to native words, especially if there is a good typological fit in both category and ordering.

(5) Very strong cultural pressure: heavy cultural borrowing.
    Structure: Major structural features that cause significant typological disruption: added morphophonemic rules; phonetic changes (i.e., subphonemic changes in habits of articulation, including allophonic alternations); loss of phonemic contrasts and of morphophonemic rules; changes in word-structure rules (e.g., adding prefixes in a language that was exclusively suffixing or a change from flexional toward agglutinative morphology); categorial as well as more extensive ordering changes in morphosyntax (e.g., development of ergative morphosyntax); and added concord rules, including bound pronominal elements.

English has been in both casual and more intimate contact with other languages, as we shall see in the course of this book. Even in the Old English period (and before), different contact situations developed between English and other languages.

3.5.1.1 *Latin and Celtic*

The juxtaposition of Latin and Celtic tells us much about language contact in the early days. All of the signs suggest that the native population did not adopt Latin in any significant numbers, but preserved their own Celtic tongues, probably owing to social and physical separation from the Romans. The lexical survivals from Latin suggest that it functioned as the language of the military and administration. It was no doubt reserved for use in the towns and major settlements that the Romans themselves established. If any Celts did learn Latin, they were most likely artisans and the few others who were forced into communication with the Romans.

In a discussion of the vital factors determining adoption of a new language by conquering invaders or subjugated peoples, Leith (1983) focuses on numerical strength, the extent of intermarriage, the degree of resistance encountered and the degree of centralization and military strength, along with the extent to which the invaders and invaded share an international written culture and religion. It is apparent that the Romans and Celts intermarried relatively little, and did not share a religion (the latter being a barrier to the former, of course). Furthermore, we know that the Romans were a highly centralized, culturally sophisticated and organized culture, possessing (at least for a considerable time) unprecedented military strength. The Celts, on the other hand, were dispersed by the Romans to the extreme areas of the country and lived in smaller clan structures. They were neither well organized administratively or militarily, nor did they have anything particularly culturally superior to the Romans (at least in the eyes of the Romans themselves – their sophistication in the arts and crafts and in learning is well known to us today). No doubt these are the reasons why the scant linguistic influence that there was in this period of contact was largely in one direction, from the Romans to the Celts.

The Latin influence on English vocabulary began even before there was such a language as English, while Latin was in contact with the Germanic dialects on the continent. These words largely suggest the cultural sophistication of the Romans, e.g. *street, wine, butter, pepper, cheese, silk, copper, pound, inch, mile*. Once the Romans settled in Britain, other words were adopted that reflect the Romanization of the islands, including some well-known and still used place names. For instance, *caster* became *ceaster* 'fortified settlement, town' and survives in place names such as Lancaster, Exeter, Manchester, Doncaster and Chester.

The Christianization of Britain (from the sixth century) brought with it the adoption of another series of Latin words, e.g. *bishop, candle, creed, font, mass, monk, priest*. It has been ascertained that over 400 words from Latin were in Old English before the Norman conquest, though most of them have not survived until today. This was, however, only the first wave of Latin influence on English. There were several others, which we will discuss at the appropriate stages below.

By contrast with Latin, fewer than twelve Celtic words are thought to have been in English before the twelfth century. These divide into two types – popular words learned by the Anglo-Saxons in daily contact with the Celts, and words introduced by the Celtic missionaries in northern England. Popular words include *bannock, bin, brock* (badger), *crag, luh* (loch), *cumb* (deep valley), and religious words include *cross* and *clugge* (bell, clock). Copious place names provide evidence of the contact between the Celts and the Anglo-Saxons: *Kent* comes from Celtic *canti* or *cantion* (of unknown meaning); there is considerable Celtic influence in place names in the West and South-West, e.g. *Devon* (from Celtic *Dumnoni*, a tribal name); *Cumberland* means 'the land of the Cymry or Britons'; and the place name *London* can be traced back to Celtic origins, as can the first element in **Winchester** and **Salisbury**. But it is in the names of hills, rivers and places near such phenomena that the Celtic names survive primarily: thus, the

Thames is a Celtic river name, and various Celtic words for river and water are preserved in the names *Avon*, *Esk*, *Usk*, *Dover* and *Wye*. However, place names can also be the symbol of superficial interaction, and in no way require any intimacy on the part of the contact groups. It has been suggested that the limited influence of Celtic on the language stems from the fact that the Celts were a submerged race in the Old English period. Once again, it appears that they were neither sufficiently well organized or centralized, nor militarily or culturally superior, so that their influence was extremely limited.

In these instances we can talk about prestige borrowing *vis-à-vis* Latin and casual or superficial contact between the languages (Celtic), which resulted in only minor lexical borrowings and no influence on language structure. This would accord with Stage 1 on Thomason and Kaufman's borrowing scale.

3.5.1.2 *The Scandinavians*

By contrast, the contact between Old English and Old Norse was much more intimate. Significant numbers of Scandinavians made England their home at this time. Even those who came to plunder would sometimes remain. The 1,400 Old Norse-based place names in England bear witness to the strength of Scandinavian settlements. Most of them are in the Danelaw area, in the North and East of England. The majority of the new settlers were Danes, although there were considerable Norwegian settlements in north-west England and a few of the northern counties, and Swedes figured largely in later settlements. The settlement we are talking about was extensive in both scope and duration, lasting over two centuries. The invaders settled as farmers and intermarried with the indigenous English, adopting their customs and entering into the everyday life of the community. In settlement areas like these conditions were ripe for pervasive Scandinavian influence on the English language.

The amalgamation of the two races was largely facilitated by the close kinship existing between them. Apart from continuing to observe certain native customs, the Scandinavians adapted themselves on the whole to the English way of life – that is, they assimilated. The Scandinavians seem to have grouped themselves first in concentrated centres: Lincoln, Stamford, Leicester, Nottingham, York and Derby were focal centres of Scandinavian influence.

Concerning the relationship between the two languages, it would appear that there are places where the Scandinavians gave up their language early, while in other communities the Scandinavian language kept hold for a remarkably long time. In some parts of Scotland, Norse (known as Norn) was still spoken as late as the seventeenth century.

Since the ways of life and the respective languages of the English and the Scandinavians were not as different at that time as they are now, some linguists claim that they were mutually intelligible. The result was a linguistic fusion, which is almost without parallel in the world, although, in fact, the subsequent fusion of Danish and Norwegian in the Norway of the late middle ages shows many similarities. It is more commonly the case that one language takes over in a situation like this, or that they coexist, functioning side by side in some sort of diglossic distribution.

Because of the similarity between Old English and the language of the Scandinavian invaders it is sometimes difficult to say whether a word in Modern English is a native word or is borrowed from Norse. Many of the more common words of the two languages were either identical or extremely close in form, and if we did not have Old English literature from the period before the Scandinavian invasions it would be impossible to say of many words that they were *not* of Scandinavian origin. In certain cases, however, there are reliable criteria for recognizing a borrowed word.

The most reliable are based on differences in the development of certain sounds in the North Germanic area. One of the easiest to recognize is the palatalization of /sk/. In Old English, /sk/ became /ʃ/ long before it did in Modern Scandinavian. Consequently, while native words like *shall*, *fish*, etc. have /ʃ/ in Modern English, words which are borrowed from Scandinavian retain /sk/ as in *sky*, *skill*. Old English *scyrte* has become *shirt*, while from the corresponding Old Norse *skyrta* we get *skirt*.

The character of Scandinavian loan words

Once the Danes had begun to settle peaceably on the island and enter into normal community relations with the English, Scandinavian words began to enter in large numbers into the English language. However, it is very difficult to divide the borrowed words into classes. While the Romans were considered superior to the Celts, the Scandinavians did not bring English into contact with a superior, or even significantly different, civilization. For this reason, the loan words resulted from everyday contact and are very basic in character: *birth*, *egg*, *guess*, *root*, *scale*, *seat*, *sister*, *skirt*, *sky*, *tidings*, for example. The new words fill no real linguistic gap, as words resulting from the introduction of Christianity did. They simply found their way into the language as a result of the mixing of the two races. The Scandinavian and English languages were used side by side and any loss or retention must have been the result of pure chance. Many examples could be cited, but two suffice to illustrate this phenomenon: as late as the fifteenth century there were two words for *egg* in use in English, *ey*, the Old English word, and *egg*, the Scandinavian word; there was also a rivalry for a time between the OE word *niman* (compare Modern German *nehmen*) and the Scandinavian word *take*.

Rather than just influencing the very open classes of lexical roots, however, Scandinavian influence extended to such key morphological classes as the pronouns, prepositions, adverbs and even a part of the verb *to be*, demonstrating the more intimate intermingling of the two languages. We can summarize this point as follows:

Pronouns:	*they, them, their* (OE *hie, him, hiera*)
Prepositions:	*till, fro* (as in *to and fro*)
Infinitive marker:	*att*, survives (as a blend with 'do') in the word 'ado', as in the title *Much Ado about Nothing*
Be:	*are*

Thus the phrase *they are* is completely Scandinavian. The number of borrowed words from Scandinavian stands at about 900 even if we only consider the words for which the evidence is totally convincing. On top of this are words that are still part of the everyday dialect of people from the north and east of England, not to mention the north-east of Scotland. For example, the sentence *The bairns are lakin out ont'street* ('the children are playing in the street'), which can be heard in Humberside to this day, is very close indeed to the equivalent Modern Swedish sentence *Barnen leker ute på gatan.*

We have already noted the large number of Scandinavian place-names indicating the extensive Scandinavian settlement in England. More than 600 place-names like *Grimsby, Whitby, Derby, Rugby* survive, all of which end in *-by*, the Scandinavian word for farm or town. This word is also preserved in *bye-law* (town law). Some 300 names like *Althorpe, Linthorpe, Bishopsthorpe*, incorporate the Scandinavian word *thorp* (village), and an almost equal number contain the term *thwaite* (isolated piece of land): *Braithwaite, Langthwaite*. In some districts of Yorkshire and Lincolnshire as many as 75 per cent of places have Scandinavian place-names. A similarly high percentage of Scandinavian personal names has been found in medieval records of these districts. Names ending in *-son* conform to the characteristic Scandinavian patronymic system, as opposed to names ending in *-ing*, the OE equivalent, cf. *Browning*.

But how intimate was the contact between Old Norse and English? Some commentators have suggested that Old Norse was largely responsible for the simplification of English morphology, that is, the shift in English from a synthetic to an analytic type, which proceeded apace in the Middle English period, as we shall see in the next chapter. We have already seen that this cannot be the case, as this shift was most likely propelled by language-internal forces that started with the fixing of stress on the initial or root syllable of a word. It seems highly unlikely that Old Norse could change the typology of English when Old Norse itself was almost identical in type. Thomason and Kaufman (1988) provide persuasive evidence that Old Norse did not influence the structure of Old (and then Middle) English. They argue that the 'Norse influence on English was pervasive, in the sense that its results are found in all parts of the language; but it was not deep, except in the lexicon. . . . What Norse did was to add a few subtleties of meaning and a large number of new ways of saying old things, often by replacing an English item of similar but not identical sound' (pp. 302–3). In other words, the influence of Old Norse on English was probably the equivalent of Stage 2 on their borrowing scale. They suggest that Norse influence on particular pursuits such as farming was extensive, but that it was not the trigger of the major structural changes in English in the Middle English period. We will have more to say about this in the next chapter.

Suggested Readings

Bean, Marian C. (1983) *The Development of Word Order Patterns in Old English*. London: Croom Helm.

Cassidy, F. G. and R. N. Ringler (eds) (1971) *Bright's Old English Grammar and Reader*. New York: Holt, Rinehart and Winston.

Millward, Celia M. (1989) *A Biography of the English Language*. New York: Holt, Rinehart and Winston.

Partridge, A. C. (1982) *A Companion to Old and Middle English Studies*. Totowa, NJ: Barnes & Noble Books.

Quirk, R. and C. L. Wrenn (1955) *Old English Grammar*. London: Methuen.

4   Middle English

Timeline: The Middle English Period

1066	Battle of Hastings; Norman Conquest
1095	First Crusade
1170	Assassination of Thomas à Becket
1204	King John loses lands in Normandy
1258–65	The Barons' War
1337–1453	The Hundred Years War
1346	Battle of Crecy
1346	Battle of Poitiers
1348–1351	The Black Death
1362	Parliament opened in English
	The Statute of Pleading (English becomes the official language of legal proceedings)
1340–1400	Geoffrey Chaucer
1381	The Peasants' Revolt
1415	Battle of Agincourt
1476	Caxton introduces the printing press
1489	French no longer used as the language of Parliament
1509	Henry VIII ascends the throne

4.1   Social and Political History

4.1.1   Political History: The Norman Conquest to Edward I

After reigning for 24 years, Edward the Confessor died childless in 1066, with no obvious successor. Although Harold, son of Godwin, was elected to the throne, it was not long before his claim was challenged. William, Duke of Normandy, with which England had enjoyed close ties since the time of Æthelred, was a second cousin to the late king and had expected to succeed him. He therefore invaded England and took the throne by force of arms, landing his army at Pevensey Bay in September 1066. Harold was killed at the ensuing Battle of Hastings, and William was crowned King of England on Christmas Day, 1066. The reign of William the Conqueror brought with it enormous changes to the social, political, religious and linguistic fabric of the British Isles.

William I died leaving three sons: Robert Curthose, who became Duke of Normandy, William Rufus, who succeeded his father to the English throne, and Henry, later Henry I. Curthose has been characterized as downright incompetent and Rufus as a merciless and detested extortionist and schemer. When William II Rufus died under suspicious circumstances in a hunting accident, his youngest brother Henry I (1100–35) acquired the throne, and eventually also took Normandy from his brother Robert (1106). When Henry I's only legitimate son, William, died, the only possible successor was his daughter Matilda, who was married to the German emperor, William V. On the death of the emperor, Matilda returned to England and Henry forced his vassals to recognize her as the next ruler of the country. He then married her to Count Geoffrey Plantagenet of Anjou. She bore him a son, the future Henry II, thus establishing the Angevin dynasty.

After Henry's death in 1135, Stephen of Blois, the son of William the Conqueror's daughter, was favoured by the English over Matilda and the future Henry II; he reigned until his death in 1154.

Henry II succeeded Stephen, becoming Duke of Poitou, Normandy and Aquitaine (through his marriage to Eleanor the ex-wife of the French king, Louis VII). His entire reign was spent defending his French property against the King of France. Thus, until the reign of King John all kings of England were essentially continental.

By diplomacy Henry II subjected the Welsh, Scottish and Irish to his sovereignty, and he married his third-eldest son Geoffrey to the heiress of Brittany. The counts of Auvergne and Toulouse also surrendered in the south of France, and Henry became the most powerful ruler in Europe. However, by the end of his life, Henry's sons were conspiring with Philip of France against him. Philip's goal was the destruction of the Angevin Empire. Richard I succeeded Henry II in 1189 and reigned for ten years. Though he is renowned as the Lionheart, he was in fact a miserable statesman and administrator, who spoke little or no English and spent only six months in total on English soil. When he died without heirs in 1199 the barons and nobles supported his brother John, who was duly crowned king, while Philip of France supported the claim of Arthur of Brittany. King John (1199–1216) was the least successful member of the Angevin dynasty, a complete failure both at war and at home. When he eloped with the daughter of one of Philip's vassals, he eventually had to forfeit his fiefdoms to Philip, and at the end of the war with France in 1205 he had lost all possessions in northern France. Philip had taken all the Angevin Empire except Aquitaine itself, and the English barons (with lands on both sides of the Channel) were also forced to forfeit lands to Philip and therefore became exclusively 'English' for the first time. The loss of land incurred the wrath of the baronage and in 1215 the Magna Carta was signed.

This marked the end of the period of northern French domination and the beginning of southern French domination with the accession of Henry III. The French language dominated in England until the reign of Edward I (1272–1307), the first king for generations to have a good command of English.

Later in this chapter (section 4.4.1) we will discuss the reversal of fortune of the French language and the re-establishment of English.

4.1.2   Social History

4.1.2.1   The Establishment of Towns and Burghs and the Beginnings of Social Stratification

The High Middle Ages (about 814–1300) saw the gradual waning of the feudal system in England and the beginning of towns and burghs. There are two interesting theories about the direction of development of the urban middle class in the Middle Ages. Pirenne's (1936) long-established theory is that boroughs had developed from walled manorial or feudal enclosures after long-distance trade had revived in the tenth and eleventh centuries, and merchants and artisans began to make their homes around established settlements – in other words, creating suburban trade centres. At first incoming traders lived apart in the suburbs, and not as part of the existing feudal order; indeed there was great tension between feudal lords and the merchants and traders. Eventually the merchants became strong enough to challenge the established system and develop a new social, economic and legal order, generating a new urban patriciate along with it. These new wealthy urbanites enjoyed social, political and economic power based on control of the wholesale and long-distance trades of the town. In other words, according to Pirenne the new civic merchant class developed separately from the original feudal masters, and most often in opposition to them.

By contrast, Hibbert (1983) believes that the development was not as unidirectional as Pirenne had thought. While trade was not a requirement of a feudal society (since most feudal settlements were largely self-sufficient), it nevertheless naturally grew out of the feudal system, and was indeed promoted by feudalism to a certain extent. In other words, it was promoted by the landowners. It is natural for all settlements to need some goods and services that have to be bought in from a distance. Rather than resist the development of towns, feudal lords actually encouraged them, and, as evidence from medieval documents would suggest, certain sections of the land-owning feudal aristocracy themselves grasped the initiative and developed gradually into merchant traders and guildsmen.

In the earlier stages of the development of the town a class emerged between the lords on the one hand and the agricultural workers, petty traders, craftsmen, porters and the like on the other. This intermediate class consisted of large free-holders, certain tenants, lower nobles and prominent administrators who had the initiative and were accustomed to high office. It is this group, Hibbert argues, that led the movement towards freedom from feudal control and developed new power based on economic and political opportunity, of which they were in a position to take advantage.

The upshot of this historical debate is crucial to the sociolinguistic interpretation of language change in the Middle English period and beyond. What it implies is that there was movement both from above and from below into a new middle class whose status depended on economic and political opportunity and which enabled increased social mobility for men of initiative and/or means. We will see below that mobility was the key to the standardization of English, and that merchants, tradesmen and members of city government had a central role to play in the establishment of a standard code.

4.2 Linguistic Developments: Middle English Sounds and Structure, with Particular Emphasis on the Breakdown of the Inflectional System and its Linguistic Typological Implications

During the Middle English period a number of very significant changes became more and more visible in the English language. The major changes from Old to Middle English are the loss of inflections, and with it the development of more fixed word order. As in the Old English period, language contact led to borrowing, but its scale was far greater during this period than it had been before.

4.2.1 Major Changes in the Sound System

4.2.1.1 The Consonants

Consonantal changes in the system are slight during this period, a characteristic feature of English. Certain voiced consonants became voiceless and other voiceless consonants became voiced; consonants could occasionally also be lost completely (see chart below). Thus, /w/ was lost before a following /o/ if it came after another consonant: OE *swa* > ME *so* (*so*); OE *hwa* > ME *ho* (*who*). In addition, ME lost consonant clusters beginning with /h/, so that *hring* became *ring* and *hrof* became *rof* (> *roof*). Significantly, both of these consonants were glides, i.e., not obstruents, among which change was limited to the feature of voice.

4.2.1.2   Consonant Changes from Old to Middle English

In the following table the first group of examples represents forms which lost initial h- preceding a resonant (l, n and r); the second set shows the loss of a final consonant; the third shows the simplification of the cluster /sw/, while the last pair reflects the voicing of voiceless consonants in some dialects:

Old English		Middle English		Meaning
hlaford	[hlaːvord]	lord	[lɔːrd]	lord
hnappian	[hnæpjan]	nape	[napə]	nap
hlæne	[hlæːnɛ]	leane	[lɛːnə]	lean
hnutu	[hnʊtʊ]	nute	[nʊtə]	nut
hring	[hrɪŋg]	ring	[rɪŋg]	ring
hrof	[hroːf]	rof	[roːf]	roof
drivan	[drivan]	drive	[driːvə]	drive
lihtlic	[lɪxtliç]	lightly	[lɪxtli]	lightly
anlic	[aːnliç]	onli	[ɔːnlɪ]	only
swuster	[swʊstɛr]	suster	[sʊstər]	sister
fæder	[fæder]	vader	[vadər]	father
self	[sɛlf]	zelf	[zɛlf]	self

4.2.1.3   Vowels in Stressed Syllables

There was also little change in the vowels in stressed or accented syllables. Most of the short vowels, unless lengthened (see below), passed unchanged into ME. But short æ was lowered to [a] and y was unrounded to i (OE *cræft* > ME *craft*; *brycg* > *brigge*, bridge). The other short vowels a, e, i, o, u remained unchanged, as in OE *catte* > *cat*; *bedde* > *bed*; *scip* > *ship*; *folc* > *folk*; *full* > *ful*.

Amongst the long vowels, the most important change was the raising and rounding of long a > o: OE *ban* > ME *bon* ('bone'), *bat* > *bot* ('boat'). [yː] was unrounded to [iː]: OE *bryd* > ME *bride*, *fyr* > *fir* ('fire').

Long æ in OE represented two sounds:

(1)   Long e (long a in West Germanic) appears as long e in ME, unchanged from OE (except in West Saxon): non-WS *ded* > *ded*; *slepan* > *slepen*.

(2)   In many words æ was a sound resulting from the i-umlaut of a. This was a more open vowel, appearing in ME as e (OE *clǣne* > *clene*, *dǣlen* > *delen* ('deal').

These sounds were subsequently raised, and are now identical with [iː]: *clean*, *deal*, *deed*, etc.

Other OE vowels preserved their quality in ME: *medu* > *mede* ('mead'); *fíf* > *fíf* ('five'); *bok* > *bok* ('book'); *hus* > *hus* ('house').

OE diphthongs were all simplified and all the diphthongs of ME are new formations resulting chiefly from the combination of a simple vowel with the following consonant ([j] or [w]), which vocalized. Though the quality did not change in ME, the quantity of OE vowels underwent considerable change. OE long vowels were shortened late in the OE period or early in ME when followed by a double consonant or by most combinations of consonants (*gretter* with short e developed as the comparative of OE *great* (with long e); OE *axian* with long a became *asken* with short a in ME. The changes are not noticeable in spelling, but they are very significant, since they determine the development of these vowels in later stages.

4.2.1.4   *Vowels in Unstressed Syllables*

The general obscuring of unstressed syllables in ME is a most significant sound change, since it is one of the fundamental causes of the loss of inflection. Before the end of OE, every unstressed /a/, /e/, /o/ and /u/ tended to become an <e> in spelling, presumably pronounced as /ə/ (schwa): OE *oxa* > ME *oxe*; OE *foda* > ME *fode*; OE *nacod* > ME *naced*. Unstressed /ɪ/, on the other hand, remained unchanged (as in British English *shilling*). When /ə/ was final in ME it was eventually lost, hence the modern forms *ox*, *food*; often the <e> was retained in spelling, though it was not pronounced. Certain endings in which /ə/ was followed by a consonant, especially the possessive and plural -*es* and preterite -*ed*, regularly syncopated, so that here, too, /ə/ is lost (e.g. *botes* > *boats*). Exceptions are sounds ending in a sibilant, e.g. *busses*, *vases*, *rushes*, etc., or verbs ending in an alveolar sound (*wedded*, *wetted*), where [ə] or [ɪ] is still encountered in the modern forms.

4.2.1.5   *Lengthening and Shortening*

(1)   Lengthening occurred before the consonant clusters ld, mb, nd in late Old English: OE [ʧɪld] > ME [ʧiːld], *child*. Lengthening did not occur if a third consonant followed, as in [ʧɪldrən], *children*, with a following liquid.
(2)   Lengthening of a, e and o took place in open syllables of disyllabic words. Open syllables end in a vowel, while closed syllables end in a double

consonant (word-medially). In disyllabic words a single consonant between the vowels goes with the second syllable and leaves the first syllable open; two or more consonants make the syllable closed. This is illustrated, for example, in OE [namɛ] > ME [nɑːmə], *name*. Moreover, where in OE the quantity distinction was clearly present, i.e. where there was a length distinction between long and short vowels, in ME this develops into a qualitative distinction: long vowels are more tense and short vowels more lax; there is no significant distinction in actual quantity any more.

(3) Shortening occurred in Early Middle English in two environments:

  (a) before double consonants and consonant clusters, except the clusters above that caused lengthening: OE *cepte* [keːptɛ] ('he kept') > ME *cept* [kɛpt]; and

  (b) in the first syllable of a trisyllabic word: OE *hæligdæg* [hæːlɪjdæj] ('holiday') > ME *halidai* [hɑlɪdei].

4.2.1.6 Summary Table of Vowel Changes from Old to Middle English

Sounds		Examples		Meaning
OE	**ME**	**OE**	**ME**	
[ɑː]	[ɔː]	ban [bɑːn]	bon [bɔːn]	bone
[æ]	[a]	þæt [ðæt]	that [ðat]	that
[æː]	[ɛː]	sæ [sæː]	se [sɛː]	sea
[y]	[ɪ]	synn [syn]	sinne [sɪnə]	sin
[yː]	[iː]	hydan [hyːdɑn]	hiden [hiːdən]	hide
[æə]	[a]	hearm [hæərm]	harm [harm]	harm
[æːə]	[ɛː]	stream [stræːəm]	streme [strɛːmə]	stream
[ɛo]	[ɛ]	heofon [hɛovɔn]	heven [hɛvən]	heaven
[eːo]	[eː]	beon [beːon]	ben [beːn]	be/are

4.2.1.7 The Formation of Middle English Diphthongs

This phenomenon involves changes in the consonants as well, as the glides [w] and [j] and the voiced velar fricative develop into the second member of the new diphthongs.

Source	New	OE	ME	Meaning
ɑ + w	ɑʊ	clawu [klawʊ]	clawe [klɑʊə]	claw
ɑ + ɣ	ɑʊ	gnagan [gnɑːɣan]	gnawe [gnɑʊə]	gnaw
æ + j	ɛɪ	dæg [dæj]	dai [dɛɪ]	day
ɛ + j	ɛɪ	weg [wɛj]	wei [wɛɪ]	way
ɛː + w	ɛʊ	neawe [nɛːwə]	newe [nɛʊə]	new

iː + w	iʊ	stiweard [stiːwæərd]	steward [stɪʊard]	steward
ɔː + w	oʊ	growan [groːwɑn]	growen [groʊən]	grow
ɔ + ɣ	oʊ	boga [bɔɣɑ]	bowe [boʊə]	bow
ɑː + ɣ	oʊ	agan [ɑːɣɑn]	owen [oʊən]	owe
OFr	ɔɪ	OFr joie	ME joie	joy

4.2.2 Major Morphological Changes from Old to Middle English

4.2.2.1 Loss of Inflections

As we mentioned in the previous two chapters, one of the major changes that English underwent in its history was the typological change from a synthetic to an analytic language. This change (as indicated earlier) began when the fixing of stress caused attention to be drawn away from the inflectional information at the ends of words. Where originally distinctive vowels were pronounced with their full values in these endings, by the end of the Old English period, unstressed vowels were being reduced to [ə]. As we will see below, this change, coupled with the reduction of other sounds, caused the loss of the grammatical endings in the Middle English period. We can summarize the changes across the inflectional spectrum with the following overview, in turn, of the noun, adjective and pronoun.

Nouns

The distinctive endings *-a, -u, -e, -an, -um*, etc. of Old English were reduced to <e>/[ə] by the end of the twelfth century. The progression – beginning with the phonologically most complex ending – was approximately (where V = 'vowel'): [Vm] > [Vn] > [Ṽ] > [ə] > [Ø]. In the noun there is one inflectional relic left in the singular, the genitive *-es*, while one form serves for all in the plural:

	OE		**ME**	
	Sing.	*Plur.*	*Sing.*	*Plur.*
N	stan	stan-as	ston	ston-es
A	stan	stan-as	ston	ston-es
G	stan-es	stan-a	ston-es	ston-es
D	stan-e	stan-um	ston	ston-es

Adjectives

Adjectives lost all distinction between the strong and weak declensions, except in monosyllabic adjectives ending in a consonant, e.g., in *yong* vs. *yonge*; strong adjectives of this type have *yong* in the singular and *yonge* in the plural.

Pronouns

The very complex system found in OE (see previous chapter) was radically reduced, most visibly by the complete loss of the morphological expression of the dual number; nevertheless, substantial differentiation among case forms is retained in this category, in stark contrast to what is seen in the noun and adjective:

		First person	**Second person**	**Third person**
Sing.	N	I	thou	he she it
	A	me	thee	him hir hit
	G	my, min	thy, thyn	his hir his
	D	me	thee	him hir him
Plur.	N	we	ye	they
	A	us	yow	hem
	G	oure	youre	hir
	D	us	yow	hem

With these changes, especially in the third person singular and plural, there is considerably less overlap in the pronouns than there was in Old English, and thus less room for confusion.

Prepositions

Once the levelling of inflections set in, distinctions of meaning previously expressed by morphological endings now had to be expressed in other ways: prepositions filled many gaps left by the loss of inflections. New prepositions were formed by

(1)   conversion, e.g. *along* < the OE adjective, and *among* < OE *gemong* ('in a crowd');
(2)   compounding, e.g. *out + of > out of, in + to > into*;
(3)   borrowing, e.g. *till* < ONorse, *except* < Latin, *according to, around, during* < French.

4.2.2.2   *Other Changes in the Morphological System*

Conjunctions

Coordinators typical of ME were *ac* ('but') and *or* ('or') from OE. *That* developed during this period, although *þe* survived until the thirteenth century. Also inherited from OE were the common conjunctions *gif* ('if'), *þeah* ('though') and *ær* ('before').

New subordinators were needed and developed primarily from other parts of speech, frequently supported by *þat* because the identity of the initial elements was clearly not that of a 'conjunction'. Thus, for example, from interrogative adverbs and pronouns came *when that, which that, how that*; from other parts of speech we get *after that, because that*. Compare also *soone as þat*, as soon as, *til þat*, etc. By the time of ME the OE correlative conjunctions *ge . . . ge* were in the process of dying out.

Adverbs

These were formed primarily by adding a final *-e* to adjectives in OE. With the gradual loss of the final *-e* in ME this died out, and the distinction between adjective and adverb was lost, leading to the addition of the suffix *-lic* instead. It had originally been an adjective-marking suffix, but adopted the function of an adverb marker. This explains why many adjectives end in *-ly* (for example, *lovely*).

4.2.2.3   Verbs

In comparison with the declined morphological classes, the verb reflects lesser degrees of change. As in OE, there are still strong and weak verbs in Middle English (the examples here are *to drink, hope, sing*, and *love*):

Middle English strong and weak verbs

		Strong	**Weak**
Sing.	1	drinke	hope
	2	drinkest	hopes
	3	drinketh	hopeth
Plur.		drinke(n)	hopen
Sing.	1	drank	hopede
	2	dronke	hopedest
	3	drank	hopede
Plur.		dronke(n)	hoped(e(n))
Sing.	1	synge	love
	2	syngest	loves
	3	syngeth	loveth
Plur.		synge(n)	love(n)
Sing.	1	sang	lovede
	2	songe	lovedest
	3	sang	loved(e)
Plur.		songen	lovede(n)

4.2.3 *Middle English Syntax*

In what follows, glosses are not supplied if the meanings are obvious.

(1) The adjective was still placed before the noun with single adjectives: *an erþely servant*; *a gentyl and noble esquyer*. However, some adjectives followed nouns, especially if translated from French or Latin. When nouns had multiple single-word modifiers one sometimes preceded the noun and the rest followed:

> a gode wyt and a retentyff
> meny cites and touns, faire, noble and ryche
> bosomy bowes grene

(2) Phrasal modifiers typically followed the words they modified:

> þe zennes þet comeþ of glutounye and of lecherie
> *the sins that come from gluttony and from lechery*

(3) Articles developed: *a* from 'one' and *þe* from the demonstrative. *þe* was used for uniqueness (*the sun*) and definiteness/givenness (*the man I know*).

(4) The *of*-possessive was an innovation of ME. It was supported (if not originally triggered) by the French possessive with *de*:

> aftyr þe lawes of oure londe
> *according to the laws of our land*

> depness of sunne
> *deepness of sin*

(5) Group possessives are just appearing in ME and they are typically made up of possessive + noun + noun modifier:

> the Dukes place of Lancastre

> Criste, þe keyng sonn of heven
> *Christ, the king's son of heaven*

(6) Prepositions occasionally follow objects, especially if the object is a pronoun:

> he seyd him to
> *he said to him*

(7) Prepositions follow an object when the object is a relative pronoun or a verb is passive:

> the place that I of speak
> preciouse stanes þat he myght by a kingdom with
> þes oþir wordis of þis biscop ouȝte to be taken hede

(8) There are not as many compound verbs as in present-day English, but they do start appearing in ME. The perfect tense became common in ME with *be* and *have* as auxiliaries, though *be* became less used for the perfect the more it became identified with the passive:

> ðou havest don our kunne wo
> *you have done our family woe*

> I am com to myne ende
> *I have come to my end*

(9) The progressive developed in OE, though it was fairly rare, and usually found in translations from Latin (Baugh and Cable, 1993: 287). In the course of Middle English it begins to develop, though its exact source is not certain. It may directly result from an *-ande* construction, or it may result from a fusion of the verb and the present participle as adjective, and the verb + *on* + the gerund. The present participle and gerund both ended in *-ing*, which meant that confusion was possible.

participle:	for now is gode Gawayne goande ryȝt here
gerund:	I am yn belding of a pore house
perfect progressive:	We han ben waitynge al this fourtenyght

(10) The verb *to be* develops as a passive auxiliary; *by* develops as the agent marker:

> (men) that wol nat *be* governed *by* hir wyves

(11) By ME the modals *shall* and *will* are associated with the future, as well as the quasi-modals *be going to*, *be about to*.

(12) *Do* began 'explosive' growth, and its use varied dialectally and over time. It had four major functions:

(a) as a pro-verb (as in OE); that is, one that substitutes for a verb in a sentence such as: *He likes apples and I do, too.*

(b) as a causative in some dialects (e.g. ME **make** or **have**)

(c) periphrastically as an alternative to simple tenses in late ME: *And in the nyght next after folwynge he did carye grete quantitee of Armur to the Guyldehalle*

(d)   in negatives and interrogatives, though this was just beginning:
      Fader, why do ye wepe?
      Father, why do you weep?

4.2.3.1   Word Order

Early Middle English had similar sorts of variation in word order to those we
discussed for Old English in the previous chapter. Thus for example in Chaucer's
Treatise on the Astrolabe, we find the following:

> This tretis . . . wole I shew the
> O   V   S
> and as well consider I thy busi pryere in special to learn the Tretis of the Astrolabe
>   X   V   S O

As the grammatical endings are lost in Middle English word-order patterns
become more fixed, and by the end of the period, with the few minor exceptions
listed above, word order within clauses was not remarkably different from that
of Modern English. There is one major exception, however, which is that pronominal objects often preceded the verb, producing the SOV order that was
fairly common in Old English, but is rarely, if ever, encountered in Modern
English. SOV order was also found in dependent clauses and clauses with more
than one verbal element:

> I wol yow al the shap devyse/Of house and site
> If a man will þe harme
> who haueþ þe in þe putte ibroute?
> *who has you in the well put?*

4.2.4   The Lexicon: Loan Words from French

William I's forceful conquest of the country had the consequence that he replaced the English nobility with new, French nobles and appointed Normans to
high positions in the military and the church. This state of affairs was to continue
for a number of generations. Once important posts such as that of archbishop
were all Norman, the lower echelons soon also filled with Frenchmen, as huge
numbers flocked to Britain to take advantage of the situation. In fact, of all the
English bishops only Bishop Wulfstan remained in office.

When we bear in mind that French was associated with higher social status,
while English was the language of the masses, it is not surprising to discover that
the original native terms for animals, and for livestock in general, were retained:

ox, sheep, swine, deer, calf. French words – *beef, mutton, pork, bacon, venison, veal* – on the other hand were used for the flesh of these animals, eaten mostly by the higher classes (the lower classes subsisting largely on a diet of grains and pulses). A similar lowly Saxon/privileged French dichotomy can be seen in the fact that *master, servant, bottle, dinner, supper* and *banquet* are all of French origin.

The fact that we can determine semantic fields of borrowing suggests that contact between the French and the English is of a completely different nature from that between the Scandinavians and the English.

In industrial civilization the French-speaking strangers were clearly superior to the native population and it is probably for this reason that nearly all the typical designations of tradesmen and artisans are of French origin. While *smith* and *baker* were OE titles, *butcher, barber, carpenter, draper, grocer, mason* and *tailor* were all borrowed from French. Even the Anglo-Saxon word *shoemaker* gave way to the French *cordwainer* or *corviser* for a considerable time.

The core family relationships: *mother, father, sister, brother, son, daughter* all kept their Germanic names. However, non-nuclear family relationships expressing more complex social relations were eventually designated by French names or hybrids: *uncle, aunt, cousin, nephew, niece* are all French replacements of English terms: *grandmother, grandfather, grandson, granddaughter*, etc. are all hybrid forms which eventually came into the language (a process that was completed by the Elizabethan period). The terms *father-in-law, mother-in-law* still display native English words, but they are in fact loan translations, or **calques**, from Old French.

4.2.4.1 Numbers and Parts of the Body

Numbers did not lose their original, native names, and parts of the body also largely kept their English terms. This is because such terms are core words, and usually immune to borrowing except in situations of extremely long and intense contact. One notable exception here is the word for *face*: while in OE there were a number of words, e.g. *onlete, onsene* (cf. Modern German (poetic) *Antlitz*, Modern Swedish *ansikte*), the French word *face* was borrowed in the late thirteenth century as the colloquial term. Literary borrowing of French only really gained pace in the thirteenth and fourteenth centuries, English writers freely borrowing French words, since they were sure of a familiarity with French on the part of their readers. While large numbers of French words came into the language through this process, many filled no real communicative need and have since become obsolete.

Much has been written about the lexical fields in which words were borrowed from French. The following brief list (which is intended to be illustrative, rather than exhaustive) indicates some of the other areas of activity in which French superiority is assumed, and prestige borrowing took place:

Government and administration: *parliament, bill, act, council, county, tax, custom*
Law and property: *court, assize, judge, jury, justice, prison; chattel, money, rent*
Titles: *prince, duke, marquis, viscount, baron*
War: *battle, assault, siege, standard, banner, fortress, tower.*

4.2.4.2   Two French Sources

The French words that came to England were from two separate dialect areas. The Norman Conquest brought with it Northern dialect, the French of Normandy and Picardy. When the Angevin dynasty began in the middle of the twelfth century, however, the dialect of Central France became the norm in court and fashionable society. Pronunciation differed considerably between the two dialects, often leading to the same word being borrowed twice, in the two different forms:

NF had [w] where CF had [g]
NF had [k] where CF had ch [tʃ]
NF had ch [tʃ] where CF had [s]
NF: catch, warden, warranty, launch, wage
CF: chase, guardian, guarantee, lance, gauge

In our discussion of creolization in Middle English below we will have more to say about the effects of French influence on the language during this period.

4.3   Middle English Dialects

There are many uniquely fascinating features about the language of Middle English that make it worthy of detailed study in its own right. In comparison with Old English, for example, where documentary evidence in the form of surviving texts is scant, we have a wealth of texts that have come down to us from the Middle English period. We will have more to say about the literary aspects of these texts in the next section. To a linguist, the most fascinating aspect of these Middle English texts is that they document widespread variation in the language of the early Middle English period, unrivalled in any other period of the language before or since. This then leads to an equally fascinating contrast with the late Middle English period, when we detect the development of a standard form of English, being used in texts from diverse regions of the country in a variety of document types and over a period of time (McIntosh *et al.*, 1986).

However, although we are conforming with normal practice here and discussing the five notional primary dialects of Middle English, we must stress that the dialectal picture of the time was in practice much more complex than this overview would suggest. The research of Angus McIntosh and others on the dialects of Middle English in particular supports the claim that this period of the language was rich in dialect diversity.

There are a number of reasons for this variety in the texts in the early Middle English period, the chief of which is that there was at that time neither a standard variety of English being used in texts, nor even a dominant scribal or spelling tradition, in contrast to the West Saxon of the late Old English period.

Traditionally we isolate five major dialects of Middle English, all of which are defined in relation to Old English dialects:

Middle English dialect	**Old English antecedent**
Northern	Northumbrian
Midland	Mercian
East Anglian	
South-eastern	Kentish
South-western	West Saxon

The Northern dialect area of Middle English extends from the middle of Yorkshire to Scotland. The Midlands area, which extends from London to Gloucestershire, is traditionally split into East Midlands and West Midlands. East Anglian is posited as a separate dialect area, as a number of texts display markedly different forms from those found in East Midlands dialects. The South-eastern dialects cover an area that is closely related to the extent of Kentish in the Old English period, while the South-western dialect area correlates with the OE West Saxon region, and dialectologists occasionally also separate out a Middle South dialect area.

Some of the features used to distinguish dialects are as follows:

(1) OE long a continues to appear as letter <a> or as <ai> in northern dialects, though it appears fairly rapidly in southern ME texts as <o>:
Northern *ham, haim*; Midland *hom(e)*

(2) Long and short y in OE has various realizations in Middle English:
  <u> in the South West, middle South and south-west Midlands
  <e> in the South East
  <i> elsewhere
OE *brycg* 'bridge' > *brugge, bregge, brig(ge)*.

(3) OE *æ* as <a> in all dialects except in south-east and west Midlands where it also occurs as <e>: *dæg* or *dey*.

The following texts are intended to be illustrative of some of the major dialect contrasts in Middle English. The examples are not intended to be exhaustive or to represent the five major dialect divisions discussed above, as these are in fact abstractions and oversimplifications and are not found in pure form in real texts. Instead, the texts are chosen to provide an indication of the extent of variation of Middle English forms.

Northern[1]

The York Lay Folks' Catechism (York), 1357

1   This er the sex thinges that I have spoken of,
    These are the six things that I have spoken of,

2   That the lawe of halikirk lies mast in
    that the law of the holy church lies most in

3   That ye er al halden to knawe and to kun
    that you are all held to know and to learn

4   If ye sal knawe god almighten and cum un to his blisse:
    if you shall know God almighty and come unto his bliss:

5   And for to gif yhou better will for to kun tham,
    and for to give you better will to learn them,

6   Our fadir the ercebisshop grauntes of his grace
    our father the archbishop grants by his grace

7   Fourti daies of pardon til al that kunnes tham,
    Forty days of pardon to all who learn them,

8   Or dos their gode diligence for to kun tham . . .
    or who make a good effort to learn them . . .

9   For if ye kunnandly know this ilk sex thinges
    For if you clearly know these same six things

10 Thurgh thaim sal ye kun knawe god almighten,
    through them you shall know God almighty,

11 Wham, als saint Iohn saies in his godspel,
    who, as Saint John says in his gospel,

12 Conandly for to knawe swilk als he is,
    clearly to know such as he is,

13 It is endles life and lastand bliss,
    it is endless life and eternal bliss,

14 To whilk blisse he bring us that bought us. amen
    To which bliss he might bring us that bought us. amen

West Midland

The York Lay Folks' Catechism: Wyclif's version

1   These be þe sexe thyngys þat y haue spokyn of
     These are the six things that I have spoken of

2   þat þe law of holy chirche lys most yn.
     that the law of holy church lies most in.

3   þat þey be holde to know and to kunne;
     that they are held to know and to learn;

4   yf þey schal knowe god almy3ty and come to þe blysse of heuyn.
     if they shall know God almighty and come to the bliss of heaven.

5   And for to 3eue 3ow þe better wyl for to cunne ham,
     And in order to give you the better will to learn them,

6 · Our Fadyr þe archiepischop grauntys of hys grace,
     our father the archbishop grants by his grace

7   forty dayes of Pardoun to alle þat cunne hem
     forty days of pardon to all that learn them

8   and rehercys hem . . .
     and rehearse them . . .

9   For yf 3e cunnyngly knowe þese sexe thyngys;
     For if you clearly know these six things,

10   þorw3 hem 3e schull knowe god almy3ty.
     through them you shall know God almighty.

11   And as seynt Ion seyþ in his gospel.
     And as Saint John says in his gospel

12   Kunnyngly to know god almy3ty
     clearly to know God almighty

13   ys endles lyf, and lastynge blysse.
     is eternal life, and lasting bliss.

14   He bryngge vs þerto, þat bow3t vs
     Let him bring us to this, that bought us

15   With hys herte blod on þe cros Crist Iesu. Amen.
     with his heart's blood on the cross of Christ Jesus. Amen.

Here we detect variation in the forms of the verb *to be* between Northern *er* and Midland *be* (line 1). The vowel in *halikirk* (Northern) and *holy chirche* (Midland) (line 2) illustrates the fact that the change from *a > o* typical of Middle English had not reached the Northern dialect area, as does the vowel contrast in *mast/most* (line 2) and in *halden to knawe/hold to know* (line 3). In this last example we also see that the final schwa has been lost in the Midlands dialect, but not yet in the Northern variety. This is illustrated again in line 4, where there is also a possible contrast in the vowel quality between Northern *cum* and Midland *com*. There is a contrast in the palatalization of the consonants in Middle English between *halikirk* (Northern) and *holy chirche* (Midland) (line 2) and Northern *sal* and Midland *schal* (line 4).

The Scandinavian influence can be seen in the Northern preposition **til** *al* in contrast to **to** *alle* in the Midland version (line 7). Line 7 also shows a contrast between the verb form with -s ending typical of Northern English and the absence of the ending typical of Midland English in *kunnes tham* vs. *cunne hem*. Here we also note the contrast in the use of the Scandinavian *th-* form of the pronoun *tham* versus the older *hem* pronoun in the Midland dialect version. There are several examples in this brief text of the contrast between the older *-and* form of the participle in Northern English, and the more progressive *-yng* form in Midland *kunnandly* vs. *cunnyngly* (line 9); *conandly* vs. *kunnyngly* (line 12); *lastand* vs. *lastynge* (line 13).

Finally, there is the significant contrast between the progressive Northern 3rd person singular present tense ending -s in *saies*, which contrasts with the more conservative -*þ* ending in *seyþ* (line 10).

Western

John Trevisa: *Dialogue between a Lord and a Clerk*

Clericus   þeus bokes of cronyks buþ ywryte yn Latyn, and Latyn ys
Clerk   *These books of chronicles are written in Latin, and Latin is*

yused and understonde a þys half Grees yn al þe nacions and londes of
used and understood on this side of Greece in all the nations and landes of

Europa; and comynlych Englysch ys noȝt so wyde understonde, yused and
Europe; and commonly English is not so widely understood, used and

yknowe, and þe Englysch translacion scholde no man understonde bote
known, and the English translation should no man understand but

Englyschmen alone. þanne how scholde þe mo men understonde þe cronyks
Englishmen alone. Then how should the more men understand the chronicles

þey a were translated out of Latyn, þat ys so wyde yused and yknowe, into
that were translated out of Latin, that is so widely used and known, into

Englysch, þat ys noȝt yused and yknowe bote of Englyschmen alone?
English, which is not used and known except of Englishmen alone?

Dominus   þes question and doute ys esy to assoyle; vor ȝef þeus cronyks
Master   *This question and doubt is easy to resolve; for if these chronicles*

were translated out of Latyn into Englysch, þanne by so meny þe mo men
were translated out of Latin into English, then by so many the more men

scholde understonde ham as understondeþ Englysch and no Latyn.
should understand them as understand English and not Latin.

This text was written alongside Trevisa's *Polychronicon*, which was finished in 1387. It is written in the Western dialect of Gloucestershire. Typical of Western dialect is the voicing of initial /f/ (*vor* instead of *for*). Throughout the text we see the use of *-þ* as the present plural (indicative) ending (cf. *buþ* 'be'). Past participles begin with the prefix *y-* (*ywryte, yknowe*). As in the Midland example, an old form *ham* is used as third-person plural pronoun.

Southern

Dan Michel: *Ayenbite of Inwyt*[2]

1   Nou ich wille þet ye ywyte hou hit is y-went:
    Now I will that you know how it is went

2   þet þis boc is y-write mid engliss of kent.
    that this book is written with English of Kent

3   Vor uader and uor moder and uor oþer ken
    for father and for mother and for other kin

4   ham uor to berȝe uram alle manyere zen
    them for to preserve from all manner sin

5   þet ine har inwytte ne be lue no uoul wen.
    that in their conscience not remain (any) foul spot.

6   'Huo ase god' is his name yzed
    'Who is like God' is his name said

7   þet þis boc made god him yeue þet bread
    that this book made God him give the bread

8   of angles of heuene and þerto his red
    of angels of heaven and thereto his counsel

9   and onderuonge his zaule huanne þet he is dyad.   Amen.
    and receive his soul when that he is dead.   Amen.

10 Ymende, þet þis boc is uolueld ine þe eue of þe holy
    Remember that this book is completed on the eve of the holy

11 apostles Symon an Iudas, of ane broþer of þe cloystre of sanyt austin of
    apostles Simon and Judas, by a brother of the abbey of Saint Augustine of

12 Canterberi, Ine þe yeare of oure lhordes bering.   1340.
    Canterbury, in the year of our lord's birth.   1340.

The most remarkable thing about this text is that it tells exactly who wrote it, where and when, a fact that is of great importance to historians of the language. It was written by a monk from St Augustine's Abbey in Canterbury. The fact that it is in poetry form for the most part means, however, that the syntax has been distorted (as does the fact that it tries to mimic the syntax of the original French version, *Somme des vices et des vertues*). It is a much more reliable source of information on variation in pronunciation. The spelling of /f/ as <v> or <u> suggests strongly that this sound was voiced in the Kentish dialect in which the monk writes, as does the use of <z> for /s/. Other Kentish features are spelling of Old English /y/ as <e>, as in the word *ken* and the indication of a long diphthong <ya> from Old English *ea* as in *dyad*. Finally, *æ* is still a front vowel, as indicated by the spelling <e> as in *þet* and *red*.

The grammar is clearly Southern with very few exceptions: the first person singular pronoun is *ich* and *ham* and *hare* are used in the third person. Plural present indicative ends with *-eþ*. The infinitive usually ends with *-e*. The past participles have the *y-* prefix and the past participle of strong verbs usually omits the final *-n*. The present participle is either Southern *-inde* or Midland *-ing*. The *-en* plural does appear but *-es* plurals are more common.

4.3.1   *Linguistic and Literary Achievements*

4.3.1.1   *Middle English Literature*

As we mentioned above in our discussion of Middle English dialects, a relatively large quantity of ME literature survives, especially after 1250. Printing presses developed in very late ME, which helped to preserve texts from this period. Considering the low level of literacy, the amount of literature surviving is in fact astonishing.

4.3.2   *Language*

During the Middle English period three major literary languages were used, Latin French and English, the last of which lagged far behind the first two. There was, of course, also literary activity in Irish, Scots Gaelic, Welsh and Cornish at the time.

Apart from a few religious admonitory texts, literature from 1150 to 1250 was generally written in French under the patronage of the court. The *Ancrene Riwle* and *Ormulum*, both religious works, are examples of the survival of Old English literary tradition.

For most ME writers in English, their own dialect was the medium of communication. A number of vaguely defined schools of literature arose:

(1) The West Midlands are associated with the *Katherine* group of religious prose and later with alliterative poetry, e.g. *Piers Plowman* and the work of the *Pearl* poet.
(2) Richard Rolle's mystical works were composed in the Yorkshire dialect.
(3) Barbour's *Bruce* can be generally described as 'Northern'.

Eventually, towards the end of the period, the London dialect began to prevail and was used even by some non-native writers. Chaucer was from London, but John Gower was from Kent and John Lydgate from Suffolk, and these two writers also used London English.

While much of the writing in English consists of translations from French and Latin, there were exceptions; thus, for example, *Everyman*, a late-ME morality play, is considered to be a translation from Dutch.

4.3.3 Genre

The overwhelming bulk of ME literature consists of religious and didactic works, and there is a heavy proportion of verse compared with prose. Since literacy was so scarce, verse was used for all sorts of texts because it is easier to memorize for oral retelling. Moreover, though prose writing had developed in OE it was destroyed after the Conquest and England was in effect starting all over again. Poetry precedes prose in most cultures. Native alliterative verse was largely abandoned in favour of syllable-counting, rhymed verse. Heroic poetry gave way to new forms, particularly the romance. Drama appeared for the first time by the end of ME as did shorter lyric poems. We do not yet find the novel, the short story, the biography or autobiography, however.

Surviving secular prose consists of much legal work: codes of laws, wills, etc. There are also handbooks on astronomy, mathematics, political theory, medicine, husbandry and etiquette. Personal letters also have survived from this period, those of the Celys and the Pastons, for example.

Most medieval chronicles were written in Latin or French or in verse, but the Anglo-Saxon Chronicle continued to be produced until 1154; John Capgrave's late-ME work *Chronical of England* (from the Creation to 1417) was written in prose. Romances were frequently written in verse, but Thomas Malory's *Morte D'Arthur* from the late fifteenth century is a romance in prose. Thomas Usk's political allegory *Testament of Love* was also in prose, and Sir John Mandeville's account of his travels is also probably to be counted as prose.

From 1250 to the mid-fourteenth century the increasing rift between England and France is reflected in the growing body of literature in English. Although religious literature continues, secular literature now comes into its own. *Gesta Romanorum*, from the late thirteenth century, is a good example of the very popular *exempla*, or short tales with a moral.

From 1350 to 1400 individual writers, including Geoffrey Chaucer (1340–1400), come to the fore. His works include *Troilus and Criseyde* and *The Canterbury Tales*. William Langland (1362–87) is the author of *Piers Plowman*, and John Wyclif (d. 1384) was the putative translator of the Bible and author of a large amount of prose, particularly sermons. The anonymous *Sir Gawain and the Green Knight* and three allegorical and religious poems were written by the same unknown author. All are proof of the secure position English had attained by the mid-fourteenth to fifteenth century, and this period is often called the imitative period, since many writers emulated Geoffrey Chaucer. It is a transition period between the language of Chaucer and Shakespeare and its foremost authors have been much neglected, though they carry English literary tradition into the Renaissance.

Secular verse is classified according to subject matter, which can be described in geographic terms as: Britain (Arthur), England (English or Germanic heroes), Greece and Rome (Alexander the Great and the Trojan War), and France (Charlemagne and his knights). There are some that do not fit these categories, e.g. tales of the long-suffering wife (*The Wife's Lament*). All genres of secular verse were borrowed directly or indirectly from French.

The mystics are also important in the fourteenth century. Richard Rolle, Walter Hilton and the author of *The Cloud of Unknowing* are good examples of male mystics; female mystics include Dame Julian of Norwich, who wrote *Revelations of Divine Love* in the late fourteenth century, and the author of the *Book of Margery Kempe* (from about 1430).

4.4   Sociolinguistic Focus: Social Stratification, Multilingualism and Dialect Variation. Language Contact: the Myth of Middle English Creolization

4.4.1   English Re-established

While we can be fairly sure about the number and influence of powerful Normans in England, the Frenchmen of lower classes are harder to talk about with much certainty. It is clear that considerable numbers of Normans and Frenchmen came to England in the years after the conquest and settled side by side with the English, but it is difficult to tell in the earlier periods of French influence in which contexts French, and in which English, was spoken and written. However, we can be sure that French was the language of the court and English was the language of the people, so that there must have been diglossia in England at the time, with French as the High language and English as the Low language.

While we are not sure how many Frenchmen came to England at this time, we do know that their superior position meant that they were able to maintain their own language. Indeed, for two hundred years after the Norman Conquest French remained the language of the upper classes in England, and the members of the upper classes may have tried to acquire some knowledge of English in order to converse with the people. Churchmen, at least at the lower levels, needed knowledge of English, though kings and queens most often used the services of an interpreter. The language of the lower class remained English, and we can assume that a lowly Norman soldier marrying an English girl would switch to English as his everyday language. In the beginning only people of Norman origin spoke French, but eventually through intermarriage and association with the ruling class numerous people of English extraction recognized the prestige of speaking French and began to use it. Eventually, facility with French was founded not on an ethnic but on a class basis. Knowledge of French could be found amongst the middle class. Knights tended to use French, even when their mother tongue was English. Town-dwellers, tradesmen and merchants began to speak French for instrumental purposes, especially in the larger and more important commercial centres. Even clerks, stewards, bailiffs and sometimes free tenants could speak French, probably partly as a consequence of the fact that various transactions and services were conducted in that language. However, it must be stressed that speakers of French amongst the non-nobility were undoubtedly in a small minority, so that all degrees of mono- and bilingualism were present in England before the loss of Normandy in 1204.

If we compare this situation with that of the Scandinavian invaders which we discussed in the previous chapter, we observe that in the latter case no loss of social status accrued to the speaking of English: Old Norse was not a prestige language. Though the Scandinavian language was in such intimate contact with English that it even influenced parts of the grammar, the types of vocabulary borrowed from Old Norse cannot be put together under distinct cultural and social rubrics. The opposite is true of the influence of the French invaders on the English language

As long as England remained in possession of lands on the continent and the English nobility was united with its continental relations by ties of property, kinship and business, there was a real need to continue using French amongst the governing class in England. Had England remained in control of the two-thirds of France which they once held, French might have remained in use in England for ever. But soon after 1200 conditions were to change. In 1204 King John lost Normandy, England's vital possession abroad, in a dispute over his bride Isabel of Angoulême, as we mentioned in the beginning of this chapter. The French king Philip I confiscated Normandy and the nobility was forced to relinquish possession of French estates. Rivalry began to develop between England and France, which culminated in the Hundred Years War.

This development naturally meant that English and French interests could no longer be the same, and it ultimately resulted in the re-establishment of English. When Louis IX declared that it was impossible to show allegiance to both England and France, the nobles were forced to declare themselves either English or French.

The split with France was not so straightforward, however, since many English nobles had land in southern France as well, and a new influx of southern French noblemen was encouraged by the close ties between the English and French royal families. Henry III, his half-brother Richard of Cornwall, Louis IX of France and Louis's brother Charles of Anjou were all linked in marriage to the Count of Provence. All of the wives' families and retinue came to England with them during Henry III's reign (1216–72). Henry III himself bestowed high office on many Frenchmen. Matthew Paris, a contemporary chronicler, states that London 'was full to overflowing, not only of Poitevins, Romans and Provençals, but also of Spaniards who did great injury to the English'.

Moreover, French had been an important literary language in England, and thanks to royal patronage a considerable body of French literature was produced in England from the beginning of the twelfth century.

Henry's favouritism caused great resentment amongst the native English. Eventually the barons and the middle class united against the French, the opposition resulting in the Provisions of Oxford (1258) and the ensuing Barons' War (1258–65). During this time the French were driven twice from England. When peace was finally established and Edward I (1272–93) ascended the throne, England was a nation aware of its national identity. All of the events leading up to this moment, though initially slowing down the spread of English, ultimately led to the awareness of the necessity of the adoption of English as the language of English affairs.

However, this process was not so easily carried out, as France was in the cultural ascendancy in Europe in the thirteenth century, and in high society a knowledge of French was essential. This naturally arrested the progress of English for some time, at least in English court circles. However, it is to be noted that the nobility's use of French was a matter of culture and fashion, that is, a sociological choice, rather than an economic and political necessity, as it had been throughout the twelfth century. The nobility chose to maintain French as the language of society, administration and commerce. Many of the fashion-conscious or ambitious had to learn French as a foreign language and the maintenance of French was therefore becoming increasingly artificial. It did, however, persist until the end of the thirteenth century as the language of parliament, the law courts and administration, although the accuracy of the French used was often open to question – a clear indication that its use was no longer 'native'. Eventually, the use of English began to spread even amongst the nobility. Henry

III's son Edward I spoke English well, and soon it was used by influential clergy, the legal profession and parliament. By the middle of the thirteenth century foreign-language instruction books had to be written, presumably to teach the children of the nobility French, since their native language was by this time undoubtedly English.

By the end of the thirteenth century the attitude had developed to one of advocating English as the language of Englishmen. The following extract from the Prologue to *Cursor Mundi*, written about the year 1300, exemplifies this impatient attitude on the part of the English:

þis ilk bok es translate
This same book is translated

Into Inglis tong to rede
Into English language to read

For the love of Inglis lede.
For the love of the English language.

Inglis lede of Ingland,
English language of England,

For the commun at understand.
For the common people to understand.

Frankis rimes here I redd
French rhymes here I read

Comunlik in ilka sted;
Commonly in the same place;

Mast es it wroght for Frankis man,
Most is it made for French man,

Quat is for him na Frankis can?
What is for him who no French can (speak)?

In Ingland the nacion
In England the nation

Es Inglis man þar in commun;
Is English man there in common;

þe speche þat man wit mast may spede;
The speech that one knows most may speed;

Mast þarwit to speke war nede.
Most therewith to speak was need.

Selden was for ani chance
Seldom was for any chance

Praised Inglis tong in France;
Praised English tongue in France;

Give we ilkan þare langage.
Let us give to each his language.

Me think we do þam non outrage.
I do not think we do them any outrage.

To laud and Inglis man I spell
To the ignorant and English man I write

þat understandes þat I tell.
Who understands what I say.

Soon a knowledge of English was common at all levels of society. Although even the church and the universities began to allow its use in certain circumstances, eventually they had to ban the use of English in order that a knowledge of French and Latin might not be lost altogether. But the need to ban a language is always a sure sign that that language is alive and thriving.

Inevitably after such a separation, Anglo-Norman French turned out not to be 'good' French. While Ile-de-France French had gained ascendancy in the thirteenth century, the French spoken in England was predominantly Norman with an admixture of other Northern elements, and it eventually evolved in Britain into a nondescript register of its own, the butt of many a mocking poem and remark by the French or English speakers of French who were fortunate enough to have studied in France itself. Even Chaucer makes fun of the Prioress:

And Frensh she spak ful faire and fetishly
After the scole of Stratford atte Bowe
For Frensh of Paris was to hir unknowe.

As well as the gradual loss of French possessions, anti-French feeling was stirred up by the Hundred Years War (1337–1453), begun by Edward III's invasion of France in retaliation for French interference in Scotland. The English had mixed success in the Hundred Years War, but after Edward III's death and the success of Jeanne d'Arc (1429), the death warrant for the use of French in England was finally signed.

4.4.1.1 *Language and the Rise of the Middle Class*

During the latter part of the ME period, serfdom and villeinage died out, the lot of the ordinary labouring Englishman improved and a new middle class developed. The plague (1348–50) caused a death rate of approximately 30 per cent, certainly higher among the poorer classes than the rich. This resulted in a shortage of labour, and a concomitant increase in wages and the unification of the peasants whose campaign for better wages and working conditions culminated in the Peasants' Revolt (1381). The result was an increase in the importance of English, since the poor people now had more say in the affairs of the country. Moreover, the plague probably eradicated many of the educated teachers who could instruct in French and Latin, thereby paving the way for the rise of English in schools.

The growth of the English urban system brought with it an expansion of the power base of the craftsmen and merchant class, and by the beginning of the fourteenth century everyone knew English again. The literature (with or without apology) appears in English as well as in French (which had not completely died out at court and in educated circles, even in Chaucer's time). However, mirroring its use at court, French did remain the language of the legal profession and the church until 1362. The people who spoke French in the fourteenth century were undoubtedly bilingual and the standard of French increasingly reflected this state of affairs.

Throughout the fourteenth century, English was used at occasions of important pronouncements. Thus, in 1337 Edward III's consultation with parliament about the invasion of France was conducted by a lawyer in English. In 1362 the Chancellor opened Parliament with a speech in English, and by 1388 English was gaining on Latin as the language of the town councils and guilds. When Richard II was deposed in 1399 the articles of accusation were read to Parliament in Latin and English, while Henry IV made his speeches and his speech of accession in English. In 1362, after five years of the use of English in the London and Middlesex sheriff's court, Parliament enacted the Statute of Pleading which stated that all lawsuits should be conducted in English, since 'French is much unknown in the said realm'. This constitutes the official recognition of English.

Eventually, English people who could speak French became the exception, rather than the rule. It became a language to be used when travelling to France, rather than at home, and knowledge of French was purely a fashionable or cultural custom in the fifteenth century.

Latin and French were both, however, still competitors with English as the medium of writings in the fourteenth century. French had rivalled the unstable medieval Latin for quite some time. But finally, in the fifteenth century, English succeeded in displacing them both. English letters began to be written by 1420 and are the rule by 1450. Henry V (1413–22) promotes the use of English in writing by example, and by about 1425 English has been generally re-adopted. Wills also follow the general linguistic development: the wills of Henry IV, V and VI are all written in English.

Towns and guilds eventually adopted English as the language in which their records should be written. After 1485 Parliament publishes statutes and petitions in English and French and by 1489 French is completely eradicated as the language of Parliament.

The following is a good example of the written English of the period.

Richard Rolle's *The Bee and the Stork*

The bee has thre kyndis. Ane es, þat scho es never ydill, and scho es noght with thaym
The bee has three kinds. One is that she is never idle and she is not with them

þat will noghte wyrke, bot castys them owte and puttes thaym awaye. Anothire es, þat
that will not work, but casts them out and puts them away. Another is that

when scho flyes scho takes erthe in hyr fette, þat scho be noghte lyghtly overheghede in
when she flies she takes earth in her feet, that she be not lightly raised too high in

the ayere of wynde. The thyrde es, þat scho kepes clene and brychte hire wyngez. Thus
the air of wind. The third is that she keeps clean and bright her wings. Thus

ryghtwyse men þat lufes God are never in ydyllnes; for owthyre þay ere in travayle,
righteous men that love God are never in idleness; for either they are in toil,

prayand, or thynkande, or redande, or othere gude doande, or withtakand ydill men and
praying, or thinking, or reading, or other good doing, or reproving idle men and

schewand thaym worthy to be put fra þe ryste of heven, for þay will noghte travayle.
showing them worthy to be put from the rest of heaven for they will not work.

Here þay take erthe, þat es, þay halde þamselfe vile and erthely, that thay be noghte
Here they take earth, that is they hold themselves vile and earthly, that they be not

blawen with þe wynde of vanyte and of pryde. They kepe thaire wynges clene, that is,
blown with the wind of vanity and of pride. They keep their wings clean, that is,

þe twa commandementes of charyte þay fulfull in gud concyens; and thay hafe othyre
the two commandments of charity they fulfil in good conscience; and they have other

vertus unblendyde with þe fylthe of syn and unclene luste.
virtues unblended with the filth of sin and unclean lust.

(From Fisher and Bornstein (1984), pp. 158–9)

4.4.2 *The Development of Standard English*

Once the French were forced to withdraw from positions of power, this brought about the increased social mobility for Englishmen noted above. Many Englishmen from various parts of the country moved to London to improve their social lot. These were naturally speakers of diverse dialects. It would appear that the Southern English and the Northern English dialect speakers understood the East and West Midlands speakers better than they did one another.

In the thirteenth century the East Midlands became the most important economic centre because of its wool and corn exports. In the fourteenth century the majority of people lived south of the Humber, 85 per cent of them rurally. The East Midlands area was the most densely populated and the least ravaged by the Black Death (1348–1400). More and more officers of London city government came from the Midlands and the North.

By the end of the fourteenth century, membership of social classes was more fluid, because of the plagues and related developments (see above). This is clearly shown by events of the beginning of the fifteenth century, when Henry IV wanted to win the support of the middle classes by giving them offices of state, household and council seats.

London eventually became the commercial and cultural capital, and it clearly had a central role to play in the emergence of a standard dialect in Britain. However, the dialect that developed into the standard is not simply the London dialect, but rather it is essentially East Midlands with some Northern and Southern influence.

Until the late fifteenth century, authors wrote in the dialect of their region (*Sir Gawain and the Green Knight* and *Piers Plowman* were written in the West Midlands dialect, *The Owl and the Nightingale* and *The Ancrene Riwle*, *Ayenbite of Inwit* (Dan Michel, Kentish, 1340) in Southern, *Bruce* in Northern, while John Gower and Geoffrey Chaucer wrote in a London/East Midlands variety.

4.4.2.1 *The Evolution of ME 'Standard' English*

It appears there were three types of 'standard' English in the ME period, only two of which were London types.

(1) The first appears to be based on spoken dialects of the Central Midlands, especially Northamptonshire and Huntingdonshire and Bedfordshire. These dialects were spread by the Lollards, followers of John Wyclif, the religious reformer who was born in Yorkshire and studied at Oxford, therefore using a Midlands dialect in his writings (*c*.1350). The Midlands Standard dwindled in importance by about 1430.

(2) Up until 1370 London was an Essex dialect (as the English proclamation of Henry III in 1258 attests). After 1300 changes occurred in this variant, as can be seen from Chaucer's writings, involving the adoption of linguistic features from the Central Midlands.

(3) After 1430 a large number of documents are written in Chancery Standard, which show more Midlands features than the earlier London type and are very different from Chaucer's English. It is this dialect, and not its predecessors, that became the basis of Modern Standard English.

Five particular morphological features of the Southern dialect have become important in differentiating the three major ME dialects. This is over and above variation in pronunciation, which certainly also existed, and indeed still exists today.

(1)   *Buth* is the dialectal form of *be* in the third person plural, present tense. Old English has two verbs for *be*, *beon* and *wesan*, and ModE *be* is an amalgamation of the two. Trevisa's use of *buth* is Southern, as is the ending *-th*. By the end of the fifteenth century *be* and *is/are* denote subjunctive and indicative respectively: 'If this be treason, we are all traitors.'

(2)   The inflection of the verb for third person plural present is *-th*, cf. *holdeth*. Other dialects use either *-en* or Ø (*holden* or *hold*).

(3)   Dialects differ in the ending of the third person singular present tense verbs, which is either *-th* or *-s*. Southern is characterized by *-th*, while Northern has *-s* (*seemeth* vs. *seems*).

(4)   The third person plural pronoun was *they*, *their*, *them* in the North, vs. *hy*, *here*, *hem* in the South; the use of the initial *th-* is distinctive. In the South the *h-* was often dropped, so that *a* could also be the equivalent of *he*.

(5)   In the formation of the past participle *y-* is prefixed to the past stem (*y-knowe*, 'known'; *y-left*, 'left'). ME dialects differ in that some use this prefix, while others make use of only a suffixed form (*risen*) or an inflection combining a suffix and medial vocalic change, retaining OE ablaut (*taught*).

The changes in the dialectal base of the eventual standard can be explained in large part by immigration into the capital, which began in the thirteenth and fourteenth centuries because of a concentration of economic power there. After 1066 London became a national centre of training and commerce, and Westminster, its neighbour, but a separate entity, became a great ecclesiastical centre, ideally suited as the home of the national administration on account of its scriptorial resources. Most of the immigrants came first from Norfolk, then Essex, Hertfordshire and the Home Counties, which is reflected in the Essex and East Anglian characteristics of the fourteenth-century texts. But in the fourteenth century there was a fresh influx of immigrants from Bedfordshire and Northamptonshire, while those from the Home Counties decreased; immigration from Norfolk continued. This explains the first change in the London dialect and its continuance explains the second change. The Northern influence is explained by the fact that northerners held high office: northern linguistic forms were present in the Central Midlands dialect. The East Anglian influence ceased after the middle of the fourteenth century, though immigration continued, because the area was considered peripheral, while in the Central Midlands the easily understood standard was developing. In sum, standard English in its written form was an upper-class dialect developed in London in the late Middle English period mainly on the basis of the influential dialect of East Midlands immigrants.

A major reason for the standardization of the Chancery Standard was that William Caxton adopted it, probably in about 1476, since he set up his printing press in Westminster and not in London. Caxton probably did more to standardize English in his time than any other individual, since it was expedient for him to edit the works he printed to resolve the dialect variants in order to gain the broadest readership possible for his publications. Strong dialectal traits disappeared from written works by the mid-fifteenth century and by the end of the seventeenth century most orthographical variants had been standardized.

A standard spoken form of the language probably extends far back in history, but it is not until relatively recently that evidence of it can be cited. For example, the population was mobile from the tenth century onward, in pilgrimages, crusades, universities, inns of court, royal households. All of these factors suggested a need for a non-localized form of speech that could be used by any and all taking part in population movements. However, not until the sixteenth century is there definite evidence of a spoken standard with Puttenham's statement that London English had become a kind of standard (from *The Arte of English Poesie*, 1589):

> Ye shall therefore take the usuall speach of the court and that of London and the shires lying about London within 60 myles, and not much above.

Despite the fact that there was an accepted standard form of English, these early versions of 'standard' English were not 'standard' in the modern sense: during the ME period English is much more restricted in acceptable variations in *pronunciation* than is Early Modern English. The early eighteenth century saw a move to 'fix the pronunciation' which was guided by traditional speaking conventions. Dr Johnson urged people to follow the written words. Thus, spoken standard English was probably very much influenced by an earlier standard written language. But all of this is anticipating the next stages of the history of English, which are described in the following chapters.

4.4.3   *Middle English Creolization: Myth?*

In recent years, the focus of historical linguistics has shifted, caused partly by a rediscovery of language as a social phenomenon. The Structuralists had been wont to speak of variation as 'free variation'; that is to say, where a speaker could choose amongst a number of possible linguistic elements in a particular utterance, these choices were simply recorded as such, and no principles were proposed to determine why a particular choice was made. More recent studies of language variation recognize that variation is often rule-governed or principled; that is, psychological and social factors frequently influence choices amongst alternatives.

A sub-field of modern sociolinguistics concerns the structure and development of pidgin and creole languages, that is, languages that are not fully fledged standardized languages, but are in various stages of development. The very fact that they are still developing allows us to view the processes of linguistic change which are happening at a perceptible rate, something which Structuralists and historians of standard European languages such as English had not hitherto felt to be possible.

Sociolinguists feel that it is possible to use what is happening in present-day languages and dialects as a window onto the past. If we recognize that the development of pidgins and creoles (also known as 'contact languages') is part of the larger issue of 'contact-induced language change', then we can see that there might be similarities between what is going on now in certain parts of the world, and what went on in early periods of English.

About twenty-five years ago, a number of linguists attempted to draw parallels between the creolization process and what happened to Middle English after close contact with Scandinavian and French. It is worth dwelling on this discussion at this point to illustrate what insights modern theory can give us into past states of language. It is also something of a cautionary tale, since it shows that it is dangerous to take over an argument, however appealing it might be, without careful consideration of the factual evidence at hand.

This whole debate revolves around two crucial questions:

(1)   How are pidgins, creoles and other contact varieties defined?
(2)   What hard evidence do we have from the contact situations occurring in the history of the English language to warrant the claim that English has been at any stage a pidgin, a creole or some other definable contact variety?

4.4.3.1   *Definitions*

In chapter 1 we looked at the typical development of creoles that emerge out of contact between two or more languages and become the native language of a set of speakers, usually converging eventually on the mainstream language with which they come to have greater contact. This diagram is based on numerous case histories of the typical development of pidgins and creoles (see Romaine, 1988, for an excellent overview of the topic).

In contrast to pidgin and creole specialists, Bailey and Maroldt (1977), who were the first to make the claim that Middle English was a creole, used the term loosely. They do provide definitions of creole, pidgin and broken English (p. 67), but their definition of creole is idiosyncratic, and they fail to acknowledge that broken speech (or code-switching) is much more common than fully fledged pidgins. Their arguments have been called contradictory and their data selective by Thomason and Kaufman (1988), but their work is worth discussing because it allows us to look more closely both at the definition of such interim varieties of language on the one hand, and at the degree of contact between English, Old Norse and French, on the other.

Unfortunately, scholars of pidgins and creoles do not even agree amongst themselves about the basic definitions of these varieties (which is part of the reason why there is so much special pleading in the discussion of the status of Middle English). Bearing this caveat in mind, we can define a pidgin and a creole roughly as follows.

Pidgin

A pidgin is a reduced form of language that is the product of contact between speakers of two different languages who are not familiar with each other's language. It is often functionally reduced, in that it is usually used for instrumental purposes, such as barter or trade, though it can eventually cover a number of communicative situations. It is not, however, ad hoc simplification (such as the broken English that tourists use in one-off encounters), but it has to be learned and it crucially demonstrates some degree of conventionalization or crystalliza-tion. Another crucial criterion in the definition of pidgins is that they are not the native language of any community; it might be the case that a few isolated children learn a pidgin, in which case it still remains a pidgin. A pidgin is unlikely to stabilize if the standard language remains accessible, as is the case in Germany today with regard to the German language of immigrant workers (cf. Fennell, 1997).

Creole

The description of a creole is more complex than that of a pidgin.

(1) A creole acquires native speakers, retains stability, simplification and unin-telligibility to standard speakers, but *expands* because of its nativeness, that is to say, it develops ways of fulfilling all the communicative functions its speakers require of it. However, a language can creolize for some groups, but stay a pidgin for others, so there is no smooth transition of the one to the other.

(2) A creole can develop out of a reduced form of the old language (e.g., French Indian Creole), but this is a marked 'break' with the standard.

(3) Creoloid fossilization of inadequately learned languages can take place on the basis of lower stability of the system as a whole. This is quite a weak

form of creolization and is not the same as creolization as it is described in
(1) above.

(4)   Creolization always involves an extreme mixture of the systems of two or
more languages (cf. Thomason and Kaufman, 1988).

4.4.3.2   *Pidgins and Creoles in England?*

It is possible that at various stages in the early history of English a number of
short-lived pidgins may have existed in England, perhaps spoken by the following:

(1)   Celtic speakers of the first to third generation speaking English;
(2)   First- to third-generation Scandinavian speakers in the tenth and eleventh
centuries;
(3)   Bilingual speakers of French in the eleventh to thirteenth centuries.

However, there is no evidence of any of these contact varieties having stabilized
sufficiently to become even a form that we can classify as a stable pidgin.

There are diagnostics for determining that a variety is a creole (Mackey, 1982).
While Middle English does display regularization (simplification) of forms, there
is no actual *loss* of the inflectional system (in fact, endings were required in
places where they had been absent or ambiguous in Old English). Thus:

Nouns:	ME retains the genitive case and its use was even extended during this period. Datives exist well into the fourteenth century, and ME also retains marking for number.
Pronouns:	ME retains gender and case distinction, which is marked more clearly than before because of the loans from Scandinavian (see above).
Adjectives:	There is inflection in the expression of comparison, which is preserved and extended to polysyllabics in the vernacular (*bountifuller*). The adjective and adverb are formally distinguished by ME (see above).
Verbs:	While creoles do not have tense distinctions, ME expands the OE tense system and develops passives, etc.

Focusing on simplification in inflection as a defining criterion of creolization, we
know that it can be caused by extensive contact with similar languages or dialects,
or by the absence of a norm or standard, or by both.

There is no doubt that there was simplification in ME and that contact with
Scandinavian and French is the most likely reason for it. Nevertheless, it is doubtful
whether we can justify an assumption that there was a stable pidgin or creole
English in thirteenth-century households, because we have no real record of the
linguistic behaviour of bilingual individuals.

The enormous influence of Scandinavian and French on the ME lexicon is also without question. And furthermore, there is evidence of contact-induced change even in phonology, with new phonemes developing where there is a gap. Hence we note the phonemicization of /v/, /z/ and /ʒ/ in English, and the addition of the diphthongs /oi/, /ui/. However, English did not develop French-like rounded vowels /yː/ or /ʏ/, or nasal vowels, so that we can hardly say the phonemic system was extensively affected by contact with French.

Finally, we recall from our earlier discussion that most – up to perhaps 90 per cent – of English speakers did not give up using English, and that widespread use of French was limited to the upper echelons of society. For all these reasons then, we must assume that French is unlikely to have caused creolization.

So if French was not the cause of creolization, might it be the case that Scandinavian affected English so much towards the end of the Old English period that we can talk of creolization in Middle English? We have seen that there was a great concentration of settlers in the Danelaw. However, the Old Norse that was used there was largely a spoken and not a written standard, unlike French at a later stage. Consequently there was no target norm at which speakers could aim, and a resulting **Ausgleichssprache** ('compromise dialect') could have developed (as it did in eighteenth-century Afrikaans, for example). Changes in ME were the result of the reduction and inherent redundancy in the OE system that we have already discussed, though there is evidence that this was speeded up and even triggered in the odd instance in the Danelaw, because of the special communicative needs faced there. Some of the changes that have been noted are:

(1)   the loss of grammatical gender;
(2)   the expansion of the strong masculine of nouns;
(3)   the loss of article and adjectival inflection (although there was regularization of the noun inflection).

All of these changes originated in the East Midlands and spread south.

Thomason and Kaufman and the arguments for and against creolization in Middle English

Thomason and Kaufman admit that there is no doubt that Norse influence on the English language was extensive, indeed, that the extent of influence reaches 2 or 3 on their scale. However, their own data suggest that pidginization is unlikely on both structural and social grounds. The structural reason they give is that Norse and English were so close to each other that there was already a high degree of mutual intelligibility that did not necessitate dramatic reduction on communicative grounds. And socially, there was no need for a reduced form of language with which to communicate on an *ad hoc* and instrumental basis. What was needed was a language that was equal to all communicative functions, as the

Norse were *settlers* in Britain, so that the same interim communicative imperative that induces the development of pidgins and creoles simply was not there.

Like us, Thomason and Kaufman stress that any simplification that took place in English was a result of the move from a synthetic to an analytic language that had begun already in the shift from Indo-European to Germanic. Their data show that this breakdown in the case system, which is typically cited as characteristic of Middle English, was already well advanced in the Northumbrian English of the Lindisfarne Gospels, suggesting that language contact had nothing to do with the change. In fact, they show that the Southern English dialects, which had greater contact with French, displayed much more conservatism than the Midland and Northern dialects, so that, if anything, the reverse is true!

With French, the question of creolization seems altogether more unlikely than with Scandinavian, in fact, since the conditions for creolization simply were not present. There were only two languages in contact, both of which were being spoken by native speakers, and there was nothing to stop normal bilingualism from developing. Bailey and Maroldt maintain that it was the French, the conquerors, not the English-speaking conquered, who were forced to shift, and this most definitely does not fit into the typical pattern of pidginization and creolization.

A key factor in all of this is that there were never huge numbers of speakers of French in England, and even they began to give up French by 1235 at the latest. There is no evidence to suggest that large numbers of the native English population learned French between 1066 and 1250, and after 1250 there was no motivation to do so in any case, because, as we say in our discussion of the political and social history, once lands had to be forfeited back to France, the nobility in England had no reason to feel anything other than English. The dialects in English that were most in contact with French underwent no simplification that can be traced to French; in fact, as we have said, they are the most conservative of the ME dialects, and no doubt would have been so with or without French contact. Simplifying traits in Standard English are imported from the East Midlands, and sometimes these traits originated in the north. The massive French influence on English vocabulary, followed by the mild influence on English morphology and syntax, and the practically trivial influences on English phonology, took place at a time when there were hardly any competent French speakers around to influence the language in the first place.

In purely linguistic terms, the influence of French on English is thus neither extreme nor special. It is similar to normal degrees of influence of Swedish on Finnish – that is, English has borrowed heavily from the French lexicon, but there is no obvious structural change that can be pointed to. In phonology, English has phonologized certain allophonic pairs, though Thomason and Kaufman claim these are not from French or Norse. It has borrowed word-formational elements; for example the affix -*abel*, from French through loan words, became an affix in its own right in the late fourteenth century. As far as word order is concerned, it is impossible to prove French influence, with the exception of a few fixed phrases that do not affect the system as a whole. And there is definitely no influence on concord. In fact, the data suggest that while a few English learned French, virtually all Norman and Angevin French speakers learned English within 250 years of the Conquest and their *French*, not their English, suffered as a result of this.

Thus, when Bailey suggests that 'creolization' is happening all the time, he means simply structural interference from one language on another. To him any kind of analytic development in a language is taken as evidence of foreign interference. But this does not have to be the case, and interference does not equal creolization. The influence of Russian on Finnic languages spoken within Russia can be shown to have proceeded for a thousand years, yet one can by no means speak of 'creoles' in that instance of intensive language contact. Heavy lexical influence and some structural influence (including some phonological phenomena) did indeed occur, but the indigenous languages are still recognizable as 'Finnic' with a Russian component. Thus Thomason and Kaufman maintain that there is neither disruption of the linguistic system, nor abrupt influence of French on English. Instead we are dealing with gradual change that was already evident in the northern OE of the Lindisfarne Gospels, as a consequence of the change that had set in during the shift from I-E to Germanic; that is, the fixing of stress on the nuclear syllable causing the gradual erosion of the morphological endings and the case system. All the evidence, then, points to only superficial French influence, which is stronger in the south than in the north, but which in no way can be interpreted as 'creolization'.

On the sociolinguistic history of /h/-dropping in English

At this stage it would be useful to apply the ideas of language contact-induced change by focusing on one particular feature of English, that of /h/-dropping, in the context of ME, as discussed by J. Milroy (1983).

In British English, /h/-dropping is a generally stigmatized phenomenon. Little research has been done on the basis of spelling variants, which could shed light on the history of this feature in English, though there is evidence of the general instability of the sound /h/. Earlier scholars (Dobson, 1968) did not relate the dropping of /h/ with the insertion of non-historic /h/, but modern sociolinguistic theory clearly points to hypercorrection in this instance. Eliza Doolittle's famous line is a clear example of this relationship: 'In 'Artford, 'Ereford and 'Ampshire 'urricanes 'ardly hever 'appen.' Milroy cites Skeat's view that the Anglo-Normans were instrumental in /h/-dropping because of their inadequate command of English. But he points out that this is less than likely to be true, and more likely due to the fact that speakers had inadequate French.

Changes involving /h/ are typical of those that sociolinguists observe in contact situations, associated in the first place with simplifications arising out of contact between French and English, and subsequently diffusing into everyday English. By 1300 the loss of initial /h/ is noted in eastern England from Kent and Surrey to Lincolnshire – this loss, according to Milroy, was variable in some lects and possibly categorical in others.

The progression of the loss of /h/ seems to have proceeded from pre-sonorant environments through pre-glide environments to pre-vocalic environments (although we do not know the precise order of vowels):

(1) Loss before sonorants: /h/, which was present in OE, is lost in the clusters /hn/, /hl/, /hr/ in the ME period, and is categorical since then in all dialects (cf. the discussion of [hrof] > [rof] above.
(2) Loss before glides: /h/ is lost before /w/ in some ME dialects and now generally in Anglo-English including standardized forms. That is, most speakers do not differentiate between *which* and *witch*. However, this feature is not stigmatized.
(3) Loss before vowels: /h/ is lost before vowels in some ME dialects, probably categorically then or subsequently. Now its loss is general in many Anglo-English dialects, but the phenomenon is variable and stigmatized.

The social and regional diffusion of the loss of /h/ can be interpreted historically according to contact situations and socially according to Labov's (1972) model of social diffusion. Early ME /h/ loss takes place in the regions that were most important commercially and administratively, and is noted in formal and learned texts. In ME, then, we can infer that /h/ loss probably carried a certain amount of prestige. Lower orders were probably the last to be affected by the change, because of less frequent contact with the Anglo-Norman aristocracy. Anglo-Norman was probably /h/-less and restructuring was subsequently caused by contact with French phonology. This transfer could well have been seen as more prestigious than the conservative English retention of /h/. Once /h/-less pronunciation was established in the middle-order English of the South-East and the East Midlands, Milroy proposes the following pattern of diffusion in later centuries:

(1) spread to lower-middle and lower orders of society;
(2) spread from the centre of political influence to other regions, initially those of relatively high commercial and political importance;
(3) spread from populated (urban) areas to more remote (rural) regions.

Despite moves towards standardization, evidence of /h/-loss from 1300 to 1600 remains considerable. This certainly cannot be due to Anglo-Norman scribes, and in fact, documentary evidence suggests that it was a middle-class phenomenon at that time. Evidence from rhymes and similar material leads Milroy to conclude that it was not stigmatized.

By the eighteenth century, however, Milroy maintains /h/-loss is considered a vulgarism, and was the subject of overt social commentary. Although it had spread fairly generally in the sixteenth century, at one point it seems to have become associated with ignorance and lack of education, which caused socially conscious people – the middle class – to avoid it. The shift in attitude is likely to be associated with the spread of literacy, education and printed books, and therefore it probably began to be stigmatized in the sixteenth century. It is conceivable that the upper and middle classes used it as a stylistic variable, dropping it in informal styles and keeping it in formal ones, but in the absence of evidence this can only remain an enlightened hypothesis.

Milroy also suggests that while London vernacular speakers lost /h/, some rural ones retained it, and this is the case today. Scotland and many northern English dialects have always been /h/-ful, and therefore we can posit a history of gradual restoration of a lost or variable segment, leading towards eventual standardization. The end of the process is the general perception that an /h/-less form (where it is etymologically present, e.g., *an hotel*) is no longer a variant to be used by 'polite' speakers, and areas colonized from the sixteenth century onward appear to be /h/-ful – particularly Ireland and North America. We shall return to the question of the spread of English in general in later chapters.

4.5 Conclusion

The application of sociological principles to individual linguistic phenomena, such as the occurrence or non-occurrence of /h/, is but one avenue open to students of the history of the language – but one that is critical for an understanding of key aspects of language change. Global issues, on the other hand, such as literacy, education, the status of language X vs. Y in society (in this instance English vs. Norman French), and internal changes of linguistic systems as a whole, set the stage for such studies. The history of ME has been shown to be a combination of internal change and greater external influence (albeit primarily lexical) than took place in the OE period. And, as a consequence of linguistic awareness, the seeds of standardization were also sown in this period. This aspect of the history of the language will consequently be a large concern of the following chapter, in which we discuss the development of Early Modern English.

Notes

1 This discussion and that of the Midland dialect, below, are expanded from Freeborn (1998: 202–3). My glosses throughout.

2 This text is also discussed in Fisher and Bornstein (1984: 113–17). Again, the glosses
   are my own.

Suggested Readings

Blake, Norman F. (ed.) (1992b) The Literary Language. In Blake, Norman F. (ed.) (1992a),
   pp. 500–41.
Fisher, John Hurt (1996) *The Emergence of Standard English*. Louisville, KY: The Univer-
   sity Press of Kentucky.
Millward, Celia M. (1989) *A Biography of the English Language*. New York: Holt,
   Rinehart and Winston.
Milroy, James (1992b) Middle English Dialectology. In: Blake, Norman F. (ed.) (1992a),
   156–206.
Thomason, Sarah Grey and Terence Kaufman (1988) *Language Contact, Creolization,
   and Genetic Linguistics*. Berkeley, CA: University of California Press.

5 Early Modern English

Timeline: The Early Modern English Period

1509	Henry VIII
1534	Act of Supremacy
1536	Small monasteries dissolved
	Statute incorporates all of Wales with England
1539	English translation of Bible in every church
1547	Edward VI
1553	Mary Tudor
1554	Mary marries Philip of Spain
1558	Elizabeth I
1559	Act of Supremacy restores laws of Henry VIII
1574	First company of actors; theatre building begins
1577	Sir Francis Drake plunders west coast of South America
1584	Colonists at Roanoke
1600	English East India Co. formed
	Population of England c.2.5 million
1603	James I
1607	London Co. plants colony at Jamestown
1611	King James Bible
1616	Death of Shakespeare
1625	Charles I
1639	English established at Madras
1642–6	Civil War
1648	Second Civil War
1649	Charles I beheaded
	Charles II
	Commonwealth established
1653	Cromwell becomes Lord Protector
1660	Charles II restored to throne

1689   William and Mary proclaimed king and queen in England and Ireland
1690   Population of England *c.*5 million
1700   Population of England and Scotland 7.5 million
1707   Union of England and Scotland as Great Britain
1727   George II
1760   George III
1775–83   American War of Independence
1776   American Declaration of Independence
1783   British recognize US independence
1789   George Washington inaugurated as first US President

5.1   Social and Political History

5.1.1   *Historical and Political Background*

The Early Modern English (EME) period was a time of tremendous political, economic, technological and social change in Britain that was to change the size, shape and functioning of the world and with it the English language.

After Henry VIII dissolved the monasteries, beginning in 1536, and following his infamous disagreements with the papacy in Rome, England became a Protestant country, with the monarch as the head of the Church of England. By 1539 there was an English translation of the Bible in every church, marking an important milestone in the history of the use of Latin in the British Isles. Despite Mary Tudor's attempts to restore Catholicism in Britain, which were aided by her marriage to Philip II of Spain, Elizabeth, the Protestant daughter of Henry VIII, ultimately triumphed. In 1559, a year after she ascended the throne of England, the Act of Supremacy restored the laws of her father, and with this the centrality of Protestantism in England.

Cultural activity flourished during this period; England saw the establishment of the first company of actors and the building of theatres in 1574. This was the period of William Shakespeare (1564–1616), who straddled the Elizabethan and Jacobean periods and who, in the eyes of many, represents the pinnacle of English literary achievement. The Elizabethan Age was the age of colonial expansionism, with Drake plundering the west coast of South America in 1577 and trade renewed and expanded from the Baltic to the Mediterranean. To the west, in 1584 the first British colonists reached Roanoke in North America, though it was not until the reign of James I that the first permanent settlement was established at Jamestown in 1607. To the east, India was also a coveted target of British expansionism, and the English East India Company was founded in 1600.

The reign of James I was fraught with difficulties for the monarchy as a whole, though it engendered many significant historical events, including, in 1611, the publication of the King James Version of the Bible. Its purpose was to provide a politically more acceptable alternative to the Geneva Bible and to shore up the position of the king, while at the same time criticizing the clergy and casting aspersions on 'Popish persons', to which the dedication bears witness. This translation became the Authorized Version and was used overwhelmingly in Britain, at least until the New English Bible was brought out in the 1960s. In linguistic terms the King James Bible is especially important both as an example of the potential of English prose and as an instrument of standardization, about which we will have more to say below.

The history of the King James Bible is just one indication that this was a time of great uncertainty for the monarch, as church and state officials and their opposition quarrelled at home, and radical elements challenged the authority of the king, the church and the nobility. The Gunpowder Plot exemplifies how precarious political life in Britain was during James's reign, since even the Catholics, who might have expected support from James, were disenchanted by his lack of interest.

5.1.1.1 *Internal Instability and Colonial Expansion*

Throughout this period England's overseas possessions continued to expand. Virginia became the first Crown Colony in 1624, Maryland was founded in 1634 and Maine was joined to the Massachusetts Bay Colony in 1652. By 1639 the English were established in Madras, India, so that English colonial possessions stretched across the globe.

Yet at home the struggle of the monarchy continued; it was a time of extreme domestic crisis, culminating in the Civil Wars of 1642–6 and 1648 and the execution of Charles I the following year. Oliver Cromwell then proceeded to launch an invasion of Ireland and his troops took Scotland in 1650, demonstrating a kind of internal colonialism. In 1653 Cromwell was named Lord Protector of England.

It was not until 1660 that the monarchy was restored in the person of Charles II. During his reign England expanded its territorial holdings into Africa, and the English annexed the New Netherlands in America, where they renamed New Amsterdam as New York. After James II succeeded his brother in 1685 another period of instability ensued, which was ultimately resolved in the proclamation of William of Orange and Mary as king and queen in 1689.

After Queen Anne succeeded William III in 1702 the Union of England and Scotland as Great Britain was formed (1707). At this time the parliaments of the two countries were united, not to be separated again until 1999. Following this, in the reign of George I, Ireland, too, was declared inseparable from England, though the Act of Union of Great Britain and Ireland was not signed until 1801. Despite Scottish and Irish resistance (Charles Edward Stuart, the Young Pretender, was defeated at the Battle of Culloden in 1746), the English maintained their colonial grasp on these countries until the modern period. This had important consequences both for the English language and for the indigenous languages of these countries, as we shall see below.

The end of the period we have designated as the Early Modern period is marked by the separation of America from Britain. The Boston Tea Party in the reign of George III has become a symbol of this time of great strife between the British colonial powers and the American colonists, which led to the American Revolutionary War of 1775–83. While America declared itself independent of Britain in 1776 it took seven more years of battle until the British finally recognized its status in 1783. Six years later George Washington was inaugurated as the first President of the United States, followed by John Adams in 1797. In the last year of this period, the American federal offices moved from Philadelphia, Pennsylvania, to Washington in the District of Columbia, which is still the seat of the US Government today.

5.2 Linguistic Developments: The Variable Character of Early Modern English

By the Early Modern English period the structure of the standard language was very close to its structure in Present-Day English (PDE). There were still some significant changes to come, such as the Great Vowel Shift, but with regard to short vowels, consonants, morphology and syntax, changes were slight. What is noticeable to a present-day reader of Early Modern English is its comparative variability. In the period from 1500 to 1700, there was considerable free variation of forms in comparison with Present-Day English. This is hardly surprising in a language that was only just beginning to be accepted as a legitimate medium of communication in science, the arts, and administration. By 1700, however, English had stabilized and texts written after that period are remarkably easy for a modern reader to comprehend.

5.2.1 *Phonology*

By Early Modern English the consonants had come to resemble those in PDE to a great extent. Many of the forms that were still permitted in the Standard subsequently developed further, but in almost all cases these variants can still be heard today in regional and social varieties. By 1800 the inventory of consonants was the same as it is in PDE.

5.2.1.1 *Consonants*

(1) The post-vocalic allophones of /h/, that is, [ç] and [x], disappear or become [f] (usually after rounded back vowels such as in *cough* and *trough*) in most dialects except for Scots: ME [sɪçt] → EME [sit] → PDE [saɪt]. The <gh> spellings in words such as *sight, through, rough* and *cough* are thus relics of the earlier fricative.

(2) After low back vowels and before labial or velar consonants /l/ was lost in pronunciation (as in *almond, folk, palm*), but not after other vowels (*film, hulk*) or before dental or palatal consonants (*belch, malt*). The -*l* in *fault, vault* was added later, by analogy for example with Latin *falsus*, English *false*; *thought* and *fault* were rhyming words during the earlier periods (cf. ME *faute* < Fr). Today the /l/ in *almond, palm*, etc. is still (or again) pronounced in a number of British and American dialects, partly as a result of certain dialects retaining this older pronunciation, but partly because of an increase in spelling pronunciation, as a result of widespread literacy.

(3) The stop elements /t/ and /d/ were frequently lost in a consonant cluster which contained /s/: *castle, hasten, handsome, landscape*. Again, this change has been reversed in some words in PDE, where spelling pronunciation has taken over.

(4) Late seventeenth-century /k/ and /g/ were no longer pronounced initially before /n/: *knee, knight, gnome*. In the eighteenth century /w/ was lost before /r/ in word-initial position: *wreak, wrong*; this is a development reminiscent of the loss of /h/ before /r/ after the Old English period, and it is worth noting that both /w/ and /h/ are glides. Up until fairly recently both elements of the cluster in words like *knock* and *knee* could still be heard frequently in varieties of North-east Scots, and vestiges remain today.[1]

(5) In the consonant cluster [ŋg], [g] was lost word-finally, making [ŋ] a phoneme because it now contrasted word-finally with /n/ (*win, wing*). In unstressed syllables [ŋ] itself also tended to become [n] in some dialects (*winnin'* vs. *winning*). In the nineteenth and even in the early twentieth century this /g/-dropping was common in both the lower and the upper classes, but it eventually became a stigmatized form and is now only used by the lower classes in Britain. Where it is found elsewhere it does not carry the same stigma that it does in Britain. Thus it can be compared in many ways to the phenomenon of /h/-dropping, discussed in the previous chapter.

(6) Loss of /r/ before /s/ is a process that started in Middle English: barse > *bass* (fish). By the late seventeenth–early eighteenth century it was regularly dropped in unstressed syllables and even in stressed position following a

back vowel (*bar*). During the eighteenth century, /r/ was lost in Standard English before a consonant and word-finally (i.e. post-vocalically, or non-prevocalically). This lack of rhotacism has become a symbol of the difference between Standard British English and other varieties and will be discussed separately in the context of US English.

(7)   Unstressed vowels were reduced to [ɪ] or [ə] in Middle English and this continued in EME. During this period, the palatal glide, or semi-vowel, [j] developed before an unstressed vowel in medial position, when it occurred after the primary stress. Words like *tenure* and *peculiar*, which were originally pronounced [tɛnər] and [pəkjulər], began to be pronounced [tɛnjər] and [pəkjuljər]. If the preceding consonant was /s/, /z/, /t/, /d/, the consonant fused with the following /j/ to produce a palatal fricative or affricate (*nation, pressure, seizure, creature, ancient, lecture, soldier, gradual, grandeur*). This was also a source of the modern phoneme [ʒ] since *usual* came to be pronounced [juʒuəl]. Thus all fricatives now occur in a voiced/voiceless pair.

Once again, this is a feature that seems to be reversing in certain varieties of Present-Day English. Rosewarne (1994) shows that in Estuary English the palatal glide is being lost in words such as *super* and *new*, both of which would have a glide in conservative or general RP (the loss no doubt reinforced to some extent by American pronunciation).

(8)   When it followed the primary stress and preceded /r/, /d/ became /ð/: *father, mother, slither, gather*. This change did not occur in loans from French (or from Latin via French), e.g. *modern*, or in comparatives (*wide, wider*).

5.2.1.2   *Vowels*

The modern Standard British English system arose as a result of the Great Vowel Shift together with a number of later changes. The few changes that are observed in the set of long vowels are limited to the mid-central low-back quadrant. The raising of /ɔː/ to /oː/ left a vacant slot that was later filled by the monophthongization of the Middle English /au/, present, for example, in the word *law*. At a later stage, the lengthening of the vowel before /r + t/, as in *fort*, added to the increased occurrence of this phone. A new long /ɑː/ arose from a series of developments connected with short /a/.

Up to the mid-sixteenth century ME short vowels retained their original qualities, but later short /a/ raised to /ɛ/ while /eo/ lowered to /ɛo/ and /ɪʌ/ centralized and lowered to /ɪʊ/. Though the basic relations among the vowels persisted, they were now phonetically quite different. The primary phonological development was present-day /ʊ/, which in the seventeenth century resulted from a split in the old Middle English /u/ class. Most often Middle English /u/ became /ʌ/, but in a certain number of lexemes, particularly in labial environments (such as *pull, bull, wool*) it remained as /ʊ/. The /ʊ/ and /ʌ/ classes were then expanded by the development of /uː/ from Middle English /oː/. Most items in the class lowered along with /uː/, but some merely shortened. Those that shortened early fell in with /ʌ/ when it developed; those that shortened after this change had taken place remained as /ʊ/, (e.g. *book, hook*). A general rule (though always allowing for exceptions) is that PDE /ʌ/ or /ʊ/ words with these <oo> spellings are from Middle English /oː/ and those with <u> spellings are from Middle English /uː/ (Lass, 1987).

The remaining changes can be summarized as follows:

(1)   Final [ə] came about during the course of the Middle English period from a variety of vocalic sources and continued weakening. By the EME period this reduced vowel was lost, although a vestige of it remains in the spelling in Modern English.

(2)   The earlier rounded vowel /ʊ/ was unrounded and lowered somewhat, resulting in the mid-central /ʌ/, /ə/, as in *hum* and *cup*.

(3)   When followed by a nasal (usually in combination with a velar element) /ɛ/ was raised to /ɪ/, as in *wing, single, thing, link, singe*, etc.

(4)   A minor development is that of /ɔ/ to /o/ after /l/, as in *old, cold*, etc. The slight raising and rounding of this vowel is clearly induced by the presence of /l/, which tends to increase labiality in adjoining back vowels.

5.2.1.3   The Great Vowel Shift

As the Great Vowel Shift is intimately connected to sociolinguistic issues, this phonological phenomenon is explored separately in section 5.4 below.

5.2.2   Morphology

5.2.2.1   Nouns

Nouns were essentially the same as in PDE. There were two cases: common, and possessive (old 'genitive'). The same mutated plurals existed, originally Ablaut forms: *mice, feet*, etc.

Possessive *-s* was frequently interpreted as a contraction of *his*, a phenomenon that was also observed in late Middle English: *As red as Mars his heart*. This interpretation then led to the frequent writing out of the full possessive, now extended to all persons by analogy: *Ann Harris her lot*; *the said Daniel Williams my heirs*, etc. Group genitives differed, as the possessed would appear immediately following the possessor, with other elements (in this case a prepositional modifier) following: *The King's Crown of England*. The possessive apostrophe did not appear with any consistency until 1700: *God's plenty* vs. *Gods plenty*.

A few *-n* plurals remained – *shoen, housen, eyen, kine* – while, especially at the beginning of the period, some uninflected plurals were still being used: *al his waipon* ('all his weapons').

5.2.2.2 *Pronouns*

The main change to be noted is the development of the second person personal pronoun. By the early seventeenth century the distinction between the nominative *ye* and accusative *you* case of this pronoun had been obscured, and the use of *you* became significantly more frequent, though both forms were still found for either case. While this coalescence is to some extent due to the reduction of the case system, it also follows partly from the fact that the vowels in these two forms were unstressed, so that they could be pronounced almost identically as [jə] or [jʌ]. We will have more to say about the use of personal pronouns in section 5.4.4 below.

In the older varieties, the pronominal determiner *mine* was frequently used before a vowel: *in myne opinion*, whereas later varieties use *my* as in Modern English.

The relative pronouns *which* and *who*, now reserved for use with non-human and human antecedents respectively, could be used interchangeably until about the middle of the seventeenth century: *men, which* vs. *men, who*.

The pronoun *who* was still used as an indefinite pronoun throughout the period:

> *Who kills a Man kills a reasonable creature.*

5.2.2.3 *Adjectives and Adverbs*

All inflections of adjectival forms have been lost by the EME period, with the exception of the comparative *-er* and *-est*; indeed, it could be argued that *-er* and *-est* are no longer inflections, but simply markers of the comparative and superlative, respectively. One thing that is notable (given its persistence in varieties of PDE) is that double marking often occurred in this category, as well as with the superlative, as in:

> *more surer on my head;*
> *In my poore opinion, this will be the most fittest for this is like man and wife, without blemish unto other.*[2]

In PDE such double markings are to be heard in casual and sometimes even in more formal speech, particularly, though not exclusively, in the United States:

Mike Krzyzewski is the most winningest coach in Duke basketball history.

Early Modern English adverbs frequently appeared without the *-ly* marker, as in *neere cast away* 'nearly cast away', a construction that is still in use in PDE.

5.2.2.4 Verbs

There are some differences in comparison with PDE, but the tendency towards the preponderance of weak verbs is stronger. More than one hundred verbs (of an earlier total of 300) that had been strong in Old English had become weak during Middle English, such as *help, brew, climb*; in addition, verbs such as *bide, crow, flay, mow, dread* and *wade* all became weak in the Early Modern English period. Many of the remaining strong verbs either became weak or varied in their conjugations at this time. In general the EME period was one in which the language showed considerable variation, not just in morphological form, but also in pronunciation, spelling and vocabulary choice.

The third person singular present tense regularly ended in *-eth* in Middle English in the South and South-East of England, e.g., *giveth, loveth, telleth, doth*. By the fifteenth century forms with *-s* also occur. This was the normal ending in Northern dialects, and throughout the sixteenth century its use increases, particularly in colloquial speech. During the first half of the seventeenth century *-s* was the universal ending in spoken language, though *-(e)th* was retained in written English, and was particularly tenacious in higher frequency words such as *hath*.

In the written language the third person plural had no separate ending because of the loss of the *-en* and *-e* endings in Middle English. The third person singular ending *-s* was therefore frequently used also as an ending in the third person plural: *troubled minds that wakes; whose own dealings teaches them suspect the deeds of others*. The spread of the *-s* ending in the plural is unlikely to be due to the influence of the northern dialect in the South, but was rather due to analogy with the singular, since a certain number of southern plurals had ended in *-(e)th* like the singular in colloquial use. Plural forms ending in *-(e)th* occur as late as the eighteenth century.

5.2.2.5 The Spread of Northern Forms

It is important to understand that a number of Northern and Midlands morphological features spread at the expense of those in Western and Southern dialects. In Middle English the North and East Midlands dialects developed third person singular feminine pronouns with initial [ʃ] (e.g. *sho*), which made it easier to differentiate them from masculine and plural pronouns (see charts in chapter 4). By Early Modern English these were the forms that had prevailed in general usage. Similarly, the third person plural pronouns beginning with þ- had been acquired in the Northern dialects under the influence of Old Norse, as we also saw in the previous chapter. Again, by Early Modern English these forms had spread through Northern and Midlands dialect into the dialects of the west and south.

Most marked of all the forms that prevailed from northern and Midlands dialects was the third person singular present tense verb ending *-(e)s*. In the East Midlands and Southern dialects the ending was *-(e)th*. There was some variation in Early Modern English, but eventually the northern and Midlands ending prevailed, and the *-(e)th* ending was ultimately reserved for religious text and is now archaic.

5.2.3   Syntax

5.2.3.1   Periphrastic **do**

Do was variously and variably used as a filler or as an emphatic particle, but stabilized after Shakespeare's time. It is now used as a support for negation, a yes–no question marker and an emphatic particle, as well as being a main verb in its own right. Until about 1700 positive declarative sentences with *do* were in free variation with those without *do*: *we did approach*; *seamen doe call*; *the seas doe mount* (none of which has an emphatic function in its context).

Negation
In Early Modern English negatives could be formed either with or without *do*, post-auxiliary negation becoming more and more common until about 1700, when it was the standard:

> *I doubt it not*   (*Romeo and Juliet*, III.v.52)
> *I do not doubt you*   (*2 Henry IV*, IV.ii.77)
> *I do not sue to stand*   (*Richard II*, V.iii.129)
> *Or if there were, it not belongs to you*   (*2 Henry IV*, IV.i.98)

Barber (1997) lists several examples of negation without *do*-support in the period spanning 1500 to 1700. For example: *we gave not*; *I deny not*; *I know not*.

We must also note here that multiple negation, common both in Old English and in Chaucer's day, was proclaimed taboo in the eighteenth century. The basis of the proscription was the mathematical (not linguistic) argument that two negatives make a positive, rather than that the use of multiple negatives simply makes the negation more emphatic.

Yes–No questions
In Shakespeare's time these constructions could be formed either by subject–verb inversion, as in other European languages, or by subject–auxiliary inversion. WH-questions patterned the same way:

> *Came he not home tonight?*   (*Romeo and Juliet*, II.iv.2)
> *Do you not love me?*   (*Much Ado about Nothing*, V.iv.74)
> *What sayde he?*   (*As You Like It*, III.ii.221)
> *What do you see?*   (*A Midsummer Night's Dream*, III.i.120)

5.2.3.2 Progressive Verb Forms

As we saw in the previous chapter, Baugh and Cable (1993) discuss the fact that in Old English there were participial forms such as *he wæs on lærende* (he was teaching), but they were almost always found in translations from the Latin. Progressive forms increased slowly throughout Middle English and, according to Görlach (1991: 101), although they were rare in Southern English, they were otherwise widespread in fifteenth-century dialects. Their use has generally expanded mainly since the sixteenth century.

Such expanded verbal constructions remained optional until 1700 and semantic contrasts only became consistently differentiated in the eighteenth century.

5.2.3.3 Passives

The passives as we know them are a rather recent innovation. Like the progressives above, they are examples of the shift towards analytic formulations; that is, they display phrasal characteristics, as opposed to conveying essential information in morphological or inflectional form.

A sentence like *The house is on building (a-building)* was capable of passive meaning in certain circumstances. This meaning is attested from the fourteenth century on. Eventually, however, the preposition *on* is lost in this construction, and *The house is building* becomes ambiguous between an active and passive interpretation, which leads to the need for an auxiliary marker of passive status: *The house is **being** built* (i.e., a form of *be* + past participle). The OED cites 1769 as the first instance of such a construction. Such passives were not accepted until the early 1800s in grammatical commentaries, and then only in the present and simple past, according to Baugh and Cable. In the future and imperfect, the progressive passive is still rare, though *The book could have been being read* and *The patient must have been being examined* are now possible formulations.

Görlach (1991: 101) points out that the choice of auxiliaries was determined by the syntactic properties of the main verb, and *be* dominated with intransitive (change of state or mutational) verbs until 1700, and could be found well into the nineteenth century. The restriction of *be* helped reduce its ambiguity after it had become obligatory with the passive.

5.2.4   Sample Text

Clearly the language of a text from 1500 or 1600 differs markedly from the language of a present-day English text. However, as the following text, 'The Phrenzy of J. D.' by Jonathan Swift, suggests, by the late seventeenth and early eighteenth century, the language was much closer to that of Modern English:

> I took Mr Lintot home with me, in order to have our wounds drest, and laid hold of that opportunity of entering into discourse with him about the madness of this person, of whom he gave me the following remarkable relation:
>   ... That about two months since, he came again into the shop, and cast several suspicious looks on a gentleman that stood by him, after which he desired some information concerning that person. He was no sooner acquainted, that the gentleman was a new author, and that his first piece was to be published in a few days, but he drew his sword upon him; and had not my servant luckily catched him by the sleeve, I might have lost one author upon the spot, and another the next sessions.

What is immediately remarkable about this passage is the fact that it is very easy for a modern reader to understand. There are a number of features which vary from present-day English, but these might be considered more anomalous than radically different, and in any case do not interfere with the comprehension of the text:

(1)   There are some differences in the spelling: *phrenzy* has <ph>, where present-day English has <f>;

(2)   The past participle of *dress* is given as *drest*, not *dressed*, which could again be considered a difference in spelling;

(3)   The past tense of *catch* is *catched* rather than *caught*, which does represent a true paradigmatic difference (but one that is still frequently heard in the speech of children and in several dialects);

(4)   In the clause *he came **again** into the shop*, the adverb immediately follows the verb, whereas in idiomatic present-day English it would most likely follow the prepositional phrase.

(5)   ***Upon** the spot* would be ***on** the spot* in present-day English, reflecting the fact that prepositional usage has changed in the past two or three hundred years.

Clearly none of these differences is major, and it would be accurate to say that the core grammar of English had developed almost completely by the eighteenth century.

5.2.5 *Vocabulary*

One area of significant change in the language over this period was the lexicon; this was in response to the remarkable expansion of experience resulting from colonialism and improvements in communication, both of which allowed English speakers to come into contact with ideas and phenomena that they had not en- countered before, and provided the impetus to change the vocabulary to account for these developments.

The vocabulary of William Shakespeare illustrates a number of trends in the language of the EME period. Firstly, the lexicon expands dramatically, incorpor- ating many new words which are quite common, even indispensable, today, e.g., *agile, critical, demonstrate, emphasis, horrid, impertinency, modest, prodigi- ous, accommodation, apostrophe, assassination, dextrously, frugal, misanthrope, obscene, pedant, premeditated, reliance, vast*. In the late sixteenth century a number of words enter the language from the Romance languages as a result of developments during the Renaissance: *ambuscado, armada, barricade, bastinado, cavalier, mutiny, palisado, pell-mell, renegade*.

One difference between many of the borrowed words in use at the time of Shakespeare and those in use now is that in Shakespeare's time their meaning was much more faithful to the meaning in the source language. Over time, how- ever, their meaning shifted, so that, in a frequently cited example, *communicate*, which now means 'to talk' or 'to exchange information' at that time meant 'to share with others'. In *A Comedy of Errors*, for example, we encounter the following lines from Adriana, in which she clearly shares the strength with her husband:

> *Thou art an elm, my husband, I a vine.*
> *Whose weakness married to thy stronger state*
> *Makes me with thy strength to communicate.*

Another example of this kind is the verb *expect*, which at that time meant 'await', as in *The Merchant of Venice*, when Lorenzo utters the words: *Let's in and there expect their coming.*

5.2.6 *The Anxious State of English: The Search for Authority*

Early Modern English was the period of the Renaissance, the revival of learning that had begun when the Crusaders became curious about the knowledge of the Arabs they were fighting against and it was discovered that much of their science had been translated from classical Greek and Latin texts. By the middle of the fifteenth century the modern languages of Europe were being advocated as a medium of learning, and English eventually became acceptable both in and out of academe.

This was not without its problems, however, as the modern vernaculars were not considered adequate at the beginning of the Early Modern period to the communicative tasks in the academy, medicine and the law, which had previously been carried out by Latin and Greek. The greater portion of the EME period is therefore a time when the English language is being expanded to fulfil the communicative needs of its users, while at the end of the period scholars are particularly interested in standardizing the language, fixing it for all time in an authoritative state of perfection, as befitted the Augustan Age. Though it was acknowledged as a legitimate literary medium, English in fact still wavered in status into the seventeenth century. Scientific and even some literary works were still written in Latin. For example, Sir Francis Bacon, John Milton and Sir Isaac Newton all wrote major works in Latin. Nevertheless, its use declined in this period and the use of vernacular languages became established throughout Europe.

The Early Modern English period is well known as the 'Age of Linguistic Anxiety'. During this time speakers felt a need to regulate and control language. As is often the case when use of a language ceases (as French did at the end of the Middle English period), the demise of Latin coincides with the borrowing of huge numbers of Latin words into English in order to fill perceived gaps in the language. There was a vast influx of new words and expressions, some of which caught on, and some of which quickly passed out of usage. While many writers borrowed judiciously and were careful to document the need for this practice in their writing, a number of them directly attacked others' choice of words, accusing them of using 'inkhorn terms', which to them seemed to be unreflective coinages. The fact of the matter is that there is little rhyme or reason dictating which words were adopted, such as *recapitulate*, and which were rejected, such as *reencephalize*, both of which originally were used to mean the same thing. While most words were borrowed directly from Latin, some were borrowed from Greek via Latin or French, such as *anachronism*, *climax*, *pathetic*, *system* and *antithesis*.

Paradoxically, the Early Modern period was also a time when writers looked backward in language, not just forward. Edmund Spenser, for example, an admirer of Chaucer, is a writer who incorporated archaized forms into his writing. Sir John Cheke attempted to rewrite the Bible using only English words. Many felt that the latinization of English was leading to its degeneration and harked back to the purer 'Saxon monosyllables'.

It was also difficult to say at this time whether a word was coming into the language from Latin directly or via French, since Latin words were being borrowed by their thousands into French at the same time, and French was definitely still an influence on English. This sometimes led to double borrowings: French *fait* was adopted into English as *feat*, while Latin *factum* was adopted into English later, as *fact*. *Confiscate*, *congratulate*, *exonerate* were based on the Latin past participle (*confiscatus*, etc.), and not on French infinitives (*confisquer*, *congratuler*, *exonerer*).

5.2.6.1 *Dictionaries and the Question of Linguistic Authority: Swift's and Johnson's View of Language*

In response to the fact that so many new words were coming into the language, English language dictionaries were devised for the first time to explain difficult, rare and borrowed words, e.g. Robert Cawdrey's *A Table Alphabeticall*, 1694; John Bullokar's *An English Exposition*, 1616; Nathaniel Bailey's *An Universal English Dictionary*, 1721 onwards, and the *Dictionarum Britannicum*. In 1747 Samuel Johnson planned *A Dictionary of the English Language*, which was published in April 1755 in two volumes, comprising 2,300 pages and about 40,000 entries. Its original purpose was to 'fix' the language and establish a standard for the use of words and their spelling:

> The chief intent is to preserve the purity and ascertain the meaning of our English idiom; and this seems to require nothing more than that our language be considered so far as it is our own; that the words and phrases used in the general intercourse of life, or found in the works of those whom we commonly style polite writers, be selected, without including the terms of particular professions, since, with the arts to which they related, they are generally derived from other nations.
>
> (Dr Johnson, 1747, *The Plan of a Dictionary of the English Language*, p. 4)

While Johnson's achievement in the dictionary is universally acclaimed, in his preface to a 1970 reproduction of Johnson's dictionary, Robert Burchfield describes him as 'insular, prescriptive, and unscientific':

> More than most contemporary or later dictionaries, it displays a cluster of personal beliefs, and precepts that stand far from the kind of objectivity that lexicographers count among their primary aims.
>
> (in Johnson, 1970, p. 7)

Nevertheless, Burchfield still regards it as 'an outstanding example of literary lexicography'. Johnson restricts himself largely to words used from about 1580– 1660, and he appeals to usage as well as to his own good taste in fixing his standards. Moreover, as the above quotation illustrates, he takes upper-class usage as his standard in most cases, therefore not merely reflecting his own use of the language.

Johnson's dictionary can also be seen as part of a dialogue that had begun at the beginning of the Early Modern English period, when it was suggested that an English Academy was needed to regulate the use of the language, along the lines of the academies in France and Italy. This discussion became even more earnest after the Restoration of Charles II, and later received the support of John Dryden and John Evelyn. While the Royal Society was founded in 1664, its members were never enthusiastic about regulating the language, despite repeated abortive attempts to set up regulatory committees. Although the subject of language improvement and language regulation was brought up repeatedly in the seventeenth century, nothing tangible came out of the discussion.

At the beginning of the eighteenth century, Jonathan Swift sent to the Earl of Oxford, the Lord Treasurer of England, *A Proposal for Correcting, Improving, and Ascertaining the English Tongue*. Part of this much-quoted text is as follows:

> My Lord, I do here in the name of all the learned and polite persons of the nation complain to your Lordship as *first minister*, that our language is extremely imperfect; that its daily improvements are by no means in proportion to its daily corruptions; that the pretenders to polish and refine it have chiefly multiplied abuses and absurdities; and that in many instances it offends against every part of grammar.

Swift's proposal was again to set up a group of experts who would arbitrate and legislate in matters linguistic – an academy in all but name. Swift's proposal did earn considerable support by such important figures as Addison. Baugh and Cable (1993: 253–64) and others make much of the opposition to the proposal made by the Whig John Oldmixon, who not only attacked the idea of an academy, but attacked the work of Swift himself as illustrative of vulgar language. Such visceral personal attacks are common throughout the Early Modern English period, as was mentioned in the discussion of inkhorn terms. Oldmixon must be given credit, however, for his assertion in *Reflections on Dr Swift's Letter to the Earl of Oxford, about the English Tongue* that languages change inexorably: 'I should rejoice with him, if a way could be found out to *fix our Language for ever*, that like the *Spanish* cloak, it might always be in Fashion.' The upshot of all the discussion was that no academy of the English language was ever formed.

Not that the lack of an academy has ever stifled discussion of the decline of language, even to the present day. There are many self-appointed gurus of language who love to lament the drop in linguistic standards from their own version of 'the good old days'. Milroy and Milroy (1991) have documented the centrality of the 'complaint tradition' in maintaining the authority of an elite linguistic code.

Samuel Johnson weighed into the argument about an academy in the 1750s. In the preface to his dictionary (1755) he discusses the status of the language at the inception of the project:

> When I took the first survey of my undertaking, I found our speech copious without order, and energetick without rules: wherever I turned my view, there was perplexity to be disentangled, and confusion to be regulated; choice was to be made out of boundless variety, without any established principle of selection; adulterations were to

be detected, without a settled test of purity, and modes of expression to be rejected or received, without the suffrages of any writers of classical education or acknowledged authority.

(p. 1)

Johnson clearly felt there was a need for the work he was doing. However, as to the question of fixing the language, Johnson was considerably more objective than the supporters of the academy:

> Those who have been persuaded to think well of my design, require that it should fix our language, and put a stop to those alterations which time and chance have hitherto been suffered to make in it without opposition. With this consequence I will confess that I flattered myself for a while; but now begin to fear that I have indulged expectation which neither reason nor experience can justify. When we see men grow old and die at a certain time one after another, from century to century, we laugh at the elixir that promises to prolong life to a thousand years; and with equal justice may the lexicographer be derided, who being able to produce no example of a nation that has preserved their words and phrases from mutability, shall imagine that his dictionary can embalm his language, and secure it from corruption and decay, that it is in his power to change sublunary nature, or clear the world at once from folly, vanity, and affectation.

Johnson goes on to talk about the nature of language change in a way that is at once insightful and naïve, liberal and elitist, but on the whole very modern in its approach, in comparison to the thoughts of his contemporaries:

> Total and sudden transformations of a language seldom happen; conquests and migrations are now very rare; but there are other causes of change, which, though slow in their operation, and invisible in their progress, are perhaps much superior to human resistance, as the revolutions of the sky, or intumescence of the tide. Commerce, however necessary, however lucrative, as it depraves the manners, corrupts the language; they that have frequent intercourse with strangers, to whom they endeavour to accommodate themselves, must in time learn a mingled dialect, like the jargon which serves the traffickers on the *Mediterranean* and *Indian* coasts. This will not always be confined to the exchange, the warehouse, or the port, but will be communicated by degrees to other ranks of the people, and be at last incorporated with the current speech.

The above paragraph illustrates Johnson's awareness of the effects of language contact on language change, while the extract below has as its theme the changing nature of society and human thoughts and their effects on language:

> There are likewise internal causes equally forcible. The language most likely to continue long without alteration, would be that of a language raised a little, and but a little, above barbarity, secluded from strangers, and totally employed in procuring the conveniences of life; either without books, or like some *Mahometan* countries, with

very few: Men thus busied and unlearned, having only such words as common use requires, would perhaps long continue to express the same notions by the same signs. But no such constancy can be expected in a people polished by arts, and classed by subordination, where one part of the community is sustained and accommodated by the labour of the other. Those who have much leisure to think, will always be enlarging the stock of ideas, and every increase in knowledge, whether real or fancied, will produce new words, or combinations of words. When the mind is unchained from necessity, it will range after convenience; when it is left at large in the fields of speculation, it will shift opinions; as any custom is disused, the words that expressed it must perish with it; as any opinion grows popular, it will innovate speech in the same proportion as it alters practice.

Not only is Johnson aware of external and internal factors that effect language change, such as language contact and class divisions in speech; he is also aware of the mechanism of semantic shift, and the operation of fashion and fad on linguistic usage:

As by the cultivation of various sciences, a language is amplified, it will be more furnished with words deflected from their original sense; the geometrician will talk of a courtier's zenith, or the eccentrick virtue of a wild hero, and the physician of sanguine expectations and phlegmatic delays. Copiousness of speech will give opportunities to capricious choice, by which some words will be preferred, and others degraded; vicissitudes of fashion will enforce the use of new, or extend the signification of known terms. The tropes of poetry will make hourly encroachments, and the metaphorical will become the current sense. . . . As politeness increases, some expressions will be considered as too gross and vulgar for the delicate, others as too formal and ceremonious for the gay and airy; new phrases are therefore adopted, which must, for the same reasons, be in time dismissed.

If one forgives Johnson some of the sins of his generation and some of the excesses of his rhetoric, his linguistic insight into the process of language change is remarkable. He came full circle from believing he could fix the English language to understanding the complexities of language change. Perhaps these changes in attitude, coupled with a certain amount of realism and perhaps the spirit of empiricism which Francis Bacon had inspired, are the reasons why an English academy was never founded.

5.3   Linguistic and Literary Achievement

As we have chosen to define it, the Early Modern English period scans three hundred years or so. We have seen how, in that time, the status of the English language varied as the vehicle for learning, science, administration and literary activity. At the start of the period it was just beginning to be used as such, by the middle of the period it was being expanded and improved, and by the end of the period the need was felt to fix it in its state of perfection and to regulate it, just as soldiers, politicians and scientists of the late eighteenth and early nineteenth centuries wished to rule and regulate the rest of their environment.

The fortunes and functions of the English language are reflected in the literature produced throughout the Early Modern English period. For the first century or so this period was marked by the Renaissance, the rebirth of culture and scholarship, when interest was rekindled in classical scholarship, particularly the works of Caesar, Homer, Ovid, Plutarch, Plato and Virgil, whose works were translated into English at this time. Influential religious works, such as those of Calvin and Martin Luther, were also studied in translation, both activities providing English with important sources of loan words, and models for a style of rhetoric that was much more sophisticated than anything seen in English before.

The Renaissance was a period of strong Italian influence, flowing through to France, Spain and then England. The influence of Petrarch on Shakespeare is well documented, his sonnets and the novelle of Boccaccio in particular influencing English style for many years.

The court of Elizabeth I (1558–1603) inspired or witnessed many great works, including the lyrics of Sir Philip Sidney (*Astrophel and Stella*), Edmund Spenser (*The Faerie Queene, The Shepheardes Calendar, Amoretti*) and William Shakespeare (the Sonnets), and the plays and pageants best represented by the works of Christopher Marlowe (*Tamburlaine the Great, The Jew of Malta, Dr. Faustus*) and again, of course, Shakespeare. The range of Shakespeare's plays runs the gamut from fantasy and satire, to searing tragedy in plays such as *A Midsummer Night's Dream*, *Measure for Measure* and *Hamlet*. The live performance of plays became extremely popular during the reign of Elizabeth, with the first public playhouse being built by James Burbage in 1576, and the second, the Curtain, following in 1585.

This was a very flowery and elegant period of English prose, perhaps best illustrated in the works of Shakespeare. Other writers such as John Lyly (*Euphues, The Anatomy of Wit*) were less refined proponents of this elegant style. It was also, on the other hand, a period when writers enriched English by the use of a lively, racy style (particularly pamphleteers such as Robert Greene, Thomas Nashe and 'Martin Marprelate').

This period was followed by the Jacobean period, named in reference to the reign of James I of England (James VI of Scotland) (1603–25). Even at the end of Elizabeth's reign the mood had turned sombre and dour and, as we mentioned earlier in the chapter, this mood was exacerbated by James's anxiety over the monarchy in very troubled times. This was obviously reflected in the literature, and the whole period has been described as one of 'self-consciousness', both linguistic and literary. The style of writing became less elaborate. Francis Bacon introduced the essay form. The King James Version of the Bible, which we have already discussed in its sociopolitical context, must also be mentioned here as a mark of high literary achievement.

Jacobean poetry is best represented by the works of Ben Jonson and John Donne, the latter being the most important of the metaphysical poets. The sombreness of such works is echoed in the melancholy of Jacobean drama, and scathing satire abounds even in the comic plays such as Ben Jonson's *Volpone* or John Marston's *The Malcontent*. Tragedy is represented by such plays as Webster's *The Duchess of Malfi*, Ford's *'Tis Pity She's a Whore*, and *The Changeling*, by Middleton and Rowley. It is argued that Shakespeare produced his finest work in the Jacobean period, his tragedies and romances.

Since we have divided up the Early Modern period in such a way that it spans 300 years, we cannot do justice to the literary history of the entire period. Perhaps we need to mention that the Early Modern period ends in the eighteenth century with the Enlightenment, also known as the Age of Reason, which is inextricably linked with such cataclysmic events as the French and American Revolutions. The turn of century into the nineteenth sees the return of the romance, typified by the poetry of John Keats and Percy Shelley, and the Gothic novels of Horace Walpole (*The Castle of Otranto*) and Mary Shelley (*Frankenstein*), which takes us into the Modern era.

5.4   Sociolinguistic Focus

5.4.1   *Variation in Early Modern English*

Although the introduction of a standard is, in terms of the accessibility of the written word, a generally welcome development, it nevertheless has great drawbacks. One clear drawback is that it privileges those that can use it, and leaves those who cannot at a disadvantage. In other words, the standard develops a 'gate-keeping' function on the social level, barring those who fail to meet the standard from advancement of various sorts.

The existence of a written standard also obscures the fact that there are other varieties of English competing with it, which are used in various functions every day, but which are not the vehicle of print communication. It goes without saying that there were regional and social varieties of Early Modern English, but their underrepresentation in the written record makes it difficult to talk about them with great certainty.

In a recent work, Barber (1997) illustrates how EME varies across a number of dimensions, including time, social group (class), religious group (e.g., Puritan English), occupation (merchant, rogue, vagabond), social context of speech (e.g., whether formal or informal, according to the speakers' relationship to one another), and whether a text is spoken, written, or written text intended for oral delivery.

Most of the time written work of the period is produced in the (near) standard, which is natural, but occasionally writers of poetry and literature provide an (albeit impressionistic) glimpse of regional dialect for literary effect. Among the classic examples cited by Barber are Edmund Spenser's reproduction of northern speech in *The Shepheardes Calendar* from 1579, and Edgar's generally 'rustic' speech in *King Lear*, when he wishes to disguise himself in order to help his father.

The attitudes of commentators towards particular types of language in the EME period varied, as with Richard Verstegan's 1605 *A Restitution of Decayed Intelligence*, in which regional variation is discussed:

> We see that in some seueral partes of *England* it self, both the names of things, and pronountiations of words are somewhat different and of this different pronountiation one example in steed of many shal suffise, as this: for pronouncing according as one would say at *London, I would eat more cheese yf I had it/* the northern man saith, *Ay sud eat mare cheese gin aye hadet/* and the westerne man saith: *Chud eat more cheese an chad it.* Lo heer three different pronountiations in our own countrey in one thing and heerof many the lyke examples might be alleged.
>
> (Barber, 1997: 12)

While many commentators before have cited George Puttenham's (1589) *The Arte of English Poesie* in order to demonstrate that there was an emerging regional standard in England at the time, Barber points out that Puttenham makes social commentary also. 'The poet must use the language of the educated classes, not of artisans. And he must use the present-day language, not that of Chaucer and other older poets.' He continues:

> neither shall he take the termes of Northern-men, such as the vse in dayly talke, whether they be noble men or gentlemen, or of their best clarkes all is a matter: nor in effect any speech vsed beyond the riuer of Trent, though no man can deny but that theirs is the purer English Saxon at this day, yet it is not so Courtly nor so currant as our Southerne English is, no more is the far Westerne mans speech: ye shall therefore take the vsuall speech of the Court, and that of London and the shires lying about London within lx. myles, and not much aboue. I say not this but that in every shyre of England there be gentlemen and others that speake but specially write as good Southerne as we of Middlesex or Surrey do, but not the common people of euery shire, to whom the gentlemen, and also their learned clarkes for the most part condescend.
>
> (Barber, 1997: 13)

Apart from giving evidence of regional speech, Puttenham also shows that regional varieties can be spoken by people of all social classes (even 'gentlemen', scholars and noblemen). We know that even up to the time of Gladstone prominent British gentlemen were known to speak with regional accents, though they might be fully competent in the written standard. (Indeed, we might argue that the Labour government of the 1990s has reinforced regional English in parliamentary debate.) Barber suggests (p. 13) that the word *condescend* at the end of the passage from Puttenham might imply that gentlemen would speak Standard English amongst themselves, but shift to the regional varieties when talking with their inferiors. While this could indeed be the case, the evidence appears more strongly in favour of bidialectalism: Standard English in formal written and regional English in spoken and written informal communication.

5.4.2 Standardization

During the Early Modern English period there were a number of significant changes in society that influenced the direction of linguistic development. Baugh and Cable (1993) single out four for special discussion: the introduction of the **printing press**, access to **education, increased communication**, and **social stratification**.

5.4.2.1 The Printing Press

Caxton introduced the printing press to Britain in 1476. By 1500 over 35,000 books had been printed, though most were in Latin. However, by 1640 there were approximately 20,000 titles available in English. This clearly had an impact on both literacy and the uniformity of the language, most directly on the standardization of spelling, and perhaps indirectly on the differences among dialects. By Shakespeare's time up to half the population of London was literate. And during the seventeenth and eighteenth centuries the rise of the middle class brought with it an increase in leisure time for reading and a general interest in education and learning. Books became both cheap and accessible.

5.4.2.2 The Renaissance and the Protestant Reformation

As we said in section 5.2.6, Early Modern English was the period of the Renaissance, when the value of classical Greek and Latin texts was re-established and influenced the languages of Europe. By the middle of the fifteenth century the modern languages of Europe were being advocated as a medium of learning, and it eventually became acceptable to use the vernacular, both in and out of the academy.

The Protestant Reformation helped spur on the acceptance of English in religious contexts, since one of its fundamental beliefs was that the vernacular, not Latin, should be the language of the church.

5.4.2.3 *English Established*

From the sixteenth century onwards, English flourished again, though, like the other vernacular European languages of the period, it took time for it to establish itself as a recognized medium in fields where Latin had been the dominant force before. For a long time, the vernacular languages had been considered inferior to Latin and not equal to expressing abstract and complex thoughts. Moreover, like the other European languages, English needed to establish a regular and uniform orthographical system, and to expand its vocabulary to meet the increased demands caused by the demise of Latin and by developments in science and new discoveries throughout the burgeoning Empire. During the sixteenth century a large number of classical works were translated into English, so that they were available to the monolingual middle classes and non-academics in general. William Wyclif's campaign against the Latin of the church during the Protestant Reformation did much to assist the establishment of English as the accepted form of communication in all fields. Moreover, given the more widespread use of the printing press, it rapidly became obvious that English-language books sold better, so that market forces (a modern term applicable to this period) did much to strengthen the position of the vernacular language.

Orthography

The advent of the printing press accelerated the process of standardization, as, once the language was set down in print, its conventions became fixed. Indeed, it is arguable that, because the sound system of the language has developed quite dramatically since Chaucer's time, while the spelling rules that were subsequently devised have remained relatively static, the printing press is in part directly responsible for the lack of correspondence between sound and symbol in the English writing system.

The word *orthography* means 'right writing'. Since there was no accepted system of spelling in the Middle Ages, writers used to spell words as closely as they could to the way they pronounced them. By the middle of the sixteenth century, a modicum of standardization was present in the language, and books on spelling and usage became common. Chomsky and Halle (1968), for example, make frequent reference to John Hart's commentary, which was written in 1570. And Richard Mulcaster (1582) provides a list of 7,000 of the most common words in English, advocating consistency in spelling, and influencing later scholars such as Dr Johnson, whose own dictionary is a good illustration of the standards existing in the middle of the eighteenth century. From his time onward, the spelling of English words has changed very little, so that it is hardly a problem for modern readers to read Early Modern English texts.

5.4.3 *The Great Vowel Shift*

The Great Vowel Shift radically altered most of the English long vowel system, and although spelling had been pretty much fixed by Johnson's time, more recent phases of the Great Vowel Shift have rendered the spelling system of English less phonetic in character. This change is one of the many reasons why the Great Vowel Shift should be looked at in detail at this point.

The Great Vowel Shift can be studied purely from the structural point of view, that is, without recourse to social issues. In the following treatment of this important set of changes in the English language, however, the purely linguistic or phonological discussion inevitably leads on to the sociolinguistic, as our discussion will show.

5.4.3.1 *Phonological Change*

From the point of view of the structure of English alone it is very interesting to view the radical changes in the long vowels since Chaucer's time, most of which changed dramatically in the late Middle and Early Modern English period and some of which are still changing in the present day.

As we saw in the previous chapter there was little change in the quality of vowels from Old to Middle English in accented syllables. The most important change in the long vowels was from *a* to *o* – for example, *baːn* > *bɔːn* (bone), *baːt* > *bɔːt* (boat). The long *æ* in Old English spelling represented two sounds: in certain words it stood for /aː/ in West Germanic. It represents a close /eː/ outside the West Saxon area and remains /eː/ in ME (North-West Saxon *ded* > *ded*; *slepan* > *slepen*). In many words OE /æ/ resulted from the i-umlaut of /a/. This was a more open vowel and appears as /ɛː/ in Middle English (OE *clæne* > *clene*; *dælan* > *delen*). The two sounds have now become identical: *deed, clean*.

Other long vowels of OE preserved their original quality in ME (*med* > *mede*; *win* > *wine*; *boc* > *bok*; *hus* > *hus*). OE diphthongs were all simplified and all ME diphthongs are new formations, resulting chiefly from the combination of a simple vowel with a following /j/ or /w/, which vocalized.

In most instances, while the quality of vowels did not change, their quantity, or length, did. OE long vowels were shortened late in the OE period or early in ME, when followed by a double consonant or by most combinations of consonants (OE *great* > *gretter*; OE *axian* > *asken*; OE *bacan* > *baken*; OE *etan* > *eten*). While they are not particularly noticeable changes in themselves, they nevertheless determined the subsequent development of the English vowel system.

The Great Vowel Shift began in about the fifteenth century and was largely completed by the late sixteenth or early seventeenth century. One interpretation of this shift has it that in the first stage the phoneme /iː/ as in *wine* and *tide* developed a series of 'slurred' pronunciations with the preceding on-glide [ɪi] and [əi]. Similar on-glides developed for the long close back vowel [uː]: [ʊu] and [əu]. During the second stage the mid-close vowels /eː/ and /oː/ raised to /iː/ and /uː/, and [ɪi] and [əu] became phonemes. Middle English /ɛː/ and /ɔː/ raised to /eː/ and /oː/, and /aː/ was raised to /ɛː/:

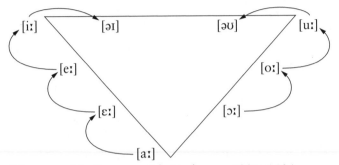

(Compare this diagram with Aitcheson, 1991: 153.)

This system-wide set of related shifts is known as a chain shift (the First and Second Germanic Consonant Shifts discussed in chapter 2 are further examples of chain shifts in English, though these are in the consonant system). Each non-high vowel rises one height, and the high vowels, which are unable to rise any further, become diphthongs. The 'chain' aspect is the systematic interconnection: it does not imply that one change preceded another directly (in time), but that there is a system-wide coordinated movement in which each chain triggers or implies another.

In the usual terminology (coined by André Martinet) there is a mixture here of a **push chain** and a **drag chain**. This all began with the raising of the mid vowels /eː/, /oː/, which had two effects: it 'pushed' up the high vowels /iː/, /uː/ and left a space, which dragged up the lower vowels /ɛː/ and /ɔː/ to fill the empty /eː/, /oː/ positions. And when /ɛː/ raised to /eː/, this left the slot open for /aː/ to move into. Everything except the raising of /aː/ was complete by the mid-sixteenth century. The developments can be charted as follows:

	ME	1550	1600
bite	iː	ei	ai
beet	eː	iː	iː
beat	eː	eː	eː
mate	aː	aː	eː
out	uː	ou	au

boot	oː	u	uː
boat	ɔː	oː	oː

Later developments brought the vowels more in line with PDE. Thus, /ɑi/ monophthongized to /aː/, so *weight* and *mate* fell together as /ɛː/, then /eː/. Before this /eː/ in *beat* raised to /iː/ so that *beat* and *beet* fell together. These developments began in the late sixteenth to early seventeenth century and were not completed until the eighteenth century.

While these structuralist and functionalist descriptions (Lass, 1987) are interesting in themselves, in that they tell us how the changes proceeded through the linguistic system, they do not enlighten us as to why the change might have begun, that is, *why* the vowels began to shift in the first place, and *how* they spread to be gradually adopted by more and more people.

Such a discussion necessitates a brief consideration of the study of linguistic variation, which is involved in the correlation of linguistic variables (such as the choice amongst a number of variants of the same vowel) and social factors (such as the age, gender and social class of the speaker). If we look at correlations between linguistic and social features, and assume that they are not constant, but shifting, we may be able to pinpoint the source and mechanism of spread of an innovation throughout the members of a speech community. There are two important issues to bear in mind here, which (after Labov, 1972) sociolinguists refer to as the *actuation problem* (How does a language change start?), and the *implementation problem* (How does a language change spread?).

There is evidence in the dialects around London in the early sixteenth century that the vowels in the words *mate* and *meet* merged, so that these two words became homophones. In the seventeenth century, however, it is documented that, instead of the merger of *mate* and *meet*, the vowels in *meat* and *meet* merged and the word *mate* was distinct. If it were the case that the second option *replaced* the first, then a situation would have existed in EME where a vowel merger was being reversed. This is a theoretical impossibility, and so another explanation has to be found.

It would appear that, rather than replacing the *mate/meet* merger, the merger of *meat* and *meet* actually occurred alongside it. In other words, two separate systems were operating at the same time. We have here a classic case of variation: there are two alternating realizations of English sounds, or linguistic variables, and we need to consider on what principle they were distributed. Where they apparently differed was in their *social* distribution: that is, there seems to be a correlation here between linguistic choice and social class. Evidence from sources such as Shakespeare's plays suggests that in the dialects around London, especially Kent and East Anglia, there was a tendency in the lower classes to substitute higher, long mid-close vowels in words where long mid-open vowels would be expected in London Middle English, i.e., /eː/ and /oː/ instead of /ɛː/ and /ɔː/

(Dobson, 1968: 608–18, 674–8). In other words, the lower classes were merging *meat* and *meet*. Since these lower-class dialects surrounding the capital were stigmatized, speakers with social aspirations opted to distance themselves from them by means of their speech. They did not manipulate their language consciously, however: we would argue that their sensitivity to this marker was below the level of consciousness – what sociolinguists would call 'change from below'. People whose social status was not in question maintained the distinction between ME /eː/ and /ɛː/ words. This seems to have caused the social climbers to adopt even higher vowels in Middle English /eː/ words in order to maintain their social difference from the lower class (Samuels, 1972: 41–2). Eventually, a redistribution of words with long vowels would take place in the system and the shift would have begun. Subsequently, Middle English /aː/ would move to /eː/, through a drag chain mechanism. Later sound changes have obscured the distinction, but it is still marked in our spelling system. Words pronounced in London with the Middle English /eː/ are generally spelled with *ee* while London Middle English /ɛː/ words are often spelled with *ea*. The system that the lower class had first adopted eventually developed into the preferred, prestige system, while the system that originally carried prestige became stigmatized. (This in itself is proof that no linguistic token is inherently prestigious or stigmatized, but rather becomes so by convention, which may change over time.)

Thus we can see that the Great Vowel Shift is indeed a mixture of push and pull or drag factors, as described in the discussion of the structural aspects of the changes above. However, we also are able to hypothesize that the change is *motivated* by social stratification. That is to say, it was caused by the increase in social differentiation typical of the swelling urban population in and around the capital at the time (compare the discussion in Leith, 1983).

It is important to note that the entire chain shift was not caused by these social factors, however. Further internal changes in the English vowel system as a whole resulted from the vowel shift, and can be seen as a structural adjustment of the system as a result of the initial changes. Phonologists point out that the Great Vowel Shift produced a very unbalanced system of three front vowels, two back vowels and no low vowel. The system readjusted to compensate for this uneven distribution. Short /a/ was lengthened in a few words like *father*, providing a new source of /aː/. Certain dialects developed *l*-deletion in words such as *almond* and *palm*, the accompanying lengthening also producing long /aː/. In other dialects of English, such as in the United States and Canada, short /ɔ/ in words like *not*, *hot* and *got* was also lowered and unrounded, and eventually lengthened to produce more instances of /aː/. The consonant /r/ was lost except prevocalically in parts of England, Wales, the eastern and southern United States, Australia and other parts of the world, causing compensatory lengthening of the preceding vowel, and thereby providing another source of long /aː/ in words like *park* and *garden*.

5.4.4   Case Study: Power and Solidarity Relations in Early Modern English

We said above that one drawback of having a standard language is that it becomes the medium of the vast majority of writing, so that we have very little evidence of dialectal variation in English once the standard had established itself. We do have some (though scant) evidence of regional dialects in English from Early Modern English times, however. What is even more difficult to find is evidence of how the language functioned in face-to-face contact, since we have neither audio nor video evidence of such interactions, as we do today. This is not to say, however, that we have no evidence at all of the use of language in Elizabethan society. One place that we can look is at dramatic monologue, which, although admittedly stylized, does afford us some insights into the way people talked to each other. And a second source of such information is personal letters, which were addressed from a first person to a second person or persons, thus requiring such elements as address forms, and often featuring terms of endearment, salutations and the like.

One aspect of sociolinguistic interaction that has been studied is address forms, and particularly titles and pronouns of address. We have already discussed the fact that in the Middle and Early Modern English period the development of soil management and crop rotation, the rationalization of husbandry and the mechanization of farming, coupled with other progressive agricultural techniques, led to far greater productivity by farmers and agricultural workers towards the end of the EME period. This freed up people to work in the newly developing industrial sector. Gradually, the number of people living in rural areas began to diminish and urbanization began in earnest. With this urbanization and dynamism in social status developed extreme consciousness of social status. It was still the case that status was *ascribed*, rather than *achieved*, and noble birth still afforded prestige and high social status. It was also a time, however, when social mobility was developing, that is, when status could be achieved, so that even in the lower ranks of society forms of address were of considerable importance and changed in value over the period.

For example, *gentle* from French *gentil* originally denoted a person of noble birth and came to describe anyone with manners and good social graces. Eventually, *gentleman* acquired considerable social significance, as it implied privilege. But by the sixteenth century, as entrepreneurs and the educated could climb social ladders, the meaning of *gentle* extended from its original scope, that is, referring primarily to owners of land (cf. the British English term *landed gentry*); by 1580 *gentleman* referred to any man who could live comfortably without having to work for a living.

The term *master* also increased in usage, possibly due to Elizabethan uncertainty about the applicability of titles in general, and sensitivity about matters of rank and status.

People tended to situate one another on the social scale so that titles and occupational terms like *parson* and *cook*, generic terms like *man* and *woman* and *gentleman*, and terms of relationship like *husband*, *wife*, were frequently used in direct address. (A parallel can be drawn here with French society, where even today people are given deferential titles such as *Monsieur le facteur* ('Mr Postman'). Condescension, even insult, could be conveyed by the use of an inappropriate term. *Fellow* used to mean 'one who lays down a fee', i.e. a partner in business, but by the fourteenth century it had acquired the connotation of polite conde-scension, and by Shakespeare's time it was used to refer to any man who was not of greatly inferior status. *Goodman* originally referred to the owner of an estab-lishment, but as the term *gentleman* expanded down the social scale it pushed *goodman* with it and by Shakespeare's time it could be used as a term of abuse (Leith, 1983).

In an analysis of four of Shakespeare's dramas (*Macbeth*, *King Lear*, *Hamlet* and *Othello*), Brown and Gilman (1989) looked at politeness strategies in Early Modern English, concentrating on the use of forms of address, including titles, names and address pronouns. They found elaborate politeness rituals of the period that were highly sensitive to rank and hereditary status. Indeed, in the four plays they analysed they found over a hundred forms of address, excluding first names and pronouns in isolation, which included:

(1) Names with honorific adjectives: *valiant Othello, worthy Macbeth, good Hamlet, good Iago.*
(2) Unadorned titles: *general, captain, sir, madam, my lord, your Grace, your Majesty.*
(3) Adorned titles: *good my lord, gentle lady, my dread lord, sweet lord, good my liege.*
(4) Names alone: *Macbeth, Guildenstern.*

Not every title meant the same thing in every social pairing. For example. *sirrah* was a title that was derogatory when used towards an adult by another adult of higher status. When said to a child, however, it was a term of affection (rather like *pal* or *buddy* in some varieties of Modern English).

The elaborate ritual of address in Early Modern English led people to use the highest title an addressee merited whenever they addressed him or her for the first time. It was also considered polite to vary the formulation of the honorific within a single conversation, as with *your lordship* vs. *my honourable good lord.*

First names

For Elizabethans, greater intimacy was required than in present-day English before personal names could be used. In a perfect illustration of this fact Blake (1983: 35) quotes Falstaff signing a letter thus:

> *Thine, by yea and no: which is as much as to say, as thou usest him,* Iacke Falstaffe *with my familiars:* Iohn *with my Brothers and Sister:* Sir Iohn, *with all Europe.*

In general it was much less common to use first names alone, and the use of first name plus last name was a frequent occurrence, which could mark either intimacy, or mild condescension. As Blake points out (ibid.), in plays such as Shakespeare's names were used for a purpose, often to heighten dramatic or comic effect, but in general we can take Shakespeare's usage as a rough guide to face-to-face interaction.

Pronouns of address

In Early Modern English there were still two competing personal pronouns (*thou*, *you/ye*) that could be used to address a single person. Though it is generally said that *thou* is the pronoun denoting intimacy, while *you* is the pronoun that is neutral or polite, in practice the patterns of usage were much more complex. The *unemotional* use of *thou* vs. *you* was indeed governed by social status: *you* was used by the upper class and *thou* was used by the lower class as a reciprocal form of address. However, in non-reciprocal situations, *you* was directed up the social scale and *thou* down the scale. That is, kings, courtiers, the nobility in general, country gentlemen, professionals and some tradespeople would use *you* as the base pronoun of address amongst equals, while servants, shepherds, farmers, seamen and clergy of the lower ranks would use *thou*.

The variations in the use of pronouns were not all explicable in terms of status alone, however. Brown and Gilman observe an *expressive* or emotive use of pronouns; that is, when *you* is expected and *thou* is used, this is an indication that the exchange is emotionally charged. It is a frequent occurrence in such circumstances that a speaker will change from *you* to *thou*. However, unlike in German or French, or indeed in the majority of languages where this sort of switch is possible, once the shift was made from *you* to *thou*, the speaker could then go back to using *you* in a later address, or even later in the same speech. Brown and Gilman refer to this feature as the 'easy retractability' of expressive *thou*. It might indeed be the case that this very variability contributed to the ultimate demise of the use of *thou* in English; since other formulations could convey the same semantic and pragmatic nuances as *thou*, it was not necessary to maintain this pronoun. This is supported by the fact that not every shift from *you* to *thou* can be accounted for, suggesting that, at least in places, *thou* and *you* were in free variation. A further development in the history of the address pronoun in English is that 'thou-ing' came to be associated with Quakerism, and since this was often accompanied by persecution, perhaps this also provided one of the final nails in *thou*'s coffin (though vestiges of it remain in some English dialects). Ultimately *you* prevailed as the universal second person pronoun in English, and only in dialects do we have any possibility of distinguishing between singular and plural second person forms (e.g. *yous* in parts of Britain and the USA, and *y'all* and *all y'all* in the southern United States).

A further contrast between Early Modern English and present-day English politeness conventions is in the formulation of indirect requests. Such indirect requests are used to mitigate the force of the request and its inherent threat to the 'face' of the addressee, as when one says 'I think I need a hand to lift this', rather than stating baldly 'Help me lift this'. At the beginning of Early Modern English such indirect requests were not formulated using *could, would, might*, etc.; this usage did not occur until the nineteenth century. Instead, they involved phrases such as *I pray you, Prithee, I do require that, I do beseech you, so please your lordship, I entreat you, If you will give me leave*. Fascinatingly, the word *please*, which is considered the quintessential politeness expression in Present-Day English, did not occur until the seventeenth century, developing as it did out of *If you please* and similar phrases. It is interesting that a word which adults spend so much time teaching their children is *not* a core word of English, or even of Germanic. The other Germanic languages also developed their formulations for *please* relatively late and from completely different sources. German, for example uses the word *bitte*, which derives from the verb *to ask*, while Swedish uses the formulae *var så god (och)*, which is literally *be so kind and . . .*, and *snälla*, which means *nice person*.

Other linguistic features than direct forms of address could also signal levels of power and solidarity amongst Early Modern English speakers. For example, greetings such as *Well met* and *How now* indicate familiarity, and contrast with more neutral salutations such as *Good morrow*. Expressions such as *How do*, or just *Now* or *Now then* are common conversational openers in Yorkshire to this day. We might compare this with the Present-Day Standard English use of a deferential 'Good morning' greeting to one's superior and a reciprocal 'Hi' to one's colleague and equal.

Two final politeness formulations in Early Modern English we might mention are imperatives with pronouns and imperatives without verbs. While in Present-Day English imperatives are formed without pronouns, in Early Modern English constructions such as *Go you, Take thou* were possible and appear to have been more polite than imperatives without pronouns. In Present-Day English we do still use verbless imperatives such as *Shh!* and *Hush!* and *The keys, now!*, but they were more common in Shakespeare's plays. Expressions such as *Peace, Kent!* and *Thy story quickly* were considered just as brusque, if not downright rude, as they are today.

5.5 Conclusion

Our overview of the changes in Early Modern English has brought us much closer to the language we recognize as English today. Any student of Shakespeare, Marlowe or Bacon will naturally have some difficulty in understanding what the author intended in the language. However, these differences strike one more as idiosyncratic variations from our present-day system, than as a radically different linguistic system. As we will see in the following chapters, the changes that follow in the Modern English period are all in the direction of regularization.

Notes

1 Derrick McClure (personal communication) assures me that until very recently all of the various transitional variants from /kn/ to /n/ could be heard progressively in the fishing villages going north to south down the east coast of Scotland.
2 The Earl of Nottingham to James I regarding choices of flags for the Union of England with Scotland. Cited in Cannon, 1988, p. 259.

Suggested Readings

Barber, Charles (1997) *Early Modern English*. Edinburgh: Edinburgh University Press.

Blake, Norman F. (1983) *Shakespeare's Language: An Introduction*. London and Basingstoke: Macmillan.

Brown, Roger and Albert Gilman (1989) Politeness Theory and Shakespeare's Four Major Tragedies. *Language in Society*, **18**: 2, 159–212.

Görlach, Manfred (1991) *Introduction to Early Modern English*. Cambridge: Cambridge University Press.

Leith, Dick (1983) *A Social History of English*. London: Routledge and Kegan Paul.

6 Present-Day English

Timeline: Present-Day English

1837	Queen Victoria
1840	Penny post introduced in Britain
1844	First telegraph line used between Washington and Baltimore
1865	Atlantic cable completed
1876	Alexander Graham Bell invents the telephone
1877	Edison invents the phonograph
1878	David Hughes invents the microphone
1879	London opens its first telephone exchange
1895	Marconi invents radiotelegraphy
	Auguste and Louis Lumière invent the motion-picture camera
1899	First magnetic sound recordings
1899–1902	Boer War
1900	R. A. Fessenden transmits the human voice via radio waves
1901	Marconi transmits radiotelegraph messages from Cornwall to New Zealand
	End of Queen Victoria's reign
1903	Orville and Wilbur Wright's first successful flight
	Ford Motor Company founded
1914–18	World War I
1921	British Broadcasting Corporation founded
1924	British Imperial Airways founded
1925	John Logie Baird transmits a picture of a human face via television
1928	John Logie Baird demonstrates first colour television
1929	Teleprinters and teletypewriters first used
	First scheduled TV broadcasts in Schenectedy, New York
	First talking pictures made
1936	BBC London television service begins
1938	Lajos Biró invents the ball-point pen
1939–45	World War II

1942	First computer developed in the United States
	Magnetic recording tape invented
1946	Chester Carlson invents Xerography
1947	Transistor invented at Bell Laboratories
1948	Peter Goldmark invents the long-playing record
1951	Colour TV introduced into USA (15 million TV sets in USA)
1952	Accession of Queen Elizabeth II
1958	First stereophonic recordings
1968	Intelsat communication satellite launched

Introduction

The structure of this chapter differs to some extent from that of earlier chapters. First of all, the reader will note that the section 'Linguistic and Literary Achievements' is lacking. Linguistic change is discussed in sections 6.2–6.4, in the context of historical change, dialects, and language in society in the modern period. For the earlier, formative periods, some discussion of literary work is crucial for an understanding of the use of language at those times. PDE differs from the English of 1800 only in relatively minor ways, however (with the exception of differences to be discussed in section 6.2). Since that time there has also been a veritable explosion of writing and publishing, and, as this book is not intended as a literary history, space does not allow for a discussion of what is now a fully developed discipline in its own right. Section 6.3 is therefore essentially devoted to the English dialects of England.

Secondly, the table of dates (above) will strike the reader as more technologically and internationally oriented, and less a 'Who's who in politics in the British Isles'. This is a characteristic of the modern period in general, the globalization of society and the shrinking of the world, brought about by vast technological change. In linguistic terms, structural change (phonological, morphological, syntactic) from EME to PDE is minor in comparison with the changes that took place between OE and ME. Consequently, section 6.2 is mostly concerned with lexical change and current trends. Finally, we examine the use and status of English across the British Isles – from the earliest periods to the present, and we end with a sociolinguistic profile of multilingual Britain today.

6.1 Social and Political History

6.1.1 The Age of Revolutions, Wars and Imperialism

The changes in society since the late eighteenth century have been nothing short of revolutionary. On the political level, there have been numerous revolutions that have fundamentally altered the way society functions. The French Revolution, with its emphasis on fraternity and equality, and the American Revolution, with its emphasis on human rights and democracy, have had a dramatic effect on life in the western industrialized world and beyond. The Industrial Revolution enabled the western industrialized world itself to develop, and brought about dramatic changes in the way people lived their lives. It led to changes in occupation, the urbanization of society and the development of the class system, but it also brought with it significant changes in communication, both in terms of transport and linguistic information exchange. The late eighteenth century and much of the nineteenth century saw the continued expansion of the British Empire, a period when earlier colonialism truly became an age of imperialism. Captain Cook explored the Pacific during this transitional time, and the first penal colony in Australia was opened in Botany Bay in 1786. The heyday of the Empire – on which the sun never set – was clearly the second half of the nineteenth century; by the end of the period the sleeping giant, the United States, began to stir, expanding into the Caribbean and all the way across the Pacific Ocean in the wake of the Spanish–American War. Further American territorial expansions in the Pacific region followed World War II; America's influence on Europe can also be described as a cultural and economic 'invasion' (some term it cultural 'imperialism') following the two world wars.

The First and Second World Wars brought with them cataclysmic change on all levels, political, economic, social and cultural. In the last quarter-century, the European Union, which has its roots in the tensions of the world wars, has developed into another revolutionary force for change, not just within Europe, but in the whole world. While after World War II the British Empire began to shrink dramatically, British involvement overseas has continued on an economic basis. But perhaps the biggest change has been that, starting in World War I and accelerating in pace since the end of World War II, the United States has vastly increased its influence across the world, politically, economically and culturally. Especially since the collapse of the Soviet Union (1991), the United States has functioned *de facto* as the world's policeman; its role as the world's banker – secure through the 1950s and into the 1980s – is now being successfully challenged by the might of the European Union's banks. Finally, we must talk about the effects of the Technological Revolution, resulting from the development of the microchip, which has changed and is still changing the way people conduct their lives. This is also a form of social and cultural imperialism (although now introduced by corporations, not countries), as the terminology used in reference to most electronic, computer- and Internet-related subjects has entered the languages of the world from English.

6.1.2 *Urbanization, Industrialization and Social Stratification*

While everyone is aware of the Industrial Revolution, it is not so widely realized that it could not have taken place without a parallel revolution in agriculture. The Agricultural Revolution was just as significant in the development of English as was the Industrial Revolution, and, like its better-known partner, did not occur without physical and emotional hardship.

The major factor in the increase of agricultural output was the revolution in farming techniques and animal husbandry wrought by the introduction of fertilizers, the draining of marshlands, the enclosure of farmlands and the development of agricultural machinery. The enclosure movement was ultimately of particular importance to the history of the English language, as it involved the consolidation of smallholdings and widely separated parcels of land into large estates. Increased output could be achieved by the adoption of modern farming methods and large-scale production. The idea behind the improvement of agriculture was to eradicate hunger from Europe. The last major famine in Europe came in the 1840s, with the failure of crops (particularly potatoes) all across Europe from Ireland to Eastern Germany.

With the increase in agricultural production came a marked decline in the number of people employed in farming. Since people were no longer bound to the soil to eke out a meagre living, and since food supplies were becoming more reliable and food surpluses quite common, a fundamental change took place in employment patterns. More and more people took work in industry, commerce and finance. The proportion of people living in the country declined dramatically as farming improved and urban life with its concentration of employment opportunities became more attractive. In Great Britain in 1851 approximately half of all citizens lived in rural communities. By 1891 this number had dropped to 28 per cent and by 1911 it was only 22 per cent of the population.

Thus, in a social push-and-pull relationship, the Agricultural and Industrial Revolutions caused the large-scale movement of people away from the country and into towns and cities, causing fundamental changes to demographic patterns that had held for thousands of years. This radical change had tremendous social consequences, among which were the restructuring of social classes in Britain (and Europe as a whole) and the weakening of the status of the landed aristocracy, the foundation of whose power had been their role in agriculture. In the decades after 1815 the seat of power shifted to industry, and with its decline in economic power came the decline of the aristocracy in political and social status.

With the demise of the landed gentry came also the demise of the peasantry, who had, of course, earned their mean living off the gentry's land. The consolidation of land and the development of large estates caused the uprooting of thousands of small subsistence farmers who had no choice but to move – either into the city, or to a different country altogether. The factory system attracted a large number of people and was responsible for the new wave of urbanization. Though there had been towns and cities before, their size had been contained by limitations in manufacturing and agriculture. With the industrial and agricultural revolutions, full rein was given to the expansion of towns. Whereas in 1800 there had been only one city (London) with more than 100,000 inhabitants in the whole of England (Manchester had 77,000, Liverpool 82,000, Birmingham 71,000, for example), industrialization now brought with it massive urban expansion. By 1931, two-thirds of the inhabitants of England and Wales lived in towns of over twenty thousand inhabitants.

Unlike the United States, which has never had a recognized geopolitical centre, the population of Britain had its centre in London: whereas in 1700 there had been about 500,000 people in the capital city, by the early 1860s there were three million or more, and close to five million at the beginning of the twentieth century. Economic and political power was centred on London, which became the heart of the British class-based society, though all the larger British cities mirrored London's social make-up to a greater or lesser extent. The interesting thing about urbanization is that, on the one hand, it promotes diversity, as it brings different population groups together into the centre, causing contact amongst a greater variety of forms of language and culture; on the other hand, however, it leads to uniformity of behaviour, since as people come together they accommodate to one another, developing compromise forms of behaviour, including communication, in order to maximize the intelligibility of their utterances and to achieve the greatest amount of social acceptance by their interlocutors. The growth of the middle class and the general increase in affluence since the Second World War particularly have led to the breakdown of close-knit communities and the development of diffuse networks of social interaction, which tend to promote uniformity of speech patterns and less emphasis on face-to-face interaction.

The general spread of literacy that followed the introduction of compulsory education in 1870 in Britain also led to the levelling of dialect and slowed down the pace of linguistic change. Improved communications have also had an enormous impact on the language, especially in the twentieth century, and social mobility has been a most important factor in the standardization of the language and the development of rules of English grammar and usage. The explosive growth of technology – in particular in the communications industry – over the last quarter of the twentieth century caused another great shift of large sections of the work-force. The transferability and spread of communications technology across the globe (accompanied or even assisted by the universal comprehension of Computer- and Internet-Speak) is a development that might be written about a century from now in the way that we write about the Industrial Revolution today.

6.2 Linguistic Developments

In the previous chapter we pointed out that the core structure of the English language as we know it today was fairly well established by the eighteenth century. Since that time, while some changes in the structure have indeed occurred, they are comparatively minor in nature. Unlike in the Early Modern English period, there are few changes in phonology and even fewer in morphology and syntax, with major changes taking place (as ever) in the lexical stock of English; in the following sections we discuss relevant changes in all of these domains except phonology. The changes that have taken place in this last-named component are minor. Phonological features are discussed in terms of their presence in various English dialects.

6.2.1 Morphology and Syntax

6.2.1.1 Morphology

In the domain of morphology there are really only two developments that can be mentioned as in any way significant.

By the modern period the remnants of the original case system were limited to the forms of the pronoun: e.g., *him*, *her*, *them*, *whom*. The first three of these examples are retained in PDE as combined accusative/dative forms (direct/indirect objects). The last, *whom*, is used by speakers conscious of 'correctness' (prescriptivists) as a direct object (*Whom did you see yesterday?*), but more often with a preposition (*of whom*, *to whom*, *with whom*). In everyday speech, even in 'good' publications such as leading newspapers, such usages are giving way to *who* – i.e., with no case marker. It is still possible, depending on word order, to hear or read *whom* in the language of non-prescriptivists. Thus, the following might be heard:

> To whom were you speaking?
> For whom did you buy this?

But most people use the following:

> Who were you speaking to?
> Who did you buy this for?

In other words, distance allows the use of the unmarked form (and note the resulting dangling prepositions: a mortal sin in relatively recent school grammars!); in general, the case-marked form is still heard more in Britain than in America.

The other development worth mentioning again is that English increasingly makes greater use of periphrastic comparatives and superlatives than inflectional ones. We saw in the previous chapter that even where inflectional forms in *-er* and *-est* were possible and even common, they began to be replaced by *more* + adjective and *most* + adjective in PDE. Transitional forms – or non-standard, doubly marked constructions – occur as well, and are seen as 'incorrect' by educated speakers: *more* + adjective-*er*, *most* + adjective-*est*: *This is the most snazziest car I've ever seen.*

6.2.1.2 *Syntax*

As in the morphological component, changes in the realm of syntax are often a function of quantity, rather than quality: that is, certain structures have expanded in number and frequency of occurrence during the PDE period. We can summarize the most striking phenomena as:

(1) The progressive passive, which had begun in the late eighteenth century (see chapter 5), expanded in frequency of use during the Present-Day English period. Sentences such as the following are now quite common:

> *John's car is being serviced today.*
> *This child was constantly being bullied at school.*

(2) The 'get-passive' (e.g. *He got beaten up*) also developed in the nineteenth century. We note, however, that this construction is still felt by many speakers to be rather colloquial; it is less likely to be used in print than in everyday speech, though it can appear in more informal types of written text, such as sports commentaries: *Forest got badly beaten in their clash with Manchester United this afternoon.*

(3) The use of periphrastic *do* that had expanded along with the fixing of SVX word order was finally established in the Modern English period. This development, then, took more or less a thousand years to complete.

(4) Expanded premodification is more common in modern English than in earlier varieties (cf. Fennell, 1986):

A Foreign Office travel advisory has been issued for tourists travelling to Turkey.
It's an immediately obvious in detail model.[1]

A related type of premodification is found in constructions where a gerund is used as an adjective, a feature that is used frequently in other Germanic languages such as German, but which has not been used to the same extent in English until recently:

Pat Cash, the come-backing Australian tennis player, won again at Wimbledon yesterday.
Claire X is a rapidly becoming confused mother of four.[2]

In Fennell (1986) I suggest that use of this structure has increased because of the contact between German and English in the United States. In this instance contact has not caused the borrowing of a new phenomenon; rather it has caused an increase in the frequency of an existing feature.

(5)   Increasing use of nominalizations is found in Modern English. Fairclough (1989: 111) has discussed the role of this construction in obfuscating agency. In a newspaper headline such as the following, there is no mention of who is responsible for lorries shedding their loads:

Quarry load-shedding problem.

(6)   Modern English verb phrases (VPs) can now be much longer than they were in earlier periods. Indeed, Celce-Murcia and Larsen-Freeman (1999) demonstrate that there are forty-four possible combinations of verb forms in English. When we add infinitival constructions and phrasal equivalents of auxiliaries (*to be able* for *can*, for example) verb phrases can become very long indeed:

He appears to wish to be able to carry on being examined by the same doctor.

Freeborn (1998) calls these constructions *catenatives*, in reference to the chaining together of verbal elements. Thus, we see that the system is still developing these analytic constructions in the verb phrase.

(7)   Modern English displays an increased frequency of phrasal verbs and verb + particle constructions: *run across* (= 'meet'); *put up with* (= 'tolerate'). Such combinations were found in Old English (though prefixing of verbs was far more common then) but have significantly increased in quantity in PDE.

(8)   There has been an increase in the choice of *do have* as opposed to *have got* in British English, no doubt as a result of American influence. *Do you have?*

in British English once meant 'do you get at repeated intervals?', as the following dialogue illustrates:

Customer to butcher: *Have you got any pheasant?*
Butcher: *No.*
Customer: *Do you have pheasant?*
Butcher: *Occasionally.*

I doubt whether such a contrast in meaning is universally sustainable with these constructions in contemporary British English.

(9) Finally, the use of preterite verbal forms instead of the corresponding perfect is becoming more common, especially in the spoken language: *I bought a new car* vs. *I've bought a new car.*

6.2.2 The Lexicon

The lexicon is the most changed aspect of English in the PDE period. This is largely due to the development of scientific–technological vocabulary and, at the end of the twentieth century especially, the rapid progress of computer/communications technology and computer literacy. Borrowing has become a less important source of new words than in the previous period, although, as the chart below demonstrates, it is still a significant source of lexical enrichment. What is interesting is that the languages from which English borrows reflect the level of cultural or economic importance of the country or countries in question. Thus, for example, although there have been a number of Japanese loan-words in the last few years (*karaoke, tamagochi, hibachi*, etc.), they have been relatively few in number and specific to Japanese culture. Beyond borrowing, the systems of register and acceptability are changing, so that previously unacceptable slang and taboo words are now in use in written as well as spoken media. Thus, although such words have always existed, they were formerly an 'invisible' component of one's vocabulary, whose visibility is now increasing.

6.2.2.1 Colonialism, Contact and Borrowings

There are at least two 'standards' of English, especially where the lexicon is concerned: the national and the international. New dictionaries aim to reflect this fact and do not claim to be the dictionary of American or British English, as they often did in the past. There will always be overlaps between the two standard lexica, however, as culture-specific borrowings can appear in the English of distant countries, as we will see in the next chapter. The following is a partial list of loan-words into English from the nineteenth and twentieth centuries from languages and cultures as far apart as France and China. Only a few can be assumed to have been borrowed during eras of colonialism, while most are culture-specific and generally (though by no means exclusively) refer to tangible phenomena rather than abstract concepts. Some words, such as *piranha* and *samba* have been borrowed from other languages via the language named in the list (in the above cases from Brazilian and Portuguese):

Some loan-words into English in the past two centuries

French	19th century	*café, surveillance, hangar, chauffeur*
	20th century	*limousine, déjà vu, rotisserie, courgette*
Italian	19th century	*bravura, lasagne, vendetta, diva, spaghetti*
	20th century	*gorgonzola, ciao, al dente, paparazzi, dolce vita*
Spanish	19th century	*mustang, ranch, rodeo, vamoose, cafeteria, bonanza*
	20th century	*macho, machismo, salsa, fajita, burrito*
Brazilian		
Portuguese	19th century	*piranha, samba*
German	19th century	*schnapps, poodle, semester, kindergarten, lager*
	20th century	*Doberman, gestalt, Luftwaffe, abseil, blitz*
Russian	19th century	*vodka, samovar, dacha, pogrom, borzoi*
	20th century	*kalashnikov, glasnost, perestroika, gulag*
Urdu	19th century	*pyjamas, yoga, tandoori, sitar, gymkhana, khaki*
	20th century	*samosa*
Hindi	19th century	*pukka, chapati, thug, raj, poppadom*
	20th century	*biriani, tikka, balti*
Arabic	19th century	*Islam, wadi, yashmak, jihad*
Celtic	19th century	*poteen, sporran, colleen, ceilidh*
	20th century	*corgi*
Japanese	19th century	*hara-kiri, tycoon, jujitsu, sumo, tofu, kimono*
	20th century	*dan, bonsai, karate, kamikaze, origami, shiatsu, karaoke, hibachi*
Chinese	19th century	*kow-tow, chop-suey*
	20th century	*chow mein, shih-tzu, mahjong, gung-ho, dim sum, wok*

(Adapted from Freeborn, 1998)

6.2.2.2 Neologisms

The journal of the American Dialect Society, *American Speech*, keeps a careful watch on the new words coming into the language in a column called *Among the*

New Words. The following list contains a number of words – and their definitions, where deemed necessary – that were discussed in *American Speech* in 1997 and 1998:

Euroskeptic	
klingon	(in the sense of an unexplained icon that appears on a computer screen)
mickey	(unit of computer mouse distance, approx. 0.005 inch);
Schwarzeneggerian	
alcopop	
crippleware	(demonstration software that lacks the full features of the program)
netrepreneur	(Internet entrepreneur)
net-savvy	

Not surprisingly, the majority of words on this list are related to computing, reflecting the rapid pace of technological advancement and application of computing to daily life. Others (e.g. *Schwarzeneggerian*, *alcopop*) refer to cultural phenomena (a film star and a new type of drink, respectively), while *Euroskeptic* is clearly a political term, in this instance in reference to British politicians who are opposed to the integration of the UK in the EU. What is remarkable about much of the new vocabulary is that it does not involve borrowing, but rather combining or blending existing words (e.g. *alcopop* = *alcohol* + *pop*; *crippleware* = *cripple* + *ware*; *Euroskeptic* = *Europe* + *skeptic*). Thus we see that the method of lexical enrichment that was the primary method in Old English is still productive today. In addition, orthographic practices are adapted or invented in order to be eye-catching and memorable. Thus, many new product names consist of blends that have an interesting orthographic twist: they can use capitalization in the middle of a word, as for example in the name *SmartLinks* (cf. the passage below).

There are other ways in which the language enriches the lexicon. For example, there are many examples of functional shift which can add completely new words to the language, or create words with slightly different nuances from existing words. For example, the verb *give* is a core word of English, with the noun *gift* deriving from it. However, a recent development is the derivation of a new noun *gifting* from *gift*, as in *Diamond jewellery makes great Christmas gifting*, which seems to suggest the act of giving a gift, rather than just giving – quite a subtle but suggestive difference. From the noun *parent*, in a similar fashion, derive the verb *to parent* and the new noun *parenting* (performing the functions of a parent), as in: 'The midwife is very knowledgeable about *parenting*'. While many commentators deplore such usages, they nevertheless are widespread across the language and signal living processes that will continue to enrich a language and expand its lexical base.

Nouns are also frequently derived from phrasal verbs, though, once again, this can be an indirect process. To *black out* (cut, extinguish, cease, cover, make dark), for example, leads to the noun *black-out*, from which derives, by analogy, the noun *brown-out* (a short-term interruption in electrical service to prevent a black-out), as in *Storm-hit Washington is having another brown-out*). Adjectives can also be derived in this way: *to knock out* leads to something being a *knock-out idea.*

Another word-formational process that is productive in the creation of neologisms is that of affixation; certain prefixes and suffixes have become noticeably productive, including:

un-	*un*-American, *un*-English, *un*-freedom
-ee	*franchisee, contractee*; this suffix (originally a French passive suffix) is now productively used in everyday speech, especially in the United States, expressing the passive partner for any agentive noun;
-ize	*burglarize, regularize, hospitalize*

Finally, several linguists have noted that present-day English also exhibits a tendency to use acronyms, particularly with reference to military and governmental institutions, e.g. UNPROFOR, UNICEF, NALGO, UNESCO, etc. Such formations are also frequently employed in the creation of names of corporations, as in AMOCO (technically a combination of an acronym and a blend, from *American Oil Company*).

6.2.2.3   Illustrative Texts

The following texts have been chosen to illustrate many of the points listed above. The first is an extract from a computer manual, while the second is a piece of popular fiction. While one is fact and the other fiction, they both illustrate the importance of technical vocabulary in Present-Day English. What is particularly interesting here is that those members of society who are not conversant with computer technology are clearly incapable of reading a novel such as Clancy's, let alone a manual like the one for McAfee Office 2000, presenting another significant communication gap between various types of English speakers (particularly generational).

McAfee Office 2000 User's Guide

Creating the SmartLinks database
The SmartLinks database stores information about the relationship between files on your computer. It stores names and locations of all files needed by the operating system. For each application, the SmartLinks database stores information about all the files that the application needs to run correctly, including icons, dynamically linked

libraries (DLLs), and other executable files, as well as operating system files that are used by the application. This information makes the SmartLinks database a complete, cross-referenced record of how executable and system files are used on your computer.

Putting UnInstaller to work

UnInstaller uses safe and simple wizards to perform its major tasks. When you use an UnInstaller wizard to clean up your hard disk or manage applications, at each step you see what you are specifying, and you can go back to previous screens and change options if you change your mind.

Even if you are an expert computer user, UnInstaller wizards can automate tasks, such as removing junk files, that would otherwise be time-consuming or error-prone. . . .

To run an UnInstaller wizard, click its button in the main UnInstaller window.

(p. 181)

Tom Clancy (1993) *Red Storm Rising* (London: HarperCollins) p. 378

'It's going to be a busy day, troops,' the captain said; he always let the attack center crew know as much of what was going on as possible. The more they knew, the better they could do their jobs. 'I saw a pair of Bear-Fs, one due north, the other west. Both a good way off, but you can bet they're dropping sonobuoys. XO, take her back down to five hundred feet, speed knots. We'll let them come to us.'

'Conn, sonar.'

'Conn, aye,' McCafferty answered.

'We got some pingers, active sonobuoys to the northwest. We count six of them, all very faint.' The sonar chief read off the bearings to the signal sources.

'Still no active sonar signals coming from the target formation, sir.'

'Very well,' McCafferty returned the mike to its holder. *Chicago*'s depth was changing quickly, as they dove at a fifteen-degree angle. He watched the bathythermograph readout. At two hundred feet the water temperature began to drop rapidly, changing twelve degrees inside of seventy feet. Good, a strong layer to hide under, and cold water deep to allow good sonar performance for his own sensors.

6.3 Modern English Dialects

Since we will treat American dialects separately in the following chapter, we will deal with the English dialects of England in this section, then with the dialects of the rest of the British Isles in section 6.4 below.

Modern (British) English dialects have been divided into two types, **traditional** and **modern** dialects (cf. Trudgill, 1990). The traditional or rural dialects of English are those spoken in rural areas, usually by older, less educated people, often involved in traditional occupations such as farming and fishing. The modern or urban dialects, including Standard English, are associated with the Home

Counties (the six counties around London where Standard English is more often encountered), urban and metropolitan areas, and places where English developed only relatively recently, such as parts of Wales and western Cornwall, which used to be Celtic-speaking areas. These mainstream modern dialects are also associated with younger people and with middle- and upper-class speakers. The major difference between traditional and modern dialects is that the latter are not so different from each other, or from Standard English, as are the former.

6.3.1 Traditional Dialects

Basing his findings on the Survey of English Dialects, Wakelin (1984) posits four dialect areas in England: the North, The West Midlands, the East Midlands and the South-West. For Wakelin the North is separated off from the rest of the country by a line running from the Humber to the Ribble, north of which words like *cows*, *goose*, *loaf*, *coal*, *eat*, *ground*, *blind* and *wrong* can be pronounced [kuːz], [ɡɪəs], [lɪəf], [kʊəl], [ɪət], [grʊnd], [blɪnd], [raŋ].

Wakelin has made a particular study of the dialects of the South-West, which are characterized by rhoticity (pronouncing /r/ both pre-consonantally and post-vocalically), voicing of initial fricatives (previously a generally southern characteristic, see chapter 4) as in *seven* and *sir*; omission of initial /w/ in words like *woman*; and the use of *be* or *bin* for *am*.

Trudgill (1990) posits three traditional dialect areas based on the Survey of English results. These are: North (North and Lower), Central (Western and Eastern) and South (Eastern and Western). See map 6.1 for details.

Each of these areas can be subdivided down to regional and county level.

Traditional English dialects can be marked off from each other by such phonological features as those in the following chart, which are those that Trudgill uses as his defining criteria:

long	[laŋg] vs. [lɔŋ]
night	[niːt] vs. [naɪt]
blind	[blɪnd] vs. [blaɪnd]
land	[lɔnd] vs. [land]/[lænd]
arm	[arm] vs. [aːm]/[ɑːm]
hill	[ɪl] vs. [hɪl]
seven	[zɛvən] vs. [sɛvən]
bat	[bat] vs. [bæt]

Trudgill finds that there is still a basic distinction in traditional dialects between the South and the North. He proposed thirteen distinctive areas on the basis of the above test criteria (see table 6.1).

Map 6.1   Traditional dialect areas
Source: Trudgill (1990), p. 33.

The southernmost pronunciation of *long* as *lang* defines the boundary between North and South, while the South is subdivided into two areas: Central and Southern. The Southern dialects pronounce *bat* with [æ], not [a], in the east. In the west they are rhotic. The Central dialects have short [a] in *bath, path*, while the South has long [aː]/[ɑː].

While Trudgill does not mention it as one of his basic criteria, I would include here the general northern [ʊ] pronunciation in words like *cup* and *butter*, though Lowland Scots and Scots have [ʌ] in such words.

Table 6.1   Dialect divisions

	Long	*Night*	*Blind*	*Land*	*Arm*	*Hill*	*Seven*	*Bat*
Northumberland	lang	neet	blinnd	land	arrm	hill	seven	bat
Lower North	lang	neet	blinnd	land	ahm	ill	seven	bat
Lancashire	long	neet	blined	lond	arrm	ill	seven	bat
Staffordshire	long	nite	blined	lond	ahm	ill	seven	bat
South Yorkshire	long	neet	blinnd	land	ahm	ill	seven	bat
Lincolnshire	long	nite	blinnd	land	ahm	ill	seven	bat
Leicestershire	long	nite	blined	land	ahm	ill	seven	bat
Western Southwest	long	nite	blined	land	arrm	ill	zeven	bat
Northern Southwest	long	nite	blined	lond	arrm	ill	seven	bat
Eastern Southwest	long	nite	blined	land	arrm	ill	seven	bat
Southeast	long	nite	blined	lænd	arrm	ill	seven	bæt
Central East	long	nite	blined	lænd	ahm	ill	seven	bæt
Eastern Counties	long	nite	blined	lænd	ahm	hill	seven	bæt

Source: Trudgill (1990), p. 32.

6.3.2   Modern Dialects

While the words *long*, *right*, *blind*, *hand* and *seven* can be used to differentiate traditional dialects of English, they contain features that are receding and are not diagnostic of the dialect of the majority of the population. Instead, therefore, Trudgill (1990: 50ff.) uses the following set of features that are distinctive in modern dialects.

Vowel of *but*
Southerners pronounce this vowel as /ʌ/, while northerners pronounce it as /ʊ/ in words like *but, cup, butter, some, luck*. Indeed this sound is a major North/South marker.

/r/ in *arm*
The change from a rhotic to a non-rhotic dialect began in the South-East of England, around London, East Anglia and the South Midlands area, and it is a change which continues to spread in present-day English. Parts of the country still retain post-vocalic /r/ as a distinctive feature of their dialect, though this /r/ is not of the same quality in every dialect. In the South-West of England and parts

of Lancashire /r/ is retained (though it is declining). Other areas such as the south coast of England and counties such as Oxfordshire, Berkshire and Hampshire still feature /r/, though it is far more common in older than in younger speakers, reinforcing its recessive character.

/ŋg/ vs. /ŋ/ in *singer, wringer*

As we saw in our discussion of Middle English, once /ŋ/ became phonemicized the final /g/ sound in these words was no longer pronounced in most English dialects. However, this older pronunciation remains indicative of the dialects of Liverpool, Manchester and Birmingham.

Vowel sound in *new, few*

In most dialects of English, including the standard, the /j/ glide has been lost in words like *rude* and *super*. In Norfolk and parts of Suffolk, Essex, Cambridgeshire, Northamptonshire, Bedfordshire, Leicestershire, Lincolnshire and Nottinghamshire, however, this change has spread to [u] after all consonants: thus, here, *few* is [fu] and *pew* is [pu].

Final /ɪ/ in *coffee, toffee*

While in the rest of the country words ending in <ee>, <ey> or <y> are pronounced with a final /i/ sound, in the central North, central Lancashire, northwest Midlands and central Midlands this final syllable is pronounced with /ɪ/ or /ɛ/ or a sound in between these two: thus, *needy* is pronounced [nidɛ], for example. Trudgill (1990: 60) makes the interesting observation that the areas where this pronunciation is heard are all near large coastal cities – Liverpool, Hull and Newcastle.

The vowel of *gate*

In most Southern and Midlands areas, this sound is pronounced as a diphthong, in line with changes in the vowel system we discussed under the Great Vowel Shift in chapter 5. However, in the North and the far South-West, a monophthongal pronunciation of this sound has been retained (as the change has not yet reached these areas): thus in the area around Middlesbrough, for example, *gate* is pronounced [geːt].

/l/ in *milk*

In a large portion of south-east England this /l/ sound has become /w/ in words like *fill, milk, hole, ball*, etc. This recent development is spreading very quickly, and Trudgill (1990: 62) predicts that this is a change like the one involving the other lateral, /r/, which might lead to the complete loss of /l/ in these words in

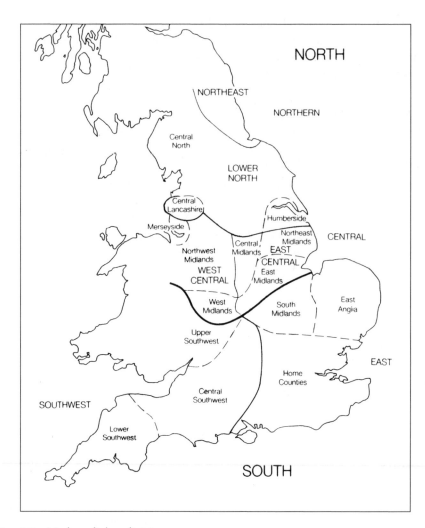

Map 6.2 Modern dialect divisions
Source: Trudgill (1990), p. 63.

the next couple of centuries. This sound is particularly indicative of so-called Estuary English, which we will discuss below.

On the basis of such sound patterning, Trudgill produces a map of the Modern Dialect divisions (see map 6.2).

His interpretation of these divisions leads him to suggest that, whereas with the traditional dialects the old North–South boundary was the most significant, with the modern dialects the boundary between Central and Southern assumes greater importance.

6.3.3 *Received Pronunciation (RP): The Social Background*

Throughout the history of the English language standardization has proceeded in tandem with the reverse trend: localization in both the written and the spoken language. We saw above that when dictionaries appeared in the eighteenth century, they constituted a move to fix and standardize the language. However, it was not until Victorian times that the notion of the 'Queen's English' developed, that is, the drive for uniformity in spoken English.

As we mentioned at the beginning of this chapter, in the early nineteenth century industrialization led to the further development of towns, and much of the rural work-force moved to these areas. After the Education Act prescribed a minimum education for all children, the ensuing increase in literacy meant that the standard could be disseminated more widely, with schoolteachers playing a central part in the standardization process. Improved road, rail and canal communications meant that people were geographically more mobile and that dialects came into contact with one another, which naturally led to a certain amount of accommodation and, ultimately, levelling. Language attitudes were still very strong, however, prompting George Bernard Shaw to write: 'It is impossible for an Englishman to open his mouth without making some other Englishman hate or despise him.' During this period people with social ambitions were quicker to espouse a more standard form of speech (a major premise of Shaw's *Pygmalion*).

Received Pronunciation emerged along with the Imperial Civil Service and the establishment of the British education system. The Education Act of 1870 established English public schools, where middle and upper classes mingled for the first time. As a typical elitist reaction to this, at the same time preparatory schools developed, where the children of the upper echelons of society were brought together and educated separately from the other classes. This segregation resulted in a dramatic change in speech patterns. Before the Education Act, most upper-class English men and women (including prime ministers like Gladstone and Peel) kept their local dialect when speaking, and the use of spoken local dialect was not stigmatized. However, by 1890 this situation had changed and accent levelling was applied both from above, by parents, teachers and employers, and from below, by peer pressure from the other boys to conform. The use of non-standard English became a marker of lack of education. And not just standard grammar and vocabulary were required, but also standard pronunciation, the so-called Received Pronunciation (RP). This term entered into British common vocabulary at the end of the nineteenth century to refer to the educated accent of London and the Home Counties. In 1917, Daniel Jones, a phonetician, described this accent as Public School Pronunciation, though it was not restricted to public schools. RP spread via the Army and the Imperial Civil Service throughout the

Empire, and became a symbol of authority and the model for English-language instruction throughout British territory.

However, because RP was associated with authority, material wealth and success, it also simultaneously engendered dislike and rejection, since many saw it as a marker of elitism and snobbery. During World War I telephones were first used on a wide scale, and recorded and electronically broadcast speech were also widely available for the first time. In 1921 the BBC was founded, and for years before, and most importantly during, World War II, there were frequent radio broadcasts of leaders' speeches. During the war the BBC assumed enormous importance as a means of spreading information on the progress of the fighting – and propaganda from both sides. The BBC had a global and imperial attitude towards English and from the outset there was serious debate about how words were to be pronounced; a British broadcasting authority made rulings about such matters through the Advisory Committee on Spoken English, which included high-profile authorities on language. (The Committee issued judgements on such matters as whether there are two or three syllables in the word *medicine*, opting for two!) The first Director General of the BBC, Lord Reith, who was from Scotland, argued strenuously in favour of RP in the belief that it would cause least offence to the listeners. Moreover, the BBC was regarded as a vehicle to promote English as an international language, and it was exactly this RP variety that was to be the target form.

In Britain the BBC was responsible for the spread of RP as the pronunciation associated with public schools, universities, the professions, government and the Church. Yet only about 3 per cent of the population actually spoke RP. Even in Hollywood films of the 1930s this more 'refined' accent was aspired to.

There were actually two types of RP, unmarked RP and marked RP; Professor Alan Ross coined the terms 'U' and 'non-U' (popularized by Nancy Mitford) for these kinds of English, which were concerned with the 'linguistic demarcation of the *upper* class'.

But during the middle part of the twentieth century attitudes towards RP and non-standard dialects began to change. In the 1960s people began to feel more positive about their regional dialects, conceding less prestige to the dialect of London and the Home Counties. A variety of reasons have been suggested for this change. In a well-known discussion of British pop song pronunciation, Peter Trudgill has suggested that the Beatles, with their Liverpool accent, had a very strong influence on British linguistic attitudes. While they clearly did have some effect, it is much more likely that attitudes to local dialects improved along with improving local conditions. And it is certainly the case today that the regionalization of Britain is having a strong effect on attitudes towards language. One powerful indicator of the rehabilitation of regional language and a concomitant drop in the prestige of RP is the proliferation of regional accents now heard on the BBC. Until the late 1990s the BBC national news was still read by predominantly

RP speakers. However, partly in response to political devolution, the 1999 revamping of the programme has Huw Edwards, who has a marked Welsh accent, as a principal news reader, and virtually all regional news programmes are broadcast in the appropriate regional accents. On ITV, the independent channel, the most popular news reader of the past decade has been Trevor McDonald, a Caribbean Briton, who has careful RP-like pronunciation, but displays the slightest hint of his Caribbean origins (if only in his hypercorrectness).

Having examined in outline form the history of RP, let us now examine the linguistic features of this mode of speech. It will strike the reader that the following discussion is limited, where phonology is concerned, to the vowels; it is here that RP is most clearly delimited.

6.3.3.1 Characteristics of RP

The Vowels

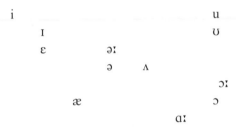

As well as the above vowels, there are five diphthongs (falling, in terms of sonority; rising, in terms of tongue height): /ei/, /ai/, /au/, /ou/, /ɔi/. There are also four centring diphthongs which appear in RP where rhotic dialects have /r/: [ɪə] *here*; [ɛə] *there*; [ɔə] *more*; [ʊə] *poor*.

RP cannot, however, be described as a global English phenomenon, as it varies according to age of speaker, region and style. In the table below, we show the pronunciation of three sample words (*home*, *white*, *poor*); the generational differences can be summarized as follows, where 'conservative' = the older age range, and 'advanced' = the younger generational range:

	home	*white*	*poor*
Conservative	ou	ʍ	ʊə
Neutral	əu	w	ʊə
Advanced	ɜːʊ	w	ɔː

The regional variants of RP tend to follow regional characteristics in general. For example, northern RP mirrors northern dialects in that it uses /ʊ/ where RP uses

/ʌ/; Welsh RP distinguishes between *flew* [flɪu] and *flu* [flu]. In general, RP still distinguishes between [ə] and [ɪ]; however, there are regional exceptions to this. The Prime Minister, Tony Blair, for example (originally from north-eastern England) typically uses [ə] in words such as *noted, wanted,* and even *sordid*. There are also RP dialects that do, and some that do not, differentiate between [æ] or [a] and [ɑː] in words like *photograph, plastic, translate*.

Lexicon and Grammar

In terms of vocabulary, more conservative varieties tend to eschew American words, while more advanced RP speakers feature American lexical items. On the grammatical level there are a number of variants within RP:

I haven't seen it	(Southern)
I've not seen it	(Northern, including Scots)
She sent it him	(Northern)
She sent it to him	
She sent him it	(Southern)
I want it fixed	(RP)
It needs fixing	(Northern)
I want it fixing	(RP)
It needs fixing	(Midlands and Northern)
I want it fixed	(RP)
It needs fixed	(Scottish)

(Trudgill, 1990)

6.3.4 *RP, Estuary English and 'the Queen's English'*

There is currently some debate on the status of, and relationship between, RP and 'Estuary English'. The phonetician David Rosewarne coined the term Estuary English in 1984 to describe a variety of present-day English that is a mixture of local south-eastern English pronunciation and non-regional or supraregional speech. He suggests that it would lie in the middle of a continuum with RP at one end and popular London speech at the other; in other words, between Cockney and the Queen's English. His research suggested that the accent occurred most commonly in the suburbs of Greater London and in Essex, north of the Thames, and Kent, south of the Thames Estuary. This was probably a result of the movement of speakers of popular London English eastwards from Victorian times through the blitz and then onto modern housing estates in the region. Estuary English spread during the 1980s and 1990s into Norwich and as far west as Cornwall, south of a line from the Wash to the Avon. It is not restricted to any one class, and has been identified as spoken by a number of notable public figures, such as members of parliament and prominent business people and entertainers. It is characterized as being more appealing to the masses than RP, which some consider 'snobbish' and indicative of the old school and the establishment.

Characteristics of Estuary English (EE)

(1)   Phonemically, Estuary English is a mixture of 'London' and general RP forms.

(2)   EE uses /w/ where RP uses /l/ in final position or in a final consonant cluster:
thus *milk* [miwk] and *faulty* [fɔwti].
(This renders the sentence 'Fowty books have been supplied in error' ambiguous between 'faulty' books and 'forty' books.)

(3)   Glottal stops frequently replace RP /t/ as in:
ne(ʔ)work, sta(ʔ)ement, sea(ʔ)belt, bi(ʔ), bu(ʔer).
However, glottal stop substitution in EE is not as frequent as it is in Cockney.

(4)   The palatal /j/ is not pronounced in words such as *consume, presume, assume, suitable*, while it is pronounced in more conservative forms of RP.

(5)   While /r/ is pronounced in EE, it is different in quality from /r/ in RP, and is pronounced 'without retroflexion' (Rosewarne, 1994: 5), which can sound more like a /w/.

(6)   Final vowels such as /iː/ in *tea* and *me* are noticeably longer than in RP, and might become diphthongized [mɪiː].

(7)   Intonation patterns are different from RP, and function words that are not normally stressed in RP can be stressed in EE, so that a sentence such as *Totters have been in operation FOR years* (Rosewarne, 1994: 6) is easily misunderstood as *Totters have been in operation FOUR years* by non-EE speakers.

(8)   EE is characterized by a rise/fall sentence intonation, giving it a kind of 'sing-song' character.

(9)   There is a greater use of question tags, such as 'don't I?' and 'isn't it?' (realized in Cockney as [ɪnɪt]) than in RP.

(10)   Certain vocabulary items are indicative of EE, such as *cheers* instead of *thank you* or *goodbye*. The word *basically* is used frequently. *There you*

go is used to signal something that is offered, rather than *Here you are.*
Excuse me is used where RP might use *Sorry.*

(11)   *There is* is used invariably with singular and plural.
(12)   There is frequent use of Americanisms and American discourse patterns,
       such as asking on the telephone 'Who's this?', rather than 'Who's that?'
       or 'Who's speaking?'

While many commentators disagree with him, Rosewarne suggests that EE is
an indication of the way RP is headed. A. C. Gimson suggested that Jones's
original term 'RP' be subdivided into **conservative**, **general** and **advanced RP**,
and suggested that the younger generation was using the advanced RP, which he
felt was the way RP would develop. However, in the past few decades, RP has
had to be democratized; that is, it has had to accept some regional forms (what
Trudgill termed 'regionalized RP'), with even the general RP of the BBC giving
way to local forms, including EE.

One of the reasons why Rosewarne believes EE is the direction in which RP is
headed is that children in state secondary schools and children in private schools in
southern England are tending to accommodate to one another and emerge from
school speaking Estuary English. It is suggested that EE constitutes a linguistic
middle ground. The more affluent classes accommodate downwards in order
to increase their popular appeal (such as Nigel Kennedy, the violinist), while
the working-class group accommodate upwards in the hope of sounding more
'sophisticated'. The point is that the EE-speaking group is now far larger than the
advanced RP-speaking group, and, Rosewarne claims, it is also more influential.
As Rosewarne puts it, 'these developments may be seen as the result of the
development of less exclusive linguistic networks in Britain. It is a sign that the
class barriers are coming down' (p. 8).

The advance of EE is also regarded as merely the latest step in the long history
of London influence on the English language. Rosewarne contends that popular
and prestigious accents only began to diverge noticeably from each other in the
eighteenth century. At this point it was London speech that was the impetus for
'Standard' English to lose non-prevocalic /r/. In the immediate linguistic past,
that is since the 1940s, popular London speech has increasingly been influencing
RP. The spread of final /l/ as /w/, a feature of EE, is considered by Rosewarne as
analogous to post-vocalic /r/; this makes perfect sense from the phonological
point of view, as both are liquids and prone to change.

While EE is spreading within England, and may indeed cross the Welsh border,
Rosewarne does not feel that it will spread into Scotland, Ireland or internationally, as his research has suggested that EE does not meet with strong approval
abroad. Matched-guise testing showed that teachers internationally still rate RP
most highly, followed by 'General American', Australian English and, in last
place, Estuary English.

6.4　Sociolinguistic Focus: English in Scotland, Ireland and Wales – Multilingualism in Britain

The role of English in England is clearly dependent on dialect, the social prestige of RP and EE, and changing population profiles across the island. The role and status of English in Scotland, Ireland, and Wales – originally Celtic-speaking countries – differ markedly from the English situation, especially given interaction with indigenous languages; but the three are very different, and the status of English differs greatly from one to another.

6.4.1　English in the British Isles

6.4.1.1　English in Scotland

The history of the English language in Scotland is a fascinating one, and without parallel in the world. In Scotland, a dialect of English evolved into a separate language, Scots, which then, because of dramatic political changes, lost its position of dominance to Standard English. Despite this, spoken Scots survived, although most believed it was simply an inferior dialect of English. There have been two earlier attempts to revive it as a literary language and at present there is another similar move to develop Scots as a separate language, particularly by those with Scottish nationalist leanings, who wish to make the most of the new independence of the Scottish parliament from Westminster and the dominance of the English.

In order to understand the developments fully, we need to go back briefly to the origins of English in Scotland.

The original inhabitants of Scotland are believed to be the Picts, who lived in the North-East of the land. Using the almost forty known ogham inscriptions, which have not to this day been satisfactorily deciphered, as evidence, conventional scholarship has held for over fifty years that the Picts spoke a non-Indo-European language along with some form of Brythonic Celtic. The suggestion is that the non-Indo-European language was merely a survival and used for ceremonial purposes only. Recently, however, some scholars (e.g. Forsyth, 1995) have come to believe that the ogham inscriptions are basically Old Gaelic, some perhaps in or with some Pictish (British Gaelic), and in some cases with Norse elements added. However, even more recently Cox (1999) suggests, quite controversially, that at least some of the ogham inscriptions in north-east Scotland are written in a form of Old Norse, possibly from the twelfth century. As the ogham script is essentially an Irish script, the question would then pose itself, why would Old Norse speakers use a Gaelic script? Cox suggests that it was probably the case that Norse-speaking clerics would have learnt about ogham and other Celtic learning traditions in what were fundamentally ecclesiastically Celtic establishments in Scotland, while the impetus for actually writing inscriptions may have come from Norway, where runes were used for memorial inscriptions. Cox's suggestion is, then, that the clerics would have learnt ogham and adapted it to Old Norse. Thus we see that even scholarship on pre-historic language samples in Britain is still a lively and thriving activity.

Whatever the outcome of the discussion of the nature of Pictish, however, we are reasonably sure that the Irish invaded the North of Britain, bringing a variety of Celtic with them that was different from that of the Britons (see chapter 2); the Romans referred to them as *Scoti*. The Picts eventually learned Scots Gaelic, giving up Pictish completely for Old Irish, whose speakers were literate and who had developed their own literary tradition.

Eventually the Picts and the Scots merged into the Gaelic-speaking kingdom of Alba, which the Anglo-Saxons called *Scotia* or Scotland. Alba pushed south-wards soon after it was founded and annexed the Southwest in the late ninth century. Soon after, Dun Eideann (Edinburgh) and then the entire Lothian area as far as the River Tweed came into Scottish possession, bringing Gaelic speakers into contact with the Anglo-Saxons of Northumbria. In 1018 Malcolm II defeated the Saxons at Carham to consolidate the Scottish hold on Anglo-Saxon territory. This territory, Old English-speaking, was loosely associated with Scotland for a considerable period, that is, during the reigns of Malcolm II (1005–34) and Macbeth (1040–57), who were both Gaelic-speaking kings.

The attempts of Malcolm III (1057–93) to modernize the Scottish monarchy along English lines were carried forward by his son David I (1124–53). A major result of this modernization was that Old English gained in prestige. Old English was particularly promoted through the establishment of the burghs, an Anglo-Norman innovation, and the courts, guilds and other institutions were also Old English-speaking. Large numbers of Old English-speakers also fled into Scottish territory to escape the tyranny of William the Conqueror and the anarchy of the reign of his son-in-law Stephen (and many were captured by the Scots as slaves). Dutch, Flemish and Scandinavians also immigrated to Scotland, both directly and via England, and as they were speakers of Germanic languages, one assumes it was easier for them to learn English than Gaelic.

Thus from the start in Scotland Old English was associated with modernity, with trade and commercial opportunity, enterprise and prosperity. While Old English did not become the official language of Scotland, David I and his imme-diate successors did prefer it to Gaelic.

The position of English suffered no setback when the Celtic royal line died out with Alexander III (1249–86) and his granddaughter the Maid of Norway, and the throne passed to Lowland families, the Balliols, the Bruces and the Stewarts. In fact, as a consequence, the monarchy itself began to identify with Lowland Scotland, rather than the Gaelic-speaking Highland region, especially when the seat of government moved from Perth to Edinburgh, deep in earlier Old English-speaking territory. Under James I (1406–37) the Acts of his predecessors were translated from Latin into Lowland Old English, not Gaelic, and his own legislation was written in Old English, and during the reigns of Robert II (1371–90) and Robert III (1390–1406) the Lowland language was used in poetry and developed into a flourishing literary vernacular. Though Gaelic was still used over more than half of the area of Scotland, particularly in the Highlands, where it was the language of culture, it was Old English that Scotland used in its transactions within the mainstream of European culture.

In the late fifteenth century English began to be referred to as *Scottis*. Gavin Douglas, the poet, was the first person to insist that Scottis was a distinct language from *Inglis*. This assertion was made on political grounds, but also because Douglas had lived in England and was aware of the sometimes striking differences between the two varieties. This change of name reflects a difference in Scottish national self-awareness. The Lowlanders had now claimed the term Scottish, which used to refer to the Gaelic of the Highlands (and Ireland), as their designation for the language. This was clearly a shift in perception, since up until this point Scottishness had been associated with the Gaelic language; now the term *Scottis* was being applied to English, suggesting that the linguistic centre of Scottish identity had shifted.

At this point, Scots could have become a separate standard language, though this was not to be: Chancery English became standardized and universal but standardized written Older Scots did not. Older Scots did show signs of standardizing, however, as the vernacular was beginning to broaden its scope in the fifteenth century, and a number of dialectal varieties of Scots were beginning to be suppressed. Furthermore, there was remarkable literary activity in Scots. The fifteenth and early sixteenth century mark the Golden Age of Scots literature, the period of the 'makars' (= makers or poets), Robert Henryson, William Dunbar, Gavin Douglas and Sir David Lyndsay. Barber (1997: 37) points out that official documents, private letters, contracts, sermons, pamphlets and works of scholarship were also all written in Scots. However, the development of this variety of Older Scots into a standard was interrupted for several reasons.

Firstly, it had an uneasy relationship with 'English English' south of the border. Until the late fifteenth century the OE-derived language spoken in the south of Scotland was referred to as *Inglis*, while the term *Scottish* was reserved for Gaelic. Added to this, there was intimate cultural contact between Inglis and English, and the Scottish vernacular literature of William Dunbar and Robert Henryson had close affinity with the earlier English poetry of Chaucer, Gower and John Lydgate. This made it harder to separate the literary status of the one from the other. Secondly, the standard never gained enough prestige to be used as a language of education. There were no grammarians to regularize Scottish forms, and orthographical conventions were widely variable. Thirdly, the southern variety began to influence Scots because of the many printed books that circulated in southern English. Fourthly, unlike with other languages, such as Welsh, there was no translation of the Bible into Scots. This meant that literacy, which was usually based on reading the Bible, centred on English English.

The main reason for the lack of standardization, however, was the collapse of real Scottish political autonomy after the defeat at Flodden in 1513, which was immediately followed by the Protestant Reformation. James IV (1488–1513) and most of the Scottish nobility were lost at Flodden, and this led not only to political decline but to a decline in cultural life as well. James V (1513–44) could not complete the promised national revival before his early death, after which the Protestant reform movement provided a new threat to the use of Scots.

The Union of the Crowns (1603) shifted Scotland's political power southward: the Authorized Version of the English Bible was used on solemn occasions while Scots remained the language of every day. Devitt (1989: 71) shows that shifts into English between 1520 and 1659 followed in an orderly sequence from religious treatises through official correspondence, private records and personal correspondence down to public records.

The Reformers used English for their confessions of faith and for theological works, and the Geneva Bible they used was also in English. When James VI left to become James I of England he took his court with him. The court naturally shifted to using English, and with this came the end of royal support of literary activity in Scots. This was especially the case after 1603 and the Union of Crowns, and even more so after the Union of Parliaments in 1707. Although Edinburgh did become a centre of cultural and economic achievement, it was fashionable to use English there, often to the explicit exclusion of Scots features. Henry VIII, Edward VI and Elizabeth I helped the reformers in Scotland as a way of suppressing the Catholic monarchy and this meant that Protestantism triumphed, leaving English as the political and cultural language of the day. From the eighteenth century onwards the use of Scots was disparaged, particularly in Scottish schools.

Scots survived as a spoken medium of communication, however, particularly in intimate conversations. It also persisted as a language of poetry and fiction, though no major literary figures emerged again until the eighteenth century, which witnessed a revival of literary Scots, spearheaded by Robert Fergusson (1750–74), Robert Burns (1759–96) and Sir Walter Scott (1771–1832). However, even Burns and Scott could not effect the revival of Scots as a national language, and, indeed, literary activity in Scots dwindled until Hugh MacDiarmid (C. M. Grieve) began writing after World War I. Other writers such as William Soutar, Douglas Young, Sydney Goodsir Smith and Alexander Scott also attempted to revive literary Scots, producing a synthetic, not a vernacular, variety which was referred to as 'Lallans' (McClure, 1988; Romaine, 1985).

Certainly in the twentieth century much academic attention has been paid to Scots. There are a number of reference works, dictionaries, grammars and readers, including the *Scottish National Dictionary*, and *A Dictionary of the Older Scottish Tongue* (Aitken). A linguistic survey of Scotland has been carried out at the University of Edinburgh, the major centre for research on Scots, and Mather and Speitel have compiled the important *Linguistic Atlas of Scotland*. Nevertheless, Murison (1971: 179) was pessimistic about the future of Scots as a language:

> The stark fact remains that the Scots language is in a bad state of decay and will assuredly pass into such a vestigial condition as to be virtually dead.

He could not know then that in 1999 Scotland would regain a significant amount of independence in the form of a separate parliament in Edinburgh. To what extent this important political development will affect the future of Scots is anybody's guess. There is no doubt that interest in the revival of Scots as a literary language is growing. The Scots Leid (language) Society in Perth is active in lobbying for increased status for Scots both in Scottish private and public life and in the school curriculum; the University of Aberdeen has a Scottish writer-in-residence and a specialist in vernacular Scots whose role is to promote creative writing in Scots at school and university level; and the Scottish Nationalist Party apparently has plans to bring Scots into the school curriculum on a larger scale, should it gain majority control of the Scottish parliament. In the meantime, however, teachers in Scotland are gearing up to teach about Scots in the English-language classroom. Historically, it has proven very difficult to revive languages, once they are on their way out. However, since Scots has always been so healthy as a spoken form of communication, thriving in a number of regional dialects, it is certain to survive in the meantime. Scottish educational and political policies of the future – but especially the crucial will of the people, its speakers – will be the final arbiters of the fate of this variety.

6.4.1.2 English in Wales

Southern Pembrokeshire has been English-speaking since the medieval period, which is traditionally attributed to Henry I establishing an English-Flemish settlement there in 1108. This is an example of linguistic colonialism, which theory gains support from the fact that the border of this county is completely straight, and man-made looking, as opposed to other borders which follow the natural contours of some geographical boundary such as a river or hill range. Many place-names in the area end in -*ton* suggesting that this was an English–Flemish settlement with a preponderance of English-speakers. The Gower peninsula was also anglicized early, before the fifteenth century, which suggests that it was another English settlement area. Elsewhere in Wales change was gradual, but in the Gower peninsula and in southern Pembrokeshire there is no evidence of this. Instead it would seem that the two areas were well insulated from the surrounding

Welsh-speaking areas, because there is significantly little Welsh influence on the English of these two areas.

As was the case in Scotland, Royal Burghs were set up in North Wales, and these excluded Welsh speakers by charter. Trade and commerce revolved around English-speaking townspeople and it was this, rather than the number of English settling in Wales, that was the main reason for the spread of English. For hundreds of years in Wales towns served as the focal point for English activity and anglicization, and this increased the divide between the small but wealthy and influential English-speaking gentry and the masses of Welsh-speaking rural peasants.

The Tudor dynasty's intent was to unite the kingdom, and as part of their strategy the prestigious speech of the strong commercial centres was backed up by law. Thus people who could afford to do so were moved to educate their children to speak English, and education itself became an ever more important tool in the spread of the language. In contrast to the situation in Scotland, by the fifteenth century English seems to have been established as a medium of education in Wales. However, the major reason for the shift to English in Wales is that the Acts of Union (1536 and 1542) required that English should be the only language in Wales with legal and administrative status, and any non-English speaker was excluded from holding a position under the Crown, which forced people to learn English in order to prosper in Elizabethan Britain, which was a time of great individual opportunity.

Hence, the Welsh gentry who supported the new regime learned English and became functionally bilingual. Those that did not remained monolingual Welsh-speakers. In any case, by the seventeenth century English had spread into significant areas of Wales. Even church services were held in English in the eastern part of the country (Radnorshire, Breconshire and Monmouthshire), where communication was facilitated by the rivers Severn, Usk and Wye. A number of Welsh-speakers worked for the Tudors in the Inns of Court, and had their children educated in Latin and English, either in Wales or in England. The gentry who left Wales were considered progressive entrepreneur types, while those that stayed behind were more concerned with Welsh culture, supporting the Welsh tradition of literacy in the face of the encroachment of English. Thus, once again, English was the language associated with modernism, opportunity and entrepreneurial spirit.

The Bible and the Divine Service were translated into Welsh in 1563, thus creating a linguistic double-edged sword. On the one hand, this helped maintain the Welsh language, but on the other it permitted Welsh to be identified as the language of religion, thus diverting it away from any political importance. As it was deemed a language that was less than important, it survived most strongly among the peasantry. In fact, by the end of the eighteenth century the Welsh peasantry still had not become very anglicized. Anglicization was contained mainly on the eastern side of the country, and monolingual English-speakers were separated from the monolingual Welsh-speakers in the west by a small buffer zone of

Welsh–English bilinguals. However, eventually English did begin to spread into the Welsh Marches in the eighteenth century.

What is interesting about the situation in Wales is that the two monolingual communities did not mix as communities, but bilingualism developed from individual to individual, and therefore took place much more gradually. Progressively, English entered more and more communicative domains in the eastern regions, from the commercial and public to the personal and private, while its influence in the West remained restricted. But eventually industrialization dramatically changed patterns of language use throughout Wales. The Education Act of 1881 promoted English in universal primary education and through this the working class became more anglicized. Education, commerce and industrial expansion in south-east Wales eventually made the use of English inevitable, and by 1872 there was not a single Welsh-medium school left in Glamorgan. Apart from its promotion of English, the Education Act also led to a demotion and stigmatization of Welsh in these areas.

The need to recruit workers into industry in the South-East also changed patterns of movement within the country, with workers coming first from the Welsh-speaking areas of the West and then the North. At the same time that this reinforced Welsh as the language of the chapel and home, English soon developed as the language of the workplace. Once this source of labour dried up, however, new migration developed from outside Wales. By 1901 67 per cent of migration into Wales was from the South-West of England and the anglicized Welsh Marches. Because of the sheer numbers, then, there was no need for new immigrants to learn Welsh. Furthermore, this mixing caused an increase in mixed marriages, which led to even faster decrease in the number of Welsh–English bilinguals, leading to the eradication of Welsh in many areas. That the rise of English in Wales took place at the expense of Welsh goes without saying. The number of monolingual English-speakers rose from 63 per cent in 1921 to 81 per cent in 1981, and the entire population of Wales now speaks English: there are no monolingual Welsh-speakers left.

While Wales held on as a diglossic country until World War II, the war itself caused tremendous social upheaval, changes in agricultural practice and depopulation of the Welsh-supporting rural areas. At first the prestige of Welsh in the Non-conformist chapels helped slow its demise, but nowadays religion is of much less significance in Wales, and the church can no longer act as a force for the maintenance of the Welsh language. There are Welsh-language societies, the BBC has had broadcasts in Welsh for a number of decades – both on television and on radio – and literature and poetry are still being produced in Welsh. This, it is hoped, will help keep the language alive, and the recent devolution vote can be viewed as a positive step towards Welsh-language maintenance. But, again, as in the case of Scots in Scotland, it will be the speakers, and the desire to keep the language alive as a first language, that hold the key.

6.4.1.3 *English in Ireland*

There are three major historical periods of English influence in Ireland. The first is during the Anglo-Norman period when Henry II landed his Pembroke-based Anglo-Norman troops in Ireland (1171). However, English had little prestige at the time and they were soon gaelicized by the Irish. The Statutes of Kilkenny (1366) tried to reinforce the position of English by stating that all Englishmen were to use English surnames, English language and English customs, or forfeit their lands. However, the law proved not to be effective. In the 1550s there was Roman Catholic opposition to the Reformation and Irish Gaelic was championed over English: language was a weapon, and Irish Gaelic was seen as a long-established symbol of Catholic Ireland, while English was the language of Henry VIII's Protestant country. English was most definitely in a state of decay in Ireland in the sixteenth century. In 1578 an English lord chancellor reported that 'all English, and the most part with delight, even in Dublin, speak Irish, and greatly are spotted in manners, habit and conditions with Irish stains'. By the end of that century there was almost no more English in Ireland, much to the disgust of visiting English dignitaries.

The second wave of influence was in the seventeenth and eighteenth century, when the English colonized Ireland by instituting the plantations. In this two-hundred-year period there was strife between the Protestant English and the Ulster Scots and the landowners, as the planters competed with the native Irish. The consequences of these differences persist today. Irish Gaelic became synonymous with Roman Catholicism and English with Protestant supremacy. As English power grew in the towns in the eighteenth century, the English language came to dominate there, and the Irish ruling classes learned to use English in order to increase their influence over the English overlords. Even in the Independence movement of the 1790s there were many English-speaking Irish.

In 1801 the Act of Union made Ireland part of the United Kingdom, triggering a third wave of English influence, since from this point it was deemed desirable to speak English, and speaking Irish was considered by most Irish people to be a barrier to progress. The Anglo-Irish aristocracy became even more English and (like the Scottish aristocracy two hundred years before) they began to send their children to England to be educated.

In the early part of the twentieth century, Irish writing in English became extremely popular and extremely well regarded, with writers such as J. P. Synge, Sean O'Casey and W. B. Yeats at the forefront. Synge particularly represented rural Irish English, often with wonderful comic effect, and all three authors used Educated Hiberno-English in such a way as to establish Irish English as a true literary medium.

Some of the traits of present-day Irish English include: constructions such as *I am after finding it, He do be living in Cork*; answers to a question with a formulation such as *indeed*, or *indeed not* instead of a direct 'yes' or 'no'; word stress that is often on a different syllable than in Standard English English.

The expansion of English in Ireland occurred at the expense of Irish. In 1800, fewer than 50 per cent of the people in Ireland had English as their first language, but in 1851 only 23 per cent had Irish as their first language, and the census of 1861 records only 2 per cent of children under the age of 11 as monoglot Irish speakers.

The rapid decline of Irish was caused by:

(1) the expansion of the railways out from English-speaking Dublin and Belfast;
(2) the spread of education, first in unofficial 'hedge' schools and then in the national schools from 1831, where English was promoted and the use of Irish actively discouraged;
(3) dramatic demographic change caused by famine and the massive emigration to America and other countries from 1830 to 1850. The famine particularly decimated the Irish-speakers in the west of Ireland, possibly halving the number of speakers.
(4) the association of English with progress, modernization and an international voice. As we will see with South Africa in chapter 8, even nationalist politicians in Ireland preached their message in English, in the knowledge that it would bring them a wider audience.

Only after the Easter Uprising of 1916 was there a return to regarding Irish as the language of Ireland, and a symbol of Irish identity, but by this time it was too late to save the Irish language as a national language. By 1900, more than 85 per cent of the Irish were monoglot English speakers, with about 10 per cent bilingual in Irish and English, and only 5 per cent monoglot Irish speakers. Today there are virtually no monoglot Irish speakers left, and while there was some attempt to bring back Irish in the schools (see figures in chapter 2), fewer than 100,000 have knowledge of Irish from birth.

And English continues to consolidate its position in Ireland. Certainly Ireland's position in the European Union today is aided by the fact that it is an English-speaking country. Ireland was in on the technological revolution from an early stage, and, particularly in the area around Dublin, there has been dramatic development as a consequence, making Dublin an extremely international capital with excellent international communications. All of this reinforces the position of English.

Irish English dialects
The Anglo-Norman influence on Ireland held in only a few places, giving way to Irish in all other areas. Only in northern Dublin county and in Wexford did it persist, no doubt bolstered by the fact that there had been Germanic-speaking

settlements in the east since Viking times. English in Ireland is referred to as Hiberno-English, and there are three main varieties of it:

(1) Rural Hiberno-English, the most conservative and gaelicized variety, spoken in the countryside and in the west.
(2) Urban Hiberno-English, more mixed in character because of contact with outsiders, though perhaps preserving some original Anglo-Norman features in the big cities.
(3) (a) Educated Hiberno-English, more influenced by Standard English, though still with some rural characteristics.
     (b) Modern Educated Hiberno-English, influenced by the media, and in particular the newsreaders of RTE, the television company, and by Dublin-educated teachers and other influential members of the community.

The situation in Northern Ireland is quite different. There is a distinction between Northern and Southern Hiberno-English, with the major dividing line falling between Bundoran (north of Sligo) in the west and Carlingford Loch (north of Dundalk) in the east.

In the Northern area, Ulster Scots is spoken in the North-East, and is heavily influenced by Lowland Scots. There is then a Mid-Ulster dialect spoken in the Lagan Valley, south Tyrone, north Monaghan and north Fermanagh. The English in the north and east of Ulster is most influenced by Scottish and Anglo-Irish, while in the west there is greater influence from Irish. The Ulster Scots regard themselves as a distinct group, even to this day, and this identity is reinforced by their literary links with Scotland from the time of Burns (1759–96), and by the tradition of sending their children to Scottish universities. However, it has been suggested that Ulster Scots may be showing signs of decline.

6.4.2   Immigrant Varieties of English in Britain

6.4.2.1   Immigration to Britain in the PDE Period

Britain has been a destination for immigrants and refugees throughout its history: Angles, Saxons, Jutes, Danes, Norwegians, Normans, Flemings, Germans, Walloons, Dutch, Huguenots in 1685, French Catholics and aristocrats during the Revolution.

World War II was an important cause and catalyst of migration. After 1941 the government made it easier for colonial subjects to enter Britain without documentation, and the shortage of labour made it easy for them to find employment. While efforts were made to repatriate them after the war, many either did not want to go, or came back because of the lack of economic opportunities in the West Indies.

There has also been considerable migration within the British Isles in the past two centuries, from Ireland to England and Scotland and from Wales to England. Between 1820 and 1910 almost five million Irish left Ireland, most for the United States, but many also for England and Scotland. About three per cent of the population of England were Irish-born according to the census of 1861, and seven per cent of the population of Scotland. In 1801 Britain and Ireland were formally united under one parliament, but the union was dissolved in 1921 with the creation of the Irish Free State. However, even after this the British government allowed unrestricted movement between Britain and Ireland; Irish citizens are not treated as aliens, but have full citizenship rights, including the right to vote. In 1984 British citizens were accorded full voting rights in Eire. But despite these close ties, the Irish were not always welcome in Britain, and they met with considerable hostility in England and Scotland. They were regarded with dislike by working-class Britons who felt they were keeping down wages by being willing to work longer for less money than the British workforce. Moreover, they were Catholic, which brought with it religious antagonism, especially in fiercely Protestant areas of Scotland (Layton-Henry, 1992).

In general, whenever there is large-scale immigration there is resentment, hostility and violence, especially in the areas where immigration is focused. This was the case between 1870 and 1914, when about 120,000 Russian and Rumanian Jews migrated to the East End of London. Poverty, unemployment, overcrowding and crime were all blamed on the Jews, though they had been rife before the Jews ever arrived in the East End. But anti-Jewish sentiment was pushed even at government level, in the shape of a number of Conservative back-benchers. There were repeated reviews of immigration, which repeatedly found that it was not at a sufficient level to be harmful or to need special action. However, the feelings persisted and in 1905 the Aliens Act was passed, giving the Home Secretary the power to refuse entry to people who could not support themselves or their dependants, or to those who would be likely to be a burden to society because of ill health or a criminal past. Nevertheless, the principle of asylum was reaffirmed. The law was not changed until 1914 when the Aliens Restriction Act was passed, giving the Home Secretary complete power over immigration. This was amended after the war and then in 1920 a new Aliens Order was passed, and renewed every year until the Immigration Act of 1971.

The next major period of immigration to Britain occurred during and after World War II, when over 120,000 Polish ex-servicemen were resettled in the country. This happened very smoothly, largely because of the acute labour shortage after the war, resulting in the rapid absorption of the Poles into the British economy, but also because the government had instituted positive measures to integrate them, in marked contrast to their treatment of other groups.

6.4.2.2   *Colonial Immigration and Language*

As subjects of the British Empire, colonial immigrants had the right of access to Britain and full rights of citizenship, including the right to vote, the right to work in the civil service and the right to serve in the armed forces. Many colonial immigrants, especially those from the West Indies, felt British and were optimistic about their reception in the Mother Country.

However, they suffered a number of disadvantages, partly because of the history of the conquest and enslavement of African, Indian and Caribbean people. The authorities and the people of Britain felt superior and were off-hand with them, because of this history of subjugation, and the colonial migrants also reacted according to their experience of subjection.

Until the middle of this century Britain proudly pursued a policy of the free movement of capital and labour within the Empire, and made no restrictions on colour, as many other countries had done, largely out of fear of a flood of Indian immigrants. There had already been small settlements of black people in port towns such as Liverpool and Cardiff, as well as in Manchester and the East End of London. These settlements were established mainly by colonial seamen, especially in World War II. In the early 1950s it was discovered that there were no accurate estimates of the size and composition of the non-white community in Britain. Estimates were provided by the police in 1953, according to which there were about 40,000 non-whites living in Great Britain, the largest groups being West Africans (15,000), Indians and Pakistanis (9,300) and West Indians (8,600).

The 1987 Local Education Authority Language Census recorded 172 different languages spoken by students enrolled in British schools.

There has been a lot of research on Celtic-speaking communities, but virtually none on speakers of other European languages, South Asian languages such as Tamil and Sinhala, African languages such as Hausa and Yoruba, or East Asian varieties of English such as Singaporean and Malaysian English.

Immigrants came either as refugees seeking asylum (Vietnamese, Tamils), or for economic reasons (from Pakistan, India, Bangladesh, the Caribbean). It is not a simple matter to separate out these reasons, however. There is also a distinction to be made in Britain between long-established immigrant communities, such as South Asian, Italian and African immigrants, and more recent arrivals, such as Vietnamese.

There are even differences within groups: Bangladeshis are different from other South Asians, in that they arrived from East Pakistan between the 1950s and 1960s and clung firmly to the 'myth of return', only sending for their wives and children much later. Thus, many Bangladeshi children were born in Bangladesh and therefore needed greater support in language teaching. They still form one of the largest linguistic minorities in the Inner London Education Authority.

Patterns of settlement are also important. If an immigrant group settles within a limited geographic area, it can form dense and multiplex social networks, which can act as norm-enforcing, and identity- and language-reinforcing, mechanisms. Examples of such groups are Spanish, Turkish, Greek and Vietnamese immigrants living in London. If they are spread out thinly, only loose networks form and identity and language are harder to maintain. This is true of Panjabis, Ukrainians, Poles, Tamils and Sinhalese (though there are some dense Polish and Panjabi settlements outside London). Furthermore, communities with little or no contact with their home country have a harder time sustaining their cultural and linguistic identity than those which have close connections. Lithuanians, Latvians and Ukrainians were in this position before the break-up of the Soviet Union. It would be interesting to see what the impact of the loosening-up of travel restrictions has been on these communities in Britain. We must also realize that patterns of language use change from generation to generation, depending on circumstance. While it is imperative for newer groups to develop facility in English, often to the detriment of their home language, more established ethnic groups may well place greater emphasis on maintaining the mother tongue (such as the Slavic communities). Just as the 'Roots' phenomenon sparked off interest in the 'new ethnicity' in the United States, this has also happened in Great Britain amongst particular immigrant groups, and the burgeoning numbers of community-based language classes bear witness to this development.

As the Minority Languages Project in the mid-1980s showed (see table 6.2 for national representations), in many communities the church, mosque, gurdwara or temple plays a central role in their social life and welfare. There are often extensive secular organizational networks on top of this. Ethnic groups frequently develop an extensive ethnic economy, e.g. restaurants, travel agents, grocery stores, clothing shops and video stores.

The age at which immigrants come to this country has an effect on how well they learn English, which in turn has an effect on how they are perceived by Standard English speakers. Most immigrants will not learn Standard English but some regional variety of it. And the younger the immigrant is on entering school the closer his or her language is likely to be to the local target variety. Children born in this country are even more likely to acquire a local variety. However, even the local variety they learn might be disadvantaged and non-standard. Giles and Bourhis (1976) found that immigrants who accommodate linguistically to a local style might actually decrease their perceived status. Children might become doubly disadvantaged on the grounds of skin colour and dialect.

It is generally accepted that children learn best through the medium of their mother tongue, and for this reason special provision has to be made for immigrant children in areas with a particular ethnic concentration. Special classes might be provided for children from a similar ethnic background, or there might be ESL

Table 6.2   A typology of recent migrations to Britain

Migrant labour		Political refugees
Ex-colonial	Bengali	East-African Asian (1968–73)
	Panjabi	Vietnamese Chinese
	Gujerati	(1979–82)
	Hong Kong	Tamils (1980s)
	Chinese	Yugoslavs (1990s)
	West Indians (1960–75)	Kosovars (1999)
	Hong Kong Chinese (1990s)	
	Greek and Turkish Cypriots (1960–75)	
European origin	Italians (from nineteenth century, but most since 1950), Portuguese, Spanish (from 1960)	Polish, Ukrainian and other East European (1945–50)

Source: Adapted from Linguistic Minorities Project (1985) p. 31.

(English as a Second Language) teachers who go from school to school. In any case, it has been suggested that children should not be isolated from mainstream groups, but integrated in the classroom as soon as possible. In general Britain does not support bilingual education. Whenever instruction in the home language is given, it is to foster *transitional* bilingualism, that is, facility in the dominant host language only, even at the expense of the mother tongue.

The Afro-Caribbean speech community is a particularly interesting case. The Caribbean was subject to multiple colonial powers throughout history: Dutch in Surinam, Spanish in Cuba, French in Guadeloupe, and British in Barbados. Sometimes a succession of different colonial powers governed a Caribbean region, e.g. St Lucia and Trinidad. What unites all Caribbeans therefore is their shared experience of political and economic conditions.

Linguistic variation in the Caribbean is the result of multilingual contact. Speakers of different African languages were deliberately separated from each other by slave-masters so they would not be able to plot their escape. They therefore needed to develop a means of communication with some urgency. Thus, first, pidgins developed and then, when they became the native tongue of slave children, they creolized. This took place in the Caribbean between 1600 and 1800. While much work has been done on the impact of European languages on the Caribbean, we know less about the influence of African languages. What we can say is that English and French were often the lexifier language, but Niger–Kordofanian languages most likely formed the grammatical base. While European languages are generally recognized as the official national languages of Caribbean countries, the majority of the people speak some variety of creole. There is a continuum from very basilectal to very acrolectal varieties, and there is much code-switching between creole and the European languages. Moreover, the European languages have a long written tradition, while the creoles continue the African oral tradition of story-telling and language games. Since education is largely through the medium of English or French, a truly diglossic situation often occurs, where English or French is the High language and creole (Patwa) is the Low language.

The history of Afro-Caribbean Britons is similar to that of West Africans, since the slaves often came from Africa to Britain by way of the West Indies. Some also came as sailors in the late nineteenth and early twentieth centuries, and some of the first black settlements in Britain were in large ports such as London, Liverpool and Cardiff. The most significant immigration from the West Indies occurred in the 1950s when serious labour shortages in Britain led to West Indians immigrating and finding work with such concerns as the National Health Service and London Transport. Between 1955 and 1961 about 200,000 West Indians settled in Britain, notably in Brixton and Haringay, but all over the country in industrial areas.

A continuum of forms of British Black English (BBE) is spoken, from acrolectal varieties to recognized creoles, which moreover vary from one group or individual to another, as well as varying from speech situation to speech situation. Sutcliffe (1982) demonstrated that, just as white speakers vary their language from one situation to another, so Jamaican Britons can vary the lects they use, depending on the social situation, and they code-switch into and out of them for a variety of reasons. He demonstrates that there is a continuum of lects with examples from a survey of British Black English speakers from Bedford. Here is a small illustrative extract from a recording of Patricia, a British-born black girl who was aged 13 in 1974:

> But mm . . . Oh God mi mummy come down. She say 'What you doin' 'ere?' An started tellin' me off, an se . . . and after she said 'I never know'. mmm – she knew the man name. 'I never know 'e started takin' pint, he usually has halves.' An se, I say 'Is it a pint cup?' And den after she say 'Patricia. A wa yuh do? Di man mos a rab yuh, yuh know.' And mm – she mm – she start cussin me. But when I tell im dat de other man . . . after I realise dat dis mus be di mm, half, di half pint one, I say: 'I don' . . . he don[t] rob me at all. Cos di oder one must pay me, mm, full, you know, a pint for di half pint.' An – mm – she just burs' out laughing an mi uncle start say 'You mus' come 'ere more often. A wi get more money.'
>
> (Sutcliffe, 1982: 132)

This passage demonstrates a number of features that are quite common in British Black English: the lack of dental suffix /t/ and /d/; reduction of consonant clusters, *mus', don', tellin'*; the use of *say* to introduce indirect speech; [d] for /ð/ in *dat, dis*; use of *mi* for *my*; /h/-dropping. This list can be compared with the list of features discussed for African-American Vernacular English in chapter 7. However, the text is still readily intelligible, and represents a form that is reasonably close to Standard English. Compare this with another of Sutcliffe's transcriptions of Patricia, in which there are considerably more Jamaican Creole features, suggesting a lect which is much nearer the other end of the acrolect–basilect continuum:

> . . . try to open dis box and 'i white boy cut imsel' . . . den after suddenly di boy was (. . .) bandage an doin' it up fi 'im an suddenly dis ting dis op . . . 'im dis go so like . . . im open i . . . dis kin' a box . . . coffin an ma . . . 'im close . . . 'e mouth was close den an 'im . . . 'im stan' up so an get out di grave . . . I mean 'i coffin, an den after 'e open 'e mout' an 'e walkin down like 'at . . . an go-in aaah! showin' 'e teet' . . . an di blood dis drippin' down di mout in it? (. . .) an 'en after 'e jus' take di bwoy han' an jus' gon suck out di blood.

> (Sutcliffe, 1982: 129)

In this instance Patricia is talking excitedly about what happens in a horror film, and she uses many more BBE features, including *'e* and *'im* for *he*, *him* and *his*; *in it?* as a tag question, *bwoy* for *boy*, etc. It is clear that not every black Briton uses all the BBE features all of the time.

While the above examples are from the 1970s, it is not the case that British Black English has disappeared. V. K. Edwards (1984, 1986) has worked extensively on the language of West Indian children in Britain and has found that West Indians' reading comprehension is considerably less than that of other children of the same age, and this despite the fact that more than three-quarters of the children participating in the study were either born in Britain or had been resident here for over five years. This suggests that the influence of West Indian English is one that extends beyond recent immigrants. Edwards suggests that West Indian speech is sufficiently different from Standard English to cause dialect interference, particularly on the grammatical and phonological levels.

In purely linguistic terms, Caribbean variants of English in use by the first generation of immigrant groups can continue into the second. The language of children of the third generation (and not infrequently of the second) generally is that of the community at large, while 'Caribbeanness' is often still reflected in isolated linguistic features. However, elements of the original Caribbean variant are amply present in the linguistic inventory of the speaker (for example, the phonological system that makes up the 'Caribbean accent') and they can be and are used for effect, for example in expressing ethnic or group solidarity. The influence of African-American Vernacular English (AAVE) is also felt in Britain, however, depending on context: thus, in some modern black British musical genres – especially rap music – elements of AAVE are readily recognized. As this particular genre had its genesis in America, this will not come as a complete surprise; it is unlikely, however, that this one genre on its own will contribute greatly to the further development of British Black English in the future.

In the next chapter we explore the English of the United States. Some of the issues treated in that chapter – including the language of immigrant ethnic groups within the country – will bear some resemblance to the British situation. The present status of the language of one major American population group, the African-Americans, is of particular interest to linguists, as the issue is one of convergence with local dialects or divergence from them; this stands in contrast to the situation in Britain, where one essentially finds convergence, even if it is incomplete.

Notes

1   *Antiques Roadshow*, PBS Washington, DC, 2 August 1999.
2   *ITN World News*, PBS Washington, 2 August 1999.

Suggested Readings

Freeborn, Dennis (1992) *From Old English to Standard English: A Course Book in Language Variation Across Time*. Ottawa: University of Ottawa Press.
Ihalainen, Ossi (1994) The Dialects of England since 1776. In: Burchfield, Robert (1994) *The Cambridge History of the English Language, Vol. V: English in Britain and Overseas: Origins and Development*. Cambridge: Cambridge University Press.
Kallen, Jeff (ed.) (1997) *Focus on Ireland*. Amsterdam: Benjamins.
McClure, J. Derrick (1988) *Why Scots Matters*. Edinburgh: The Saltire Society.
Sutcliffe, David (1982) *British Black English*. Oxford: Blackwell.
Trudgill, Peter (1990) *The Dialects of England*. Oxford: Blackwell.
Wakelin, Martyn F. (1984) Rural dialects in England. In: Trudgill, P. (ed.) (1984) *Language in the British Isles*. Cambridge: Cambridge University Press.

7 English in the United States

Timeline: America in the Modern Period

1607	Jamestown, Virginia, is established as the first permanent English settlement in America
1620	The Pilgrims arrive at Plymouth Rock on the *Mayflower*
1670	English settlement in Charles Town, later Charleston, South Carolina
1680s	Welsh Quakers settle in large numbers in Pennsylvania; first German immigrants in America
1729	North and South Carolina become Crown Colonies; Benjamin and James Franklin publish 'The Pennsylvania Gazette'
1756–63	The French and Indian War in North America
1774	Parliament passes the Stamp Act, unifying the colonies against the British
1775	The East India, or Tea, Act prompts the Boston Tea Party
1776	The Declaration of Independence; the Revolutionary War begins
1783	The Treaty of Paris successfully ends the Revolution
1789	George Washington is inaugurated as first US president
1803	The Louisiana Purchase doubles the size of US territory
1812–14	War of 1812 between the USA and Britain
1819	Florida purchased by the USA from Spain
1824	Erie Canal opens, strengthening east–west trade, but increasing the isolation of the south
1828	The Baltimore and Ohio Railway opens
1837	The electric telegraph demonstrated by Samuel Morse
1848	Gold discovered in California; Gold Rush 1849
1861	Civil War begins with the Confederate attack on Fort Sumter
1863	Emancipation of the slaves is proclaimed, as of 1 January 1863
1865	General Lee surrenders to Grant at Appomattox; President Lincoln is assassinated, five days later
1867	Alaska is purchased from Russia, becoming the 49th state in 1959
1869	The first transcontinental railroad is completed

1876	Alexander Graham Bell patents the telephone
1903	Orville and Wilbur Wright make the first successful manned flight at Kitty Hawk, North Carolina
1908	Henry Ford introduces the mass-produced Model T
1914	Panama Canal opened
1914–18	World War I
1924	The National Origins Act marks the official end of large-scale immigration to America; from this point on numbers are restricted and quotas are introduced
1939–45	World War II

7.1 Social and Political History

7.1.1 Settlement and Language

The development of English in the United States is not, of course, synonymous with the development of *language* in the United States, since there were already indigenous Native American languages when the European settlers first arrived. Indeed, the native peoples of America spoke approximately one thousand different languages or dialects, representing language families and groupings as diverse as Na-Dene, Eskimo-Aleut, Algonkian, Iroquoian, Salishan, Penutian, Uto-Aztecan, Yuman, Coahuil, Siouan and Gulf. The history of the Native Americans has been well documented; we are aware that they were slaughtered, dispossessed and displaced by the white settlers, often taken as slaves, and, in some cases, whole tribes were eradicated. While today Native Americans can be found across the country in many cities and states, just under half of them live on reservation lands. As far as their languages are concerned, the number of Native Americans still speaking them has been decimated, particularly as a result of the eighteenth- and nineteenth-century expansion of European settlers. Only about two hundred different native languages survive, of which Navajo is the healthiest, though still with significantly fewer than 100,000 speakers. In many regions of the world such a small number of speakers would be signalling a critical stage in the life of a language, even the probability of eventual language death. Some of the language families or groupings, such as Penutian and Salishan, are now represented by fewer than 1,500 speakers and, needless to say, many are featured in the UNESCO Red Book on Endangered Languages.

The language that the British brought with them to America, beginning with the first settlement in Jamestown, Virginia, in 1607, is Early Modern English, and is largely the English of South-East England. Its subsequent development in America is affected by a number of factors, which we can summarize as follows:

(1) The source of the original British dialect;
(2) Maintenance of contact with the 'home' country;
(3) Patterns of settlement;
(4) Influences of languages other than English caused either by immigration from other countries, or by contact with speakers of other languages within America;
(5) Social and geographical mobility.

Simplifying for the sake of clarity, we might say that settlement of America occurred in three very broad stages. Firstly, the original thirteen colonies were established on the Eastern Seaboard, moving into the mountainous regions of the East (such as the Appalachian and Allegheny Mountains), only rarely as far as the Mississippi. Secondly, settlers pushed into the deep south (west and south-west of Georgia), and then northwards into the Ohio Valley and the Midwest; and finally movement was possible into the Southwest and the West in general, including the Pacific Northwest (see map 7.1). A major reason why settlement occurred in stages was the sheer size and geographical complexity of the country: sections could only be opened up as ways were found to negotiate mountain ranges, navigate rivers, and cross deserts and snow-filled valleys. For example, as we shall see below, the opening up of the Erie Canal was instrumental in the populating of the Midwest, while the coming of the transcontinental railroad helped considerably in the opening up of the Far West, as well as in improving communications and mobility generally across America.

The settlement of the original thirteen colonies was important for dialectologists, who can say with some certainty from which areas in Britain and in mainland Europe these colonies were settled, and what the relationship was between these colonies and with Britain, at least until American independence in 1776. The original colonies extend from Maine in the North as far south as Georgia, and have traditionally been divided into New England, the Middle Atlantic States and the South Atlantic States. There follows a brief summary of American settlement, indicating the major sources and time-scales of immigration.

7.1.2 Settlement by Region

7.1.2.1 The Original Thirteen Colonies

Although we speak of three 'distinct' American dialect areas to begin with – those associated with the thirteen original colonies – boundaries are somewhat fluid in the South but clearer in the North. The smallest of these dialect areas is the 'south Atlantic' region, essentially comprising Georgia. This was the last of the original thirteen colonies to be settled. As part of a policy to empty England's bulging prisons, debtors were deported to Georgia, ostensibly to give them a new start, but mainly to decrease the burden on English government coffers.

Georgia stands alone, then, as representative of the south Atlantic dialect region until the purchase and annexation of Florida by the United States from Spain in 1819. As the other two regions (especially in reference to their early colonization) are substantially larger than the south Atlantic, they are the main focus of this part of the study.

Mid-Atlantic

Jamestown, the first permanent settlement of English speakers in America, was mostly settled by speakers of south-eastern English dialect, though there was some admixture of other dialects, and all social classes were represented in Virginia. From Virginia the colonists also moved south and settled North Carolina, which later received a large number of German, Scottish and Scots-Irish settlers. In South Carolina there were English, Irish and Welsh settlers and a significant number of French Huguenots and Dutch, both directly from the Netherlands and from New Amsterdam (now New York). In addition to the ethnic and linguistic mix of colonists, South Carolina also witnessed an influx of different religious groups: Quakers from Louisiana, Baptists from Massachusetts and Irish Catholics.

The Middle Atlantic states were settled quite differently from New England and the south Atlantic states, as from the outset their population was mixed in character, and did not have the solid English core of the other areas. The exception was initially Maryland, which had been an essentially English colony; however, its English population was eventually joined by settlers from Pennsylvania, who were largely Scots-Irish and German. In 1664 the English seized New York from the Dutch, who had occupied the Hudson Valley for about 50 years. New York was always mixed in its population, for apart from the English and Dutch there was also a large influx of Palatinate Germans in the early eighteenth century, while Connecticut and other New England territories also provided settlers to the Middle Atlantic. New Jersey was largely English, with direct settlement on the Delaware River and secondary settlement from New England in the East.

Pennsylvania was populated by a mixture of English, Welsh, Scots-Irish and Germans, with the Quaker William Penn providing leadership from 1681. Because the Quaker movement was largely organized in the North of England and in parts of Wales and Scotland, Philadelphia did not have the same dialect base as New England or some parts of the south Atlantic states. In the early eighteenth century there was a wave of Ulster settlement, though many Ulstermen and -women moved on when they encountered large settlements by the English (whom they were often trying to avoid in emigrating in the first place!), and moved on into the mountains and down into the Southwest. Immigration into Pennsylvania by the Scots-Irish continued throughout the eighteenth century.

As in New York, another phase of German immigration into Pennsylvania began in the early eighteenth century, when Palatinate Germans (mostly Anabaptists) settled the farmland in the Susquehanna and Lehigh valleys. These groups mostly lived separately from the English-speaking population, and some have maintained a colonial variety of German to this day, which is generally referred to as Pennsylvania Dutch (from *Deutsch*) or Pennsylvania German. Scots-Irish immigrants were also later compelled to move further south into the hills and the Carolinas since German settlers had claimed so much of the best farmland.

New England

The settlement of New England began around Massachusetts Bay in 1620 and, in the general search for land, extended to Connecticut in 1634, followed shortly by coastal Maine, Rhode Island and, eventually, New Hampshire. The majority of the settlers came from the eastern and south-eastern counties of England, with a significant number of Puritans from East Anglia. Boston became the cultural and linguistic focal centre of eastern New England, though western New England developed differently from the coastal area.

New England is clearly a much more compact geographic region than the area that is called the 'Mid-Atlantic' region. This is one reason why the settlement patterns were so much more complex in the latter: it was much larger, and offered greater expanses of land for settlement and development. The two regions were not isolated from one another, however, as we shall see in the following discussion of one of the key linguistic features characteristic of them.

The pronunciation of /r/ in the mid-Atlantic–New England dialect regions

It is striking today to see that some of the characteristic features of the Mid-Atlantic dialect areas still reflect their origins directly. Thus, for example, parts of Tidewater Virginia are recognized for the /r/-less, or non-rhotic, character of their dialect, that is to say, speakers do not pronounce /r/ when it does not precede a vowel ([paːk], [kaːt], for *park*, *cart*, etc.). While most English dialects were still rhotic in the early seventeenth century, those of south-eastern England, the major source of Virginia settlement, had already developed /r/-lessness and therefore this feature travelled to America with the settlers. However, the Piedmont and mountain areas of Virginia were not settled by non-rhotic speakers, but by speakers of dialects from other regions where /r/-pronouncing was preserved, and in particular by Scots-Irish speakers from Ulster, who had particularly strong /r/-pronunciation.

It was a similar situation with eastern New England; it, too, was settled chiefly by south-eastern English dialect speakers, and remains today as a non-rhotic relic area, despite the fact that the areas west of the Connecticut River Valley and New York State are both /r/-pronouncing. Interestingly, New York City, which is renowned for its /r/-lessness (pronouncing *first* as *foist*, for example) was actually a rhotic area in the beginning, and only became non-rhotic under the influence of eastern New England in the nineteenth century.

Charleston, South Carolina, is another pocket of /r/-lessness which was perpetuated because of links with England. The received interpretation of this development, which comes down to us from the dialect geographers, is that all of the three areas mentioned were plantation areas, and the wealthy traders who established these first settlements usually maintained their ties with England for a long time, often sending their sons to be educated there. Moreover, these settlements were much more static and homogeneous than the secondary settlements, which also led to the reinforcement of the features of 'polite speech' in well-to-do social circles. In other words, unlike most other Americans, the population of these areas looked to London for its norms of communication; that is, they had an *exocentric* model of speech to which they aspired, while the rest of the population developed its own *endocentric* norms of language use. In our discussion of African-American Vernacular English below, however, we will discuss more recent research which suggests that the spread of non-rhotic dialects in the South may well be in part due to over 350 years of contact between African-Americans and the white population.

7.1.2.2 *The Middle West*

The settlement of the Middle West was largely made possible by improvements in navigation. The Mississippi and Ohio Rivers were important means of mobility for the settlers. The states south of the Ohio River were largely populated by secondary settlement from the original thirteen colonies. Virginia, Pennsylvania and North Carolina provided much of the populace of Kentucky, while Tennessee contained a strong contingent of Scots-Irish from North Carolina. People from neighbouring states likewise settled Alabama and Mississippi, which also had a large number of forced immigrants in their population, that is, slaves from various parts of Africa. Louisiana had a mixed population of French, English and Scots, as did Missouri, though the French influence was always stronger in the former than the latter state.

Settlement of the Old Northwest Territory, which was north of the Ohio River, was again possible because waterways were added to overland routes as means of communication. An overland route into the territory from Pennsylvania had existed earlier; however, when the Erie Canal opened in 1825, this facilitated settlement from New England and New York, while the Ohio River carried people into the territory from Kentucky and West Virginia. For dialectologists this kind of movement is significant. Frequently rivers and mountain chains mark dialect boundaries, because they form natural barriers to communication. On the other hand, rivers can also be linguistic conduits, as in this case, where the Ohio River marks an important South–North channel and explains why there are so many southern features in this area (such as the use of *you all* or *y'all* for the plural form of *you*).

Michigan and Wisconsin were originally populated primarily by New Englanders, but in the nineteenth and early twentieth centuries both were the target of considerable immigration from Germany and Scandinavia. This was largely a result of revolution and religious persecution in Germany, and the desire or need to escape religious and political differences and general poverty in various parts of Scandinavia. Indeed, though far fewer in number than their Scandinavian cousins, about 35,000 Finns left Finland for America at the beginning of the last century, and there remains a Finnish-speaking pocket in Michigan to this day.

The flow of goods north and south along the Mississippi River made it possible for farmers in the Midwest to earn their livelihood selling staple foods to the cotton farmers of the South, who were almost exclusively involved in the production of cotton. The steamboat contributed significantly to this trade. Apart from bringing in people on regular steamboat services (both along the Mississippi and through the various canals), steamboats were also used as freighters, carrying crops and other goods, and contributing significantly to communications in general.

7.1.2.3 *The South and West*

The Louisiana Purchase of 1803 doubled the territory of the United States and stimulated the settlement of the West and the Far West. Pioneers travelled more than two thousand miles to the Pacific Northwest following the Oregon Trail, which started from Independence, Missouri, and followed the Platte River on to the Columbia and thence to Fort Vancouver. The population included settlers from Kentucky, Missouri and Tennessee, though the majority came from New England.

Settlers were able to make their way to the Southwest once the Santa Fe Trail became negotiable; it ran westward through Kansas Territory, also from Independence, Missouri.

After the signing of the Oregon Treaty in 1846, the Mormon leader Brigham Young founded Salt Lake City in Utah with a large group of Mormons from the East, primarily from New York State and New England, who were looking for a place to settle in which they could pursue their religion in freedom. From the late

1840s – especially after the discovery of gold in California – the number of people seeking land and a new life in the west grew quickly; many of these new settlers stayed in communities that had already taken hold, such as Salt Lake City, en route to California.

Texas had originally been part of the Spanish holdings in the Americas, after which it was part of Mexico; consequently, it has always been populated by large numbers of Hispanics. Indeed, southern Texas largely remains Spanish-speaking to this day. After Texas was declared an independent republic in 1836, a large number of English-speaking settlers made their home in East Central Texas; Southern Central Texas was settled by people from Alabama, Georgia, Mississippi and Louisiana. Northern Central Texas was the target of immigration from the Upper South, that is, from Arkansas, Kentucky, Missouri and Tennessee. From there, these speakers gradually moved into western Texas.

The discovery of gold in California caused a precipitous increase in its population after 1848; indeed, the number of residents swelled to over a quarter of a million within four years. Los Angeles soon became a major commercial and cultural centre, and its influence spread as far north as Oregon and central Washington State, and as far east as western Idaho, Nevada and southern Arizona. The Gold Rush brought English-speakers into Northern California in 1849, making San Francisco an important centre, though its significance was soon overshadowed by Los Angeles. Migration westwards became generally easier after the Transcontinental Railroad was completed in 1869. However, in terms of dialect development, Texas, rather than California, has had the strongest influence on the region, reaching as far north as the Great Plains and the Rocky Mountains.

The Pacific Northwest focuses on Portland, Oregon. The earliest non-native residents in this part of the country were the English, who settled around Puget Sound in 1828. Trappers and traders from New England soon made their way over to the lucrative west-coast trapping grounds. Once Oregon was settled in 1843 large numbers of English-speakers moved in from the Ohio Valley and Tennessee, followed by settlers from Missouri, Illinois and Iowa. As in the Midwest, at the end of the nineteenth century there was significant immigration from Scandinavia.

What is remarkable about the settlement of the Pacific Northwest is that the English settlers from New England brought a number of discernible northern dialect features with them (such as [ɑː] in *last* and *path*), which actually held on until at least the early twentieth century and persist even today in some very small relic areas. By comparison, the Southwest has few northern features, particularly in the area dominated by Texas.

The most important points of the preceding discussion of the settlement patterns of America are summarized in map 7.1.

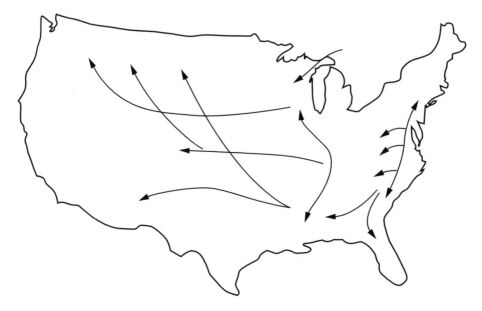

Map 7.1   Sketch map of direction of settlement of America

7.2   The Development of American English

In the following pages, we shall explore the birth of American English as a function of a variety of factors: geography, separation from Britain, experiences of the colonists in a new land, contact with other immigrants, and the development of an 'American' identity.

7.2.1   The Strength and Maintenance of Dialect Boundaries

As one might expect, American dialects are more distinctive in areas of original primary settlement that have remained relatively homogeneous, and are less distinctive as a result of dialect mixing in areas of secondary settlement, and everywhere where there has been geographical and social movement. One result of this is that, in comparison with British English and with other European languages, American English is on the whole much more homogeneous, since social and geographical mobility have been a feature of the United States almost throughout its history. The European languages, on the other hand, existed for hundreds of years before long-distance communications and physical movement were possible to any significant extent. They have consequently developed numerous local varieties that are often palpably different from one another, even over very short distances (even between neighbouring villages, in some instances).

In general, it is fair to say that dialect boundaries were at their strongest in the areas of the original thirteen colonies, that they began to become fuzzy once English crossed the Mississippi, and are rather blurred by the time they reach the west coast. It is also true that these 'traditional' American dialect features become more mixed over time, though, as we shall see below, this does not mean that there are no longer any definable dialect boundaries, or that the original dialect boundaries no longer have any significance.

7.2.2 How, Why and When American English Began to Diverge from British English

From the very beginning of the settlement of America by English speakers, the two varieties of the language necessarily began to diverge from each other. It is remarkable how quickly British travellers to America begin to comment on the differences between the varieties of English they encounter in the two countries. This divergence came about for a number of reasons, including:

(1) The physical separation of America from Britain;
(2) The different physical conditions encountered by the settlers;
(3) Contact with non-native speakers of English, both Native American and immigrant;
(4) Developing political differences between the two countries and the growing American sense of national identity.

We will deal with each of these factors in turn below.

7.2.2.1 Physical Separation

We have seen throughout our discussion of English that physical separation of one dialect from another leads to divergence, as the two groups develop differently from one another. When we consider that the only way to reach America from Britain was by ship until after World War II, and when we also realize that, even today, freighters take on average between seven and ten days to cross the Atlantic, we begin to get some idea of the enormous physical separation between the two countries.

They were also separated in other important ways, not the least of which is that, while people in Britain were socially and geographically relatively immobile throughout the settlement period (though Britain was undergoing what was, for it, dramatic change at the time), America has since its inception been a country of change, dynamism and mobility. Allowing ourselves to indulge in generalization for a moment, we might also remark that the mentality of each country was also fundamentally different. While Americans settling the frontiers needed to be pragmatic, self-assertive and adaptive, Britain has traditionally been rather conservative and nostalgic in its attitude towards its long and colourful history. Since many immigrants were coming to America to escape persecution, poverty or other hardship, or were merely trying to make a 'fresh start', they expressly wanted to leave the old life behind and work out new ways of living and new ways of prospering. Thus the general identity of the two countries was founded on wholly different premises.

One way in which this can be illustrated in reference to the language is that the British have always criticized the Americans for their linguistic innovations. To this day, they comment negatively about such phenomena as the frequent use of *-ize* to derive nouns from verbs: *hospitalize, burglarize, generalize, prioritize*, etc. (many of which are now frequently encountered in British English).

7.2.2.2 *The Different Physical Conditions Encountered by the Settlers*

When the settlers arrived in the enormous country that was to become the United States, they encountered physical conditions that were often radically different from anything they had witnessed before. The physical geography of the country was different, and they needed words to refer to the geographic features they met. The flora and fauna of the new country were also new and words had to be found to describe them also. Of course, Native Americans had lived in America for hundreds of years before the settlers, and obviously had words in their own languages for the items they encountered in their everyday lives, but which were new to the immigrants. This was particularly so in the case of names for places, rivers and other topographical features. The settlers' options were to borrow words from other languages, to make up completely new words, or to extend existing terms from English to meet their new communicative needs.

Consequently, we have words like *prairie*, *levee* and *bayou* from French to denote geographical features; place and river names such as *Manitowoc* (Wisconsin), *Chappaquiddick* (Massachusetts) and *Potomac* (Maryland) from Native American languages; and names for fauna such as *skunk, opossum, moose, raccoon*. The colonists also extended the meaning of familiar terms from Britain to cover new species of plants and animals encountered in America. Thus *oak* now refers to a different kind of tree from the British oak, and *bee* refers to what Britons would call a *wasp*, while in America *wasp* refers to something that Britons would call a *hornet*, and so on. A further method of innovation was to make new descriptive combinations to cover new phenomena, such as *bullfrog, egg plant*, etc.

7.2.2.3 *Contact with Immigrant Non-Native Speakers of English*

As we have seen, American settlers came from many parts of Europe and the rest of the world, and not just Britain. These settlers brought with them customs, items and ideas that were new to their neighbours, and as these phenomena became more widely used within American society, the words used to designate them also spread. Names for foodstuffs, architectural features and religious concepts were among the types of words that were borrowed. Foodstuffs included: *cruller, cookie, coleslaw* (Dutch); *beignet, chowder, potage* (French); *macaroni, zucchini, mozzarella, pastrami* (Italian); *sauerkraut, hamburger, frankfurter, noodle, pretzel* (German). Jewish immigrants provided words like *matzo, gefilte fish* and the expression *kosher* to designate foodstuffs as prepared within religious guidelines. A myriad of other words were borrowed into American English, covering all types of phenomena, such as *stoop* (< Dutch); *piazza, mezzanine* (< Italian). Many of the words listed here will also be familiar to speakers of British English, either through later contact with speakers of the original languages, or via American English.

Because of the large number of Hispanics living in America, particularly in the southern United States, but in all major cities across the country, there are many words from Spanish in American English. The majority of words refer to food and drink, such as *taco, tortilla, salsa, tequila, margarita, fajita, burrito* and *nachos*. However, there are others that refer to more abstract concepts such as *fiesta, siesta, macho, machismo* and *mestizo*. While some of these words have entered into general American English (and indeed into English in general, see chapter 6), others are more likely to be encountered in more Spanish-speaking parts of the country, such as southern Florida or southern Texas, New York, Chicago, San Diego or Los Angeles.

7.2.2.4 *Developing Political Differences and the Growing American Sense of National Identity*

For the first hundred and sixty years or so of American settlement, there was a close relationship between America and Britain, but it was one that increasingly became filled with tension. Americans began to feel very strongly that the British were exploiting their resources and hard work while providing little or nothing in return. While many, but by no means all, Americans were willing until this point (and even beyond Independence in some cases) to follow the fashions and styles of British society, in the eighteenth century Americans as a whole became less and less willing to be governed by the British.

Matters came to a head in the reign of King George III when in an attempt to raise revenues the fiscally embarrassed Parliament passed the Stamp Act in 1765, which had the effect of unifying the colonies against the British. While the Stamp

Act was officially repealed in 1766 and did not lead to outright rebellion, similar British actions did prompt revolt in 1773 when the East India or Tea Act prompted Boston merchants to tip tea into the harbour in a show of defiance (the 'Boston Tea Party'). Political anti-British sentiment ran very high from the mid-1760s to the mid-1770s, when matters finally came to a head. Throughout this time another major difference emerged between the Americans and the British: that is, their attitudes toward slavery.

All of these significant differences prompted the colonies in 1776 to declare themselves independent from Britain, leading to seven years of Revolutionary War between the two countries. In 1783 the British were forced to admit defeat and recognize the independence of the United States in the Treaty of Paris. Six years later George Washington was inaugurated as the first President of the United States.

Needless to say, anti-English feelings ran very high at the end of the eighteenth century, and many Americans were consequently disposed to accentuate, and even exaggerate, the differences between the two countries. Nowhere was this more evident than in the language.

Noah Webster (1758–1843) was a lawyer who turned to teaching. He wrote three elementary books on English, including a spelling book, under the title *A Grammatical Institute of the English Language*. The spelling book was subsequently published as *The American Spelling Book* and sold hundreds of millions of copies over the next hundred years, making a major contribution to the uniformity of English throughout the United States. Webster was out to prove that English in America was distinctively American, and his motives were unabashedly political. In his work *Dissertation on the English Language* (1789) he says:

> As an independent nation our honor requires us to have a system of our own, in language as well as government. Great Britain, whose children we are, should no longer be *our* standard; for the taste of her writers is already corrupted, and her language on the decline. But if it were not so, she is at too great a distance to be our model, and to instruct us in the principles of our own tongue.

As the War of 1812 attested, not everyone in America was pro-revolution (particularly in New England and the South). In 1789 there was a definite need to forge a collective American identity in the 13 colonies, and Webster felt that one way this could be achieved was through spelling reform:

> A national language is a band of national union. Every engine should be employed to render the people of this country *national*; to call their attachments home to their own country; and to inspire them with the pride of national character.

Americans still needed this, he argued, because they still clung to Britain too closely:

However they may boast of independence, and the freedom of their government, yet their *opinions* are not sufficiently independent; an astonishing respect for the arts and literature of their parent country, and a blind imitation of its manners, are still prevalent among the Americans.

In the preface to his *American Dictionary* (1828), the culmination of his work, Webster says:

It is not only important, but, in a degree necessary, that the people of this country, should have an *American Dictionary* of the English Language; for, although the body of the language is the same as in England, and it is desirable to perpetuate that sameness, yet some differences must exist.

It is well known that Webster's major direct influence on the English language in America was on spelling, which he reformed with the support and input of other prominent Americans, including Benjamin Franklin, who himself had devised a new spelling system in 1768. While these spelling reforms did not go as far as Webster (or indeed Franklin) would have wished, they are responsible for a number of significant differences between British and American spelling. They include the following:

British	**American**
honour, neighbour	honor, neighbor
traveller, waggon	traveler, wagon
fibre, theatre	fiber, theater
defence, offence	defense, offense
axe, plough	ax, plow
tyre	tire
storey	story
gaol	jail
judgement	judgment
mediaeval, oestrogen	medieval, estrogen
masque, cheque	mask, check

Some of the above spellings are also now acceptable in Britain (notably *wagon, estrogen, medieval, judgment*). Some of Webster's other changes (such as *music, physic* instead of *musick, physick*) developed in Modern British English independently.

While such changes in spelling might appear trivial to some, they are in fact extremely significant in terms of the standardization of American English. Most linguists would agree that consistent spelling is an important indicator of a standard dialect, and thus these spelling reforms lie at the heart of the claim to a different dialect (some Americans even declare it a language) from British English.

Apart from in spelling, other changes that naturally grew out of differences between the political systems of the two countries were reflected in vocabulary, such as *congress(ional), governor, gubernatorial, sheriff, caucus, presidential, senate, assembly, primary*. While many, though not all, of these words feature in British English also, they differ in their meaning in that context, and naturally there is also a difference in the frequency of use of such terms.

Since the colonies and then the United States of America have been in existence there have been almost 400 years of contact with English. There is no doubt that the varieties of English spoken in the USA today are just that, varieties of *English*. American English is not a separate language, despite the wishes of a number of observers, particularly those writing after the American War of Independence. H. L. Mencken, an American journalist, was even moved to write a work entitled *The American Language* (1919), clearly wearing his political allegiance on the sleeve of his book. But serious dialectologists have no doubt whatsoever that even today the high degree of mutual intelligibility and shared development make British and American English close dialect cousins, despite all of the political, social and cultural differences that exist between the two countries.

7.3   Language Variation in the United States

7.3.1   *Uniformity and Diversity in Early American English*

It has been reported in numerous histories of the English language that from very early on commentators remarked on the uniformity of American English in contrast to British English. Somewhat perplexingly, however, commentators (often the *same* commentators) also remark on the emerging varieties of American English. There is no doubt today that, in comparison with British English, American English is remarkably uniform. And there is likewise also no doubt that the various regions of American English have dialect features that clearly set them off from each other. So just how is it that this seeming paradox has existed since the beginning of American English, and can it be the case that diversity and uniformity coexist in this way?

Until the turn of the century the vast majority of immigrants to America were of northern European, and particularly British, origin. In the years before World War I eastern and south-eastern Europe became the primary sources of immigration to America. Since World War II South America has provided the greatest number of immigrants.

The dialects that developed in America are generally much more homogeneous than they are in Britain. This is partly because of the high degree of physical, geographical and social mobility possible during the settlement process, and partly because of the social mobility that contrasts with generations of relatively static class structure in Britain.

7.3.2 *Regional Dialect Divisions in American English*

There are still a large number of documented regional dialects in the United States, however. Three major dialect studies have attempted to delimit the dialect boundaries of the United States. These are the traditional dialect studies that were part of the *Linguistic Atlas of the United States*, Carver's (1987) discussion of lexical variation, based on the research of the *Dictionary of American Regional English*, and Labov's (1989) studies of phonological variation in the United States leading to TELSUR, the still on-going telephone survey of American dialects. We will take a brief look at each of these in turn, and discuss the ways in which they have influenced our thinking about dialects in American English.

Before there were any dialect surveys in the United States, it was generally believed that there were two main dialects, Yankee (i.e. northern) and southern. The results of the work of dialect geographers who collected their data in the 1930s and 1940s, however, suggested a three-way division in dialect areas: Northern, Midland and Southern, with the Midland area subdivided into a North Midland and a South Midland area (as shown in map 7.2).

7.3.2.1 *The Lexicon*

This division in the dialects was based largely on lexical differences amongst the different regions. The following brief list gives some indication of the areal distribution of particular lexical tokens that dialect geographers found diagnostic of particular regions:

(a)   *pail* (Northern, North Midland); *bucket* (Southern Midland);
(b)   *eave spout, eaves trough, eave troft* (Northern); *gutter, guttering, spouts, spouting* (Midland); *water trough* (Northern, Southern);
(c)   *teeter board* (Northern); *teeter totter* (Northern, Midland); *see saw* (Southern, Midland); *ridy-horse, hickey horse* (Southern);
(d)   *night crawler, angleworm* (Northern); *fishing worm, fish worm* (Midland); *redworm* (South Midland), *bait worm* (Southern, Midland);
(e)   *crick* (Northern, North Midland), *brook* (Northern); *run* (North Midland); *creek* (Midland); *branch* (Southern, South Midland);
(f)   *faucet* (Northern); *spicket, spigot, hydrant* (Southern, Midland).

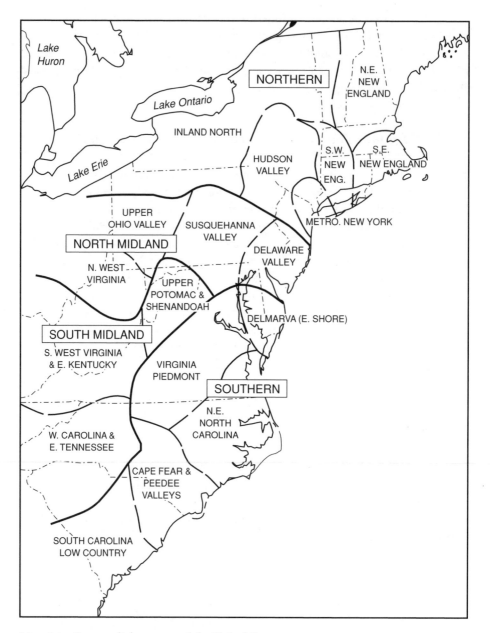

Map 7.2   Eastern dialect areas of the United States
Source: Kurath (1949), p. 75.

Another recent work on dialect boundaries has concentrated on lexical variants, and is based on data collected in the 1960s and 1970s for the *Dictionary of
American Regional English* (DARE). Carver's work on redefining dialect boundaries used a new mapping method referred to as *dialect layering*. His results show

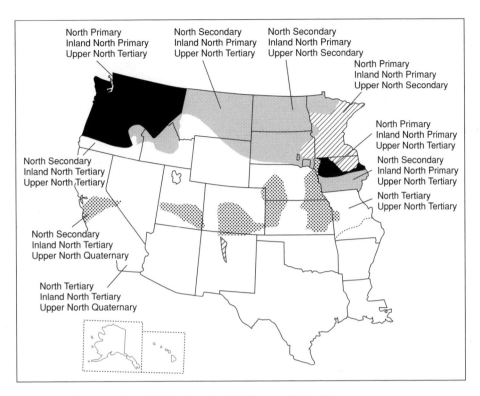

North Primary
Inland North Primary
Upper North Tertiary

North Secondary
Inland North Primary
Upper North Tertiary

North Secondary
Inland North Primary
Upper North Secondary

North Primary
Inland North Primary
Upper North Secondary

North Primary
Inland North Primary
Upper North Tertiary

North Secondary
Inland North Primary
Upper North Tertiary

North Tertiary
Upper North Tertiary

North Secondary
Inland North Tertiary
Upper North Tertiary

North Secondary
Inland North Tertiary
Upper North Quaternary

North Tertiary
Inland North Tertiary
Upper North Quaternary

Map 7.3 An example of dialect layering in Western United States
Source: Carver (1987), p. 243.

that there is some validity to the old North/South split, of which people were aware even before dialect geography. Carver's primary dialect areas are split into two, not three, divisions, Northern and Southern, while these major divisions each contain one subdivision (Lower Northern and Upper Southern), as opposed to the Northern, (North and South) Midland and Southern split of the traditional dialect geographers. Unlike the Linguistic Atlas researchers, Carver was able with the aid of computers to cover the whole of the country much more thoroughly in his research. This led him to find, for example, that there is a significant concentration of Northeast dialect features in the Pacific Northwest and that there is little regional dialect overlay in the English spoken in the Southwest. A major finding of Carver's study is that there are *primary*, *secondary* and *tertiary* regional dialect areas in the United States and that these correspond loosely to primary, secondary and tertiary settlement areas (see map 7.3). It is fairly straightforward to assume that regional dialect features will persist in areas of the longest and most stable settlement, but they will be less evident where the sources of immigration are mixed, where settlement is most recent and the population is most mobile.

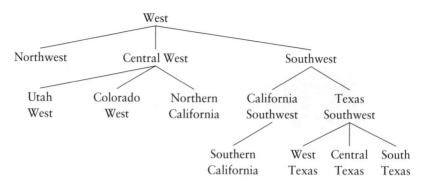

Figure 7.1 An example of dialect layering in the West, hierarchically represented
Source: Carver (1987), p. 243.

This division would link well with patterns of social networking, where more traditional, static and close-knit communities have dense and multiplex networks that reinforce and maintain local behaviours (including dialect use). By contrast, less traditional, socially and geographically more mobile groups evince loose and more diffuse and uniplex networks, which do not act as norm-enforcing mechanisms (see figure 7.1).

Such studies have been criticized by linguists for concentrating on lexical tokens, which linguists regard as the most superficial of linguistic levels. However, in a recent study of a completely different kind, which concentrates exclusively on pronunciation distinctions, Labov (1989) found patterns of change that would corroborate the basic dialect distribution found by Carver (see section 7.3.2.3 below).

7.3.2.2 *Phonology: Consonants*

With reference to the sound system in particular, the dialect geographers involved in mapping out the *Linguistic Atlas of the United States* found a number of regional variations in pronunciation, including the following consonantal phenomena (cf. Conklin and Lourie, 1983: 83–4):

Feature	Example	Pronounced	Region
intervocalic /s/ vs. /z/	*greasy*	[grisi] [grizi]	Northern Midland, Southern
/ð/ vs. /θ/	*with, without*	[wið] [wiθ]	Northern Midland
/hw/ > /w/	*whether, weather*		New York City, North Midland

/h/ deleted before /iu/	*human, Hugh*		Eastern United States, especially New York City
/l/ deleted before /p/, /b/, /f/	*help, bulb,* *wolf, gulf*		Southern
/r/ deleted after vowels	*park, car,* *sister*	[paːk] [kaː]	Eastern New England, New York City, plantation- influenced South

Differences in grammar were also found, though they were very few and largely confined to morphological variations, as the linguistic geographers tended to concentrate mostly on lexicon.

7.3.2.3 *Phonology: Vowels*

Labov's findings indicate that there are three major systematic changes in progress in the American vowel system, on account of a push–pull effect which manifests itself in two different vowel rotations. These are referred to as the **Northern Cities Vowel Rotation** and the **Southern Vowel Shift**.

The Northern Cities Vowel Rotation

This change constitutes a rotation of the place of articulation of the vowels, in which the long low vowels are moving forward and upward and the short vowels are moving downward and backward (figure 7.2). Thus the /ɔ/ in *coffee* is beginning to sound more like the /a/ in *father*. The low vowel in *pop*, on the other hand, is moving toward the /æ/ in *bat*, which itself then moves up to sound like the /ɛ/ in *bed*. The /ɛ/ then moves backward toward the /ʌ/ vowel in *cup*, which in turn moves backward.

This vowel shift or rotation starts in Western New England, goes west into northern Pennsylvania, northern Ohio, Indiana, Illinois, Missouri and Wisconsin.

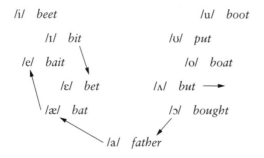

Figure 7.2   Northern Cities Vowel Shift

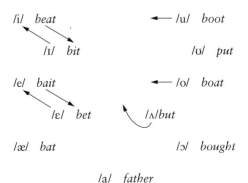

Figure 7.3   Southern Vowel Shift

It is centred on the larger cities, with the younger speakers in the larger cities such as Buffalo, Chicago, Cleveland and Detroit reflecting the most advanced stages of the shift. Phonological change that is observable in such a way (that is, inter-generationally) is valuable and rare, as sound change is usually a function of much greater lengths of time.

The Southern Vowel Shift

The Southern Vowel Shift is very different from the Northern Cities Rotation. In it, the short front vowels (*bed*, *bid*) are shifting: /ɛ/ is shifting upward and developing an off-glide, as happened with the long vowels of English; thus *bed* is pronounced as /beɪd/. The short high front vowel /ɪ/, when it changes, tends to shift downwards. The long front vowels in *beat* and *late* are shifting backward and down, and the back vowels are moving forward, as in figure 7.3. Both of these shifts are also summarized in Wolfram (1991: 85–8).

An important consequence of the radical difference in the nature of these vowel rotations is that the Northern and Southern dialects are now diverging from each other. The Southern Shift is more advanced in more traditional, core areas of the South, and is more prominent in rural than in metropolitan areas. This is because southern cities have experienced immigration from other dialect areas, while this is less commonly the case in rural areas. As we saw above, it is also the major metropolitan areas in the North that are the focus of the Northern Cities Shift.

The third major dialect division is in those areas which are not part of either of the two shifts discussed above. This dialect area is characterized by the relative stability of /æ/ and the merger of the low back vowels /ɔ/ and /a/ (as in *cot*, *caught*, *hawk*, *hock*). For this reason it is referred to as the Low Back Merger area. This area is very similar to the traditional Midland dialect area, with two major centres. One is close to Boston in eastern New England and stretches all the way to the northern border, but not too far south. The second area is in

Pennsylvania up towards the northern boundary of the Midland area east of the Mississippi River. The western boundary of this region encompasses most of the American West. There is a transitional area through Wisconsin, Minnesota, Iowa, Kansas and Arkansas down through southern New Mexico, and Arizona. The Low Back Vowel Merger is not a metropolitan feature in the West, and neither Los Angeles nor San Francisco features it.

Labov has further extended his work on the vowel changes with a large-scale study conducted as a telephone survey (TELSUR). His findings to date suggest that currently the United States can be divided into three dialect areas, the North, Midland and South (along similar boundaries to those Carver described as North, Lower North, Upper South, and South) but with a further area which he regards as the West (see map 7.4). Current maps can be accessed at http://ling.upenn.edu/phonoatlas.

While all of these different methods have turned up some differences in their findings, the major distinction still remains, that is that there is still validity in the North/South divide, which looms so large in the history and the national consciousness of the United States.

7.3.3 Social and Ethnic Dialects

We have up until this point discussed dialect mostly from the point of view of geography, but regional provenance is only one of the demographic characteristics that affect the way people speak. Others include social class, ethnicity and gender. Class boundaries have always been more important in Britain than in the United States. We saw in the previous chapter that the use of RP correlates strongly with social class in Britain; while the few are brought up speaking this prestige variant, others aspire to RP as they rise through elite educational institutions and then through society itself. There is no equivalent to RP in the United States, although the film media in the first half of the twentieth century attempted to emulate this variety: one has only to watch American films from the 1930s to hear a form of speech that strikes one as upper-class and mildly British. There do, however, persist upper-class variants of English in America that can smack – to a middle- or lower-class listener – of elitism or snobbery. We might say this of the language of the New England elite, specifically of long-established 'old Bostonian' (the Boston Brahmin) families, who do not flap 't' into 'd' in words like *better, letter, butter*. Elsewhere one might point to the classic Virginian and Charlestonian variants (especially the /r/-less variants described earlier in this chapter) as the language of an older 'cultivated' populace, traces of which can, however, still be heard in the language of the region in general. These pronunciations, as we mentioned above, may be due in part at least to the closer ties that these areas had with Britain, and with conscious exonormative behaviour.

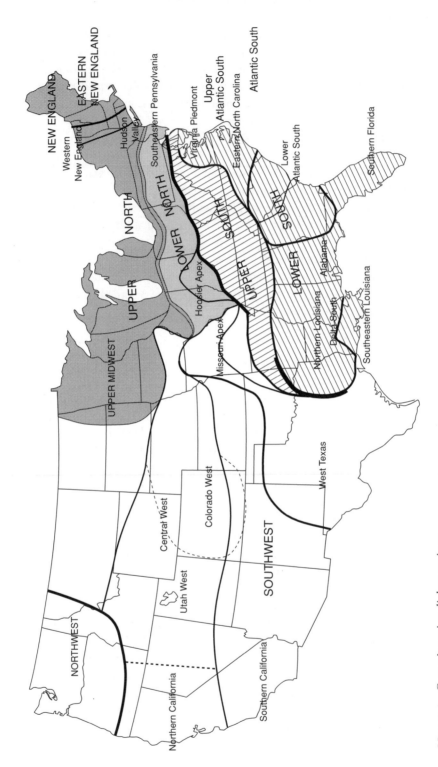

Map 7.4 Carver's major dialect regions

But in America today, class usually only comes into the picture in discussing stigmatized, rather than prestige, factors. The classic New Yorker's *Toidy Toid Street* is simultaneously a marker of lower class. And non-standard grammatical forms are particularly associated with lower-class speakers. Multiple negatives, such as *I don't know nothing* are highly marked and stigmatized.

7.3.3.1   Social Class and Language Change

We refer to forms that are clearly associated with prestige, such as standard 'school book' English, as carrying **overt** prestige, while those that carry prestige in the local culture, even though they do not conform to national prestige norms, are regarded as bearing **covert** prestige. Thus, for example, *Toidy Toid Street*, while carrying negative overt prestige, may indeed bear considerable covert prestige in a local New York youth gang.

Modern sociolinguistic studies have been particularly interested in the relationship between social class and language change. We discriminate between **changes from below** and **changes from above** the level of consciousness. Frequently, phonological change is change from below, and reflects a subconscious shift towards particular articulations. Most of the changes involved in the Northern Cities Chain Shift and the Southern Sound Shift are changes from below. By contrast, the development of non-rhotic dialects in New England, Virginia and South Carolina that we have just mentioned can perhaps be considered examples of change from above, to the extent that they involve the conscious emulation of norms of linguistic behaviour (but see also the discussion of /r/-lessness under African-American Vernacular English in section 7.3.3.3 below).

7.3.3.2   Ethnicity

It is difficult to be exact about the precise contribution of ethnicity to variation in language especially in a country that is largely made up of immigrants. Ethnicity can be closely linked to class, but also to religion and other personal characteristics. Ethnicity – whether one speaks of a difference in accent, vocabulary, or even syntax – can contribute to the formation of different language varieties. Thus, most Americans will be familiar with some aspect of such variants as New York Jewish English, Puerto Rican English, Chicano English, German English, African-American Vernacular English, etc., and would be able to imitate at least the accent of one or more of these.

There is no doubt that ethnicity does affect linguistic behaviour, but it is often more difficult to observe and measure than the effect of class or regional provenance. Some more obvious forms of influence associated with ethnicity may stem from the fact that a group is, or was at one point, bilingual. Thus, for example, Hispanic American English varieties frequently feature 'borrowed' Spanish characteristics.

More difficult to observe, though most definitely present, is the substratum effect that ethnicity can have on later generations of speakers of English belonging to that group. Labov (1972) cites the example of the raising of vowels in words like *coffee* and *dog* in New York Italian and Jewish English as an example of an ethnic substratum effect. Rather than simply borrowing Italian or Jewish vowels, however, the raising occurred when second-generation Jewish and Italian immigrants structurally hypercorrected their pronunciation of these sounds, articulating them higher in the mouth in reaction to the lower pronunciation of their parents. Since the second-generation immigrants wanted to assimilate and not be marked directly as Jewish or Italian like their non-native-speaker parents, they subconsciously adopted this higher pronunciation. Thus ethnicity played a role in this language change, but it was not the result of direct borrowing from Italian or Yiddish.

We shall explore the question of the role of ethnicity in linguistic behaviour as it pertains to variation in American English in section 7.3.3.3 below.

The ethnic community can also display features that are not related to the previous language background, but to local community norms; that is, they might identify more or less with their local community. This kind of convergence is typical of the language of many immigrant ethnic groups, and, in the long run, represents the scenario for most ethnic groups – especially for those who do not constitute large enough population groups to maintain a separate linguistic identity, but also for larger groups that are linguistically (and sometimes physically) very similar to others of their environment. Leaving aside the Pennsylvania Dutch – a closed community – we might cite the Germans and Scandinavians of the Midwest as an example of the latter. The issue of convergence and/or divergence is central to the question of African-American Vernacular English, which we examine in the following section.

7.3.3.3   *African-American Vernacular English*

African-American Vernacular English is the term used for the variants of English spoken by some, though by no means all, African-Americans. This variety or set of varieties of English has been the subject of intense research (and often intensely controversial debate) since the 1960s. Important features of the discussion of AAVE centre around its origins, its relation to other American dialects, and the question of whether it is converging towards, or diverging from, mainstream Anglo varieties of American English.

There are two main theories of its origins: the Anglicist and Creolist hypotheses. According to those who subscribe to the Anglicist theory, most distinctive features of African-American English can be traced back to dialects of English in Britain. Any features of AAVE that cannot be traced to English are then credited to the African languages spoken by the slaves in the early stages of their forced migration to America, or to the unique social circumstances in which they lived once they got there.

The Creolist hypothesis, by contrast, holds that African-American Vernacular English is the result of a creole that developed from the contact between a number of African languages and English. The argument is that slaves were separated from speakers of the same African languages from the outset, and therefore needed to develop another language as their primary means of communication. Living away from mainstream white dialect speakers, according to this theory, produced the right conditions for creolization. As social conditions improved, and African-American speakers gained access to mainstream models of American English, their language decreolized, shifting towards the mainstream linguistic norms and leaving only a substrate of linguistic features that indicate its creole origin (see diagram and discussion of the typical development of Creoles in chapter 1). Other evidence for the Creolist theory is the similarity between some features of AAVE and the Gullah or 'Geechee' creole spoken on the Sea Islands of Georgia and South Carolina.

While the Creolist hypothesis has long had its supporters, it would appear that in recent years opinions have been changing again, and linguists are split on the question of the creole origins of AAVE. In any case, most linguists would agree that AAVE is a subsystem of English that incorporates many of the rules of English of the Southern United States, but which nevertheless has a distinct set of phonological and syntactic rules. These rules would appear to be similar now to those of other dialects, but they still show traces of derivation from an earlier creole, particularly in the aspectual system (cf. Labov, 1982).

The unique features of AAVE have been summarized by Fasold (1981) as follows:

(1)   devoicing of voiced stops in stressed syllables, e.g. [lɪt] for *lid*; [sæk] for *sag*;

(2)   absence of -*s*/-*es* in third person singular, present tense:

   he sit for *he sits*; *she choose* for *she chooses*;

(3)   general absence of -*s*/-*es* in plurals (not just of weights and measures):

   four book for *four books*; *some dress* for *some dresses*;

(4)   remote *been* (i.e. used to refer to something that happened far in the past):

   I been seen him a long time ago.
   You been told her that.

(5)   absence of possessive -*s*/-*es*:

   man hat for *man's hat*; *Bill house* for *Bill's house*;

(6)   reduction of final consonant clusters followed by a vowel:

  lif' up for *lift up*; *bussing* for *busting*;

(7)   absence of *is* forms of the copula:

  She nice for *She's nice*; *He in the kitchen* for *He's in the kitchen*;

(8)   use of habitual or distributive *be*:

  Sometimes my ears be itching.
  She don't usually be there.

Although most commentators would accept these features as unique to AAVE, there are others who would question whether there are in fact individual features that are unique to Black English, while still other linguists suggest that the list of unique features is not even complete. We also ought to be aware that we have been discussing African-American Vernacular English as if it were one variety, but in fact there is regional and social variation, as one would expect, though there is a core of features that unites speakers of AAVE across the United States.

While we mentioned the controversy about the origins of AAVE at the beginning of this section, we have not yet addressed the most recent controversy surrounding this variety, the question whether AAVE is developing in such a way that it is **converging** with or **diverging** from other vernacular varieties of English (discussed comprehensively in Butters, 1989). Labov (1985: 1) asserted on the basis of his work in Philadelphia that the speech of African-Americans was developing in an independent direction from that of white Americans, and suggested that this was a result of the difference in economic status between African-Americans and whites, the socio-economic gap increasing between the two groups. Linguistically he based his argument on a couple of features found in AAVE, including *be done* in its resultative sense (*I'll be done put so many holes in him he'll wish he wouldna said it*), and the lively past time narrative use of *-s*, similar to the historical present of other varieties of English. Bailey and Maynor (1989) suggest that another feature contributing to the divergence theory is the use of habitual *be* in black speakers in the south. They propose that this form is developing a unique use along with the *-ing* suffix of verbs amongst younger, usually urban speakers of AAVE, as in *They be having on lipstick and everything*; *Her mamma . . . be getting her clothes and stuff*, thus increasing the difference of the verb-aspect system of AAVE from that of other vernacular varieties.

Such evidence for divergence is based largely on qualitative, not quantitative, differences between the linguistic systems of younger, urban speakers of AAVE and older, rural ones. But it has been questioned by a number of sociolinguists, most notably Wolfram (1987), who calls for more evidence. Other linguists have provided evidence for convergence between black and white dialects, in order to counter the divergence claim. This led Bailey and Maynor (1989) to distinguish between changes that were significant and those that were not. They argued that the evidence for divergence comes from more modern changes that have a much greater effect on the system of AAVE than those features which are regarded as evidence for convergence. Many sociolinguists remain unconvinced however. They suggest that much more important evidence for any sort of divergence is Labov's observation that black Americans are not participating in the major sound shifts delineated above (Wolfram, 1991: 116). In the meantime, however, it would appear that AAVE will persist as an ethnically marked dialect of American English, and it does not seem to be undergoing any major structural changes.

Considering the fact that there have been over 350 years of contact between African-Americans and other Americans in North America, and also considering the fact that so much contemporary work has been done on the nature of AAVE, it is surprising how infrequently linguists have considered the effect of AAVE on other varieties of American English.

In a recent article Feagin (1997) discusses the possible influence of African-American English (AAE) on Southern States English as spoken by the white community. She suggests that there are three features which may have been influenced by AAE: the lack of post-vocalic /r/, the 'southern drawl' and the use of falsetto intonation.

Feagin's strongest argument is for the influence of AAE on /r/-lessness, which is supported by a number of different types of evidence. Firstly, she questions the received wisdom (which we have discussed above) about the source of the widespread /r/-lessness in Southern States English, namely, that it developed both in New England, Virginia and the Deep South because of continued contact between the plantation owners and England through trade and because they sent their sons to be educated in English schools. While she concedes that many plantation owners did send their children to school in England (even some of their daughters), she has found that this practice was in no way as widespread as has been assumed.

Whatever its source, she points out that /r/-lessness was firmly established in the Deep South by the 1860s, and it was taken as far west as east Texas and was established in the South as a prestige pattern wherever it spread. By contrast, /r/-lessness did not spread out from its base in New England. The major difference between conditions in non-rhotic areas in the North and those in the South was, Feagin contends, the large African-American population in the latter as compared with the former area.

Feagin believes that demographic factors are very important in this argument. Until the middle of the seventeenth century white indentured labourers outnumbered black slaves in the south. In the late seventeenth century the number of black slaves increased at a rapid rate, coming for the most part directly from Africa, and eventually overtaking the white population. The question is whether English was *swamped* by an African creole-like speech at this point, or whether newer African-Americans learned their English from older blacks who had almost completely assimilated to the white speech of the plantations. In either case, their speech was most probably /r/-less, as the majority of languages spoken by the African slaves had linguistic structures that, for one reason or another, did not support the pronunciation of post-vocalic /r/.

Moreover, we recall from our discussion of the settlement of the South above that not all white speakers came from /r/-less dialect areas of Britain; indeed, many came from Scots and Irish backgrounds, with very strongly constricted /r/. They could therefore not reliably have been the source for the spread of /r/-lessness. For these reasons Feagin claims that the /r/-lessness which developed in the speech of whites came about as a result of contact with AAE.

Southern drawl, which Feagin defines as 'the elaboration of vowels which interacts with a wide intonational drop', is another feature that she suggests is connected with the long association between the white and the black communities. Feagin is convinced that in this instance AAE intonation is related to its creole origin, and that it could in fact be a question of substratal influence here. The same is also suggested for the use of falsetto, used most notably amongst African-Americans, but also found in the speech of working- and upper-class teenagers in the American South. Women apparently use falsetto to express pleasure and surprise in greetings, while men use it for emphasis when talking about such topics as football and hunting, or when telling jokes. Feagin maintains that falsetto may have been brought to the South by Africans, maintained by African-Americans and borrowed into some areas of white English.

The reason for this borrowing, Feagin claims, might be tied up with the notion of covert prestige. While southern middle- and upper-class whites were not completely isolated at the time in question, their lives were nevertheless more rural than urban, and it was not so easy to meet up with other whites. Documentary evidence indicates that white children in the South before the Civil War mingled relatively freely with black slaves and their children, often having a single black slave of the same age that they kept their entire lives.

After the period of slavery, African-Americans made up over half the population in South Carolina, Louisiana and Mississippi, close to half the population of Georgia, Alabama, Florida and Virginia, and between 30 and 40 per cent of the population in North Carolina, Texas and the District of Columbia. Many of the middle- and upper-class whites in these areas, but most particularly children, had extensive contacts with African-Americans, and Feagin (pp. 136–7) cites many first-hand accounts of this.

The point is that this intimate contact with children began at an impression-able age, and there are records from the nineteenth and the first part of the twentieth century of white middle- and upper-class parents expressing serious concern that their children's speech was 'too' close to that of black children, particularly in phonological and morphosyntactic features. While there is less information about the contact between AAE speakers and white working-class children, Feagin assumes they may have worked side by side with slaves and have been influenced by their speech.

In any case, Feagin believes that the most important point of contact was between African-Americans and white children. Citing Trudgill's work on covert prestige (1974) she points out that children can be great facilitators of language change, and not necessarily in the direction of local prestige forms. She points out that conditions in the South were also consistent with white children acquiring features of AAE.

Feagin is not the only person to have suggested that AAE may have had influence on American English in general. Wolfram and Schilling-Estes (1998: 178) point out that contact between black and white speakers for generations may have resulted in each group picking up features from the other. Wolfram (1974) showed that Anglo-Americans and African-Americans in the Deep South both use copula deletion (e.g. *She my friend*; see table of AAVE features above). However, what is remarkable is that despite the fact that white speakers prob-ably borrowed this feature from African-Americans, they do not use it in exactly the same way, suggesting that even when there is borrowing amongst ethnic groups, subtle patterns of differentiation can still be maintained. Thus features might persist or even spread in the community, but their distribution or fre-quency may change at the same time.

In the next section we look at the issue of the persistence of dialect features in a different way, by examining how change is resisted in traditional dialects.

7.3.3.4 *Traditional Dialects and the Resistance to Change*

Since the World Wars there has been considerable change in the types of popula-tion movement in the United States. Internationally, the source of immigration has shifted considerably; while there are still new immigrants from the traditional source countries Ireland, Britain, Germany, etc., in the last forty or fifty years the majority of immigrants have come from Mexico, Puerto Rico, most Central and South American countries, Vietnam and Cambodia. In the past twenty years there has also been a marked increase in the South Asian population of the United States, and most recently there has been immigration from the countries of the former Yugoslavia.

On a national level, movement patterns have also changed from those that were observed during the original settlement of the United States. A notable example is that, from the end of World War I, considerable numbers of African-Americans moved from the South, either along the East Coast to cities such as Washington, Philadelphia and New York, or inland to the cities of the Midwest, particularly Chicago, Cleveland and Detroit.

Such changes have had important consequences for the character of American English. For example, the large groups of Hispanic Americans found in Texas, Florida and California (as well as in major cities in the rest of the United States) have now developed their own varieties of English, influenced particularly by Spanish. While there were always large numbers of Spanish speakers in America, it is only really in the last forty years or so that Hispanic American varieties have been recognized. This phenomenon is similar to the development of African-American identity: African-Americans moving from the South to the cities of the North took with them southern dialect features, which eventually became associated with them as an ethnic group in the North. Consequently, these features have shifted from being regional to ethnic markers.

A further movement of people that is worthy of mention in this chapter is the massive influx of Northerners and Midlanders to the southern United States since World War I, and particularly in the last couple of decades. With the general availability of air-conditioning, which allows people to live and work more comfortably in the hot southern summers, the southern United States began to attract many Northern and Midland Americans who were looking for employment and improved living and working conditions. This in-migration has resulted in dialect mixing on a grand scale in places such as Houston, Texas, Miami, Florida, and the Raleigh–Durham–Chapel Hill area of North Carolina (known as the Research Triangle). This is another example of the phenomenon known as dialect swamping, and it is recognized as a threat to traditional dialects, as increased contact between people from different areas is known to lead to dialect levelling, as we have observed throughout this work. Such large in-migrations coupled with the increase in mobility in the population in general have been observed to create conditions of **dialect endangerment** (Wolfram and Schilling-Estes, 1998).

In a paradigm study of the dialect of the Outer Banks in North Carolina, a series of barrier islands off the south-east coast of the state, Wolfram and Schilling-Estes concentrated on the dialect of the island of Ocracoke. This small island, which was traditionally a fishing island, has increasingly expanded its tourist trade to the extent that it is swamped with tourists from the mainland from the spring to the late autumn. The island is renowned for its traditional dialect, which some have even claimed contains relics of the Elizabethan English of the earliest inhabitants; this dialect has been maintained on Ocracoke because of its insular character – it has been effectively separated from the mainland for hundreds of years, connected only by boat traffic. The Ocracoke dialect features a number of distinctive local words and expressions such as those in the list below (not exhaustive):

catawampus	in a diagonal position, crooked, not square: *The boxes in the General Store were piled up all catawampus.*
fladget	a piece of something; used mostly in reference to food or wounds: *He cut a fladget of skin off his finger.*
dingbatter	a non-islander.
meehonkey	a local version of hide-and-seek.
mommuck	to harass or bother: *He got a mommuckin' from his brothers.*
of the morning/ evening, etc.	in the morning(s): *We would go hunting of the morning.*
quamish	sick to the stomach: *Felt quamished on the ferry.*

One of the major phonological features of Ocracokers' dialect is the pronunciation of the diphthong [aɪ] as something like [ɔɪ], as in 'hoi toide' for 'high tide' (giving Ocracokers their nickname 'Hoi toiders'). Another characteristic feature of pronunciation is [æɪ] or [ɛɪ] for [aʊ] (pronouncing *house* something like 'hice' for example).

The swamping of Ocracoke with visitors from the outside, coupled with the fact that a number of Ocracokers have left the island in search of greater prosperity, has led to the loss of the traditional dialect on the island. What is interesting from a sociolinguistic point of view, however, is that dialect features are not being lost at the same rate throughout the system. It would appear that features such as [æɪ] or [ɛɪ] for [aʊ], which are not salient markers of Ocracoke identity, are being lost at a much faster rate than features such as [ɔɪ] for [aɪ], which is a feature that is so symbolic of island identity that it has given the Ocracokers one of their nicknames. On the basis of this Ocracoke study and a related one on a post-insular community on Smith Island in Virginia, Wolfram and Schilling-Estes have discovered that symbolically important features resist loss, and in some cases even expand in their usage as traditional dialects die out. This would seem to suggest that as traditional dialects are threatened by incoming influences they undergo a period of *focusing*; that is, the burden of identity marking is concentrated on a restricted number of salient symbolic features, while less salient features are lost much sooner. Such studies may well indicate a particular way forward for traditional American dialects, though they cannot, of course, predict which features will change and when.

American English is not a monolithic language when it is examined within America. To the outside world, it is more monolithic – representative of American culture (in the broadest definition of the word). America and American English have played a large part in the emergence of English as a world language, the subject of the next chapter.

Suggested Readings

Carver, Craig M. (1987) *American Regional Dialects: A Word Geography*. Ann Arbor, MI: University of Michigan Press

Cassidy, Frederic G. (1982) Geographical Variation of English in the United States. In: Bailey, Richard W. and Görlach, Manfred (eds) (1982) *English as a World Language*. Ann Arbor, MI: University of Michigan Press, 177–209.

Fasold, Ralph (1981) The Relation between Black and White Speech in the South. *American Speech*, **56**, 163–89.

Kurath, Hans (1949) *A Word Geography of the Eastern United States*. Ann Arbor, MI: University of Michigan.

Labov, William (1991) The Three Dialects of English. In: Eckert, Penelope (ed.) *New Ways of Analyzing Sound Change*. New York: Academic Press, pp. 1–44.

Wolfram, Walt and Natalie Schilling-Estes (1998) *American English*. Oxford: Blackwell.

8 World-Wide English

Timeline: World-Wide English

1600	British East India Company founded
1605	Barbados, West Indies, claimed as English colony
1606	Virginia Company of London sends 120 colonists to Virginia
1607	Jamestown founded
1621	English attempt to colonize Newfoundland and Nova Scotia
1627	Charles I grants charter to the Guiana Company
1633	English trading post established in Bengal
1637	English traders established in Canton
1646	English occupy the Bahamas
1649	Cromwell invades Ireland
1655	English capture Jamaica
1663	Charles II grants charter to Royal African Company
1668	British East India Company gains control of Bombay
1684	Bermudas become Crown Colony
1690	Calcutta founded
1707	British land in Acadia, Canada
1710	English South Sea Company founded
1744	Robert Clive arrives at Madras
1759	British take Quebec from the French
1762	British capture Martinique, Grenada, Havana and Manila
1765–1947	British Raj in India
1770	James Cook discovers Botany Bay, Australia
1778	Cook discovers Hawaii
1784	Pitt's India Act: East India Company under government control
1786	Penang ceded to Great Britain
1790	The first penal colony established in Sydney, Australia
1795, 1806	British forces occupy Cape of Good Hope
1800	British capture Malta
1810	British seize Guadeloupe

1811	British occupy Java
1819	British settlement established in Singapore by East India Company
1822	English becomes the official language of the Eastern Cape of South Africa
	Liberia founded – Africa's oldest republic
1824	British take Rangoon, Burma
1832	Britain occupies the Falkland Islands
1840	New Zealand becomes an official colony
1842	Hong Kong ceded to Great Britain
1851	Victoria, Australia, proclaimed separate colony
1852	New constitution for New Zealand
1858	Powers of East India Company transferred to British Crown
1860	Kowloon added to British territories in South-East Asia
1861	British Colony founded in Lagos, Nigeria
1867	Federal Malay States become a Crown Colony
1884	Papua New Guinea becomes British protectorate
1885	Britain establishes protectorate over Northern Bechuanaland, Niger River Region and southern New Guinea, and occupies Port Hamilton, Korea
1886	First Indian National Congress meets
1887	First Colonial Conference opens in London
1888	Cecil Rhodes granted mining rights by King of Matabele
1890	Rhodes becomes Premier of Cape Colony
1893	Uganda united as British protectorate
	USA annexes Hawaii
1895	British South Africa Company territory south of the Zambezi River becomes Rhodesia
1898	America receives Guam and sovereignty over the Philippines
	New Territories leased by Britain from China for 99 years
1900	British capture Bloemfontein, relieve Mafeking, annex Orange Free State and Transvaal and take Pretoria and Johannesburg
	Commonwealth of Australia created
1903	British conquer northern Nigeria
1907	New Zealand becomes a dominion within the British Empire
1908	Union of South Africa established
1916	USA purchases Danish West Indies (Virgin Islands)
1917	USA purchases Dutch West Indies
1919	League of Nations founded
1920	Gandhi emerges as leader of India
	Kenya becomes British colony
1921	First Indian Parliament meets
1945	United Nations founded

1946	Philippines become independent from the United States
1947	India proclaimed independent
1957	Common Market established by Treaty of Rome
	Malaysian independence
1962–75	Uganda, Kenya, Zambia (Northern Rhodesia), Malawi, Malta, Gambia, Southern Rhodesia (Zimbabwe), Guyana, Mauritius, Nigeria, Bahamas, Papua New Guinea all become independent of Great Britain
1989	South Africa desegregated
1997	Hong Kong rule returns to China

8.1 Social and Political History: The Spread of English across the Globe

No one can dispute the fact that in the last fifty years English has become a global language. English is used all around the world by professionals and academics in international encounters; it is often the official language of international and multinational companies and industries; it is the language of the Internet.

According to a British Council *English 2000* press release of 23 March 1995, over 1,400 million people lived in countries where English has official status, and by the year 2000 over 1 billion people for whom English is not their first language will be learning English. Estimates of the numbers of English speakers are difficult to make, however. According to David Crystal (1997a) the cautious estimate is that there are 670 million native or near-native speakers of English; the most extreme estimate is that there are 1,800 million speakers; and the middle-of-the-road estimate is that there are from 1,200 to 1,500 million native or near-native speakers.

The first questions we need to ask here are **how** and **why** English has spread across the globe the way it has. The development can be divided into four (partially overlapping) phases:

(1) In the seventeenth and eighteenth centuries, English spread as a result of **British colonialism**.

(2) In the eighteenth and nineteenth centuries, English spread as the language of British leadership in the Industrial Revolution.

(3) In the late nineteenth and early twentieth centuries, English spread as the language of American economic superiority and political leadership.

(4) In the second half of the twentieth century, English spread as a consequence of American technological domination.

The first two phases of the spread of English have been summed up succinctly by Crystal (1997: 8) as follows:

> British political imperialism had sent English around the globe, during the nineteenth century, so that it was a 'language on which the sun never sets'. During the twentieth century, this world presence was maintained and promoted, almost single-handedly, through the economic supremacy of the new American superpower. And the language behind the US dollar was English.

We will see in the sections that follow that the current position of English as a global language is partly an accident of history. It would seem that English was expanding in the right geographical and technological, political, economic and cultural areas at the right time.

8.1.1 British Colonialism

English spread across the globe originally because it was the language of a world power, first in terms of military might and then in terms of technological and economic superiority. Long before the first phase, in the eleventh century, as we saw in chapter 6, English spread to Scotland partly because of the military escapades of William the Conqueror, and it was maintained there because it was regarded as the language of economic and political opportunity. It spread to Ireland in the twelfth century with the Anglo-Norman troops sent in by Henry II and, crudely stated, it eventually won out in the battle with the indigenous language, Irish, because of British colonialism in the first instance. As we mentioned in chapter 6, the final stage in the anglicization process for Ireland was the act of joining the European Community; the economic benefits which accrued from using English internationally far outstripped any possible advantages of using Irish Gaelic (and linguistic reality would preclude its successful reintroduction in any event).

But in global terms the spread of English did not begin in earnest until the sixteenth century, when the language became a tool of imperial expansion, and ended up by gaining a special place in the history of a significant number of countries. We have already traced the development of English in the United States in chapter 7. There now follows a necessarily brief account of the spread of English in other colonial areas.

8.1.1.1 Canada

John Cabot is said to have given Newfoundland its name in 1497. Canada was eventually settled in the late sixteenth century by farmers, trappers and traders who settled along the Atlantic coast. The French were also present in Canada very early, from 1530, and vied with Britain for domination until they were defeated in Queen Anne's War (1702–13) and the French and Indian War (1754–63), when British rule eventually prevailed. About 6,000 speakers of French were deported from Acadia (modern Nova Scotia) between 1755 and 1758, with most ending up in Louisiana. In their place settlers from New England, then from Ireland, England and Scotland, came to predominate in Nova Scotia. The Canadian population figures also swelled after 1776 when American supporters of Britain fled to escape the newly independent United States, and settled in Nova Scotia and then in the New Brunswick area. Thousands were attracted by the promise of cheap land in Upper Canada (beyond the Great Lakes and north of Montreal) and over 7,000 settlers had moved there by 1785. Over the course of the nineteenth century settlement proceeded westwards, as it did in the United States, eventually reaching the Pacific coast; French-speakers by and large remained in the East, however. As they moved west, settlers came into contact with native Americans across Canada, but English predominated in the end as the language of society. In North America as a whole literacy came with the languages of the settlers, the language of the largest groups dictating the linguistic future of later communities; the French of Quebec remained the main exception to the rule of English in Canada. Canadians, like New Zealanders, tend to define their identity according to what they are not. They do not want to be indistinguishable from their neighbour the United States, and they do not all want to be either English or French Canadians. The role of French in Quebec has until recently been supported by bilingual regulations governing the whole of Canada, but the position of French seems to have been slipping in recent years.

8.1.1.2 *The Caribbean*

The most widely spoken language in the Caribbean is not English, or English-based creoles, but Spanish, and other European languages are also spoken there, reflecting the complex colonial history of the region. Slaves were brought to the Caribbean from West Africa in the early seventeenth century. By the end of the American Civil War, after which slavery was abolished, there were over 4 million slaves in the Caribbean. Language was used as a tool of control in the Caribbean: the slave masters saw language as power, and presumably thought that large enough groups of slaves who spoke the same language could be dangerous or difficult to control. Therefore they implemented a policy of separating slaves with the same native language. This meant that the Africans that were brought to the Caribbean had to develop some means of communicating amongst themselves: they developed creoles, which have become the native language of the majority of speakers from the Caribbean. Literacy was limited in the early period to the languages of the colonizers, notably English and French; slaves were not educated by their masters in any event. As creoles developed and gained societal status, however, some of them came to be literary languages as well. Others, such as Jamaican Creole, have gradually developed more in line with Standard English as their speakers have gained access to education and power. There is usually a continuum of varieties in countries such as Jamaica, from the basilectal (close to pidgin) variety to the acrolectal (near native) variety. However, no creole has gained enough status to be accepted and standardized as a national language. Indeed, Görlach (1997: 18) points out that the diversity and the complex history of the Caribbean have made it very difficult to promote any kind of nation building, and most linguistic standards are exonormative, following London (and perhaps increasingly the United States). While the mesolectal varieties in countries like Jamaica, Barbados and Guyana are used frequently in spoken language, and are beginning to be used in literature, nothing like a standard has been produced in these areas, and creole is generally still stigmatized as 'patois'.

8.1.1.3 *Australia*

The first penal colony was established in Sydney in 1790, twenty years after Captain Cook set foot on Australian soil. Just as we saw in the previous chapter with the debtors who were sent to Georgia, the British government emptied its overcrowded jails by sending prisoners to Australia, over 130,000 by the mid-nineteenth century. By 1850 the population of Australia was 400,000 and by 1900 it was about 4 million (today there are about 18 million inhabitants). The majority of the immigrants came from the British Isles, with the largest proportion coming from London and Ireland, both of which have lent features to the distinctive Australian dialect. Ninety per cent of all immigrants came from Britain and Ireland, which, it has been suggested (Görlach, 1997: 27), might be the reason for the remarkable homogeneity nation-wide in Australia, in contrast to, say, the United States or Canada. However, contact between colonizers and indigenous peoples led to the borrowing of some lexical items referring to animals or cultural implements found only in Australia; otherwise the English of the colonizers was unaffected by language contact. There was no literacy prior to the arrival of the Europeans; thus literacy came to Australia with English. Beyond the linguistic features of the dialects of the colonizers, other features then also developed independently in Australia.

Until the 1940s, RP was promulgated in the media in Australia, but in the last half-century Australian English has come into its own, especially since Australia has emerged as a major power in the South-West Pacific. There is even an *Australian National Dictionary* and the *Macquarie Dictionary*, which have reinforced the status of Australian English. Over the last couple of decades Australian English has also come under strong influence from American English, as cross-Pacific ties have grown, and the vocabulary in particular has shifted accordingly.

Similarly, since World War II there has been increased immigration from a variety of non-English-speaking countries, and a number of these groups, such as the Italians, have developed distinctive ethnically marked varieties of Australian English.

8.1.1.4 New Zealand

Unlike Australia, New Zealand was not settled by convicts, and it was settled much more slowly. There was a European presence from the 1790s onwards, when whalers and traders came to New Zealand, and in 1814 missionaries began their attempts to convert the indigenous Maoris. New Zealand became an official colony only in 1840, when its population of immigrants was approximately 2,100. By 1850 it had reached 25,000 and by 1900 over a quarter of a million people had immigrated to New Zealand. The current population stands at approximately 3.5 million. On the South Island of New Zealand Scottish settlers predominated. New Zealanders are more sympathetic to the British than are the Australians, and they also like to assert their difference from Australians (with whom they are often confused abroad), and in this way have much in common with the Canadians. New Zealanders are also much more inclusive of the indigenous population; this is one reason why the language contains a large number of Maori words, in contrast to Australian English. For example, a potent symbol of New Zealand identity is the 'haka', the verbal battle ritual of the Maori warrior which the All Blacks, the New Zealand national rugby team, perform to the terror of their opponents at the beginning of each international game. On the other hand, although a number of lexical items have come into New Zealand English from US English, there is greater antipathy towards American English – and American cultural influence in general – than in Australia. As in the case of Australia, however, literacy came to New Zealand with the colonizers.

8.1.1.5 South Africa

There were already Dutch colonial settlements on the Cape of Good Hope in 1653, and British interest did not begin until the Napoleonic Wars (from 1795 on), when an expeditionary force established British control in 1806. True settlement began in 1820 when 5,000 Englishmen were given land on the Eastern Cape. By 1822 English had become the official language of the region, and attempts were made to try to anglicize the unwilling Afrikaans-speaking population, who were in the great majority. Large settlements were founded in the 1850s and 1860s, especially in Natal; after gold and diamond mining were established in the Witwatersrand area in the 1870s, there was a huge influx of Europeans into the area. By the end of the nineteenth century there were half a million immigrants in southern Africa, most of whom spoke English.

Eventually a homogeneous dialect grew up in the area, somewhat similar to Australian English in character. Afrikaans-speakers, the majority, used English as a second language, developing their own variety of English, which they took with them on the Great Trek north to escape rule by the British in 1836. Black South Africans also developed their own varieties of English, influenced by their first languages and by the fact that most had learned English as a second language originally from the missionaries. The significant population of Indian immigrants who began to arrive from 1860 also adopted this variety of English.

But English continued to be a minority language in South Africa. In 1996 fewer than 8 per cent of the population of 42 million spoke English as a native language; Afrikaans was the language of the white majority. Each language in Africa came to symbolize different things. To the blacks, Afrikaans symbolized government authority and the repression of apartheid; the native languages were disparaged by all whites to some extent, but particularly by the Afrikaners. By the same token, the use of English symbolized – in the government's view – both protest and the quest for self-determination, while for the blacks it represented a way to give their grievances an international voice. But English was also seen as the language of modernization and opportunity, so that many Afrikaners also came to be bilingual in English and Afrikaans for economic reasons. This led to the development of a continuum of dialects, which ranged from those strongly coloured by Afrikaans to those which were near RP-accented English. The development of literacy in South Africa then parallels the spread of English and Afrikaans in general. There was no native tradition of literacy when the Dutch arrived, and the development of literary Afrikaans and English was tied to levels of immigration – once enough English-speakers had settled in the country, there were two viable literary languages. The promotion of one or the other was therefore dependent on region, population mix, and governmental regulation (e.g., by means of educational policies).

The constitution of South Africa in 1993 named eleven languages as official in South Africa, English and Afrikaans among them. This extremely complex situation has inevitably led to the use of English in modern South Africa as a lingua franca: a telling statistic is the fact that almost 90 per cent of all speeches in the new South African parliament were given in English. However, it is likely that, as in India, there will be a three-language formula in South Africa, centred around Afrikaans, English and regional native African languages.

8.1.1.6 *South Asia*

There are about 40 million users of English in South Asia, making it the third-largest English-using area after the United States and Great Britain. However, this constitutes only 3–4 per cent of the whole population of South Asia. Because of the varied histories of different parts of the subcontinent, a number of distinct varieties of English have developed there that are referred to collectively as 'South Asian English'.

As we saw in chapter 5, in the year 1600 a charter was granted by Elizabeth I to form the British East India Company, and soon trading posts were operating in Madras, Calcutta and Bombay. During the eighteenth century the power of the Moguls and the European challengers for Indian sovereignty eventually waned, and the East India Company increased its control. To counteract corruption Parliament assumed control in 1784; after the Indian Mutiny, in 1858, the Company was abolished and the Crown took over. The period from 1765 to 1947 is known as the period of the British Raj; during this time English was developed into a medium of control. It took over in both administration and education, especially after 1835, when Macaulay's educational *Minute* was written to advise the government of the best language and education policy for the region, with the express aim of creating an English-based subculture in the subcontinent. The basis for this subculture was the English language; here again, language is equated with power. As it happened, the formal introduction of English for such purposes was made easier by the existence of a vast array of local languages: using one language therefore was logical, and tied all subjects to the crown, no matter what their ethnic and linguistic background was.

The subculture, to be created by the authorities, would be made up of indigenous people schooled in English, who would remain where they were (the purpose was *not* to bring them to England!) and be able to communicate with the rulers and the ruled:

> . . . a class who may be *interpreters* between us and the millions whom we govern, a class of persons Indian in *blood* and *colour*, but English in taste . . .
>
> [my italics]

Hence, when the universities were founded in Bombay, Calcutta and Madras in 1857, English was the medium of instruction. English was thus firmly entrenched as the language of education and administration in the country, and managed to hold on as an official language even after Indian independence in 1947. This was a remarkable occurrence, given the fact that English was regarded by many as the language of the colonial enemy at that time. However, with the particularly complex linguistic situation on the subcontinent, despite its bitter colonial aftertaste, English was considered the least of a number of evils and adopted as an official lingua franca, alongside Hindi. Gradually, in the 1960s, Indian educators, politicians and intellectuals came to challenge the place of English (and indeed of Hindi) in the face of so many local languages, and the 'three-language formula' was developed. According to this, a national, a regional and a local language are to be learned by all citizens. This means that English can be used as an alternative to Hindi in the North or to a regional language in the

South. English is classified as an associated official language in most states, and is an official language in several. The Dravidian-speaking areas of the South usually prefer English to Hindi, while the status of English is more varied in the North. The three-language formula allows for the learning of the local language; nevertheless, there is some feeling today that the local languages are not being promoted enough, and that English is too influential. Recently, for example, opinions were expressed in a local (English-language!) newspaper in Bengal that Bengali should be used more, and that English words should be avoided when doing so. While it is impossible to say how such local situations will develop in the future, the use of English is certain to continue.

English is also an associated official language in Pakistan, and while it is not an official language in the other areas of South Asia (Bangladesh, Sri Lanka, Nepal, Bhutan), it is widely used internationally as a lingua franca throughout the region.

The issue of literacy is more complex on the subcontinent, as there was already a millennia-long tradition of writing in Sanskrit, then in Hindi; the early spread of Islam also led to widespread writing of Urdu (in Arabic script). The introduction of English in education in the nineteenth century was therefore not a new phenomenon, but it did unite much wider segments of the populace in using the same language system than had been the case before.

8.1.1.7   *Former Colonial Africa: West Africa*

Most of Africa was divided up amongst Britain, France, Germany, Portugal, Italy and Belgium by 1914. After World War II, however, German and Italian territories were partitioned, and most of the countries of former colonial Africa gained their independence in the 1960s or later. The English language had been used sporadically on the coast of West Africa from about the end of the fifteenth century. By the nineteenth century, the increase in trade and activities in opposition to the slave trade brought English to the entire West African coast, and several English-based pidgins and creoles developed, due to contact amongst the literally hundreds of local languages. These pidgins and creoles were used alongside the standard English of the missionaries, administrators, soldiers and traders in the area. As in many other parts of the world, literacy came to this region with the English language; English is still taught and used, and is an official language in the West African countries. But alongside English, a substantial number of West Africans still speak a pidgin or creole, some of which are established written languages. Many, for example, are literate in Krio, an English-based creole which spread rapidly across the West African coast (see individual countries below). British varieties of English developed in six particular countries, each of which still has English as an official language:

(1) **Sierra Leone**.   In the late eighteenth century British anti-slavery supporters bought land in West Africa to establish a homeland for freed and 'recaptured' slaves. They came first from England, Nova Scotia and Jamaica. Sierra Leone became a Crown Colony in 1808, and was used as a base from which to retrieve captured Africans. Some 600,000 slaves were 'recaptured' in all. These ex-slaves communicated mostly in Krio. In 1896, Britain declared the hinterland a protectorate. Sierra Leone gained its independence from Britain in 1961, and most of the population of close to five million now speak Krio.

(2) **Ghana** (formerly the Gold Coast).   The Gold Coast became a Crown Colony in 1874 after the Ashanti were defeated. The modern state was created in 1957 when the Gold Coast was adjoined to the British Togoland trust territory, which had been mandated to Britain after WWI. Now named Ghana, the country gained independence in 1960. The population today stands at approximately 16 million, about one million of whom can use English as a second language.

(3) **The Gambia**.   Trading in the Gambia began in the early seventeenth century. After conflict with France, in 1816 Bathurst (modern day Banjul) was established as a British base for anti-slavery activists. The country became a Crown Colony in 1843, an independent commonwealth country in 1965, and a republic in 1970. The population of over a million largely use Krio as a lingua franca.

(4) **Nigeria**.   A British colony was founded in Lagos in 1861. In 1914 a single country was formed together with other southern and northern territories, and Nigeria became independent in 1960. It does not have a clearly defined language policy, though it is the largest and most powerful West African nation. However, since it has an extremely complex linguistic situation, with Yoruba, Igbo and Hausa being used side by side with over a hundred smaller languages, English has a significant role to play as a lingua franca. There are also widely differing varieties of English spoken in Nigeria, with most pidgin spoken in the South, and more standard-like English spoken in the North, where it was learned through schools. In 1996 it had a population of 94 million, about half of whom use a pidgin or creole form of English as a second language.

(5) **Cameroon**.   In 1919 Cameroon, which had been a German protectorate, was divided between Britain and France. The two areas merged again in 1972, retaining both French and English as official languages. French is used for most official functions, and English is used by many fewer people, though it is important in international communication. This is a highly multilingual country with a population of about 13 million people, and contact languages are particularly important here, especially Cameroon Pidgin, which is spoken by about half of the population.

(6) **Liberia**. Liberia is Africa's oldest republic, founded in 1822 with the aid of
the American Colonization Society, with the intention of establishing a homeland for former slaves. Over 13,500 black Americans immigrated to Liberia
over a period of 50 years and more than 6,000 slaves recaptured at sea were
settled there. In 1847 the republic adopted a constitution based on that of
the USA. Even during the scramble for Africa at the turn of the century,
Liberia managed to hold on to its independence. The population in 1996
was about 2.5 million, most of whom use Pidgin English as a second language, though there are also a number of English native speakers. The
language spoken in Liberia has been said to have strong links with African-
American Vernacular English.

8.1.1.8 East Africa

East Africa was visited by English ships from the sixteenth century, but was only
explored in the 1850s by the likes of Livingstone, Speke and Burton. The Imperial East Africa Company was founded in 1888, and eventually a series of colonial
protectorates was established, despite competition from other European nations.
There are six main states with a history of British rule that gave English official
status when they gained their independence.

(1) **Kenya**. Kenya was a British colony from 1920, and became independent
in 1963 after the Mau Mau Rebellion. English then became the official
language, though it was replaced by Swahili in 1974; in spite of this, English
is still an important language for the population of about 28 million.
(2) **Tanzania**. Tanzania is composed of former Zanzibar and Tanganyika.
Zanzibar became a British protectorate in 1890, and in 1919 Britain received
a mandate for Tanganyika. Tanzania was the first East African country to
become independent, in 1961. It had a population of over 27 million in
1996, and English was a joint official language with Swahili until 1967,
when Swahili was declared the sole official language. Nevertheless, English
is still considered an important language for the country.
(3) **Uganda**. Uganda was united as a British protectorate in 1893 and became
independent in 1962; its population in 1996 was over 18 million. English
is the sole official language in Uganda, but Swahili is widely used as a lingua
franca.
(4) **Malawi** (formerly Nyasaland). A British Colony from 1906, Malawi became
independent in 1964. Its population of 10 million in 1996 used English and
Chewa as joint official languages.
(5) **Zambia** (formerly Northern Rhodesia). This territory was first administered by the British South Africa Company, becoming a British Protectorate

in 1924; Zambia became independent in 1964. The population of 9 million has English as its official language.

(6) **Zimbabwe** (formerly Southern Rhodesia). Also ruled by the British South Africa Company, Southern Rhodesia became a colony in 1923. The white government made a Unilateral Declaration of Independence in 1965, but power was eventually restored to the African majority and the country became officially independent under the name of Zimbabwe in 1980. The population of about 11 million has English as its official language.

The kinds of English spoken in East Africa are different from those of West Africa, since a large number of highly skilled people settled there; a large number of white Africans were also born there, again usually in the professional classes. The schools of the region operated on the British model, reinforcing the expatriate variety of British English brought originally by the missionaries at the turn of the century. The varieties of mother-tongue English that developed in East Africa are therefore more similar in character to those in South Africa, Australia and New Zealand. In terms of literacy, this again was not an issue until English became established in East Africa. We noted above that English is official – and thus used in education – in the last four East African countries named; especially interesting for the first three countries, however, is the fact that Swahili is either official or widely used – an established African language. We contrast this with the situation in West Africa, where the major (non-English) varieties of language used are pidgin- and creole-based.

8.1.1.9 *South-East Asia and South Pacific*

In the South Pacific territories and to their west there is a mixture of Australian and British English. America entered the scene relatively late: after the Spanish–American War of 1898 the USA received Guam and sovereignty over the Philippines; Hawaii was annexed only a very short time before then, in 1893. American influence then increased in the 1940s, after the United States invaded Japanese-held Pacific islands, and after World War II, when America assumed control over several areas as United Nations Trust Territories. The Philippines became independent in 1946, but American English influence has remained strong there. The Philippines has the largest population of the English-speaking states in the region (roughly 70 million).

The British influence in the South Pacific began much as it did in Australia, when sailors reached the area at the end of the eighteenth century, most significantly, Captain James Cook of north Yorkshire in the 1770s. Missionaries were sent to the South Pacific from the 1830s. Again, literacy came with the English: first with the missionaries, then later with colonists.

In South-East Asia the British colonial empire emerged as a result of the activities of Sir Stamford Raffles, who was an administrator for the East India Company. Trading centres were established in Penang (1786), Singapore (1819), and Malacca (1824). The Federal Malay States became a Crown Colony in 1867 and English was established as the language of law and administration and was increasingly used in other communicative contexts. Here the English language was used next to and in place of a large variety of indigenous languages, some of which also had a long tradition of writing.

English rapidly became an influential language in the British territories in South East Asia. Hong Kong was ceded to Britain in 1842 by the Treaty of Nanking, and Kowloon was added in 1860. The New Territories were leased from China in 1898 for ninety-nine years. Certain territories became protectorates of Great Britain at the end of the nineteenth century, and the administration of others was later assumed by Australia or New Zealand. The variety of language used in each of these was dictated by the identity of the administrators.

The British education system brought Standard British English to these areas at a relatively early time. English-medium schools began to operate in Penang in 1816, and with increasing numbers of students, English eventually became the language of professional advancement and also the chief literary language. After the turn of the century higher education in English was also introduced and English became a prestigious lingua franca. Because of the very different historical and cultural circumstances in different parts of the region, no one South Asian English variety has emerged.

(1) **Singapore**.   In Singapore bilingual education was introduced in the 1950s, and English was used side by side with Tamil, Chinese and Malay. English was the language of government, administration and law, and was also important in the media as well as in education; its use steadily increased amongst the general population. In a survey conducted in 1975, only 20 per cent of people over 40 years of age could understand English, while 87 per cent of those between 15 and 20 years could (as it is a language used in education, this includes a level of literacy in the language); English is widely used even within the family. Singapore had a population of 3 million in 1996.

(2) **Malaysia**.   Upon Malaysia's independence in 1957 Bahasa Malaysia was adopted as the national language; in comparison with Singapore, the English language became more restricted in use. Malay-medium education was introduced, and while English remained an obligatory subject, it was treated rather as a foreign language than a second language. In spite of this, many of the more than 20 million speakers regard English as a prestigious language and continue to use it. Indeed, so effective was the switch to Malay-medium schooling that after a time the government had to redouble its efforts to

teach English as a foreign language, as the number of English-speakers was decreasing to the disadvantage of the country.

(3) **Hong Kong**. English had limited use in the territory and was associated with the government, the military, law, business and the media; Cantonese was the home language of 98 per cent of the population (6 million in 1996). English-language education has been expanded in the past decade, however, and in 1992 it was estimated that over 25 per cent of the population had at least some use of English. English and Chinese have joint official status, but Chinese is used in most spoken contexts, and there is much language mixing. It will be interesting to trace the role of English in Hong Kong in the future, since it was returned to Chinese rule in 1997.

(4) **Papua New Guinea**. There are records of British sailors in the area from 1793, and it became a British Protectorate in 1884; the region was mandated to Australia in 1920 and became independent in 1975. The variety of English used in government and administration was thus first British and then Australian English; although the Australian period was significantly longer than the British (55 years vs. 36), the current English of this region cannot be said to be very 'Australian'. Of the population of 4.5 million in 1996, about half speak Tok Pisin, an English-based creole, as a second language, and some speak it as their mother tongue. It is used nation-wide and many important works of literature have been translated into Tok Pisin. Thus there are two competing literary languages, one established by colonists of the Empire, and one that developed as a result of contact between indigenous peoples and those colonists.

8.1.2 An Overview of the Use of English throughout the World

There are a number of ways of looking at the role of English in different countries of the world. Basically, we can divide up countries according to whether they have English as a native language, English as a second language, or English as a foreign language. The first category is self-explanatory. The difference between English as a foreign language and English as a second language is that in the latter instance only, English has actual assigned communicative status within the country. All told, there is a total of 75 territories where English has a special place in society. Kachru has divided the English-speaking countries of the world into three broad types, which he symbolizes by placing them in three concentric rings:

(1) The **inner circle**:   these countries are the traditional bases of English, where it is the primary language, that is Great Britain and Ireland, the United States, Canada, Australia and New Zealand.

(2) The **outer** or **extended circle**: these countries represent the earlier spread
      of English in non-native contexts, where the language is part of the country's
      leading institutions, where it plays a second-language role in a multilingual
      society, e.g. Singapore, India, Malawi, and 50 other territories.
(3) The **expanding circle**: this includes countries that recognize the importance
      of English as an international language though they have no history of col-
      onization and English has no special administrative status in these countries,
      e.g. China, Japan, Poland and a growing number of other states. This is
      English as a *foreign* language.

   It is clear that the expanding circle is the one that is most sensitive to the global
status of English. It is here that English is used primarily as an international
language, especially in the business, scientific, legal, political and academic
communities.

8.2   English as a Global Language

8.2.1   *The Industrial Revolution*

British colonialism clearly set the stage as the first phase of the expansion of
English. The necessarily brief sketches of the development of English in various
parts of the world above illustrate how English-medium instruction was a major
tool both in reinforcing British colonial power on the one hand, and spreading
the language on the other. This role of language as the passport to knowledge
was extremely important in the second phase of the development of English as a
global language. Britain was at the forefront of the Industrial Revolution, as
steam-engines, bridge building and large-scale manufacturing and production
machinery were just some of the major technological advancements being pion-
eered there. Countries which needed this new industrial knowledge could access it
most directly via the medium of English, and this again strengthened the position
of the language internationally.
   The development of technology in the age of steam often quite literally went
side by side with the spread of English: when railway tracks were laid, telegraph
cables were laid along with them. Since English was the language in which the
telegraph system was developed, English became the international language of all
telegraph operators. This early use in international communications clearly paved
the way for the use of English in radio and telecommunications at a later stage.
   Interestingly, in Britain until after World War II, most large British industrial
companies still employed French translators, reflecting the position of French in

international trade, finance and industry. In the fifty-odd years since the war, however, the role of French has declined dramatically, and with it the hiring of multilingual secretaries. However, those companies that deal through and with Europe still frequently employ multilingual workers, particularly in French and German.

8.2.2 *American Economic Superiority and Political Leadership*

Although Britain had been the greatest political, economic and industrial power in the world in the eighteenth and nineteenth century, by the end of the nineteenth and in the early twentieth century the United States had emerged out of its splendid isolation as an economic and, ultimately, political superpower.

During this time, the countries of the world began to come together in international organizations: the League of Nations after World War I, the United Nations and side organizations (such as UNESCO and UNICEF) after World War II. And as they came together, they needed to be able to communicate; several languages were chosen as the official languages of the League of Nations and later the UN. However, it is extremely expensive to run this kind of multilingual operation: the translation and printing costs alone are prohibitive. It is not surprising, then, that a number of countries with languages of little international status (often meaning 'having small numbers of speakers') have decided to use English in their international interactions. Of course at least one important factor differentiates the UN from the earlier League: the League's headquarters were in Europe, while the UN's ended up in New York. The world's focus thereby shifted to the United States for yet another reason.

The influence of the United States, exerted by the combined weight of economic and political factors, is, finally, enhanced by the sheer size of its population: the United States has 70 per cent of all the native speakers of English in the world, excluding creoles.

8.2.3 *American Technological Domination*

The computer revolution that took over the world in the period after World War II and particularly in the 1980s and 1990s was spearheaded by American technology and American know-how. Consequently, the language of computers is English. There are economic and technical reasons why this is so. While some countries have developed versions of the most popular software such as Word with instructions in their own languages, this is a very expensive undertaking and can only be done when it is economically viable – that is, when enough software will be sold to make it worthwhile. These days it is, of course, not just technically feasible, but relatively easy to develop programming based on other languages; and, were the computer revolution beginning now (developing outside of the United States, for example), it might be a very different 'virtual' world, at least in a linguistic sense. But English has been so firmly entrenched as the computer lingua franca that it is likely to continue in this role.

Another case in point is the airline industry. In the early decades of commercial flight, American aircraft production proved to be dominant throughout much of the world. Practically all of the technology (much of it spurred on by World War II) connected to this industry was English-based, and most of it American. The most visible symbol of this phenomenon is the universal use of English in all communications between aircraft and control towers today: and, more often than not, it takes place between non-English speakers, at both ends. This is also true of other areas, such as international shipping, and indeed so important is the use of English for such professions that applied linguists have developed pro-grammes in English for Special Purposes.

8.2.4   *The Boom in English Language Teaching*

The expanding circle is of particular interest in a discussion of the global role of English because we can say that a 'country' recognizes and acts upon the per-ceived importance of English without the involvement of government. Teaching English as a Second or Foreign Language has become a huge industry all over the world in the last thirty years.

Graduates of British and American universities are going abroad in droves to teach English for a year (or more), working in countries as diverse as Japan, Nepal, Ukraine and Rumania. In the Ukrainian city of Odessa, for example, English-language teaching centres are found all over the city: the students are middle-aged, of university age, and of school age. Such trends have naturally accelerated in the former Soviet Union and Eastern Europe since the breakdown of the Eastern bloc in 1989–91, and there are no signs of their slowing down. According to the British Council website on English Language Teaching:

> The future of English matters tremendously for Britain. English language teaching earned Britain £700m last year, publishing brought in a further £1,000m. Added to these sums is the revenue generated by English language media, cultural exports and other business where English is the lingua-franca.

There are whole networks of standardized language-testing centres, often administered through a university such as the University of Cambridge or the University of Michigan, and there are commercial language-training companies in most countries. On the university level, courses providing combinations of English and business or entrepreneurial studies, for example, where English is more directly touted as a means to an end, are again proving to be a popular and expanding area. Indeed there is a whole new sub-field of English research and teaching on English for Occupational Purposes, where the emphasis is not so much on literature or conversational ability, as on issues such as how to read a technical manual or how to write a résumé.

But not everyone regards the teaching of English as a second and a foreign language as always a good thing. Often language teaching forms part of a British or American aid package to underprivileged countries, and while many see this as a positive contribution, more sceptical observers suggest that Britain and America are merely using the language as a tool to secure Anglo-American hegemony in those areas, frequently making aid contingent on assimilation to an (Anglo)-American political and cultural model. This is partly the reason why some observers view English as a 'killer' language, which we will discuss in greater detail below.

8.2.5 *The Need for a Global Language*

While we have traced the spread of English throughout the world in this chapter, we have taken it somewhat for granted and have not asked the fundamental question, why is or was there a need to develop a global language? As we have seen in earlier chapters, the idea of having English as a national language developed only gradually even within Britain, arising at first as the country emerged from hundreds of years of French domination. Its position was only really secured in the Renaissance period, when French and Latin were completely replaced by English as a language of learning, law, literature and commercial activity. Even when English expanded into the Celtic-speaking areas of Britain, this was not done with any nationalistic fervour, or indeed with any specific legal programme. But gradually, with the rise of Standard English, the nation came to associate one particular way of speaking with the identity of the nation.

However, the philosophy of one nation united under one language is a European notion that developed primarily in Germany in the nineteenth century. From this point on, national languages were considered a potent symbol of national unity and identity and were exploited in the development of national cultures and government. It is no accident that this desire for unity came at a time when Europe was particularly unstable, in the run-up to World War I, and far from unified either politically, culturally or linguistically.

The role of the standard national language was to act as a unifying force within countries, but the problem of communication between nations still remained. As we have already seen, Latin had functioned as an international lingua franca for centuries, but as with English, the use of Latin created advantages and disadvantages. While on the one hand it did allow people of different nationalities to communicate, it was nevertheless the exclusive privilege of the rich and the learned, and thus it was also a tool for elitism, serving to lend power and prestige to those who spoke it, and to subjugate and alienate those who could not.

Already in the seventeenth century there were calls for a replacement language for Latin, and this was the first time that the possibility of inventing an artificial language was suggested. Once French began to serve as a lingua franca in the eighteenth century, the need for another auxiliary language was less keenly felt. But French never did achieve full global status. During industrial expansion and the beginning of international markets in the nineteenth century, and especially in the period of great tension before World War I, a number of artificial languages were proposed as auxiliary languages, with wonderfully utopian names such as Volapük ('world language'), Novial, Ekselsioro, Mondlingvo and Europeo. The most famous of them, Esperanto, developed by the Pole Ludwig Zamenhof at the turn of the century, caught on with significant numbers of adherents around the world, and is still learned, spoken and used at international meetings today. However, neither it nor any other artificial language became the international auxiliary language that many had dreamed of. This is because a number of important factors of language use are not covered by artificial languages. They are often no easier to learn than a natural language such as English or French, and they would need to be equal to the full range of communicative functions that a natural language covers, from greetings card messages to high poetry to weather forecasts. They would need to develop a standard form that everyone could agree on and identify with, and to be capable of change (though this is very difficult, since they have no recognized society to change along with). Most importantly, they should not show bias towards any particular language or region of the world (and almost all are Eurocentric). (For an interesting discussion of the ideal artificial language, see Crystal, 1997: 17.)

In the end, utopian attempts to develop a global language by *planning*, with all the goodwill that this must entail, seem doomed to failure. The accession of English to its global position was anything but a planned development, although proponents of theories of cultural imperialism might not entirely agree with such a statement.

8.2.6 *Structural Considerations*

Umberto Eco believes that apart from by historical contingency, English expanded because it is rich in monosyllables, capable of absorbing foreign words and flexible in forming neologisms, etc. (Eco, 1995: 331).

Baugh and Cable (1993: 9–13) also discuss the structural characteristics that supposedly made English the 'right' language for global expansion. Firstly, they stress its cosmopolitan vocabulary. They point out that as a Germanic language it has affinity with the other Germanic languages structurally, but that more than half of its vocabulary is Latin-derived This means that it has much in common with the Romance languages, increasing its universal appeal. Moreover, as we have seen, English has in the course of its history been receptive to loans from a wide variety of the world's languages, from Hebrew to Malay and Irish to Chinese. This cosmopolitan lexicon is, they feel, a direct asset to a language bidding for global status. Next they discuss the relative inflectional simplicity of English in comparison with other languages and suggest that this makes it easier to learn than the 'complicated agreements' of a language such as German. Finally, they mention explicitly the fact that English has natural, not grammatical gender, which makes it more accessible to learners than, say, the Romance languages.

But even Baugh and Cable suggest that English also has 'liabilities' in its linguistic system. The first that they mention is the need to express oneself idiomatically (while admitting that English is probably no more replete with idiomatic expressions than any other language). And secondly they mention the 'chaotic' (by which they mean 'unphonetic') character of English spelling.

Other commentators have gone further than Eco and Baugh and Cable, suggesting that there is something about the structure and beauty of English that makes it better suited than any other language for the role of a global language. But no descriptive linguist could really agree with any of this. The fact is that English is a linguistic system that is as complex and as simple as any other; there are features of English that are harder or easier to learn for some speakers and not for others. But there is nothing inherent in the language that equips it uniquely for the role of a global language. The fact is that English could not have spread without the social, economic, technological and political developments of the English-speaking world of the past two centuries.

8.2.7   Global and at the Same Time Local

In spite of the realities of the use of English on a global scale, wherever English has gained societal status and has been in use alongside other, indigenous, languages, that variety of English has taken on features specific to those regions. Such features can be phonological or morphological, but most often they are lexical; in other words, the English of a given region can contain a lexical component that refers specifically to indigenous phenomena or realia. On top of this, in a multilingual country such as India, where access to English is not equal for all citizens, a variety of types of English develop in English-'knowers', 'from Pidgin English or broken English on the one hand to educated (or standard) South Asian English' (Kachru, 1983: 356).

Especially in informal and spoken communication at the lower end of this continuum, a number of typical South Asian characteristics appear in the English used.

Kachru (1983) provides a description of these features, from which the following observations are selected. On the level of phonology, typically South Asian retroflex consonants [ʈ] and [ɖ] may be substituted for English [t] and [d], and aspirated stops [pʰ], [tʰ] and [dʰ] may be substituted for the fricatives [f], [θ] and [ð]. On the grammatical level, interrogatives may be formed without subject–verb inversion: *What you would like to read?* The universal tag question *isn't it?* might be used instead of the standard English polar opposite tag, e.g. *You are going tomorrow, isn't it?* (cf. *You are going tomorrow, aren't you?*). Another feature of South Asian English grammar is the use of progressive forms with stative verbs, such as *Mohan is having two houses; I am understanding English better now.*

Perhaps the most striking differences are on the level of lexis and collocation, where South Asian characteristics might appear directly translated into English. Rather than reproduce Kachru's examples, the following text has been chosen to illustrate this point, while at the same time showing that, even in written educated South Asian English, these contrasts with standard British or American English are striking.

A River Most Foul

About 1,000 to 2,000 devotees take a dip in this river almost daily and their number swells to several *lakhs* on special occasions like *Amavasya* and *Purnima*. Moreover devotees come from neighbouring States like Punjab, Haryana and even beyond.

We do have one *ghat* known as *Khudisa Ghat* there for such purposes. It is a pity that this place is kept as *unclean and dirty* as it can be. You enter a narrow *kachcha* lane to go to this *ghat* and not only confront petty-vendors but also about 50–100 beggars on its both sides of the *ghats*. They literally bully you into *giving them alms* and can go to any extent – even hang on to your arm – for the purpose.

During floods, which are an annual feature or during rains you have to wade through knee-deep water to reach the *ghat*.

And what do you witness there? There are about a dozen *ghats* (*bathing places*) but none of them has the usual stairs where you can stand and have a normal dip.

. . . If you stroll around the *ghat complex* you notice heaps of *raddi* (consisting mostly of cardboard boxes, plastic bags, bottles and waste papers) being displayed prominently by *kabaris* in the space rented by the resident *pandits*.

[my italics]

(from *The Hindustan Times Online*, www.hindustantimes.com,
2 December 1998, by Subhash Goyal)

This text is remarkable for a number of reasons. Firstly, and most strikingly it features words from Hindi, which have no explanation in the text (except for the word *ghat*, for which a translation is provided at the fifth mention!), because the imagined audience for this piece consists of locals who are bilingual in English and Hindi. Secondly, the text is dealing with a cultural concept that is not familiar to Westerners: thousands of 'devotees' bathing in a sacred river. The occasions for such events are *Amavasya* and *Purnima*, which would have to be explained to non-Indians as well. Even though the vast majority of the text consists of standard international English vocabulary, the text cannot be understood without specific knowledge of this specialized lexis and the cultural background. There are also English lexical items in the text that are marked, for example, 'devotee', because it seems to be used in a culture-specific sense here, and 'giving them alms', which is now an antiquated phrase in British and American English. Finally, there is the classic piling up or reduplication of near-synonymous phrases, which Kachru has argued is typical of South Asian English: *the place is kept as **unclean** and **dirty** as it can be.*

By contrast with this text and in order to further demonstrate that English in India occurs not as a homogeneous variety, but as a range of lects, the following textual extract from *The Times of India* has been chosen. It is remarkable for the fact that it is almost indistinguishable from any mainstream English-language newspaper text anywhere in the world that is dealing with computer technology.

White-Collar Crime: Cops see Red

In the age of cyber-hacking and e-business, the world of white-collar crime too has a new addition: Fake Permanent Account Number (PAN) card.

Even as Delhi Police sleuths busted the fake PAN card racket – the first of its kind in the country – last week, the fact remains that white-collar crime is growing faster than the crime-beaters can keep pace with.

Police officials admit that with advancement in technology, criminals are becoming more innovative in committing new white-collar crimes. What is more alarming is that such crimes are being committed by persons well-versed with technology.

'Income-tax authorities were taken aback as they had not come across cases of fake PAN card. We believe this could just be the tip of the iceberg,' says additional commissioner of police (crime) S K Jain.

(Aditya Kant, *The Times of India*, www.indiatimes.com)

The text is striking for its use of criminal slang terms, which are strongly influenced by American English (*cops, busted*), and for the easy use of specialist terms (*cyber-hacking, e-business*). The text is by no means perfect (*well-versed *with technology*, title of the additional commissioner of police not capitalized, etc.); however, it would be very hard to attribute any of the infelicities directly to Indian influence (though the unidiomatic use of prepositions is arguably a typical error of non-native speakers). All in all, however, the text is only recognizably Indian by the use of place names and job titles, something which would be different in any variety of English. The tone and content of the piece are suggestive of a modern, informed, youthful and knowledgeable journalist, and the whole article is rather international in its character (and the imperfections in style are no worse than those that can be found in any typical contemporary English or American newspaper).

Up to this point we have seen the growth of English as a global means of communication, and the establishment of a large number of local varieties of English alongside other – native – languages. In the last part of this chapter, we need to address the question of whether the spread of English is a positive or a negative thing, and whether there is any validity to the label that has occasionally been given to English as a 'killer' language, or a 'glottophage'.

8.3   English as a Killer Language

Throughout the world, people regard English as a language of economic opportunity, though this is not a universal feeling, since some consider English a tool for the destruction of linguistic and cultural diversity. A number of commentators have seen the spread of English not as an unqualified benefit, but rather as an opportunity reserved only for the select few and a means to construct patterns of inequality both within countries and between the 'west' and the 'rest'.

The global spread of English is complex: on the one hand it appears as an unstoppable process that homogenizes culture wherever it goes: Crystal (1997a) cites the Italian word *cocacolonizzare* (to coca-colonize), while the poet Derrick Desmond rather crudely laments the 'Californucation' (sic) of world culture. On the other hand, however, the spread of English creates divisions in society, and contact with other languages causes the creation of new language varieties.

Pattanayak (1996) has suggested that in India the use of English affords improved educational opportunities for only a very small minority. On the whole it accentuates the rift between the urban and rural, the developed and the developing and the masses and the elite. He argues that since English is the almost exclusive language of science and technology, this actually prevents ordinary people from having access to and interacting with it. Because it prevents many languages sharing communication, it promotes 'alienation, anomie, and blind spots in cultural perception'. Ultimately, Pattanayak argues, English causes other cultures to wither and die, and its use by the elite to secure their position of privilege is just as much of an imposition on the people as colonialism ever was.

It has also been suggested (and it does seem to be true certainly of most Britons and Americans) that the spread of global English has led to complacency about the use of English, and has encouraged people to be lazy about learning languages. Certainly in my recent experience teaching at university in Great Britain, many of the foreign-language programmes are struggling to recruit students who wish to specialize in a foreign language, and traditional literature-based German and French programmes in particular seem to be struggling to retain student numbers. On the other hand, as we mentioned in the section on the boom in English teaching, courses that combine European languages with, for example, business studies, marketing or IT training, where the instrumental function of learning the language is transparent, are indeed attracting students. Thus, this complacency or lack of interest might not be a simple matter of students losing interest in learning languages, but rather of academics losing touch with how and why we teach them.

8.3.1 *Language Death*

There have been some extremely gloomy predictions about the fate of the world's languages in the coming century. In a much-cited article, Krauss (1992: 7) predicted that up to 90 per cent of the approximately 6,000 languages spoken in the world today would be lost by the end of the twenty-first century. Many authors blame the spread of English directly or indirectly for the death of languages, but the question remains whether English really is a 'killer' language (cf. Graddol, 1996: 196–9).

There is no doubt that English has been more directly the cause of death of languages in countries that now speak English as a native language. We saw in chapter 2 how English caused the extinction of Cornish and Manx in the British Isles, and we mentioned in chapter 7 that of the approximately one thousand indigenous languages spoken in America before its colonization by English-speakers, only approximately 200 survive today, and many of them are barely hanging on. It is also the case that in Australia perhaps as many as two hundred aboriginal languages have been lost in recent years.

But in other countries the blame cannot be so straightforwardly placed on English. For example, as Görlach (1997: 12) points out, in many colonial contexts, such as in East Africa in the nineteenth century, the missionaries, merchants and administrators frequently used an existing lingua franca, or a local language that could be made to function as a lingua franca, to communicate with the locals. Certainly in the case of East Africa this caused an *expansion* in the functional and geographical range of Swahili. Thus, even in the colonial context, the advent of English did not necessarily entail the death knell for other languages:

> In such situations the spheres of English and indigenous languages are separated by a lingua franca, and English cannot be the glottophage it proved to be in North America and Australia. On the other hand, its presence may indeed become a grievous obstacle to the development of a national language. In particular, its neutral function internally (helping to avoid a decision for or against the promotion of local languages, as in Nigeria and India), and its pragmatic advantages as a window on western technology

are brought to bear. This alleged neutrality may well become a political weapon in the hands of those that can wield it, and be underpinned by the fact that all freedom movements of the 1940s to 1960s used English for political rallies – right up to recent campaigns in Southern Africa.

(Görlach, 1997: 12)

It appears that in looking at cases of language death we must take local conditions into account. Graddol (1987: 197) illustrates this with reference to India, which, as we have seen, is a highly multilingual country with a definite language hierarchy. Very few people actually use English in India (perhaps even as few as 3 per cent or as many as 18 per cent, depending on how you define 'use English'), though it is one of the co-official languages that can be used according to the three-language formula (see above). Although many of the almost 100 recognized languages are under threat, the languages that the speakers are turning to are not English or even Hindi, the first national language of India, but rather regional languages such as Marathi and Bengali. Graddol cites work that comes to a similar conclusion about language loss in Africa.

Thus, English is not usually the *direct* cause of language death in such situations. Rather, it is a driving force in the globalization of the economy, which indirectly causes people to switch to English as a means to improve their lot in life. In other words, English is not a 'killer' language in most instances, but it could definitely be called an 'accessory to murder'.

8.3.2 *Language and Communication Technology*

The English language dominates the electronic media. Graddol (1996: 206) points out that the development of global electronic communications goes hand in hand with the development of world-wide political, commercial and economic networks. He suggests that the ensuing language loss is just one part of the process of globalization, a process by which people throughout the world become more interdependent culturally, economically and politically. An expression which one often hears in this regard is that the world has become a kind of 'global village'.

Graddol points out (205ff.) that the development of the radio telegraph was the first step in the globalization of communications. Having been patented in 1837, a telegraph service was in operation between Britain and India by 1865, and all of the intermediate posts that were needed to connect India with Britain were staffed by people who spoke English. The majority of the world's telegraph station operators came to use English, and by the 1930s, only French and German competed with English in the telegraph service, and even German fell out of use by the 1950s.

A transatlantic cable was laid in 1866, uniting Britain and America, and by the 1870s links had been established as far away as Suez, Bombay, Sydney and New

Zealand, and Britain was the international centre of radiotelegraphy, with more than half of all cables being sent via London. The telegraph sent international news, business and diplomatic information. And Britain controlled the technology, the maintenance and the actual processing of the messages. This huge communication complex made it possible to conduct international transactions of all kinds for the first time. And because English was the language of the telegraph, it became established as the language of these international activities.

When the telephone became popular in the early part of the twentieth century the telegraph service began to wane (though the last telegraph office using Morse code was not closed down until August 1999). America eventually took the lead in telephone technology, and although other countries developed considerable telephone and electronic communications systems, America continued to dominate this industry and does so still today. If English is to be seen as a 'killer' language, communication technology must be interpreted as one of its major weapons.

8.4 The Future of English

The English language has gone through some remarkable transitions since it arrived in the British Isles in the fifth century. As with all languages, always, it was impossible to predict then, as it is impossible to predict now, what the future would have in store for it. No one could foresee in the Middle Ages that English, not Latin, would be the language of learning and knowledge across the globe. No one could foresee in the eighteenth century, and even in the 1950s, that English, not French, would be the first language of international diplomacy. The future of a language is impossible to predict. However, Crystal (1997a) has suggested a number of factors that might negatively influence the role of English as a global language in the future.

Firstly, he mentions that some nations have already rejected English. As we saw above, in the 1950s Malaysia rejected English as a language of education in favour of Bahasa Malaysia, and there are many more countries where English does not find favour. Should this reaction to English develop into a world-wide trend, the future of English as a global language would be jeopardized. But this is an unlikely eventuality in the foreseeable future, if only because so many countries are dependent on the United States financially.

However, this brings us to a second factor in the potential derailing of global English. If the United States were to lose its position as an economic, political and cultural superpower, the use of English would become much less desirable in non-English-speaking countries. Language-users are fickle, as the fate of Greek and Latin, or even of Scots in Scotland, reminds us. Language teachers in Britain and the United States feel that the drop in students enrolling in German and Russian classes is a temporary phenomenon, linked to their present financial and internal difficulties. It is believed that once things pick up in these countries, students will wish to study the languages again. This could be the fate of English as a foreign language, should the English-speaking countries encounter such difficulties. Crystal points out that it would take a major change in the fortunes of the United States alone for this to happen, since the other English mother-tongue countries – including Britain – do not have enough influence on the use of English to make such a difference.

The language situation within the United States itself has also changed some-what since World War II. Especially in the last three decades, the number of Hispanic Americans who wish to continue using Spanish in America has in-creased. Although the numbers are still insufficient to warrant a real threat to the status of English as the national language of the United States, some politicians and other observers perceive the use of Spanish as a danger to their identity. Consequently, despite the fact that America has never needed to enshrine in law the fact that English is its official language, even in the face of immigration from a vast array of speakers of other languages, some states have declared an English-only policy. The arguments for doing so are usually economic (it costs a con-siderable amount of money for a state to be bilingual) and cultural (America has always regarded itself as a 'melting pot', and assimilation has been high on the American agenda). The arguments against the English-only ruling are that America is enriched by the enhanced linguistic and cultural ability of Spanish-speakers. To date it would appear that the threat from Spanish in America is making very little difference to the status of English in the country as a whole, which means that the global status of English remains stable.

Another possible threat to the global status of English is the global nature of English itself. We have seen in this chapter that where English comes into contact with other languages in countries that constitute Kachru's 'outer circle', English has begun to develop its own distinctive character. These 'other Englishes', as they have come to be called, have prompted some linguistic 'Chicken Littles' to predict that the sky will fall and that these varieties will soon diverge so markedly from each other that they will lose mutual intelligibility, thus causing the frag-mentation of English across the globe. But those commentators have failed to take into consideration the centripetal force of standard written language across the globe and the fact that education in English is also conducted through the medium of standard, not local varieties. Crystal (1997a) points out that, even if national Englishes across the globe did continue to fragment, speakers would be able to adapt to this contingency, since we are all multidialectal to a greater or lesser extent. People would simply have to add what Crystal has dubbed 'World Standard Spoken English' to their repertoire, since such differences would be less marked in written English.

In a wondrous bout of Anglocentrism Baugh and Cable said (1993) about the future of English:

> How much pleasanter foreign travel would be if we did not have to contend with the inconveniences of a foreign language. How much more readily we could conduct our business abroad if there were but a single language of trade. How greatly would the problem of the scientist and the scholar be simplified if there were one universal language of learning. And how many of the prejudices that divide nations would be avoided, how much the peace of the world would be promoted if there were free interchange of national thought and feeling – if only we could make effective the French proverb, *Tout comprendre, c'est tout pardonner.*

It is easy to think like this if one is part of the 'we' that speak English natively, but this is not likely to happen in the near future. Humans need diversity of expression just as much as, if not more than, they need directness and clarity, and the forces that promote uniformity in language are constantly countered by those that promote division and change. While English looks set to continue as an *aid* to world-wide communication for the foreseeable future, it is likely, and desirable, that it should not eradicate the splendid diversity of language and culture to be encountered across the globe. We might parody Baugh and Cable by remarking how tedious it would be if we were to travel across the globe and encounter no difference. There seems to be little danger that this will happen in the course of the next century or two.

Suggestions for further reading

Bailey, Richard W. and Manfred Görlach (eds) (1983) *English as a World Language.* Ann Arbor, MI: University of Michigan Press.

Crystal, David (1997a) *English as a Global Language.* Cambridge: Cambridge University Press.

Graddol, David (1996) Global English, Global Culture? In: Goodman, Sharon and David Graddol (eds) *Redesigning English: New Texts, New Identities.* London: Routledge.

Bibliography

Aers, David, Bob Hodge and Gunther Kress (1981) *Literature, Language and Society in England, 1580–1680*. Dublin: Gill and MacMillan.

Aitchison, Jean (1991) *Language Change: Progress or Decay?*, 2nd edition. Cambridge: Cambridge University Press.

Aitchison, Jean (1985) Language Change: Progress or Decay? In: Clark, V. P. *et al.* (eds) *Language: Introductory Readings*. New York: St Martin's Press.

Aitken, A. J. (1979) Scottish Speech: A Historical View with Special Reference to the Standard English of Scotland. In: Aitken, A. J. and T. McArthur (eds) *Languages of Scotland*. Association for Scottish Literary Studies, Occasional Papers, no. 4. Edinburgh: W. and R. Chambers, pp. 85–118.

Algeo, John (1982) *Problems in the Origin and Development of the English Language*, 3rd edition. New York: Harcourt Brace Jovanovich.

Alladina, Safder and Viv Edwards (1991) *Multilingualism in the British Isles*, Part 2: *Africa, the Middle East and Asia*. London: Longman.

Allen, Harold B. and Michael D. Linn (eds) (1982) *Readings in Applied English Linguistics*, 3rd edition. New York: Knopf.

Allen, Harold B. and Michael D. Linn (eds) (1986) *Dialect and Language Variation*. Orlando, FL: Academic Press.

Anderson, John M. and C. Jones (1977) *Phonological Structure and the History of English*. North-Holland Linguistic Series 33. Amsterdam: North-Holland.

Anttila, Raimo (1972) *An Introduction to Historical and Comparative Linguistics*. New York: Macmillan.

Arlotto, Anthony (1972) *Introduction to Historical Linguistics*. Boston, MA: Houghton Mifflin Co.

Bailey, C.-J. N. and Karl Maroldt (1977) The French Lineage of English. In: Jürgen Meisel (ed.) *Langues en Contact: Pidgins, Creoles – Languages in Contact*. Tübingen: TBL-Verlag Narr, pp. 21–53.

Bailey, Guy (1987) Are Black and White Dialects Diverging? Papers from the NWAVE XIV Panel Discussion. *American Speech*, **62**, 32–40.

Bailey, Guy and Natalie Maynor (1989) The Divergence Controversy. *American Speech*, **64**, 12–39.

Bailey, Richard W. (1991) *Images of English: A Cultural History of the Language*. Ann Arbor, MI: University of Michigan Press.

Bailey, Richard W. and Manfred Görlach (eds) (1983) *English as a World Language*. Ann Arbor, MI: University of Michigan Press.

Barber, Charles (1997) *Early Modern English*. Edinburgh: Edinburgh University Press.

Baron, Dennis E. (1982) *Grammar and Good Taste: Reforming the American Language*. New Haven, CT: Yale University Press.

Baron, Naomi (1977) *Language Acquisition and Historical Change*. North-Holland Linguistic Series 36. Amsterdam: North-Holland.

Bartlett, Robert (1994) *The Making of Europe: Conquest, Colonisation and Cultural Change, 950–1350*. London: Penguin.

Baugh, Albert C. and Thomas Cable (1993) *A History of the English Language*, 4th edition. London: Routledge.

Baugh, John (1999) *Out of the Mouths of Slaves: African-American Language and Educational Malpractice*. Austin, TX: University of Texas Press.

Bean, Marian C. (1983) *The Development of Word Order Patterns in Old English*. London: Croom Helm.

Bender, Harold H. (1922) *The Home of the Indo-Europeans*. Princeton, NJ: Princeton University Press.

Blake, Norman F. (1981) *Non-Standard Language in English Literature*. London: André Deutsch.

Blake, Norman F. (1983) *Shakespeare's Language: An Introduction*. London and Basingstoke: Macmillan.

Blake, Norman F. (ed.) (1992a) *The Cambridge History of the English Language*, vol. II: *1066–1476*. Cambridge: Cambridge University Press.

Blake, Norman F. (ed.) (1992b) The Literary Language. In: Blake, Norman F. (ed.) (1992a), pp. 500–41.

Blake, Norman F. (1996) *A History of the English Language*. Basingstoke and London: Macmillan.

Blench, Roger and Matthew Spriggs (1997) *Archaeology and Language*, vol. I: *Theoretical and Methodological Orientations*. One World Archaeology 27. London: Routledge.

Bloomfield, Leonard (1914) *An Introduction to the Study of Language*. New York: Holt, Rinehart and Winston.

Bolton, W. F. (1982) *A Living Language: The History and Structure of English*. New York: Random House.

Brooks, Cleanth (1985) *The Language of the American South*. Athens, GA: University of Georgia Press.

Brown, Roger and Albert Gilman (1989) Politeness Theory and Shakespeare's Four Major Tragedies. *Language in Society*, **18**, no. 2, 159–212.

Buck, Carl Darling (1988) *A Dictionary of Selected Synonyms in the Principal Indo-European Languages*. Chicago, IL: University of Chicago Press.

Burchfield, R. W. (1982) On That Other Great Dictionary . . . and the American Language. In: Allen, H. B. and M. D. Linn (eds) (1982), pp. 484–90.

Butters, Ronald R. (1989) *The Death of Black English: Convergence and Divergence in White and Black Vernaculars*. Frankfurt am Main: Peter Lang.

Bynon, Theodora (1978) *Historical Linguistics*, corrected edition. Cambridge Textbooks in Linguistics. Cambridge: Cambridge University Press.

Cable, T. (1983) *A Companion to Baugh and Cable's History of the English Language*. New York: Prentice-Hall.

Callary, Edward (1985) Phonetics. In: Clark, V. P. *et al.* (eds) *Language: Introductory Readings*. New York: St Martin's Press.

Cannon, John and Ralph Griffiths (1988) *The Oxford Illustrated History of the British Monarchy*. New York: Oxford University Press.

Carver, Craig (1987) *American Regional Dialects: A Word Geography*. Ann Arbor, MI: University of Michigan Press.

Cassidy, F. G. (1982) Geographical Variation of English in the United States. In: Bailey, Richard W. and Manfred Görlach (eds) (1982) *English as a World Language*. Ann Arbor, MI: University of Michigan Press, 177–209.

Cassidy, F. G. and R. N. Ringler (eds) (1971) *Bright's Old English Grammar and Reader*. New York: Holt, Rinehart and Winston.

Celce-Murcia, Marianne and Diane Larsen-Freeman (1999) *The Grammar Book*, 2nd edition. Boston, MA: Heinle and Heinle.

Cheshire, Jenny (1991) *English Around the World: Sociolinguistic Perspectives*. Cambridge: Cambridge University Press.

Chickering, Howell, Jr (1989) *Beowulf*. New York: Anchor Books, Doubleday.

Claiborne, Robert (1983) *Our Marvelous Native Tongue: The Life and Times of the English Language*. New York: Times Books.

Claiborne, Robert (1989) *The Roots of English: A Reader's Handbook of Word Origins*. New York: Times Books.

Collinge, N. E. (1985) *The Laws of Indo-European*. Amsterdam: Benjamins.

Comrie, Bernard (1989) *Language Universals and Linguistic Typology*, 2nd edition. Chicago, IL: University of Chicago Press.

Conklin, N. F. and Lourie, M. A. (1983) *A Host of Tongues: Language Communities in the United States*. New York: Free Press.

Cooper, Robert L. (ed.) (1982) *Language Spread: Studies in Diffusion and Social Change*. Bloomington, IN: Indiana University Press.

Cox, Richard A. V. (1999) *The Language of the Ogam Inscriptions of Scotland*. Aberdeen: Department of Celtic, University of Aberdeen.

Crystal, David (1992) *An Encyclopaedic Dictionary of Language and Linguistics*. Oxford: Blackwell Publishers.

Crystal, David (1995) *The Cambridge Encyclopedia of the English Language*, 1st edition. Cambridge: Cambridge University Press.

Crystal, David (1997a) *English as a Global Language*. Cambridge: Cambridge University Press.

Crystal, David (1997b) *The Cambridge Encyclopaedia of Language*, 2nd edition. Cambridge: Cambridge University Press.

Cusack, Bridget (1998) *Everyday English, 1500–1700: A Reader*. Edinburgh: Edinburgh University Press.

Danielsson, B. and R. C. Alston (eds) (1966) *The Works of William Bullokar*, vol. I: *A Short Introduction or Guiding, 1580–1581*. Leeds: University of Leeds School of English.

Davis, Lawrence M. (1983) *English Dialectology: An Introduction*. Tuscaloosa, AL: University of Alabama Press.

Davis, Norman (ed.) (1970) *Sweet's Anglo-Saxon Primer*. Oxford: Clarendon Press.

Denison, David (1993) *English Historical Syntax*. London: Longman.

Devitt, Amy J. (1989) *Standardizing Written English. Diffusion in the Case of Scotland, 1520–1659*. Cambridge: Cambridge University Press.

Dillard, Joey L. (1975) *All-American English: A History of the English Language in America*. New York: Random House.

Dillard, Joey L. (1985) *Toward a Social History of American English*. New York: Mouton.

Dillard, Joey L. (1992) *A History of American English*. London: Longman.

Dobson, Eric J. (1968) *English Pronunciation, 1500–1700*. Oxford: Clarendon Press.

Donaldson, E. Talbot (1966) *Beowulf: A New Prose Translation*. New York: W. W. Norton.

Dykema, Karl W. (1982) The English Language: Past and Present. In: Allen, H. B. and M. D. Linn (eds) (1982), pp. 20–31.

Eco, Umberto (1995) *The Search for the Perfect Language*. Oxford: Blackwell Publishers.

Edwards, John R. (1979) *Language and Disadvantage*. London: Edward Arnold.

Edwards, John (1984) Irish and English in Ireland. In: Trudgill, Peter (ed.) (1984) *Language in the British Isles*. Cambridge: Cambridge University Press, pp. 480–98.

Edwards, John (1985) *Language, Society and Identity*. Oxford: Blackwell.

Edwards, V. K. (1984) British Black English and Education. In: Trudgill, Peter (ed.) (1984), pp. 559–72.

Edwards, V. K. (1986) *Language in a Black Community*. San Diego, CA: College-Hill Press.

Fairclough, Norman (1989) *Language and Power*. London: Longman.

Fasold, Ralph (1981) The Relation between Black and White Speech in the South. *American Speech*, **56**, 163–89.

Feagin, Crawford (1997) The African Contribution to Southern States English. In: Nunnally, Thomas and Robin Sabino (eds) (1997) *Language Variety in the South Revisited*. Tuscaloosa, AL: University of Alabama Press.

Fennell, Barbara A. (1986) Left-Branching Prenominal Adjectival Constructions in Modern English: On the Interface of Syntactic Typology and Discourse Function. *Proceedings of the Spring Linguistics Colloquium*, University of North Carolina at Chapel Hill, pp. 65–72.

Fennell, Barbara A. (1997) *Language, Literature and the Negotiation of Identity*. Chapel Hill, NC: University of North Carolina Press.

Finegan, Edward (1999) *Language: Its Structure and Use*, 3rd edition. Fort Worth, TX: Harcourt Brace College Publishers.

Fischer, Andreas (1989) *The History and the Dialects of English: Festschrift for Eduard Kolb*. Heidelberg: Carl Winter Universitätsverlag.

Fisher, John H. and Diane Bornstein (1984) *In Forme of Speche is Chaunge: Readings in the History of the English Language*. London: University Press of America.

Fisher, John H. (1996) *The Emergence of Standard English*. Louisville, KY: The University Press of Kentucky.

Fishman, Joshua A., R. L. Cooper and A. W. Conrad (1977) *The Spread of English: The Sociology of English as an Additional Language*. Rowley, MA: Newbury House.

Fisiak, Jacek (1968) *A Short Grammar of Middle English*, vol. 1: *Graphemics, Phonemics and Morphemics*. Warsaw: Panstwowe Wydawnictwo Naukowe.

Flexner, Stuart Berg (1982) *Listening to America*. New York: Simon and Schuster.

Forsyth, Katherine (1995) The Ogham-Inspired Spindle-Whorl from Buckquoy: Evidence for the Irish Language in Pre-Viking Orkney? *Proceedings of the Society of Antiquaries of Scotland*, **125**, 667–96.

Forsyth, Katherine (1997) *Language in Pictland: The Case Against 'Non-Indo-European Pictish'*. Utrecht: De Keltische Draak.

Freeborn, Dennis (1998) *From Old English to Standard English: A Course Book in Language Variation across Time*. Ottawa: University of Ottawa Press.

Giglioli, Pier Paolo (ed.) (1972) *Language and Social Context*. Harmondsworth: Penguin.

Giles, H. and R. Y. Bourhis (1976) Methodological Issues in Dialect Perception: A Social Psychological Perspective. *Anthropological Linguistics*, **19**, 294–305.

Goodman, Sharon and David Graddol (1996) *Redesigning English: New Texts, New Identities*. London: Routledge.

Gordon, James D. (1972) *The English Language: An Historical Introduction*. New York: Thomas Y. Cromwell.

Görlach, Manfred (1991) *Introduction to Early Modern English*. Cambridge: Cambridge University Press.

Görlach, Manfred (1997a) *The Linguistic History of English*. Basingstoke: Macmillan. English translation of Görlach, Manfred (1994) *Einführung in die englische Sprachgeschichte*.

Görlach, Manfred (1997b) Language and Nation: The Concept of Linguistic Identity in the History of English. *English World-Wide*, **18**: 1, 1–34.

Graddol, David (1996) Global English, Global Culture. In: Goodman, Sharon and David Graddol (1996) *Redesigning English: New Texts, New Identities*. London: Routledge, pp. 181–238.

Gray, Douglas (ed.) (1988) *The Oxford Book of Late Medieval Verse and Prose*. Oxford: Oxford University Press.

Greenberg, Joseph H. (1960) A Quantitative Approach to the Morphological Typology of Language. *International Journal of American Linguistics*, **26**, pp. 178–94.

Greenough, James B. and G. Kitteridge (1901) *Words and their Ways in English Speech*. New York: Cromwell-Collier and Macmillan; paperback edn Beacon Press, 1962.

Grun, Bernard (1982) *The Timetables of History*. New York: Simon and Schuster/ Touchstone Books.

Guerber, H. A. (1986) *Myths and Legends Series: Middle Ages*. New York: Avenel Books.

Haas, Mary (1969) *The Prehistory of Languages*. The Hague: Mouton.

HarperCollins (1999) *Past Worlds Atlas of Archaeology*. Ann Arbor, MI: Borders Press in association with HarperCollins.

Hartung, C. V. (1982) Where our Grammar Came From. In: Allen, H. B. and M. D. Linn (eds) (1982), pp. 20–31.

Hawkins, John A. (1985) *A Comparative Typology of English and German: Unifying the Contrasts*. Austin, TX: University of Texas Press.

Hester, M. Thomas (1982) *Kinde Pitty and Brave Scorn: John Donne's Satires*. Durham, NC: Duke University Press.

Hibbert, A. B. (1983) The Origins of the Medieval Town Patriciate. In: Tierney, Brian (ed.) *The Middle Ages*, vol. II: *Reading in Medieval History*, 3rd edition. New York: Knopf, pp. 127–38.

Hill, David (1981) *An Atlas of Anglo-Saxon England*. Oxford: Blackwell.

Holloway, Joseph E. and Vass, Winifred K. (1993) *The African Heritage of American English*. Bloomington, IN: Indiana University Press.

Holm, John A. (1988) *Pidgins and Creoles*, volume 1: *Theory and Structure*. Cambridge: Cambridge University Press.

Howard, Philip (1985) *The State of the Language: English Observed*. New York: Oxford University Press.

Hughes, A. and P. Trudgill (1979) *English Accents and Dialects: An Introduction to Social and Regional Dialects of British English*. London: Arnold.

Ihalainen, Ossi (1994) The Dialects of England since 1776. In: Burchfield, Robert, *The Cambridge History of the English Language*, volume V: *English in Britain and Overseas: Origins and Development*. Cambridge: Cambridge University Press.

Jeffers, Robert J. and I. Lehiste (1979) *Principles and Methods for Historical Linguistics*. Cambridge, MA: MIT Press.

Jespersen, Otto (1982) *Growth and Structure of the English Language*. Oxford: Blackwell.

Johnson, Samuel (1970) *The Plan of a Dictionary of the English Language*, Facsimile Reprint of 1747 edition. Menston: Scolar Press.

Kachru, Braj B. (1983) South Asian English. In: Bailey, R. W. and M. Görlach (eds) (1985), 353–83.

Kallen, Jeff (ed.) (1997) *Focus on Ireland*. Amsterdam: Benjamins.

Keiller, Alan R. (ed.) (1972) *A Reader in Historical and Comparative Linguistics*. New York: Holt, Rinehart and Winston.

Kennedy, Charles W. (1960) *An Anthology of Old English Poetry*. New York: Oxford University Press.

King, Robert D. (1969) *Historical Linguistics and Generative Grammar*. Englewood Cliffs, NJ: Prentice-Hall.

Knowles, Gerry (1997) *A Cultural History of the English Language*. London: Arnold.

Krapp, G. P. (1960) *The English Language in America*. Reprint of 1925 version. Berlin: Unger.

Krapp, G. P. (1969) *Modern English: Its Growth and Present Status*. Revised by Albert H. Marckwardt. New York: Charles Scribner's Sons.

Krauss, M. (1992) The World's Languages in Crisis. *Language*, **68**: 1, 462–73.

Labov, William (1972) *Sociolinguistic Patterns*. Philadelphia, PA: University of Pennsylvania Press.

Labov, William (1982) Objectivity and Commitment in Linguistic Science: The Case of the Black English Trial in Ann Arbor, *Language in Society*, **11**, 165–202.

Labov, William (1985) The Increasing Divergence of Black and White Vernaculars. Introduction to the Research Reports. Unpublished manuscript.

Labov, William (1987) Are Black and White Dialects Diverging? Papers from the NWAVE XIV Panel Discussion. *American Speech*, **62**, 5–12.

Labov, William (1989) The Child as Linguistic Historian. *Language Variation and Change*, **1**, 85–94.

Labov, William (1991) The Three Dialects of English. In: Eckert, Penelope (ed.) *New Ways of Analyzing Sound Change*. New York: Academic Press, pp. 1–44.

Labov, William (1994) *Principles of Linguistic Change*, volume 1: *Internal Factors*. Oxford: Blackwell.

Lass, R. (ed.) (1969) *Approaches to English Historical Linguistics: An Anthology*. New York: Holt, Rinehart and Winston.

Lass, Roger (1987) *The Shape of English: Structure and History*. London: Dent.

Layton-Henry, Zig (1992) *The Politics of Immigration*. Oxford: Blackwell.

Lehmann, Winfred P. (1955) *Proto-Indo-European Phonology*. Austin, TX: University of Texas Press and Linguistics Society of America.

Lehmann, Winfred P. (1992) *Historical Linguistics: An Introduction*, 3rd edition. London: Routledge.

Leith, Dick (1983) *A Social History of English*. London: Routledge and Kegan Paul.

Le Page, Robert B. and Andrée Tabouret-Keller (1985) *Acts of Identity: Creole-Based Approaches to Language and Ethnicity*. Cambridge: Cambridge University Press.

Lewis, Archibald R. (ed.) (1970) *The High Middle Ages, 814–1300*. Englewood Cliffs, NJ: Prentice-Hall.

Lightfoot, David W. (1979) *Principles of Diachronic Syntax*. Cambridge Studies in Linguistics 23. Cambridge: Cambridge University Press.

Linguistic Minorities Project (1985) *The Other Languages of England*. London: Routledge and Kegan Paul.

Lloyd, Donald J. and H. R. Warfel (1956) *American English in its Cultural Setting*. New York: Knopf.

Lockwood, William B. (1969) *Indo-European Philology*. London: Hutchinson.

Lockwood, William B. (1975) *Languages of the British Isles Past and Present*. London: André Deutsch.

Lodge, R. Anthony (1993) *Le Français: Histoire d'un Dialecte Devenu Langue*. London: Fayard.

Lodwig, R. R. and E. F. Barrett (1967) *The Dictionary and the Language*. New York: Hayden Book Companies.

Machan, Tim William and Charles T. Scott (1992) *English in its Social Contexts: Essays in Historical Sociolinguistics*. Oxford: Oxford University Press.

Marckwardt, Albert H. (1980) *American English*, 2nd edition; revised by J. L. Dillard. New York: Oxford University Press.

Markey, T. L. (1982) Afrikaan: Creole or non-creole. *Zeitschrift für Dialektologie und Linguistic*, **49**, 2, pp. 169–207.

Markman, Alan M. and Erwin R. Steinberg (1983) *Exercises in the History of English*. London: University Press of America.

Markman, Alan M. and Steinberg, Erwin R. (eds) (1970) *English Then and Now: Readings and Essays*. New York: Random House.

McClure, J. Derrick (1988) *Why Scots Matters*. Edinburgh: The Saltire Society.

McCrum, Robert, William Cran and Robert MacNeil (1986) *The Story of English*. London: Faber and BBC Books.

McIntosh, Angus, M. Samels and M. Benskin (1986) *A Linguistic Atlas of Late Mediaeval English*. Aberdeen: Aberdeen University Press.

McKnight, G. H. (1928) *Modern English in the Making*. New York: D. Appleton Century.

McMahon, April M. S. (1994) *Understanding Language Change*. Cambridge: Cambridge University Press.

Mehrotra, Raja Ram (1998) *Indian English: Texts and Interpretation*. Amsterdam: Benjamins.

Mencken, H. L. (1982) *The American Language*, abridged version, ed. Raven I. McDavid, Jr. New York: Knopf.

Mesthrie, Rajend (1992) *English in Language Shift: The History, Structure and Sociolinguistics of South African Indian English*. Cambridge: Cambridge University Press.

Millward, Celia M. (1989) *A Biography of the English Language*. New York: Holt, Rinehart and Winston.

Milroy, James (1983) On the Sociolinguistic History of /h/-dropping in English. In: Davenport, M., E. Hensen and H.-F. Nielsen (eds) (1983) *Current Topics in English Historical Linguistics*. Sheffield: University of Sheffield Press, pp. 173–91.

Milroy, James (1992a) *Linguistic Variation and Change: On the Historical Sociolinguistics of English*. Oxford: Blackwell.

Milroy, James (1992b) Middle English Dialectology. In: Blake, Norman F. (ed.) (1992), 156–206.

Milroy, James and Lesley Milroy (1991) *Authority in Language. Investigating Language Prescription and Standardisation*, 2nd edition. London: Routledge and Kegan Paul.

Murison, David (1971) The Dutch Element in the Vocabulary of Scots. In: A. J. Aitken, A. Macintosh and H. Pålsson (eds) *Edinburgh Studies in English and Scots*. London: Longman, pp. 159–76.

Murison, David (1977) *The Guid Scots Tongue*. Edinburgh: Blackwood.

Myers, L. M. (1966) *The Roots of Modern English*. Boston, MA: Little, Brown and Company.

Nielsen, Hans Frede (1989) *The Germanic Languages: Origins and Early Dialectal Interrelations*. Tuscaloosa, AL: University of Alabama Press.

Nunberg, G. (1983) The Decline of Grammar. *The Atlantic*, December, pp. 31–46.

Page, R. I. (1988) *Runes: Reading the Past*. London: British Museum Publications.

Partridge, A. C. (1982) *A Companion to Old and Middle English Studies*. Totowa, NJ: Barnes and Noble Books.

Pattanayak, Debi P. (1996) Change, Language and the Developing World. In Coleman, H. and L. Cameron (eds) *Change and Language*. Clevedon: Bilingual Matters.

Pedersen, Holger (1962) *The Discovery of Language: Linguistic Science in the Nineteenth Century*, trans. John Webster Spargo. Bloomington, IN: Indiana University Press.

Pilch, Herbert (1970) *Altenglischer Lehrgang*. Munich: Max Hueber Verlag.

Pirenne, Henri (1936) *Economic and Social History of Medieval Europe*. New York: Harcourt, Brace and World.

Platt, J., H. Weber and M. L. Ho (1984) *The New Englishes*. London: Routledge and Kegan Paul.

Pope, John C. (ed.) (1966) *Seven Old English Poems*. Indianapolis, IN: Bobbs-Merrill.

Price, Glanville (1984) *The Languages of Britain*. London: Arnold.

Pyles, Thomas (1952) *Words and Ways of American English*. New York: Random House.

Pyles, Thomas and John Algeo (1982) *The Origins and Development of the English Language*, 3rd edition. New York: Harcourt Brace Jovanovich.

Quirk, R. and C. L. Wrenn (1955) *Old English Grammar*. London: Methuen.

Renfrew, Colin (1987) *Archaeology and Language*. London: Jonathan Cape.

Renfrew, Colin (1997) World Linguistic Diversity and Farming Dispersals. In: Blench, Roger and Matthew Spriggs (1997), pp. 82–90.

278 *Bibliography*

Roberts, Paul (1958) How to Find Fault with a Dictionary. *Understanding English*. New York: Harper and Row.

Robertson, S. and F. G. Cassidy (1969) *The Development of Modern English*. Englewood Cliffs, NJ: Prentice-Hall.

Robins, R. H. (1964) *General Linguistics: An Introductory Survey*. Bloomington, IN: Indiana University Press.

Romaine, Suzanne (1982) *Socio-Historical Linguistics*. Cambridge: Cambridge University Press.

Romaine, Suzanne (1983) The English Language in Scotland. In: Bailey, R. W. and M. Görlach (eds.) (1985), pp. 56–83.

Romaine, Suzanne (1988) *Pidgin and Creole Languages*. London: Longman.

Rosewarne, David (1994) Estuary English: Tomorrow's RP? *English Today*, **10**: 1, pp. 3–8.

Russ, Charles V. J. (1983) The Geographical and Social Variation of English in England and Wales. In: Bailey, R. W. and M. Görlach (eds) (1985), 11–55.

Ryan, Ellen Bouchard and Howard Giles (eds) (1982) *Attitudes Towards Language Variation: Social and Applied Contexts*. London: Edward Arnold.

Sampson, Geoffrey (1980) *Schools of Linguistics: Competition and Evolution*. London: Hutchinson.

Samuels, Michael C. (1972) *Linguistic Evolution: with Special Reference to English*. Cambridge: Cambridge University Press.

Saunders, Tim (1995) Clean English. *The New Welsh Review*, **28**, Spring, p. 102.

Sledd, James and W. R. Ebbitt (1962) *Dictionaries and That Dictionary*. Glenview, IL: Scott, Foresman and Company.

Smith, Jeremy (1996) *An Historical Study of English: Function, Form and Change*. London: Routledge.

Stephens, John and Ruth Waterhouse (1990) *Literature, Language and Change: From Chaucer to the Present*. London: Routledge.

Stevenson, Patrick (1997) *The German Speaking World*. London: Routledge.

Strang, Barbara M. H. (1970) *A History of English*. London: Methuen.

Sutcliffe, David (1982) *British Black English*. Oxford: Blackwell.

Thomason, Sarah Grey and Terence Kaufman (1988) *Language Contact, Creolization, and Genetic Linguistics*. Berkeley, CA: University of California Press.

Thompson, Sandra A. (1978) Modern English from a Typological Point of View: Some Implications of the Function of Word Order. *Linguistische Berichte*, **54**, 19–35.

Tierney, Brian (1983) *The Middle Ages*, volume 1: *Sources of Medieval History*, 4th edition. New York: Alfred A. Knopf.

Tierney, Brian (1983) *The Middle Ages*, volume 2: *Readings in Medieval History*, 3rd edition. New York: Alfred A. Knopf.

Trask, Robert L. (1996) *Historical Linguistics*. London: Arnold.

Tristram, Hildegard L. C. (ed.) (1997) *The Celtic Englishes*. Heidelberg: Carl Winter Universitätsverlag.

Trudgill, Peter (1974) *The Social Differentiation of English in Norwich*. Cambridge: Cambridge University Press.

Trudgill, Peter (1983) *Sociolinguistics: An Introduction*, 2nd edition. Harmondsworth: Penguin.

Trudgill, Peter (ed.) (1984) *Language in the British Isles*. Cambridge: Cambridge University Press.

Trudgill, Peter (1986) *Dialects in Contact*. Oxford: Blackwell.

Trudgill, Peter (1990) *The Dialects of England*. Oxford: Blackwell.

Trudgill, Peter and Chambers, J. K. (1991) *Dialects of English: Studies in Grammatical Variation*. London: Longman.

Viereck, Wolfgang (1985) *Focus on: England and Wales*. Amsterdam: Benjamins.

Wakelin, Martyn F. (1972) *English Dialects: An Introduction*. London: Athlone Press, University of London.

Wakelin, Martyn F. (1984) Rural Dialects in England. In: Trudgill, P. (ed.) *Language in the British Isles*. Cambridge: Cambridge University Press.

Wolfram, Walt (1974) The relationship of Southern White Speech to Vernacular Black English. *Language*, **50**, 498–527.

Wolfram, Walt (1987) Are Black and White Dialects Diverging? Papers from the NWAVE XIV Panel Discussion. *American Speech*, 62, 40–8.

Wolfram, Walt (1991) *Dialects and American English*. New Jersey: Prentice-Hall.

Wolfram, Walt and Natalie Schilling-Estes (1998) *American English*. Oxford: Blackwell.

Index

AAVE (African-American Vernacular English), 5, 206, 232–7
absolute universal, 44, 45
accommodation, 3–4, 185
acrolect, 4, 205, 206, 246
actuation problem, 51, 160
adjectives, 27, 41, 42, 48, 59, 62, 67–8, 77–8, 101, 104, 128, 142–3, 173, 174
adstratum influence, 50
Ælfric, Abbot, 80, 82
Æthelred the Unræd, 59, 80, 95
affixing, 77, 78–9, 87, 88, 130, 178
African-American Vernacular English see AAVE
agglutinating language, 46–8
America, 4, 5, 23, 26, 31, 133, 137, 138, 169, 174, 175, 199, 207, 208–40, 242–7, 253, 257–8, 259, 262–8
American dialects, 13, 139, 210–11
American Dialect Society, 176
American English, 5, 6, 13, 52, 60, 178, 208–40, 247, 253, 262, 263
American Revolution, 154, 169
American Speech, 176
analytic formulations, 145, 174
analytic language, 46, 48–9, 59
  shift of English to, 6, 35, 40, 76, 92, 101, 130–1
Anglia, 56
  Anglian, 85, 86
Anglo-Norman French, 120, 131, 132, 133

Anglo-Saxon, 2, 56–7, 81, 83, 85, 107, 192–3
  Anglo-Saxons, 59, 89, 192
Anglo-Saxon Chronicle, 80, 86, 115
Anglo-Saxon Heptarchy, 56–7
archaeological linguistics, 49, 51–3
archaeology, 8, 18, 40
Ausgleichssprache, 129
auxiliary language, 260
auxiliary verb, 6, 74, 75, 105, 144, 145

basilect, 4, 205, 206, 246
Bede, 56, 58, 80, 85
Benrath–Ürdingen Line, 33, 39
Beowulf, 78, 83–5
Bopp, Franz, 21, 23
borrowing, 20, 60, 78, 86–93, 106–8, 148, 174, 175
borrowing scale,
  Thomason and Kaufman, 87
Boxhorn, Marcus, 20
British English, 5, 13, 52, 95, 131, 140, 162, 175, 210, 216, 217–18, 221–2, 253–4
Bühnenaussprache, 34
Busbecq, Flemish Ambassador of Charles V, 32

Cædmon's Hymn, 85
Chaucer, Geoffrey, 1, 94, 106, 115, 116, 120, 123, 124, 144, 148, 155, 157, 158, 193
class, social, 13, 96–7, 107, 139, 149, 152, 155, 156, 157, 160–1, 169,

170–2, 180, 185–6, 189, 190, 197, 198, 201, 211, 223, 229, 231, 236, 237, 249, 253
compound verbs, 105
compounding, 35, 60, 64, 77–8, 102
Comrie, Bernard, 44
convergence, 126, 207, 232, 234, 235
Corded Ware burials, 15, 51, 52
creole, 4, 13, 125–31, 204–6, 232, 233–4, 236, 245–6, 250, 251, 253, 255, 257
Cyril, Saint, 27

Danelaw, 90, 129
Danish, 31, 32–3, 55, 58–9, 80, 91, 92, 200
Darwin, Charles, 18
diachrony, 18, 43, 44
dialect, 5, 8, 13, 92, 106, 132, 133, 139, 146, 156, 168, 191, 207
    American, 210–40
    Australian, 243
    British, 210–11
    compromise, 129
    Early Modern, 139, 145, 154, 160
    French, 108
    Germanic, 2, 20, 32–4, 56, 59, 89
    immigrant, 202
    Indo-European, 50
    interference, 206
    Irish English, 199–200
    levelling, 171
    London, 123, 160–1, 186
    Middle English, 106, 108–14, 116, 122–3, 123–5, 130, 143
    Modern, 182–4
    Modern English, 179–90
    non-standard, 186
    Northern, 143, 144
    Old English, 81, 84–5
    Southern, 143
    South African, 248
    standard, 123–5, 156
    traditional, 180–2
    Western, 143
dispersal, 52–3

divergence, 234
Do periphrases, 144–5
dominant language, 4
Donne, John, 1, 154

Early Modern English, 1, 2, 6, 13, 133, 135–67, 172, 209
East Anglia, 56, 58, 109, 124, 160, 182, 212
East Germanic, 32
Edison, Thomas, 7, 167
Edward the Confessor, 55, 57, 59, 94
English,
    American, 5, 6, 13, 52, 60, 178, 208–40, 247, 253, 262, 263
    British, 5, 13, 52, 95, 131, 140, 162, 175, 210, 216, 217–18, 219, 221–2, 253–4
    Early Modern, 1, 2, 6, 13, 133, 135–67, 172, 209
    Middle English, 1, 2, 64, 68, 71, 92, 94–134, 139–41, 143, 145, 148, 158–61, 183
    Modern English, 1, 2, 6, 13, 38, 40, 46, 59–65, 71, 72, 75, 76, 78, 86, 90, 106, 141, 142, 146, 163–6, 173–5, 178, 179
    Old English, 1, 2, 6, 8, 10, 13, 41, 44, 53, 55–93, 97, 98, 99, 101, 102, 106, 108, 109, 114, 124, 128, 129, 139, 143, 144, 145, 158, 174, 177
Estonian, 50
external change, 6, 7, 133, 152

Finnish, 19, 23, 24, 31, 36, 50, 214
First Germanic Consonant Shift, 35–8
French, 2, 9, 13, 20, 23, 29, 30, 34, 94, 96, 104, 114, 115, 116–20, 121, 126–33, 140, 164, 178, 204, 205, 211, 213, 244–5, 251, 257, 259, 260, 266
    loan words, 106–8, 140, 148, 149, 176, 218–19
    Revolution, 154, 169
fusional language, 46–8

gender
  grammatical:
    Germanic, 40
    Indo-European, 40
    Middle English, 128, 129
    Old English, 60, 64, 65, 66, 68, 77
  social, 160, 229, 261
German, 19, 20, 23, 31, 33–4, 35, 37,
    38–40, 46, 48, 62, 64, 72, 73, 78,
    91, 127, 164, 165, 174, 176, 212,
    219, 231, 257, 261, 264, 266, 267
Germanic, 2, 4, 6, 13, 19, 20, 21, 22, 25,
    27, 31–4, 34–42, 50, 55, 56, 58, 59,
    62, 65, 67, 68, 76, 78, 79, 85, 89,
    91, 98, 107, 116, 129, 158, 165,
    174, 192, 199, 261
Gimbutas, Maria, 51
Gothic, 23, 24, 32, 41, 42
government and binding theory, 44
Grammatical Word Order Language, 49, 77
Greek, 2, 16, 17, 18, 21, 23, 24, 28, 35,
    41, 42, 43, 147, 148, 156, 203–4,
    267
Greenberg, Joseph, 44
Grimm, Jakob, 21, 23, 35, 37, 38
Grimm's Law, 36–8, 43
Guthrum, 58

High German, 33–4, 38–40, 59
Hittite, 16, 42, 53
Hughes, David, 7, 167

incorporating language, 46, 48–9
Indo-European, 13, 17–18, 20, 21, 23–5,
    28, 34, 35, 36, 40, 42, 43, 49–53
Industrial Revolution, 2, 169, 170–2, 243,
    256–7
infix, 78
inflection, 41, 46, 48, 87, 97, 99, 101–2,
    124, 128, 142, 145, 173, 261
inflectional language, 6
internal change, 6, 133, 161
International Phonetic Alphabet (IPA), 11
isolating language, 46, 47
i-umlaut, 6, 62, 99, 158

Japanese, 3, 175, 176, 253
Jones, William, 21
Junggrammatiker, 43
Jutes, 17, 18, 56, 85, 200

Kurgan invasions, 51, 52

Labov, William, 222, 227–9, 232
language change, 3–7, 43, 49, 52, 97,
    126, 133, 151, 152, 160, 231, 232,
    237
language contact, 4, 7, 49, 50, 79, 86–8,
    97, 116, 130, 131, 151, 152, 246
language death, 50, 209, 265, 266
language typology, 45
language universals, 44, 45
Laryngeal theory, 53
Latin, 2, 9, 16, 21, 23–5, 28, 29, 35, 37,
    41–3, 64, 79–82, 86, 88–90, 102,
    104, 105, 112–15, 120, 121, 136,
    139, 140, 145, 148, 149, 156, 157,
    193, 196, 259–61, 267
lexifier language, 204
linguistic accommodation, 3–4, 185
linguistic reconstruction, 8, 17, 23, 27,
    31, 43
loss of endings, 99, 101–3, 128, 143
Low German, 33, 34, 38, 59

Mandrell, Ned, 30
Mercia, 56–7, 85–6, 109
mesolect, 4, 246
metanalysis, 7
Methodius, 27
Middle English, 1, 2, 64, 68, 71, 92,
    94–134, 139–41, 143, 145, 148,
    158–61, 183
Milton, John, 148
minimalist theory, 44
Modern English, 1, 2, 6, 13, 38, 40, 46,
    59–65, 71, 72, 75, 76, 78, 86, 90,
    106, 141, 142, 146, 163–6, 173–5,
    178, 179
monosyllabic language, 47
morpheme, 7, 9–10, 43, 46–9, 78

morphology, 9, 10, 35, 40–1, 76–7, 88, 92, 130, 138, 141–4, 172–3
multidialectal speakers, 268
mutation, 6, 62

neogrammarians, 43
Normans, 4, 80, 89, 94–5, 106, 108, 116, 117, 131
Norman French, 108, 120, 131
North Germanic, 6, 32, 62, 94
Northumbria, 56, 192
  Northumbrian, 85, 109, 130
noun, 6, 27, 42

Old English, 1, 2, 6, 8, 10, 13, 41, 44, 53, 55–93, 97–9, 101, 102, 106, 108, 109, 114, 124, 128, 129, 139, 143–5, 158, 174, 177
Old Norse, 32, 58–9, 79, 90–2, 117, 127, 129, 130, 144, 191

Pāṇini, 25
participle, 74, 77, 105, 112, 114, 124
past participle, 35, 38, 40, 78, 145, 146, 149
Penreath, Dolly, 30
phone, 9, 36, 43, 87
phoneme, 9, 36, 43, 61, 87, 129, 139, 140, 159
phonetics, 9
phonology, 9, 30, 50, 87, 129, 130, 132, 138, 172, 187, 226, 227, 262
Picts, 55, 56, 191, 192
pidgin, 4, 126–30, 204, 246, 250–3, 261
plural, 9, 38, 40, 47, 48, 62, 65, 66, 67, 70, 71, 99, 101, 113, 114, 124, 141–4, 165, 189, 214, 233
polysynthetic, 46, 48–9
Pragmatic Word Order Language, 49, 77
pragmatics, 10
prefixing, 10, 35, 60, 78, 88, 113, 114, 124, 174, 178
preposition, 40, 45, 64, 72, 73, 76, 87, 91, 92, 102, 104, 105, 141, 145, 146, 172, 173, 263

Present-Day English, 1, 138, 140, 167–207
prestige, 3, 5, 7, 31, 33, 39, 87, 90, 117, 132, 161, 162, 186, 191, 192, 194, 197, 198, 229, 231, 235–7
prestige borrowing, 87, 90, 108
progressive, 105, 112, 145, 173, 262
Proto-Germanic, 31, 42
Proto-Indo-European, 29
proto-language, 23, 43

Rask, Rasmus, 21, 23, 35, 37
reanalysis, 7
reconstruction, 8, 17, 23, 27, 31, 43
Renfrew, Colin, 52–3
'Rhenish Fan', 39
Romance, 20, 21, 28, 29, 147, 261
Russian, 19, 27, 47, 50, 51, 77, 131, 176, 201, 268

Sanskrit, 21, 23–4, 25, 35, 42
Saussure, Ferdinand de, 43, 53
Schlegel, August von, 46
Schleicher, August, 18, 23
Scots, 8, 56, 60, 80, 139, 182, 188, 191, 195, 197, 198, 200, 211, 212, 213, 236, 267
Second Germanic Consonant Shift, 38–40
semantics, 10, 42
Shakespeare, William, 1, 116, 135, 136, 144, 145, 147, 153, 154, 156, 160, 163, 164, 165
social class, 13, 96–7, 107, 139, 149, 152, 155–7, 160–1, 169, 170–2, 180, 185–6, 189, 190, 197, 198, 201, 211, 223, 229, 231, 236, 237, 249, 253
solidarity, 3, 162, 165, 206
Spanish, 20, 23, 29, 176, 203, 204, 215, 219, 231, 238, 245, 268
Stammbaumtheorie, 18, 35
Standard English, 5, 8, 85, 122–5, 130, 138, 139, 156, 165, 180, 191, 200, 207, 246, 250, 259, 262
standardization, 137, 156, 157, 171, 185, 194, 199, 227

Stewart, Dugald, 21
strong declension, 59
strong verbs, 59, 114, 143
structuralism, 43, 44
substratum influence, 3, 7, 39, 50, 232
suffix, 10, 42, 60, 76, 78, 88, 103, 124,
    178, 205, 234
Swedish, 9, 19, 20, 31, 32, 41, 92, 130,
    165
Swiss German, 38
synchrony, 43
syntactic universals, 45–6
syntax, 10, 41, 72, 87, 88, 104, 114, 130,
    139, 144–6, 172–5, 231
synthetic language, 59, 76

technology, 2, 13, 171, 175, 178, 256–8,
    263–7
TELSUR, 222, 227–9
Thomason and Kaufman
    borrowing scale, 87
transformational grammar, 44
Tryggvason, Olaf, 59
Turkish, 47, 203, 204
typological classification, 44–9

Ulfilas, 41
Ulster Scots, 198, 200
universal, 44, 45
    absolute, 44
    laws, 40
    syntactic, 46–7

Verner's Law, 37–8, 43
Vikings, 4, 57–9, 78, 79, 80, 199
Vortigern, 56

weak declension adjectives, 67
Wedmore, Treaty of, 55, 58
Welsh, 4, 29–30, 53, 95, 114, 187, 188,
    193, 196–7, 211
West Germanic, 6, 32, 59, 98
West Saxon, 81, 98
William I, the Conqueror, 2, 94–5,
    106
Wooton, William, 21
Wulfstan, Bishop, 80, 81, 106

yes-no question, 6, 144–5
Yiddish, 31, 32, 34, 232